Mediterranean Diet Cookbook for Beginners

1500+ Days Easy, Delicious and Wholsome Recipes for Body Management. Include 30 Days Meal Plan to Help You Live a Healthier Life

Damaris Gutkowski

Copyright© 2023 By Gilberto Bender

All rights reserved worldwide.

No part of this book may be reproduced or transmitted in any form or by any means, electronic or mechanical, including photo- copying, recording or by any information storage and retrieval system, without written permission from the publisher, except for the inclusion of brief quotations in a review.

Warning-Disclaimer

The purpose of this book is to educate and entertain. The author or publisher does not guarantee that anyone following the techniques, suggestions, tips, ideas, or strategies will become successful. The author and publisher shall have neither liability or responsibility to anyone with respect to any loss or damage caused, or alleged to be caused, directly or indirectly by the information contained in this book.

Table of Contents

INTRODUCTION — 1

Chapter 1: The Mediterranean Diet and it's Celebration of Live and Living — 2

What is the Mediterranean Diet?.............................2
Health Benefits of the Mediterranean Diet................2
The Mediterranean Food Pyramid 3
Extra Virgin Olive Oil: The Core of the Mediterranean Diet..4

Chapter 2: Eight Steps to Getting Started — 5

Living the Mediterranean Way................................6
30 Days Mediterranean Diet Meal Plan...................7

Chapter 3 Breakfasts — 9

Green Spinach & Salmon Crepes..............................9
Tiropita (Greek Cheese Pie)....................................9
Golden Egg Skillet..9
Baked Egg and Mushroom Cups............................10
Mini Shrimp Frittata...10
Morning Buzz Iced Coffee 10
Spanish Tortilla with Potatoes and Peppers 10
Buffalo Egg Cups..10
Tortilla Española (Spanish Omelet) 11
Peachy Oatmeal with Pecans 11
Summer Day Fruit Salad 11
Peachy Green Smoothie 11
Baked Ricotta with Pears 11
Spinach and Feta Egg Bake....................................12
Nuts and Fruit Oatmeal..12
Egg and Pepper Pita 12
Greek Yogurt Parfait..12
Greek Egg and Tomato Scramble...........................12
Italian Egg Cups..13
Peach Sunrise Smoothie...13
Breakfast Hash 13
Sunshine Overnight Oats.......................................13
Quinoa Porridge with Apricots..............................13
Mediterranean Muesli and Breakfast Bowl............13
Savory Feta, Spinach, and Red Pepper Muffins......14
Crunchy Vanilla Protein Bars................................14
Blueberry-Lemon Tea Cakes.................................14
Feta and Herb Frittata..14
Honey-Vanilla Greek Yogurt with Blueberries 15
Red Pepper and Feta Egg Bites.............................15
Spanish Tuna Tortilla with Roasted Peppers..........15
Creamy Cinnamon Porridge...................................15
Greek Yogurt Parfait with Granola.........................15
Smoked Salmon Egg Scramble with Dill and Chives 16
Spinach, Sun-Dried Tomato, and Feta Egg Wraps 16
Gluten-Free Granola Cereal 16
Garlicky Beans and Greens with Polenta................16
Spinach and Mushroom Mini Quiche 16
C+C Overnight Oats...17
Blueberry-Banana Bowl with Quinoa 17
Chickpea Hash with Eggs 17
Mediterranean Frittata..17
Jalapeño Popper Egg Cups.....................................17
Berry Breakfast Smoothie......................................18
Baked Peach Oatmeal 18
Mediterranean Omelet..18
Avocado Toast with Smoked Trout 18
Turkish Egg Bowl 18
Savory Breakfast Oats..19
Oat and Fruit Parfait...19
Mediterranean Fruit Bulgur Breakfast Bowl...........19
Grilled Halloumi with Whole-Wheat Pita Bread....19
Mediterranean Breakfast Pita Sandwiches..............19
South of the Coast Sweet Potato Toast...................20
Spinach Pie..20
Egg Salad with Red Pepper and Dill......................20
Oatmeal with Apple and Cardamom......................20
Cauliflower Avocado Toast 21
Quickie Honey Nut Granola...................................21
Berry Baked Oatmeal...21

Chapter 4 Beef, Pork, and Lamb 22

Saucy Beef Fingers 22
Greek-Inspired Beef Kebabs 22
Beef Brisket with Onions 22
Beef Ragù 22
Mustard Lamb Chops 23
One-Pan Greek Pork and Vegetables 23
Lamb Stew 23
Asian Glazed Meatballs 23
Tenderloin with Crispy Shallots 24
Spaghetti Zoodles and Meatballs 24
Pork Tenderloin with Vegetable Ragu 24
Pork and Cabbage Egg Roll in a Bowl 24
Beef Bourguignon with Egg Noodles 25
Meatballs in Creamy Almond Sauce 25
Red Curry Flank Steak 25
Herb-Roasted Beef Tips with Onions 25
Herbed Lamb Meatballs 26
Greek Lamb Burgers 26
Blackened Cajun Pork Roast 26
Fajita Meatball Lettuce Wraps 26
Mediterranean Pork with Olives 26
Beef Whirls 27
Herb-Crusted Lamb Chops 27
Pepper Steak 27
Roasted Pork with Apple-Dijon Sauce 27
Bone-in Pork Chops 28
Smoky Pork Tenderloin 28
Parmesan Herb Filet Mignon 28
Wedding Soup 28
Greek Lamb Chops 28
Baby Back Ribs 29
Lamb and Bean Stew 29
Lamb and Vegetable Bake 29
Braised Short Ribs with Fennel and Pickled Grapes 29
Lebanese Ground Meat with Rice 30
Greek Meatball Soup 30
Spiced Lamb Stew with Fennel and Dates 30
Smoky Herb Lamb Chops and Lemon-Rosemary Dressing
.... 30
Beef Burger 31
Pork Souvlaki 31
Moroccan Lamb Roast 31
Lamb Shanks and Potatoes 31
Southern Chili 31
Balsamic Pork Chops with Figs and Pears 32
Moroccan Meatballs 32
The Best Spaghetti Sauce 32
Kofta with Vegetables in Tomato Sauce 32
Seasoned Beef Kebabs 33
Beef Stew with Red Wine 33
Pork and Cannellini Bean Stew 33

Chapter 5 Fish and Seafood 34

Baked Monkfish 34
Balsamic Tilapia 34
Cucumber and Salmon Salad 34
Grilled Bluefish 34
Cod with Jalapeño 34
Crispy Fish Sticks 35
Tomato-Basil Salmon 35
Cod with Parsley Pistou 35
Stuffed Shrimp 35
Simple Poached Turbot 35
Mixed Seafood Soup 36
Halibut Fillets with Vegetables 36
Lemon-Pepper Trout 36
Italian Halibut with Grapes and Olive Oil 36
Parmesan Mackerel with Coriander 36
Salmon with Garlicky Broccoli Rabe and White Beans 37
Poached Octopus 37
Fried Fresh Sardines 37
Herbed Shrimp Pita 37
Baked Grouper with Tomatoes and Garlic 38
Salmon Croquettes 38
Roasted Sea Bass 38
Maple Balsamic Glazed Salmon 38
Quick Seafood Paella 38
Rosemary Salmon 39
Honey-Balsamic Salmon 39
Friday Night Fish Fry 39
Mediterranean Grilled Shrimp 39
Salmon Spring Rolls 39
Shrimp with Arugula Pesto and Zucchini Noodles 40
Linguine with Clams and White Wine 40
Fish Gratin 40
Mediterranean Spice-Crusted Salmon over White Beans 40
Catfish in Creole Sauce 41
Apple Cider Mussels 41
Mediterranean Cod Stew 41
Paprika-Spiced Fish 41
Baked Salmon with Tomatoes and Olives 41
Salmon with Cauliflower 41
Snapper with Shallot and Tomato 42
Herbed Tuna Steaks 42
Lemon Salmon with Dill 42
Tuna and Fruit Kebabs 42
Lemon-Dill Salmon Burgers 42
Shrimp and Fish Chowder 43
Southern-Style Catfish 43
Shrimp over Black Bean Linguine 43
Wild Cod Oreganata 43
Tuna Steaks with Olive Tapenade 43
Salmon Cakes with Bell Pepper and Lemon Yogurt 44

Chapter 6 Poultry — 45

- Chicken Chili Verde over Rice ... 45
- Classic Chicken Kebab ... 45
- Blackened Cajun Chicken Tenders ... 45
- Buffalo Chicken Cheese Sticks ... 45
- Cilantro Chicken Kebabs ... 46
- Chicken and Chickpea Skillet with Berbere Spice ... 46
- Chicken Legs with Leeks ... 46
- One-Pan Parsley Chicken and Potatoes ... 46
- South Indian Pepper Chicken ... 47
- Catalonian Chicken with Spiced Lemon Rice ... 47
- Ginger Turmeric Chicken Thighs ... 47
- Garlic Chicken (Shish Tawook) ... 47
- Chicken Piccata with Mushrooms ... 48
- Chicken Jalfrezi ... 48
- Apricot Chicken ... 48
- Calabrian Chicken with Potatoes and Vegetables ... 48
- Harissa Yogurt Chicken Thighs ... 49
- Skillet Creamy Tarragon Chicken and Mushrooms ... 49
- Taco Chicken ... 49
- Jerk Chicken Kebabs ... 49
- Classic Whole Chicken ... 50
- Honey-Glazed Chicken Thighs ... 50
- Brazilian Tempero Baiano Chicken Drumsticks ... 50
- Hoisin Turkey Burgers ... 50
- Chicken Marsala ... 50
- Chicken Caprese Casserole ... 51
- Whole Tandoori–Style Braised Chicken ... 51
- Grilled Chicken and Vegetables with Lemon-Walnut Sauce ... 51
- Lebanese Garlic Chicken Flatbreads ... 51
- Hot Goan-Style Coconut Chicken ... 52

Chapter 7 Beans and Grains — 53

- Spanakorizo (Greek Spinach and Rice) ... 53
- Sweet Potato Black Bean Burgers ... 53
- Barley Salad with Lemon-Tahini Dressing ... 53
- Creamy Lima Bean Soup ... 54
- Greek Chickpeas with Coriander and Sage ... 54
- Quinoa with Artichokes ... 54
- Vegetable Barley Soup ... 54
- Chili-Spiced Beans ... 55
- White Beans with Kale ... 55
- Garlic-Asparagus Israeli Couscous ... 55
- Bulgur with Chickpeas, Spinach, and Za'atar ... 55
- Wheat Berry Pilaf ... 55
- Creamy Thyme Polenta ... 56
- Rice with Blackened Fish ... 56
- Revithosoupa (Chickpea Soup) ... 56
- Quinoa Salad with Tomatoes ... 56
- Vegetable Risotto with Beet Greens ... 56
- Couscous with Apricots ... 57
- Amaranth Salad ... 57
- Puréed Red Lentil Soup ... 57
- Barley Risotto ... 57
- Greek-Style Black-Eyed Pea Soup ... 57
- Rice with Pork Chops ... 58
- Apple Couscous with Curry ... 58
- Lentils with Artichoke, Tomato, and Feta ... 58
- Lemon Farro Bowl with Avocado ... 58
- Lentils with Spinach ... 58
- Lentil and Zucchini Boats ... 59
- Lentils and Bulgur with Caramelized Onions ... 59
- Black Beans with Corn and Tomato Relish ... 59
- Lentil Pâté ... 59
- Herbed Barley ... 60
- Wild Mushroom Farrotto ... 60
- Lentil Chili ... 60
- Baked Mushroom-Barley Pilaf ... 60
- Rice with Olives and Basil ... 61
- Lemon Orzo with Fresh Herbs ... 61
- Garlicky Split Chickpea Curry ... 61
- Lentil Bowl ... 61
- Garbanzo and Pita No-Bake Casserole ... 61
- Herbed Lima Beans ... 62
- Za'atar Chickpeas and Chicken ... 62
- Moroccan Date Pilaf ... 62
- White Beans with Garlic and Tomatoes ... 62
- Quinoa with Kale, Carrots, and Walnuts ... 62
- Simple Herbed Rice ... 63
- Mediterranean Lentils and Rice ... 63
- Moroccan-Style Rice and Chickpea Bake ... 63
- Lebanese Rice and Broken Noodles with Cabbage ... 63
- Black Lentil Dhal ... 64

Chapter 8 Pasta — 65

- Tahini Soup ... 65
- Puglia-Style Pasta with Broccoli Sauce ... 65
- Pine Nut and Currant Couscous with Butternut Squash ... 65
- Mixed Vegetable Couscous ... 66
- Rotini with Spinach, Cherry Tomatoes, and Feta ... 66
- Rotini with Walnut Pesto, Peas, and Cherry Tomatoes ... 66
- Creamy Spring Vegetable Linguine ... 66
- Orzo with Feta and Marinated Peppers ... 67
- Couscous with Tomatoes and Olives ... 67
- Penne with Roasted Vegetables ... 67
- Quick Shrimp Fettuccine ... 67
- Penne with Tuna and Green Olives ... 68
- Linguine with Avocado Pesto ... 68
- Whole-Wheat Spaghetti à la Puttanesca ... 68
- Whole-Wheat Capellini with Sardines, Olives, and Manchego ... 68
- Bowtie Pesto Pasta Salad ... 68
- Meaty Baked Penne ... 69
- Chilled Pearl Couscous Salad ... 69
- Zucchini with Bow Ties ... 69
- Couscous with Crab and Lemon ... 69

Chapter 9 Pizzas, Wraps, and Sandwiches — 70

- Classic Margherita Pizza 70
- Grilled Chicken Salad Pita 70
- Grilled Eggplant and Feta Sandwiches 70
- Dill Salmon Salad Wraps 70
- Beans and Greens Pizza 71
- Moroccan Lamb Wrap with Harissa 71
- Roasted Vegetable Bocadillo with Romesco Sauce 71
- Greek Salad Wraps 71
- Sautéed Mushroom, Onion, and Pecorino Romano Panini ... 72
- Turkey and Provolone Panini with Roasted Peppers and Onions 72
- Jerk Chicken Wraps 72
- Vegetable Pita Sandwiches 72
- Cucumber Basil Sandwiches 73
- Greek Salad Pita 73
- Turkey Burgers with Feta and Dill 73
- Open-Faced Eggplant Parmesan Sandwich 73
- Margherita Open-Face Sandwiches 73
- Herbed Focaccia Panini with Anchovies and Burrata 74
- Mediterranean-Pita Wraps 74
- Mexican Pizza 74

Chapter 10 Snacks and Appetizers — 75

- Domatosalata (Sweet-and-Spicy Tomato Sauce) 75
- Vegetable Pot Stickers 75
- Black Olive and Lentil Pesto 75
- Burrata Caprese Stack 75
- Black-Eyed Pea "Caviar" 76
- Apple Chips with Chocolate Tahini 76
- Crunchy Orange-Thyme Chickpeas 76
- Garlic-Lemon Hummus 76
- Feta and Quinoa Stuffed Mushrooms 76
- Grilled Halloumi with Watermelon, Cherry Tomatoes, Olives, and Herb Oil 77
- Fig-Pecan Energy Bites 77
- Homemade Sweet Potato Chips 77
- Baked Italian Spinach and Ricotta Balls 77
- Eggplant Fries 78
- Baked Spanakopita Dip 78
- Sweet Potato Fries 78
- Herbed Labneh Vegetable Parfaits 78
- Citrus-Kissed Melon 78
- Smoky Baba Ghanoush 79
- Salmon Niçoise Salad with Dijon-Chive Dressing 79
- Garlic-Parmesan Croutons 79
- Air Fryer Popcorn with Garlic Salt 79
- Greek Yogurt Deviled Eggs 79
- Sea Salt Potato Chips 80
- Stuffed Fried Mushrooms 80
- Bravas-Style Potatoes 80
- Roasted Rosemary Olives 80
- Marinated Olives and Mushrooms 80
- Quick Garlic Mushrooms 81
- Lemon-Pepper Chicken Drumsticks 81
- Crispy Spiced Chickpeas 81
- Spicy Roasted Potatoes 81
- Dark Chocolate and Cranberry Granola Bars 81
- Goat Cheese–Mackerel Pâté 82
- Mini Lettuce Wraps 82
- Whole Wheat Pitas 82
- Pesto Cucumber Boats 82
- Crispy Chili Chickpeas 82
- Red Pepper Tapenade 83
- Cheese-Stuffed Dates 83
- Tuna Croquettes 83
- Buffalo Bites 83
- Citrus-Marinated Olives 84
- Marinated Feta and Artichokes 84
- Mexican Potato Skins 84
- Roasted Mushrooms with Garlic 84
- Red Lentils with Sumac 84
- Spanish Home Fries with Spicy Tomato Sauce 85
- Five-Ingredient Falafel with Garlic-Yogurt Sauce 85
- Steamed Artichokes with Herbs and Olive Oil 85

Chapter 11 Vegetarian Mains — 86

- One-Pan Mushroom Pasta with Mascarpone 86
- Eggs Poached in Moroccan Tomato Sauce 86
- Stuffed Pepper Stew 86
- Cauliflower Steaks with Olive Citrus Sauce 86
- Tangy Asparagus and Broccoli 87
- Moroccan Red Lentil and Pumpkin Stew 87
- Linguine and Brussels Sprouts 87
- Zucchini Lasagna 87
- Balsamic Marinated Tofu with Basil and Oregano 88
- Moroccan Vegetable Tagine 88
- Quinoa Lentil "Meatballs" with Quick Tomato Sauce 88
- Roasted Veggie Bowl 88
- Vegetable Burgers 89
- Eggplants Stuffed with Walnuts and Feta 89
- Pistachio Mint Pesto Pasta 89
- Creamy Chickpea Sauce with Whole-Wheat Fusilli 89
- Parmesan Artichokes 90
- Freekeh, Chickpea, and Herb Salad 90
- Mozzarella and Sun-Dried Portobello Mushroom Pizza 90
- Crispy Cabbage Steaks 90
- Root Vegetable Soup with Garlic Aioli 90
- Provençal Ratatouille with Herbed Breadcrumbs and Goat Cheese 91
- Baked Tofu with Sun-Dried Tomatoes and Artichokes 91
- Crustless Spinach Cheese Pie 91
- Grilled Eggplant Stacks 91
- Cauliflower Rice-Stuffed Peppers 92
- Farro with Roasted Tomatoes and Mushrooms 92
- Crispy Tofu 92
- Roasted Portobello Mushrooms with Kale and Red Onion ... 92

Pesto Vegetable Skewers 93
Asparagus and Mushroom Farrotto 93
Greek Frittata with Tomato-Olive Salad 93
Caprese Eggplant Stacks 93
Cheese Stuffed Zucchini 94
Stuffed Portobellos 94
Turkish Red Lentil and Bulgur Kofte 94
Quinoa with Almonds and Cranberries 94
Three-Cheese Zucchini Boats 94
Cauliflower Steak with Gremolata 95
Rustic Vegetable and Brown Rice Bowl 95

Chapter 12 Vegetables and Sides — 96

Rustic Cauliflower and Carrot Hash 96
Ratatouille 96
Roasted Broccolini with Garlic and Romano 96
Tingly Chili-Roasted Broccoli 96
Sweet and Crispy Roasted Pearl Onions 96
Spiced Honey-Walnut Carrots 97
Crispy Roasted Red Potatoes with Garlic, Rosemary, and Parmesan 97
Walnut and Freekeh Pilaf 97
Heirloom Tomato Basil Soup 97
Green Beans with Pine Nuts and Garlic 97
Spicy Grilled Veggie Pita 98
Braised Radishes with Sugar Snap Peas and Dukkah ... 98
Eggplant Caponata 98
Zucchini Fritters with Manchego and Smoked Paprika Yogurt 98
Roasted Harissa Carrots 99
Brown Rice and Vegetable Pilaf 99
Wild Mushroom Soup 99
Garlicky Broccoli Rabe with Artichokes 99
Air-Fried Okra 99
Radish Chips 100
Five-Spice Roasted Sweet Potatoes 100
Indian Eggplant Bharta 100
Sesame Carrots and Sugar Snap Peas 100
Spicy Roasted Bok Choy 100
Couscous-Stuffed Eggplants 101
Cretan Roasted Zucchini 101
Roasted Broccoli with Tahini Yogurt Sauce 101
Cauliflower Steaks with Creamy Tahini Sauce 101
Toasted Pita Wedges 102
Caramelized Eggplant with Harissa Yogurt 102
Braised Fennel 102
Honey and Spice Glazed Carrots 102
Mediterranean Zucchini Boats 102
Rice Pilaf with Dill 103
Zucchini-Eggplant Gratin 103
Puréed Cauliflower Soup 103
Crispy Green Beans 103
Garlic and Herb Roasted Grape Tomatoes 103
Tahini-Lemon Kale 104
Sesame-Ginger Broccoli 104
Easy Greek Briami (Ratatouille) 104
Roasted Garlic 104
Nordic Stone Age Bread 104
Roasted Vegetables with Lemon Tahini 105
Brussels Sprouts with Pecans and Gorgonzola 105
Roasted Fennel with Za'atar 105
Polenta with Mushroom Bolognese 105
Balsamic Beets 106
Grilled Vegetables 106
Mushrooms with Goat Cheese 106
Roasted Cherry Tomato Caprese 106
Mediterranean Lentil Sloppy Joes 106
Dandelion Greens 107
Broccoli Salad 107
Individual Asparagus and Goat Cheese Frittatas 107
Spanish Green Beans 107
Mini Moroccan Pumpkin Cakes 107
Cauliflower Steaks Gratin 108
Vegetable Terrine 108
Greek Garlic Dip 108
Lemon-Rosemary Beets 108
Roasted Brussels Sprouts with Tahini-Yogurt Sauce ... 109
Braised Cauliflower 109
Gorgonzola Sweet Potato Burgers 109
Steamed Cauliflower with Olive Oil and Herbs 109
Cucumbers with Feta, Mint, and Sumac 110
Savory Butternut Squash and Apples 110
Greek Fasolakia (Green Beans) 110
Sautéed Mustard Greens and Red Peppers 110
Beet and Watercress Salad with Orange and Dill 110

Chapter 13 Salads — 111

Simple Insalata Mista (Mixed Salad) with Honey Balsamic Dressing 111
Easy Greek Salad 111
Citrus Fennel Salad 111
Greek Potato Salad 111
Italian Summer Vegetable Barley Salad 112
Beets with Goat Cheese and Chermoula 112
No-Mayo Florence Tuna Salad 112
Superfood Salmon Salad Bowl 112
Israeli Salad with Nuts and Seeds 113
Roasted Cauliflower Salad with Tahini-Yogurt Dressing   113
Quinoa with Zucchini, Mint, and Pistachios 113
Tabbouleh 113
Roasted Cauliflower "Steak" Salad 114
Riviera Tuna Salad 114
Bacalhau and Black-Eyed Pea Salad 114
Roasted Golden Beet, Avocado, and Watercress Salad ... 114
Tuna Niçoise 115
Wilted Kale Salad 115
Dakos (Cretan Salad) 115
Pistachio-Parmesan Kale-Arugula Salad 115
447. Marinated Greek Salad with Oregano and Goat Cheese 115
Italian White Bean Salad with Bell Peppers 116

Citrusy Spinach Salad 116	Red Pepper, Pomegranate, and Walnut Salad 117
Insalata Caprese 116	Moroccan Tomato and Roasted Chile Salad 118
Valencia-Inspired Salad............... 116	Powerhouse Arugula Salad 118
Arugula and Fennel Salad with Fresh Basil............ 116	Watermelon Burrata Salad 118
Asparagus Salad 116	Wild Greens Salad with Fresh Herbs 118
Tricolor Tomato Summer Salad 117	Pipirrana (Spanish Summer Salad) 118
Turkish Shepherd'S Salad............... 117	Zucchini and Ricotta Salad 119
French Lentil Salad with Parsley and Mint............ 117	Traditional Greek Salad 119
Italian Tuna and Olive Salad 117	Melon Caprese Salad............... 119

Chapter 14 Desserts — 120

Strawberry-Pomegranate Molasses Sauce 120	Tahini Baklava Cups 124
Cherry-Stuffed Apples............... 120	Mascarpone and Fig Crostini 125
Poached Apricots and Pistachios with Greek Yogurt 120	Greek Yogurt with Honey and Pomegranates 125
Creamy Rice Pudding 120	Roasted Plums with Nut Crumble............... 125
Greek Yogurt Ricotta Mousse 120	Lemon Fool 125
Pears with Blue Cheese and Walnuts 121	Red Wine–Poached Figs with Ricotta and Almond 125
Olive Oil Ice Cream 121	Cucumber-Lime Popsicles 126
Chocolate Lava Cakes............... 121	Almond Rice Pudding............... 126
Karithopita (Greek Juicy Walnut Cake) 121	Honey-Vanilla Apple Pie with Olive Oil Crust 126
Avocado-Orange Fruit Salad 121	Golden Coconut Cream Pops 126
Date and Honey Almond Milk Ice Cream............... 122	Greek Island Almond Cocoa Bites 126
Grilled Pineapple and Melon 122	Koulourakia (Olive Oil Cinnamon Cookies) 127
Peaches Poached in Rose Water............... 122	Red-Wine Poached Pears 127
Pumpkin-Ricotta Cheesecake............... 122	Lemon Coconut Cake............... 127
Chocolate Turtle Hummus 122	Apple and Brown Rice Pudding............... 127
Creamy Spiced Almond Milk............... 123	Dried Fruit Compote 128
Frozen Raspberry Delight 123	Greek Yogurt Chocolate "Mousse" with Berries 128
Fresh Figs with Chocolate Sauce 123	Steamed Dessert Bread 128
Grilled Stone Fruit with Whipped Ricotta 123	Minty Cantaloupe Granita 128
Toasted Almonds with Honey 123	Red Grapefruit Granita............... 128
Grilled Peaches with Greek Yogurt............... 123	Pears Poached in Pomegranate and Wine 129
Poached Pears with Greek Yogurt and Pistachio 124	Pomegranate-Quinoa Dark Chocolate Bark............... 129
Ricotta Cheesecake 124	Olive Oil Greek Yogurt Brownies 129
Apricot and Mint No-Bake Parfait............... 124	Dark Chocolate Bark with Fruit and Nuts............... 129
S'mores 124	Chocolate Hazelnut "Powerhouse" Truffles............ 130

Chapter 15 Staples, Sauces, Dips, and Dressings — 131

Creamy Grapefruit-Tarragon Dressing............... 131	Maltese Sun-Dried Tomato and Mushroom Dressing............ 132
Parsley-Mint Sauce 131	Lemon-Yogurt Sauce............... 133
Pickled Turnips............... 131	Olive Mint Vinaigrette 133
Kidney Bean Dip with Cilantro, Cumin, and Lime 131	Skinny Cider Dressing 133
Berry and Honey Compote............... 131	Pepper Sauce 133
Lemon Tahini Dressing 132	Olive Tapenade............... 133
White Bean Hummus 132	Simple Vinaigrette............... 133
Versatile Sandwich Round 132	Herbed Oil............... 133
Tomatillo Salsa............... 132	Italian Dressing 134
Vinaigrette............... 132	Cucumber Yogurt Dip 134

Appendix 1: Measurement Conversion Chart — 135

Appendix 2: The Dirty Dozen and Clean Fifteen — 136

INTRODUCTION

As I sit down to write this foreword, I can't help but feel excited to share my passion for the Mediterranean diet with you. I grew up in a family where cooking and sharing meals was a cornerstone of our culture, and the Mediterranean diet was at the center of it all. It was not just about nourishment, but it was a way of life.

Now, as a chef and nutritionist, I have spent years researching and exploring the health benefits of the Mediterranean diet, and I am eager to share my knowledge and recipes with you. This recipe book is the culmination of my experiences, my family traditions, and my commitment to helping people take charge of their health through the power of food.

At its core, the Mediterranean diet is a way of eating that focuses on fresh, whole foods, and minimizes processed and refined foods. It is rich in fruits and vegetables, whole grains, legumes, and healthy fats like olive oil and nuts. This diet is not only delicious, but it has also been extensively researched and has been shown to promote heart health, support healthy blood sugar levels, and protect brain function.

In this recipe book, you will find a collection of recipes that embody the Mediterranean diet principles. From classic dishes like grilled shrimp with lemon and herbs to innovative twists on traditional favorites like Mediterranean quinoa salad, there is something for everyone. The recipes are easy to follow, and I have included plenty of tips and tricks to help you make the most of the ingredients and flavors.

As you embark on this journey with me, I want you to know that I am on your side. I understand that making dietary changes can be challenging, but I promise you that the benefits of following the Mediterranean diet are well worth the effort. With this book, I hope to inspire you to explore new flavors, embrace fresh ingredients, and take charge of your health. So, let's get started and discover the joys of the Mediterranean diet together.

Chapter 1: The Mediterranean Diet and it's Celebration of Live and Living

What is the Mediterranean Diet?

The Mediterranean diet is more of a cultural eating pattern than a full blown diet. It's origins come from Europe, particularly in the areas surrounding the Mediterranean Sea. It came to the attention of scientists because unlike the rest of the world, who tended to rely on similar foods (though in different quantities), this area wasn't facing epidemics of obesity, heart disease, diabetes, etc. This was jaw dropping to the era of people who were just discovering the role diet plays in overall health (Gunnars & Link, 2021). The answer was found to be in the way they eat their food.

Unlike nearly every popular diet, the Mediterranean diet isn't centered around what you can't eat. Rather it focuses on how much of something you should eat, and the type of something you should eat. Due to the geography of the area, fish is a huge part of their diet. The climate of this area is also perfect for plant growth. Thanks to this, it's easier for those in this area to get a hold of fresh food than it is for them to get a hold of anything processed.

With the fresh fruits and vegetables being in easy reach, it makes up a major portion of the diet.

What isn't so easy to get a hold of in this area is red meat. Because of that, it is severely limited. White meats are included much more in this diet, but not as often as fish.

Finally, if you are an alcohol lover, you will like this! The Mediterranean diet does include wine. Vineyards are not hard to come by in the Mediterranean region.

Health Benefits of the Mediterranean Diet

One health benefit is that people in this area just seem to live longer. Their average age of death is higher because they don't have to worry about a lot of these common killers, which will often make up the top ten deaths in places like the United States.

One of these killers is heart disease. While it makes up a significant portion of deaths in the U.S., the Mediterranean diet aids the region due to it's low-fat content. There is evidence to suggest that it doesn't lead to nearly as much plaque build up in the arteries (Gunnars & Link, 2021).

It can have a great impact on your brain as well. Diseases such as Alzheimer's are much less common in those who follow this diet. It has also shown to help with overall brain function, with those who have been on it reporting that they can think and focus better (Gunnars & Link, 2021).

It protects us against diabetes. Much of the issues with diabetes come from highly processed foods and red meat that are not common in this area. The Mediterranean diet helps with inflammation and body function, and it can have positive effects on those who already have diabetes, and help others who are at risk avoid getting it altogether (Gunnars & Link, 2021).

Finally, there are certain cancers that are linked to diet. Liver cancer, for example, can stem from fatty liver which is a result of obesity. The Mediterranean diet protects against this.

The Mediterranean Food Pyramid

The Mediterranean Diet Pyramid is basically a guide to what foods you should be eating if you want to follow the Mediterranean diet. At the base of the pyramid are the foods you should be eating the most of: fruits, veggies, whole grains, and healthy fats like olive oil. These are the foundation of the Mediterranean diet, so you should aim to eat a lot of them.

Moving up the pyramid, you'll find foods that you should eat in moderation, like fish, poultry, and dairy products. These foods are still a part of the diet, but you should be mindful of how much you're eating.

At the very top of the pyramid are the foods that you should only eat sparingly, like red meat, sweets, and processed foods. These are the foods that you should try to avoid if you can.

In addition to the food groups, the Mediterranean Diet Pyramid also emphasizes the importance of physical activity and socializing with others during meals. It's not just about what you eat, but how you eat it!

Overall, the Mediterranean Diet Pyramid is a simple and easy-to-follow guide to healthy eating. By focusing on fresh, whole foods and limiting processed and unhealthy options, you can nourish your body and enjoy delicious meals at the same time.

Foods to Eat

First of all, fruit is very important! Fruit contains vital vitamins and minerals, and in this way of eating, you don't have to limit your consumption of them! Apples, oranges and other citruses, berries, peaches, mangoes, grapes, and more are all ready and waiting for you to make them a part of your diet. A little tip if you are craving something sweet is to have cut up fruit with you. Oftentimes, this will do the trick!

Vegetables, as you might imagine, are next on the list. Like fruit, vegetables also contain items that are vital to your health. Carrots, broccoli, spinach, lettuce, onions, and more are all now a major part of the diet. It's worth noting that the traditional Mediterranean diet also includes potatoes, but there will be a difference in the level of processing between their potatoes and ours. At the end of the day, if you want to enjoy a starchy treat, it's best to be able to name all of the ingredients it contains.

Whole grains are your next item in this section. This will mean a lot of substitution. Many breaded and carb items are filled with refined grains which are stripped of their minerals and tend to harm us more than they help us. Whole wheat bread, pasta, rice, and other breaded items are all fantastic options for some of your favorite carb rich dishes.

Olive oil is a huge part of the Mediterranean diet. Because this diet is low on processed items, dressings and cooking sprays are often out of the picture. However, olives grow naturally in this area, so it's understandable that they are such a big part of the diet. You can cook with it, add it to baked goods, make dips out of it, and use it in dressing. If you're bored of the same olive oil, specialty stores often carry a wide variety of flavors!

Up next are beans. Beans can be very filling and they are a great source of protein. With the Mediterranean diet, you won't be consuming as much meat, so these will become important!

We can't forget about nuts and seeds. A lot of vitamins and minerals will come from them, and some nuts even have protein!

Finally, there are herbs and spices. They add flavor to your food and they are full of rich vitamins and minerals for your body.

Foods to Eat in Moderation

Anything listed above is something that should be a part of your diet every day. They take up a main portion of every meal. This next list, however, doesn't need to be included as often.

The most important ones on this list are fish, shellfish, and other seafood. You should be aiming to eat this at least two times a week. As discussed above, fish is a huge part of the Mediterranean diet. It provides a good source of healthy fat and protein. You should aim for fresh fish if you can!

Up next is poultry, which includes white meats such as chicken and turkey. These aren't nearly as hard on your heart as red meat tends to be. They still provide a great source of protein. You should be aiming for this anywhere from daily to weekly.

Up next are eggs. Like poultry items, eggs provide a great source of protein, but they aren't as important to the diet as items in the first category. You should also be aiming for a daily to weekly intake of this.

Next are the dairy products. This includes milk, cheese, and yogurt. Because these items have to go through some processing in order to be created, they aren't as involved in the diet, but they do

contain some much needed nutrients (like Vitamin D). They can also be a healthy source of fat in some cases. Try to aim for less processed options if possible and consume them anywhere from a daily to a weekly basis.

Finally, there is wine. Wine is a wonderful part of the Mediterranean diet, and is also something that should be consumed in moderation. That means something different to everyone. Whether you chose to have a single glass with a meal, or you chose to have a couple of drinks on the weekend with friends is up to you!

Foods That Won't Be the Main Part of the Diet

The cool thing about the Mediterranean diet is that it doesn't really eliminate foods, instead it relies on amounts and limits.

The main thing for this will be processed foods. This is incredibly hard in countries like America, where everything does seem to have a lot of processing to it, but that processing is hurting us! In countries in the Mediterranean region, it's actually harder to get a hold of processed foods than it is to get a hold of regular food types. This may link to why their health seems to be a lot better as a population.

Steer away from processed options as much as your budget will allow. White breaded items can be swapped for whole grains (which is something to consume daily) at almost no cost. Aim for fresh fruits and vegetables if you can, but if you have budget concerns, or if you know they will go bad, start reading labels very carefully. These can provide clues as to what's been processed more.

Running along the line of processed foods are candy. These should only be consumed once a week at most. They are often highly processed and even when they aren't, they still contain things that aren't very good for us. If you like sweet things, make fruit a go-to in your diet. Dates are also a fantastic way to satisfy your sweet tooth. If you are still really craving that sugar, aim for dark chocolate. It still has many great minerals for you and it hasn't been nearly as processed.

Finally, there is red meat. Red meat has been linked to a variety of issues, including raised cholesterol, heart disease, obesity, blood pressure, diabetes, etc. No one is certain on why it seems to be causing us so much trouble, but everyone can agree that it is problematic and that cutting it down in our diet would help us. The Mediterranean region has never had the same access to red meat that we do and as a result, they are in better internal shape. You should be eating this, at most, weekly.

Extra Virgin Olive Oil: The Core of the Mediterranean Diet

You may have heard before that substituting canola and vegetable oil with olive oil was a better choice. This is more than true!

Olive oil is a huge part of the Mediterranean diet. It can be cooked with, made into dips and dressings, and more. Olive oil is rich in the healthy fats you need, and finding the right kind means that you have an unprocessed oil to cook with.

When thinking of olive oil, you may just be thinking of the plain brand that ends up in every store, but there is more to it than that. If you know where to look, you can find specialty stores that sell olive oil in a variety of flavors with different processes to make them. Each one can add something amazing to your cooking!

If it is within your budget, I absolutely recommend trying out one of these speciality stores for your olive oil needs. They will have little to no processing, and their taste is impeccable.

If this isn't an option for you, then read the labels at your local grocery store carefully. Refined olive oil will be the most processed. Then there is virgin olive oil. Finally, anything labeled extra virgin olive oil will have the least amount of process, and it is associated with the most health benefits.

For extra virgin olive oil, you don't need to refrigerate it. With the other two, this is your best option. Do not store your olive oil next to the stove, as the heat can harm the potency of the oil and shorten its life. Keep it in a dark place and at room temperature. If you don't use it within a year, it may start to break down on you.

Chapter 2: Eight Steps to Getting Started

1. Eat LOTS of Vegetables

Vegetables are a major part of the Mediterranean diet. Technically, it's supposed to be a major part of all diets, but that isn't necessarily what happens. In many countries, fresh vegetables are often exalted, but they are expensive. When people think that frozen or canned items aren't good for them, they tend to leave without any vegetables. Whether it's fresh, frozen, or canned though, vegetables still have amazing benefits.

2. Change the Way You Think About Meat

We are taught that protein is vital to our diet. It is stressed to us from a young age, and it often leaves us to believe that we should consume it in every meal. This isn't true.

Meat isn't the only protein source out there. Beans, nuts, wholegrains, and even dairy all contain what we need.

Furthermore, we don't need meat with every meal. Having a protein source in our diet once a day will satisfy our body's needs most of the time.

Meat, in particular, can be dangerous if over consumed. Heart disease and it's cousins, high cholesterol, high blood pressure, obesity, and diabetes, are all associated with over consumption of meat.

3. Enjoy Some Dairy Products

People tend to over or under do it when it comes to dairy.

If you eat too little, you aren't getting enough of the vitamins and minerals that contribute to bone growth. If you are eating too much then you run the same risk that you do when you eat too much meat.

The Mediterranean diet says to consume dairy on a daily to weekly basis. You don't need it every day, but you should be having it more than once a week.

4. Eat Seafood Twice a Week

If your diet doesn't usually contain seafood, then this is a great place to start. Eating seafood twice a week can provide protein the same way meat can, and it provides you with healthy fats. Fresh fish is going to be your best bet if you can get a hold of it!

5. Cook a Vegetarian Meal One Night a Week

How much do you consume when it comes to vegetables? With the Mediterranean diet, you should be consuming them with just about every meal. Cooking in a vegetarian manner allows you to do just that, and opens your mind to more possibilities. If you want to ensure your meal is filling, add beans or whole grains…or both!

6. Use Good Fats

Olive oil! We are absolutely talking about olive oil here. Canola and other oils are extremely refined and can really hurt you in the long run. Olive oil, on the other hand, involves minimal processing and it is associated with great health benefits.

7. Switch to Whole Grains

Even though other diets have tried to eliminate them, carbohydrates are important to your diet…it's the kind of carb that will matter. White grains are extremely processed and have had all of the vital vitamins and minerals removed from them. Whole grain options let you get your carbs in while also containing what your body needs!

8. Use Fresh Fruit to Satisfy Your Sweet Tooth

Fresh fruit is incredibly sweet and full of nutrients. If you are like me and you get a sweet tooth, have something on hand from your local farmer's market! These won't contain processed additives that will do more harm than good, and they will make you feel better at the end of the day.

Living the Mediterranean Way

The Mediterranean region also has certain lifestyle aspects that will make a huge difference in how this diet works for you.

The Mediterranean region is, as a whole, more active. Their outdoor spaces are open and inviting (how could you not want to walk on the Mediterranean beach), and they have shorter commute times that usually render a car unnecessary. These mild things make a difference, and with these changes, they naturally make time for exercise too.

These changes can affect your metabolism and make a huge difference in how your body might handle things! You can try to go out for morning walks, or find some workout videos if you have an area at home. Going to a gym regularly can also be of great benefit.

The Mediterranean region is also in the habit of being social when it comes to food. Eating with the family, and having big gatherings that surround food as a culture are major. They also take time with lunch, even on the working day. Eating with people encourages you to slow down and taste what you are eating. You won't be trying to get it all down as quickly as possible.

Finally, they are wary of processed and outsourced food items. They can get everything they need rather easily, so why would they need anything processed. Processed and outsourced items can cost more in this region.

Small changes like these make a world of difference. The data proves it!

30 Days Mediterranean Diet Meal Plan

DAYS	BREAKFAST	LUNCH	DINNER	SNACK/DESSERT
1	Mini Shrimp Frittata	Grilled Bluefish	Ratatouille	Strawberry-Pomegranate Molasses Sauce
2	Spinach and Feta Egg Bake	Flatbread	Greek Potato Salad	Cherry-Stuffed Apples
3	Egg and Pepper Pita	Rustic Cauliflower and Carrot Hash	Rice Pilaf with Dill	Frozen Raspberry Delight
4	Tortilla Española (Spanish Omelet)	Walnut and Freekeh Pilaf	Classic Chicken Kebab	Fresh Figs with Chocolate Sauce
5	Peachy Oatmeal with Pecans	Air-Fried Okra	Honey and Spice Glazed Carrots	Greek Yogurt Ricotta Mousse
6	Nuts and Fruit Oatmeal	Spicy Grilled Veggie Pita	Classic Margherita Pizza	Creamy Spiced Almond Milk
7	Greek Yogurt Parfait	Brown Rice and Vegetable Pilaf	Bowtie Pesto Pasta Salad	Apricot and Mint No-Bake Parfait
8	Sunshine Overnight Oats	Radish Chips	Vegetable Pita Sandwiches	Pumpkin-Ricotta Cheesecake
9	Quinoa Porridge with Apricots	Black Beans with Corn and Tomato Relish	Quinoa Salad with Tomatoes	Karithopita (Greek Juicy Walnut Cake)
10	Golden Egg Skillet	Mediterranean Zucchini Boats	Five-Spice Roasted Sweet Potatoes	Apricot and Mint No-Bake Parfait
11	Mediterranean Muesli and Breakfast Bowl	Couscous with Apricots	Barley Risotto	S'mores
12	Oat and Fruit Parfait	Rice Pilaf with Dill	Wheat Berry Pilaf	Peaches Poached in Rose Water
13	Crunchy Vanilla Protein Bars	Quinoa with Artichokes	Margherita Open-Face Sandwiches	Grilled Peaches with Greek Yogurt
14	Gluten-Free Granola Cereal	Dandelion Greens	Zucchini Lasagna	Creamy Rice Pudding
15	Garlicky Beans and Greens with Polenta	Herbed Barley	Apple Couscous with Curry	Mascarpone and Fig Crostini
16	Spinach, Sun-Dried Tomato, and Feta Egg Wraps	Roasted Cherry Tomato Caprese	Jerk Chicken Wraps	Roasted Plums with Nut Crumble
17	Peachy Green Smoothie	Polenta with Mushroom Bolognese	Freekeh, Chickpea, and Herb Salad	Cucumber-Lime Popsicles
18	Baked Ricotta with Pears	Creamy Lima Bean Soup	Honey and Spice Glazed Carrots	Golden Coconut Cream Pops

DAYS	BREAKFAST	LUNCH	DINNER	SNACK/DESSERT
19	Spinach and Mushroom Mini Quiche	Braised Fennel	Creamy Thyme Polenta	Burrata Caprese Stack
20	Italian Egg Cups	Wild Mushroom Farrotto	Crispy Cabbage Steaks	Garlic-Lemon Hummus
21	Peach Sunrise Smoothie	Garlicky Broccoli Rabe with Artichokes	Rustic Cauliflower and Carrot Hash	Sweet Potato Fries
22	Breakfast Hash	Black Lentil Dhal	Black Lentil Dhal	Crispy Spiced Chickpeas
23	Nuts and Fruit Oatmeal	Roasted Garlic	Moroccan Red Lentil and Pumpkin Stew	Pesto Cucumber Boats
24	Blueberry-Banana Bowl with Quinoa	Chili-Spiced Beans	Caramelized Eggplant with Harissa Yogurt	Mascarpone and Fig Crostini
25	Chickpea Hash with Eggs	Zucchini-Eggplant Gratin	Greek Potato Salad	Almond Rice Pudding
26	Mediterranean Frittata	Rice with Pork Chops	Puréed Red Lentil Soup	Red Grapefruit Granita
27	Jalapeño Popper Egg Cups	Mediterranean Lentil Sloppy Joes	Arugula and Fennel Salad with Fresh Basil	Olive Oil Greek Yogurt Brownies
28	C+C Overnight Oats	Cauliflower Steaks Gratin	Eggplant Caponata	Dried Fruit Compote
29	Mediterranean Omelet	Sautéed Mustard Greens and Red Peppers	Roasted Vegetable Bocadillo with Romesco Sauce	Steamed Dessert Bread
30	Savory Breakfast Oats	Cretan Roasted Zucchini	Cucumbers with Feta, Mint, and Sumac	Black Olive and Lentil Pesto

Chapter 3 Breakfasts

Green Spinach & Salmon Crepes

Prep time: 10 minutes | Cook time: 5 minutes | Serves 1

Green Spinach Crepe:
1 cup fresh spinach or thawed and drained frozen spinach
1 small bunch fresh parsley
½ teaspoon fresh thyme leaves or ¼ teaspoon dried thyme
1 tablespoon nutritional yeast
1 tablespoon flax meal
Salt and black pepper, to taste
2 large eggs
2 teaspoons extra-virgin avocado oil or ghee for cooking
Salmon Filling:
3 ounces (85 g) wild smoked salmon
½ large avocado, sliced
2 tablespoons crumbled goat's cheese or feta
1 teaspoon fresh lemon or lime juice
Optional: fresh herbs or microgreens, to taste

Make the green spinach crepe: 1. Place the spinach, herbs, nutritional yeast, flax meal, salt, and pepper in a food processor or blender. Process well until the spinach is finely chopped. Add the eggs and process on low speed until the mixture is just combined. 2. Heat half of the oil in a large skillet and add half of the mixture. Swirl the pan so the mixture completely covers the bottom. Cook for about 3 minutes or until just set, then add the salmon and avocado. Sprinkle the crepe with the goat's cheese and drizzle with the lemon juice. Slide onto a plate and optionally garnish with fresh herbs or microgreens. Serve warm.

Per Serving:
calories: 673 | fat: 48g | protein: 44g | carbs: 23g | fiber: 15g | sodium: 762mg

Tiropita (Greek Cheese Pie)

Prep time: 15 minutes | Cook time: 45 minutes | Serves 12

1 tablespoon extra virgin olive oil plus 3 tablespoons for brushing
1 pound (454 g) crumbled feta
8 ounces (227g) ricotta cheese
2 tablespoons chopped fresh mint, or 1 tablespoon dried mint
2 tablespoons chopped fresh dill, or 1 tablespoon dried dill
¼ teaspoon freshly ground black pepper
3 eggs
12 phyllo sheets, defrosted
1 tsp white sesame seeds

1. Preheat the oven to 350°F (180 C). Brush a 9 × 13-inch (23 × 33cm) casserole dish with olive oil. 2. Combine the feta and ricotta in a large bowl, using a fork to mash the ingredients together. Add the mint, dill, and black pepper, and mix well. In a small bowl, beat the eggs and then add them to the cheese mixture along with 1 tablespoon olive oil. Mix well. 3. Carefully place 1 phyllo sheet in the bottom of the prepared dish. (Keep the rest of the dough covered with a damp towel.) Brush the sheet with olive oil, then place a second phyllo sheet on top of the first and brush with olive oil. Repeat until you have 6 layers of phyllo. 4. Spread the cheese mixture evenly over the phyllo and then fold the excess phyllo edges in and over the mixture. Cover the mixture with 6 more phyllo sheets, repeating the process by placing a single phyllo sheet in the pan and brushing it with olive oil. Roll the excess phyllo in to form an edge around the pie. 5. Brush the top phyllo layer with olive oil and then use a sharp knife to score it into 12 pieces, being careful to cut only through the first 3–4 layers of the phyllo dough. Sprinkle the sesame seeds and a bit of water over the top of the pie. 6. Place the pie on the middle rack of the oven. Bake for 40 minutes or until the phyllo turns a deep golden color. Carefully lift one side of the pie to ensure the bottom crust is baked. If it's baked, move the pan to the bottom rack and bake for an additional 5 minutes. 7. Remove the pie from the oven and set aside to cool for 15 minutes. Use a sharp knife to cut the pie into 12 pieces. Store covered in the refrigerator for up to 3 days.

Per Serving:
calories: 230 | fat: 15g | protein: 11g | carbs: 13g | fiber: 1g | sodium: 510mg

Golden Egg Skillet

Prep time: 15 minutes | Cook time: 20 minutes | Serves 2

2 tablespoons extra-virgin avocado oil or ghee
2 medium spring onions, white and green parts separated, sliced
1 clove garlic, minced
3½ ounces (99 g) Swiss chard or collard greens, stalks and leaves separated, chopped
1 medium zucchini, sliced into coins
2 tablespoons water
1 teaspoon Dijon or yellow mustard
½ teaspoon ground turmeric
¼ teaspoon black pepper
Salt, to taste
4 large eggs
¾ cup grated Manchego or Pecorino Romano cheese
2 tablespoons (30 ml) extra-virgin olive oil

1. Preheat the oven to 360°F (182°C) fan assisted or 400°F (205°C) conventional. 2. Grease a large, ovenproof skillet (with a lid) with the avocado oil. Cook the white parts of the spring onions and the garlic for about 1 minute, until just fragrant. Add the chard stalks, zucchini, and water. Stir, then cover with a lid. Cook over medium-low heat for about 10 minutes or until the zucchini is tender. Add the mustard, turmeric, pepper, and salt. Add the chard leaves and cook until just wilted. 3. Use a spatula to make 4 wells in the mixture. Crack an egg into each well and cook until the egg whites start to set while the yolks are still runny. Top with the cheese, transfer to the oven, and bake for 5 to 7 minutes. Remove from the oven and sprinkle with the reserved spring onions. Drizzle with the olive oil and serve warm.

Per Serving:
calories: 600 | fat: 49g | protein: 31g | carbs: 10g | fiber: 4g | sodium: 213mg

Baked Egg and Mushroom Cups

Prep time: 5 minutes | Cook time: 15 minutes | Serves 6

Olive oil cooking spray	8 ounces (227 g) baby bella mushrooms, sliced
6 large eggs	
1 garlic clove, minced	1 cup fresh baby spinach
½ teaspoon salt	2 scallions, white parts and green parts, diced
½ teaspoon black pepper	
Pinch red pepper flakes	

1. Preheat the air fryer to 320°F (160°C). Lightly coat the inside of six silicone muffin cups or a six-cup muffin tin with olive oil cooking spray. 2. In a large bowl, beat the eggs, garlic, salt, pepper, and red pepper flakes for 1 to 2 minutes, or until well combined. 3. Fold in the mushrooms, spinach, and scallions. 4. Divide the mixture evenly among the muffin cups. 5. Place into the air fryer and bake for 12 to 15 minutes, or until the eggs are set. 6. Remove and allow to cool for 5 minutes before serving.

Per Serving:
calories: 83 | fat: 5g | protein: 8g | carbs: 2g | fiber: 1g | sodium: 271mg

Mini Shrimp Frittata

Prep time: 15 minutes | Cook time: 20 minutes | Serves 4

1 teaspoon olive oil, plus more for spraying	shrimp, drained
	Salt and freshly ground black pepper, to taste
½ small red bell pepper, finely diced	
	4 eggs, beaten
1 teaspoon minced garlic	4 teaspoons ricotta cheese
1 (4-ounce / 113-g) can of tiny	

1. Spray four ramekins with olive oil. 2. In a medium skillet over medium-low heat, heat 1 teaspoon of olive oil. Add the bell pepper and garlic and sauté until the pepper is soft, about 5 minutes 3. Add the shrimp, season with salt and pepper, and cook until warm, 1 to 2 minutes. Remove from the heat. 4. Add the eggs and stir to combine. 5. Pour one quarter of the mixture into each ramekin. 6. Place 2 ramekins in the air fryer basket and bake at 350°F (177°C) for 6 minutes. 7. Remove the air fryer basket from the air fryer and stir the mixture in each ramekin. Top each frittata with 1 teaspoon of ricotta cheese. Return the air fryer basket to the air fryer and cook until eggs are set and the top is lightly browned, 4 to 5 minutes. 8. Repeat with the remaining two ramekins.

Per Serving:
calories: 114 | fat: 6g | protein: 12g | carbs: 1g | fiber: 0g | sodium: 314mg

Morning Buzz Iced Coffee

Prep time: 10 minutes | Cook time: 0 minutes | Serves 1

1 cup freshly brewed strong black coffee, cooled slightly	heavy cream (optional)
	1 teaspoon MCT oil (optional)
1 tablespoon extra-virgin olive oil	⅛ teaspoon almond extract
	⅛ teaspoon ground cinnamon
1 tablespoon half-and-half or	

1. Pour the slightly cooled coffee into a blender or large glass (if using an immersion blender). 2. Add the olive oil, half-and-half (if using), MCT oil (if using), almond extract, and cinnamon. 3. Blend well until smooth and creamy. Drink warm and enjoy.

Per Serving:
calories: 124 | fat: 14g | protein: 0g | carbs: 0g | fiber: 0g | sodium: 5mg

Spanish Tortilla with Potatoes and Peppers

Prep time : 5 minutes | Cook time: 50 minutes | Serves 6

½ cup olive oil, plus 2 tablespoons, divided	1 roasted red pepper, drained and cut into strips
2 pounds (907 g) baking potatoes, peeled and cut into ¼-inch slices	6 eggs
	2 teaspoons salt
	1 teaspoon freshly ground black pepper
2 onions, thinly sliced	

1. In a large skillet over medium heat, heat ½ cup of the olive oil. Add the potatoes and cook, stirring occasionally, until the potatoes are tender, about 20 minutes. Remove the potatoes from the pan with a slotted spoon and discard the remaining oil. 2. In a medium skillet over medium heat, heat the remaining 2 tablespoons of olive oil. Add the onions and cook, stirring frequently, until softened and golden brown, about 10 minutes. Remove the onions from the pan with a slotted spoon, leaving the oil in the pan, and add them to the potatoes. Add the pepper slices to the potatoes as well. 3. In a large bowl, whisk together the eggs, salt, and pepper. Add the cooked vegetables to the egg mixture and gently toss to combine. 4. Heat the medium skillet over low heat. Add the egg-vegetable mixture to the pan and cook for about 10 minutes, until the bottom is lightly browned. Use a spatula to loosen the tortilla and transfer the whole thing to a large plate, sliding it out of the pan so that the browned side is on the bottom. Invert the skillet over the tortilla and then lift the plate to flip it back into the skillet with the browned side on top. Return to the stove and continue to cook over low heat until the tortilla is fully set in the center, about 5 more minutes. 5. Serve the tortilla warm or at room temperature.

Per Serving:
calories: 370 | fat: 26g | protein: 9g | carbs: 29g | fiber: 5g | sodium: 876mg

Buffalo Egg Cups

Prep time: 10 minutes | Cook time: 15 minutes | Serves 2

4 large eggs	2 tablespoons buffalo sauce
2 ounces (57 g) full-fat cream cheese	½ cup shredded sharp Cheddar cheese

1. Crack eggs into two ramekins. 2. In a small microwave-safe bowl, mix cream cheese, buffalo sauce, and Cheddar. Microwave for 20 seconds and then stir. Place a spoonful into each ramekin on top of the eggs. 3. Place ramekins into the air fryer basket. 4. Adjust the temperature to 320°F (160°C) and bake for 15 minutes. 5. Serve warm.

Per Serving:
calories: 354 | fat: 29g | protein: 21g | carbs: 3g | fiber: 0g | sodium: 343mg

Tortilla Española (Spanish Omelet)

Prep time: 10 minutes | Cook time: 40 minutes | Serves 4

1½ pounds (680 g) Yukon gold potatoes, scrubbed and thinly sliced
3 tablespoons olive oil, divided
1 teaspoon kosher salt, divided
1 sweet white onion, thinly sliced
3 cloves garlic, minced
8 eggs
½ teaspoon ground black pepper

1. Preheat the oven to 350°F(180°C). Line 2 baking sheets with parchment paper. 2. In a large bowl, toss the potatoes with 1 tablespoon of the oil and ½ teaspoon of the salt until well coated. Spread over the 2 baking sheets in a single layer. Roast the potatoes, rotating the baking sheets halfway through cooking, until tender but not browned, about 15 minutes. Using a spatula, remove the potatoes from the baking sheets and let cool until warm. 3. Meanwhile, in a medium skillet over medium-low heat, cook the onion in 1 tablespoon of the oil, stirring, until soft and golden, about 10 minutes. Add the garlic and cook until fragrant, about 2 minutes. Transfer the onion and garlic to a plate and let cool until warm. 4. In a large bowl, beat the eggs, pepper, and the remaining ½ teaspoon salt vigorously until the yolks and whites are completely combined and slightly frothy. Stir in the potatoes and onion and garlic and combine well, being careful not to break too many potatoes. 5. In the same skillet over medium-high heat, warm the remaining 1 tablespoon oil until shimmering, swirling to cover the whole surface. Pour in the egg mixture and spread the contents evenly. Cook for 1 minute and reduce the heat to medium-low. Cook until the edges of the egg are set and the center is slightly wet, about 8 minutes. Using a spatula, nudge the omelet to make sure it moves freely in the skillet. 6. Place a rimless plate, the size of the skillet, over the omelet. Place one hand over the plate and, in a swift motion, flip the omelet onto the plate. Slide the omelet back into the skillet, cooked side up. Cook until completely set, a toothpick inserted into the middle comes out clean, about 6 minutes. 7. Transfer to a serving plate and let cool for 5 minutes. Serve warm or room temperature.

Per Serving:
calories: 376 | fat: 19g | protein: 15g | carbs: 37g | fiber: 5g | sodium: 724mg

Peachy Oatmeal with Pecans

Prep time: 10 minutes | Cook time: 4 minutes | Serves 4

4 cups water
2 cups rolled oats
1 tablespoon light olive oil
1 large peach, peeled, pitted, and diced
¼ teaspoon salt
½ cup toasted pecans
2 tablespoons maple syrup

1. Place water, oats, oil, peach, and salt in the Instant Pot®. Stir well. Close lid, set steam release to Sealing, press the Manual button, and set time to 4 minutes. 2. When the timer beeps, quick-release the pressure until the float valve drops. Press the Cancel button, open lid, and stir well. Serve oatmeal topped with pecans and maple syrup.

Per Serving:
calories: 399 | fat: 27g | protein: 8g | carbs: 35g | fiber: 7g | sodium: 148mg

Summer Day Fruit Salad

Prep time: 5 minutes | Cook time: 0 minutes | Serves 8

2 cups cubed honeydew melon
2 cups cubed cantaloupe
2 cups red seedless grapes
1 cup sliced fresh strawberries
1 cup fresh blueberries
Zest and juice of 1 large lime
½ cup unsweetened toasted coconut flakes
¼ cup honey
¼ teaspoon sea salt
½ cup extra-virgin olive oil

1. Combine all of the fruits, the lime zest, and the coconut flakes in a large bowl and stir well to blend. Set aside. 2. In a blender, combine the lime juice, honey, and salt and blend on low. Once the honey is incorporated, slowly add the olive oil and blend until opaque. 3. Pour the dressing over the fruit and mix well. Cover and refrigerate for at least 4 hours before serving, stirring a few times to distribute the dressing.

Per Serving:
calories: 249 | fat: 15g | protein: 1g | carbs: 30g | fiber: 3g | sodium: 104mg

Peachy Green Smoothie

Prep time: 10 minutes | Cook time: 0 minutes | Serves 2

1 cup almond milk
3 cups kale or spinach
1 banana, peeled
1 orange, peeled
1 small green apple
1 cup frozen peaches
¼ cup vanilla Greek yogurt

1. Put the ingredients in a blender in the order listed and blend on high until smooth. 2. Serve and enjoy.

Per Serving:
calories: 257 | fat: 5g | protein: 9g | carbs: 50g | fiber: 7g | sodium: 87mg

Baked Ricotta with Pears

Prep time: 5 minutes |Cook time: 25 minutes| Serves: 4

Nonstick cooking spray
1 (16-ounce / 454-g) container whole-milk ricotta cheese
2 large eggs
¼ cup white whole-wheat flour or whole-wheat pastry flour
1 tablespoon sugar
1 teaspoon vanilla extract
¼ teaspoon ground nutmeg
1 pear, cored and diced
2 tablespoons water
1 tablespoon honey

1. Preheat the oven to 400°F(205°C). Spray four 6-ounce ramekins with nonstick cooking spray. 2. In a large bowl, beat together the ricotta, eggs, flour, sugar, vanilla, and nutmeg. Spoon into the ramekins. Bake for 22 to 25 minutes, or until the ricotta is just about set. Remove from the oven and cool slightly on racks. 3. While the ricotta is baking, in a small saucepan over medium heat, simmer the pear in the water for 10 minutes, until slightly softened. Remove from the heat, and stir in the honey. 4. Serve the ricotta ramekins topped with the warmed pear.

Per Serving:
calories: 306 | fat: 17g | protein: 17g | carbs: 21g | fiber: 1g | sodium: 131mg

Spinach and Feta Egg Bake

Prep time: 7 minutes | Cook time: 23 to 25 minutes | Serves 2

Avocado oil spray
⅓ cup diced red onion
1 cup frozen chopped spinach, thawed and drained
4 large eggs
¼ cup heavy (whipping) cream
Sea salt and freshly ground black pepper, to taste
¼ teaspoon cayenne pepper
½ cup crumbled feta cheese
¼ cup shredded Parmesan cheese

1. Spray a deep pan with oil. Put the onion in the pan, and place the pan in the air fryer basket. Set the air fryer to 350ºF (177ºC) and bake for 7 minutes. 2. Sprinkle the spinach over the onion. 3. In a medium bowl, beat the eggs, heavy cream, salt, black pepper, and cayenne. Pour this mixture over the vegetables. 4. Top with the feta and Parmesan cheese. Bake for 16 to 18 minutes, until the eggs are set and lightly brown.

Per Serving:
calories: 366 | fat: 26g | protein: 25g | carbs: 8g | fiber: 3g | sodium: 520mg

Nuts and Fruit Oatmeal

Prep time: 10 minutes | Cook time: 7 minutes | Serves 2

1 cup rolled oats
1¼ cups water
¼ cup orange juice
1 medium pear, peeled, cored, and cubed
¼ cup dried cherries
¼ cup chopped walnuts
1 tablespoon honey
¼ teaspoon ground ginger
¼ teaspoon ground cinnamon
⅛ teaspoon salt

1. Place oats, water, orange juice, pear, cherries, walnuts, honey, ginger, cinnamon, and salt in the Instant Pot®. Stir to combine. 2. Close lid, set steam release to Sealing, press the Manual button, and set time to 7 minutes. When the timer beeps, let pressure release naturally, about 20 minutes. Press the Cancel button, open lid, and stir well. Serve warm.

Per Serving:
calories: 362 | fat: 8g | protein: 7g | carbs: 69g | fiber: 8g | sodium: 164mg

Egg and Pepper Pita

Prep time: 10 minutes | Cook time: 10 minutes | Serves 4

2 pita breads
2 tablespoons olive oil
1 red or yellow bell pepper, diced
2 zucchini, quartered lengthwise and sliced
4 large eggs, beaten
Sea salt
Freshly ground black pepper
Pinch dried oregano
2 avocados, sliced
½ to ¾ cup crumbled feta cheese
2 tablespoons chopped scallion, green part only, for garnish
Hot sauce, for serving

1. In a large skillet, heat the pitas over medium heat until warmed through and lightly toasted, about 2 minutes. Remove the pitas from the skillet and set aside. 2. In the same skillet, heat the olive oil over medium heat. Add the bell pepper and zucchini and sauté for 4 to 5 minutes. Add the eggs and season with salt, black pepper, and the oregano. Cook, stirring, for 2 to 3 minutes, until the eggs are cooked through. Remove from the heat. 3. Slice the pitas in half crosswise and fill each half with the egg mixture. Divide the avocado and feta among the pita halves. Garnish with the scallion and serve with hot sauce.

Per Serving:
calories: 476 | fat: 31g | protein: 17g | carbs: 36g | fiber: 11g | sodium: 455mg

Greek Yogurt Parfait

Prep time: 5 minutes | Cook time: 0 minutes | Serves 1

½ cup plain whole-milk Greek yogurt
2 tablespoons heavy whipping cream
¼ cup frozen berries, thawed with juices
½ teaspoon vanilla or almond extract (optional)
¼ teaspoon ground cinnamon (optional)
1 tablespoon ground flaxseed
2 tablespoons chopped nuts (walnuts or pecans)

1. In a small bowl or glass, combine the yogurt, heavy whipping cream, thawed berries in their juice, vanilla or almond extract (if using), cinnamon (if using), and flaxseed and stir well until smooth. Top with chopped nuts and enjoy.

Per Serving:
calories: 333 | fat: 27g | protein: 10g | carbs: 15g | fiber: 4g | sodium: 71mg

Greek Egg and Tomato Scramble

Prep time: 10 minutes | Cook time: 25 minutes | Serves 4

¼ cup extra-virgin olive oil, divided
1½ cups chopped fresh tomatoes
¼ cup finely minced red onion
2 garlic cloves, minced
½ teaspoon dried oregano or 1 to 2 teaspoons chopped fresh oregano
½ teaspoon dried thyme or 1 to 2 teaspoons chopped fresh thyme
8 large eggs
½ teaspoon salt
¼ teaspoon freshly ground black pepper
¾ cup crumbled feta cheese
¼ cup chopped fresh mint leaves

1. In large skillet, heat the olive oil over medium heat. Add the chopped tomatoes and red onion and sauté until tomatoes are cooked through and soft, 10 to 12 minutes. 2. Add the garlic, oregano, and thyme and sauté another 2 to 4 minutes, until fragrant and liquid has reduced. 3. In a medium bowl, whisk together the eggs, salt, and pepper until well combined. 4. Add the eggs to the skillet, reduce the heat to low, and scramble until set and creamy, using a spatula to move them constantly, 3 to 4 minutes. Remove the skillet from the heat, stir in the feta and mint, and serve warm.

Per Serving:
calories: 355 | fat: 29g | protein: 17g | carbs: 6g | fiber: 1g | sodium: 695mg

Italian Egg Cups

Prep time: 5 minutes | Cook time: 10 minutes | Serves 4

Olive oil	4 teaspoons grated Parmesan cheese
1 cup marinara sauce	
4 eggs	Salt and freshly ground black pepper, to taste
4 tablespoons shredded Mozzarella cheese	Chopped fresh basil, for garnish

1. Lightly spray 4 individual ramekins with olive oil. 2. Pour ¼ cup of marinara sauce into each ramekin. 3. Crack one egg into each ramekin on top of the marinara sauce. 4. Sprinkle 1 tablespoon of Mozzarella and 1 tablespoon of Parmesan on top of each egg. Season with salt and pepper. 5. Cover each ramekin with aluminum foil. Place two of the ramekins in the air fryer basket. 6. Air fry at 350°F (177°C) for 5 minutes and remove the aluminum foil. Air fry until the top is lightly browned and the egg white is cooked, another 2 to 4 minutes. If you prefer the yolk to be firmer, cook for 3 to 5 more minutes. 7. Repeat with the remaining two ramekins. Garnish with basil and serve.

Per Serving:
calories: 123 | fat: 7g | protein: 9g | carbs: 6g | fiber: 1g | sodium: 84mg

Peach Sunrise Smoothie

Prep time: 10 minutes | Cook time: 0 minutes | Serves 1

1 large unpeeled peach, pitted and sliced (about ½ cup)	peach low-fat Greek yogurt
	2 tablespoons low-fat milk
6 ounces (170 g) vanilla or	6 to 8 ice cubes

1. Combine all ingredients in a blender and blend until thick and creamy. Serve immediately.

Per Serving:
calories: 228 | fat: 3g | protein: 11g | carbs: 42g | fiber: 3g | sodium: 127mg

Breakfast Hash

Prep time: 10 minutes | Cook time: 30 minutes | Serves 6

Oil, for spraying	2 tablespoons olive oil
3 medium russet potatoes, diced	2 teaspoons granulated garlic
½ yellow onion, diced	1 teaspoon salt
1 green bell pepper, seeded and diced	½ teaspoon freshly ground black pepper

1. Line the air fryer basket with parchment and spray lightly with oil. 2. In a large bowl, mix together the potatoes, onion, bell pepper, and olive oil. 3. Add the garlic, salt, and black pepper and stir until evenly coated. 4. Transfer the mixture to the prepared basket. 5. Air fry at 400°F (204°C) for 20 to 30 minutes, shaking or stirring every 10 minutes, until browned and crispy. If you spray the potatoes with a little oil each time you stir, they will get even crispier.

Per Serving:
calories: 133 | fat: 5g | protein: 3g | carbs: 21g | fiber: 2g | sodium: 395mg

Sunshine Overnight Oats

Prep time: 5 minutes | Cook time: 0 minutes | Serves 2

⅔ cup vanilla, unsweetened almond milk (not Silk brand)	1 teaspoon honey
	¼ teaspoon turmeric
⅓ cup rolled oats	⅛ teaspoon ground cinnamon
¼ cup raspberries	Pinch ground cloves

1. In a mason jar, combine the almond milk, oats, raspberries, honey, turmeric, cinnamon, and cloves and shake well. Store in the refrigerator for 8 to 24 hours, then serve cold or heated.

Per Serving:
calories: 82 | fat: 2g | protein: 2g | carbs: 14g | fiber: 3g | sodium: 98mg

Quinoa Porridge with Apricots

Prep time: 10 minutes | Cook time: 12 minutes | Serves 4

1½ cups quinoa, rinsed and drained	1 cup almond milk
	1 tablespoon rose water
1 cup chopped dried apricots	½ teaspoon cardamom
2½ cups water	¼ teaspoon salt

1. Place all ingredients in the Instant Pot®. Stir to combine. Close lid, set steam release to Sealing, press the Rice button, and set time to 12 minutes. When the timer beeps, let pressure release naturally, about 20 minutes. 2. Press the Cancel button, open lid, and fluff quinoa with a fork. Serve warm.

Per Serving:
calories: 197 | fat: 2g | protein: 3g | carbs: 44g | fiber: 4g | sodium: 293mg

Mediterranean Muesli and Breakfast Bowl

Prep time: 10 minutes | Cook time: 0 minutes | Serves 12

Muesli:	Breakfast Bowl:
3 cups old-fashioned rolled oats	½ cup Mediterranean Muesli (above)
1 cup wheat or rye flakes	
1 cup pistachios or almonds, coarsely chopped	1 cup low-fat plain Greek yogurt or milk
½ cup oat bran	2 tablespoons pomegranate seeds (optional)
8 dried apricots, chopped	
8 dates, chopped	½ teaspoon black or white sesame seeds
8 dried figs, chopped	

1. To make the muesli: In a medium bowl, combine the oats, wheat or rye flakes, pistachios or almonds, oat bran, apricots, dates, and figs. Transfer to an airtight container and store for up to 1 month. 2. To make the breakfast bowl: In a bowl, combine the muesli with the yogurt or milk. Top with the pomegranate seeds, if using, and the sesame seeds.

Per Serving:
calories: 234 | fat: 6g | protein: 8g | carbs: 40g | fiber: 6g | sodium: 54mg

Savory Feta, Spinach, and Red Pepper Muffins

Prep time: 10 minutes | Cook time: 22 minutes | Serves 12

2 cups all-purpose flour
¾ cup whole-wheat flour
¼ cup granulated sugar
2 teaspoons baking powder
1 teaspoon paprika
¾ teaspoonp salt
½ cup extra virgin olive oil
2 eggs
¾ cup low-fat 2% milk
¾ cup crumbled feta
1¼ cups fresh baby leaf spinach, thinly sliced
⅓ cup jarred red peppers, drained, patted dry, and chopped

1. Preheat the oven to 375°F (190°C) and line a large muffin pan with 12 muffin liners. 2. In a large bowl, combine the all-purpose flour, whole-wheat flour, sugar, baking powder, paprika, and salt. Mix well. 3. In a medium bowl, whisk the olive oil, eggs, and milk. 4. Add the wet ingredients to the dry ingredients, and use a wooden spoon to stir until the ingredients are just blended and form a thick dough. 5. Add the feta, spinach, and peppers, and mix gently until all the ingredients are incorporated. Evenly divide the mixture among the muffin liners. 6. Transfer to the oven, and bake for 25 minutes or until a toothpick inserted into the middle of a muffin comes out clean. 7. Set the muffins aside to cool for 10 minutes, and remove them from the pan. Store in an airtight container in the refrigerator for up to 3 days. (Remove from the refrigerator 10 minutes before consuming.)

Per Serving:
calories: 243 | fat: 12g | protein: 6g | carbs: 27g | fiber: 2g | sodium: 306mg

Crunchy Vanilla Protein Bars

Prep time: 10 minutes | Cook time: 5 minutes | Serves 8

Topping:
½ cup flaked coconut
2 tablespoons raw cacao nibs
Bars:
1½ cups almond flour
1 cup collagen powder
2 tablespoons ground or whole chia seeds
1 teaspoon vanilla powder or 1 tablespoon unsweetened vanilla extract
¼ cup virgin coconut oil
½ cup coconut milk
1½ teaspoons fresh lemon zest
⅓ cup macadamia nuts, halved
Optional: low-carb sweetener, to taste

1. Preheat the oven to 350°F (180°C) fan assisted or 380°F (193°C) conventional. 2. To make the topping: Place the coconut flakes on a baking tray and bake for 2 to 3 minutes, until lightly golden. Set aside to cool. 3. To make the bars: In a bowl, combine all of the ingredients for the bars. Line a small baking tray with parchment paper or use a silicone baking tray. A square 8 × 8–inch (20 × 20 cm) or a rectangular tray of similar size will work best. 4. Press the dough into the pan and sprinkle with the cacao nibs, pressing them into the bars with your fingers. Add the toasted coconut and lightly press the flakes into the dough. Refrigerate until set, for about 1 hour. Slice to serve. Store in the refrigerator for up to 1 week.

Per Serving:
calories: 285 | fat: 27g | protein: 5g | carbs: 10g | fiber: 4g | sodium: 19mg

Blueberry-Lemon Tea Cakes

Prep time: 10 minutes | Cook time: 25 minutes | Serves 12

4 eggs
½ cup granulated sugar
Grated peel of 1 lemon
1½ cups all-purpose flour
¾ cup fine cornmeal
2 teaspoons baking powder
1 teaspoon kosher salt
1 cup extra-virgin olive oil
1½ cups fresh or frozen blueberries

1. Preheat the oven to 350°F(180°C). Grease a 12-cup muffin pan or line with paper liners. 2. With an electric mixer set to medium speed, beat the eggs and sugar together until they are pale and fluffy. Stir in the lemon peel. 3. In a medium bowl, stir together the flour, cornmeal, baking powder, and salt. With the mixer on low speed, alternate adding the flour mixture and oil to the egg mixture. Fold in the blueberries. 4. Dollop the batter into the muffin pan. Bake until the tops are golden and a toothpick inserted in the middle comes out clean, 20 to 25 minutes.

Per Serving:
calories: 317 | fat: 20g | protein: 4g | carbs: 31g | fiber: 2g | sodium: 217mg

Feta and Herb Frittata

Prep time : 10 minutes | Cook time: 30 minutes | Serves 6

¼ cup olive oil, divided
1 medium onion, halved and thinly sliced
1 clove garlic, minced
8 sheets phyllo dough
8 eggs
¼ cup chopped fresh basil, plus additional for garnish
¼ cup chopped flat-leaf parsley, plus additional for garnish
1 teaspoon salt
½ teaspoon freshly ground black pepper
4 ounces (113 g) crumbled feta cheese

1. Preheat the oven to 400°F(205°C). 2. Heat 2 tablespoons of the olive oil in a medium skillet over medium-high heat. Add the onions and cook, stirring frequently, until softened, about 5 minutes. Add the garlic and cook, stirring, for 1 minute more. Remove from the heat and set aside to cool. 3. While the onion mixture is cooling, make the crust. Place a damp towel on the counter and cover with a sheet of parchment paper. Lay the phyllo sheets in a stack on top of the parchment and cover with a second sheet of parchment and then a second damp towel. 4. Brush some of the remaining olive oil in a 9-by-9-inch baking dish or a 9-inch pie dish. Layer the softened phyllo sheets in the prepared dish, brushing each with some of the olive oil before adding the next phyllo sheet. 5. Next, make the filling. In a large bowl, whisk the eggs with the onion mixture, basil, parsley, salt, and pepper. Add the feta cheese and mix well. Pour the egg mixture into the prepared crust, folding any excess phyllo inside the baking dish. 6. Bake in the preheated oven for about 25 to 30 minutes, until the crust is golden brown and the egg filling is completely set in the center. Cut into rectangles or wedges and serve garnished with basil and parsley.

Per Serving:
calories: 298 | fat: 20g | protein: 12g | carbs: 17g | fiber: 1g | sodium: 769mg

Honey-Vanilla Greek Yogurt with Blueberries

Prep time: 2 minutes | Cook time: 0 minutes | Serves 2 to 3

2 cups plain Greek yogurt
¼ to ½ cup honey
¾ teaspoon vanilla extract
1 cup blueberries

1. In a medium bowl, stir together the yogurt, honey (start with the smaller amount; you can always add more later), and vanilla. Taste and add additional honey, if needed. 2. To serve, spoon the sweetened yogurt mixture into bowls and top with the blueberries.

Per Serving:
calories: 295 | fat: 0g | protein: 23g | carbs: 55g | fiber: 2g | sodium: 82mg

Red Pepper and Feta Egg Bites

Prep time: 5 minutes | Cook time: 8 minutes | Serves 6

1 tablespoon olive oil
½ cup crumbled feta cheese
¼ cup chopped roasted red peppers
6 large eggs, beaten
¼ teaspoon ground black pepper
1 cup water

1. Brush silicone muffin or poaching cups with oil. Divide feta and roasted red peppers among prepared cups. In a bowl with a pour spout, beat eggs with black pepper. 2. Place rack in the Instant Pot® and add water. Place cups on rack. Pour egg mixture into cups. Close lid, set steam release to Sealing, press the Manual button, and set time to 8 minutes. 3. When the timer beeps, quick-release the pressure until the float valve drops and open lid. Remove silicone cups carefully and slide eggs from cups onto plates. Serve warm.

Per Serving:
calories: 145 | fat: 11g | protein: 10g | carbs: 3g | fiber: 1g | sodium: 294mg

Spanish Tuna Tortilla with Roasted Peppers

Prep time: 15 minutes | Cook time: 15 minutes | Serves 4

6 large eggs
¼ cup olive oil
2 small russet potatoes, diced
1 small onion, chopped
1 roasted red bell pepper, sliced
1 (7-ounce / 198-g) can tuna packed in water, drained well and flaked
2 plum tomatoes, seeded and diced
1 teaspoon dried tarragon

1. Preheat the broiler on high. 2. Crack the eggs in a large bowl and whisk them together until just combined. Heat the olive oil in a large, oven-safe, nonstick or cast-iron skillet over medium-low heat. 3. Add the potatoes and cook until slightly soft, about 7 minutes. Add the onion and the peppers and cook until soft, 3–5 minutes. 4. Add the tuna, tomatoes, and tarragon to the skillet and stir to combine, then add the eggs. 5. Cook for 7–10 minutes until the eggs are bubbling from the bottom and the bottom is slightly brown. 6. Place the skillet into the oven on 1 of the first 2 racks, and cook until the middle is set and the top is slightly brown. 7. Slice into wedges and serve warm or at room temperature.

Per Serving:
calories: 247 | fat: 14g | protein: 12g | carbs: 19g | fiber: 2g | sodium: 130mg

Creamy Cinnamon Porridge

Prep time: 10 minutes | Cook time: 10 minutes | Serves 2

¼ cup coconut milk
¾ cup unsweetened almond milk or water
¼ cup almond butter or hazelnut butter
1 tablespoon virgin coconut oil
2 tablespoons chia seeds
1 tablespoon flax meal
1 teaspoon cinnamon
¼ cup macadamia nuts
¼ cup hazelnuts
4 Brazil nuts
Optional: low-carb sweetener, to taste
¼ cup unsweetened large coconut flakes
1 tablespoon cacao nibs

1. In a small saucepan, mix the coconut milk and almond milk and heat over medium heat. Once hot (not boiling), take off the heat. Add the almond butter and coconut oil. Stir until well combined. If needed, use an immersion blender and process until smooth. 2. Add the chia seeds, flax meal, and cinnamon, and leave to rest for 5 to 10 minutes. Roughly chop the macadamias, hazelnuts, and Brazil nuts and stir in. Add sweetener, if using, and stir. Transfer to serving bowls. In a small skillet, dry-roast the coconut flakes over medium-high heat for 1 to 2 minutes, until lightly toasted and fragrant. Top the porridge with the toasted coconut flakes and cacao nibs (or you can use chopped 100% chocolate). Serve immediately or store in the fridge for up to 3 days.

Per Serving:
calories: 646 | fat: 61g | protein: 13g | carbs: 23g | fiber: 10g | sodium: 40mg

Greek Yogurt Parfait with Granola

Prep time: 10 minutes | Cook time: 30 minutes | Serves 4

For the Granola:
¼ cup honey or maple syrup
2 tablespoons vegetable oil
2 teaspoons vanilla extract
½ teaspoon kosher salt
3 cups gluten-free rolled oats
1 cup mixed raw and unsalted nuts, chopped
¼ cup sunflower seeds
1 cup unsweetened dried cherries
For the Parfait:
2 cups plain Greek yogurt
1 cup fresh fruit, chopped (optional)

Make the Granola: 1. Preheat the oven to 325ºF (163ºC). Line a baking sheet with parchment paper or foil. 2. Heat the honey, oil, vanilla, and salt in a small saucepan over medium heat. Simmer for 2 minutes and stir together well. 3. In a large bowl, combine the oats, nuts, and seeds. Pour the warm oil mixture over the top and toss well. Spread in a single layer on the prepared baking sheet. Bake for 30 minutes, stirring halfway through. 4. Remove from the oven and add in the dried cherries. Cool completely and store in an airtight container at room temperature for up to 3 months. Make the Parfait: 5. For one serving: In a bowl or lowball drinking glass, spoon in ½ cup yogurt, ½ cup granola, and ¼ cup fruit (if desired). Layer in whatever pattern you like.

Per Serving:
calories: 370 | fat: 144g | protein: 19g | carbs: 44g | fiber: 6g | sodium: 100mg

Smoked Salmon Egg Scramble with Dill and Chives

Prep time: 5 minutes | Cook time: 5 minutes | Serves 2

4 large eggs	⅛ teaspoon freshly ground black pepper
1 tablespoon milk	2 teaspoons extra-virgin olive oil
1 tablespoon fresh chives, minced	2 ounces (57 g) smoked salmon, thinly sliced
1 tablespoon fresh dill, minced	
¼ teaspoon kosher salt	

1. In a large bowl, whisk together the eggs, milk, chives, dill, salt, and pepper. 2. Heat the olive oil in a medium skillet or sauté pan over medium heat. Add the egg mixture and cook for about 3 minutes, stirring occasionally. 3. Add the salmon and cook until the eggs are set but moist, about 1 minute.

Per Serving:
calories: 325 | fat: 26g | protein: 23g | carbs: 1g | fiber: 0g | sodium: 455mg

Spinach, Sun-Dried Tomato, and Feta Egg Wraps

Prep time: 10 minutes | Cook time: 7 minutes | Serves 2

1 tablespoon olive oil	1½ cups packed baby spinach
¼ cup minced onion	1 ounce (28 g) crumbled feta cheese
3 to 4 tablespoons minced sun-dried tomatoes in olive oil and herbs	Salt
3 large eggs, beaten	2 (8-inch) whole-wheat tortillas

1. In a large skillet, heat the olive oil over medium-high heat. Add the onion and tomatoes and sauté for about 3 minutes. 2. Turn the heat down to medium. Add the beaten eggs and stir to scramble them. 3. Add the spinach and stir to combine. Sprinkle the feta cheese over the eggs. Add salt to taste. 4. Warm the tortillas in the microwave for about 20 seconds each. 5. Fill each tortilla with half of the egg mixture. Fold in half or roll them up and serve.

Per Serving:
calories: 435 | fat: 28g | protein: 17g | carbs: 31g | fiber: 6g | sodium: 552mg

Gluten-Free Granola Cereal

Prep time: 7 minutes | Cook time: 30 minutes | Makes 3½ cups

Oil, for spraying	1 tablespoon toasted sesame oil or vegetable oil
1½ cups gluten-free rolled oats	1 teaspoon ground cinnamon
½ cup chopped walnuts	½ teaspoon salt
½ cup chopped almonds	½ cup dried cranberries
½ cup pumpkin seeds	
¼ cup maple syrup or honey	

1. Preheat the air fryer to 250ºF (121ºC). Line the air fryer basket with parchment and spray lightly with oil. (Do not skip the step of lining the basket; the parchment will keep the granola from falling through the holes.) 2. In a large bowl, mix together the oats, walnuts, almonds, pumpkin seeds, maple syrup, sesame oil, cinnamon, and salt. 3. Spread the mixture in an even layer in the prepared basket. 4. Cook for 30 minutes, stirring every 10 minutes. 5. Transfer the granola to a bowl, add the dried cranberries, and toss to combine. 6. Let cool to room temperature before storing in an airtight container.

Per Serving:
calories: 322 | fat: 17g | protein: 11g | carbs: 35g | fiber: 6g | sodium: 170mg

Garlicky Beans and Greens with Polenta

Prep time: 5 minutes | Cook time: 20 minutes | Serves 4

2 tablespoons olive oil, divided	or chard
1 roll (18 ounces / 510-g) precooked polenta, cut into ½"-thick slices	2 tomatoes, seeded and diced
	1 can (15 ounces / 425-g) small white beans, drained and rinsed
4 cloves garlic, minced	Kosher salt and ground black pepper, to taste
4 cups chopped greens, such as kale, mustard greens, collards,	

1. In a large skillet over medium heat, warm 1 tablespoon of the oil. Cook the polenta slices, flipping once, until golden and crispy, about 5 minutes per side. Remove the polenta and keep warm. 2. Add the remaining 1 tablespoon oil to the skillet. Cook the garlic until softened, 1 minute. Add the greens, tomatoes, and beans and cook until the greens are wilted and bright green and the beans are heated through, 10 minutes. Season to taste with the salt and pepper. To serve, top the polenta with the beans and greens.

Per Serving:
calories: 329 | fat: 8g | protein: 12g | carbs: 54g | fiber: 9g | sodium: 324mg

Spinach and Mushroom Mini Quiche

Prep time: 10 minutes | Cook time: 15 minutes | Serves 4

1 teaspoon olive oil, plus more for spraying	4 eggs, beaten
1 cup coarsely chopped mushrooms	½ cup shredded Cheddar cheese
	½ cup shredded Mozzarella cheese
1 cup fresh baby spinach, shredded	¼ teaspoon salt
	¼ teaspoon black pepper

1. Spray 4 silicone baking cups with olive oil and set aside. 2. In a medium sauté pan over medium heat, warm 1 teaspoon of olive oil. Add the mushrooms and sauté until soft, 3 to 4 minutes. 3. Add the spinach and cook until wilted, 1 to 2 minutes. Set aside. 4. In a medium bowl, whisk together the eggs, Cheddar cheese, Mozzarella cheese, salt, and pepper. 5. Gently fold the mushrooms and spinach into the egg mixture. 6. Pour ¼ of the mixture into each silicone baking cup. 7. Place the baking cups into the air fryer basket and air fry at 350ºF (177ºC) for 5 minutes. Stir the mixture in each ramekin slightly and air fry until the egg has set, an additional 3 to 5 minutes.

Per Serving:
calories: 156 | fat: 10g | protein: 14g | carbs: 2g | fiber: 1g | sodium: 411mg

C+C Overnight Oats

Prep time: 5 minutes | Cook time: 0 minutes | Serves 2

½ cup vanilla, unsweetened almond milk (not Silk brand)
½ cup rolled oats
2 tablespoons sliced almonds
2 tablespoons simple sugar liquid sweetener
1 teaspoon chia seeds
¼ teaspoon ground cardamom
¼ teaspoon ground cinnamon

1. In a mason jar, combine the almond milk, oats, almonds, liquid sweetener, chia seeds, cardamom, and cinnamon and shake well. Store in the refrigerator for 8 to 24 hours, then serve cold or heated.

Per Serving:
calories: 131 | fat: 6g | protein: 5g | carbs: 17g | fiber: 4g | sodium: 45mg

Blueberry-Banana Bowl with Quinoa

Prep time: 5 minutes | Cook time: 20 minutes | Serves 4

1½ cups water
¾ cup uncooked quinoa, rinsed
2 tablespoons honey, divided
1 cup blueberries (preferably frozen)
2 bananas (preferably frozen), sliced
½ cup sliced almonds or crushed walnuts
½ cup dried cranberries
1 cup granola
1 cup milk or nondairy milk of your choice

1. Combine the water and quinoa in a medium saucepan. Bring to a boil over medium-high heat, cover, reduce the heat to low, and simmer for 15 to 20 minutes, until the water has been absorbed. Remove from the heat and fluff the quinoa with a fork. 2. Evenly divide the quinoa among four bowls, about ½ cup for each bowl. Evenly divide the honey among the bowls and mix it in well. Top evenly with the blueberries, bananas, almonds, cranberries, granola, and milk. Serve.

Per Serving:
calories: 469 | fat: 15g | protein: 12g | carbs: 77g | fiber: 9g | sodium: 31mg

Chickpea Hash with Eggs

Prep time: 20 minutes | Cook time: 35 minutes | Serves 4

1 cup dried chickpeas
4 cups water
2 tablespoons extra-virgin olive oil, divided
1 medium onion, peeled and chopped
1 medium zucchini, trimmed and sliced
1 large red bell pepper, seeded and chopped
1 teaspoon minced garlic
½ teaspoon ground cumin
½ teaspoon ground black pepper
¼ teaspoon salt
4 large hard-cooked eggs, peeled and halved
½ teaspoon smoked paprika

1. Place chickpeas, water, and 1 tablespoon oil in the Instant Pot®. Close lid, set steam release to Sealing, press the Manual button, and set time to 30 minutes. 2. When the timer beeps, quick-release the pressure until the float valve drops, press the Cancel button, and open lid. Drain chickpeas well, transfer to a medium bowl, and set aside. 3. Clean and dry pot. Return to machine, press the Sauté button, and heat remaining 1 tablespoon oil. Add onion, zucchini, and bell pepper. Cook until tender, about 5 minutes. Add garlic, cumin, black pepper, and salt and cook for 30 seconds. Add chickpeas and turn to coat. 4. Transfer chickpea mixture to a serving platter. Top with eggs and paprika and serve immediately.

Per Serving:
calories: 274 | fat: 14g | protein: 15g | carbs: 36g | fiber: 16g | sodium: 242mg

Mediterranean Frittata

Prep time: 10 minutes | Cook time: 15 minutes | Serves 2

4 large eggs
2 tablespoons fresh chopped herbs, such as rosemary, thyme, oregano, basil or 1 teaspoon dried herbs
¼ teaspoon salt
Freshly ground black pepper
4 tablespoons extra-virgin olive oil, divided
1 cup fresh spinach, arugula, kale, or other leafy greens
4 ounces (113 g) quartered artichoke hearts, rinsed, drained, and thoroughly dried
8 cherry tomatoes, halved
½ cup crumbled soft goat cheese

1. Preheat the oven to broil on low. 2. In small bowl, combine the eggs, herbs, salt, and pepper and whisk well with a fork. Set aside. 3. In a 4- to 5-inch oven-safe skillet or omelet pan, heat 2 tablespoons olive oil over medium heat. Add the spinach, artichoke hearts, and cherry tomatoes and sauté until just wilted, 1 to 2 minutes. 4. Pour in the egg mixture and let it cook undisturbed over medium heat for 3 to 4 minutes, until the eggs begin to set on the bottom. 5. Sprinkle the goat cheese across the top of the egg mixture and transfer the skillet to the oven. 6. Broil for 4 to 5 minutes, or until the frittata is firm in the center and golden brown on top. 7. Remove from the oven and run a rubber spatula around the edge to loosen the sides. Invert onto a large plate or cutting board and slice in half. Serve warm and drizzled with the remaining 2 tablespoons olive oil.

Per Serving:
calories: 520 | fat: 44g | protein: 22g | carbs: 10g | fiber: 5g | sodium: 665mg

Jalapeño Popper Egg Cups

Prep time: 10 minutes | Cook time: 10 minutes | Serves 2

4 large eggs
¼ cup chopped pickled jalapeños
2 ounces (57 g) full-fat cream cheese
½ cup shredded sharp Cheddar cheese

1. In a medium bowl, beat the eggs, then pour into four silicone muffin cups. 2. In a large microwave-safe bowl, place jalapeños, cream cheese, and Cheddar. Microwave for 30 seconds and stir. Take a spoonful, approximately ¼ of the mixture, and place it in the center of one of the egg cups. Repeat with remaining mixture. 3. Place egg cups into the air fryer basket. 4. Adjust the temperature to 320ºF (160ºC) and bake for 10 minutes. 5. Serve warm.

Per Serving:
calories: 375 | fat: 30g | protein: 23g | carbs: 3g | fiber: 0g | sodium: 445mg

Berry Breakfast Smoothie

Prep time: 5 minutes | Cook time: 0 minutes | Serves 1

½ cup vanilla low-fat Greek yogurt
¼ cup low-fat milk
½ cup fresh or frozen blueberries or strawberries (or a combination)
6 to 8 ice cubes

1. Place the Greek yogurt, milk, and berries in a blender and blend until the berries are liquefied. Add the ice cubes and blend on high until thick and smooth. Serve immediately.

Per Serving:
calories: 158 | fat: 3g | protein: 9g | carbs: 25g | fiber: 1g | sodium: 110mg

Baked Peach Oatmeal

Prep time: 5 minutes | Cook time: 30 minutes | Serves 6

Olive oil cooking spray
2 cups certified gluten-free rolled oats
2 cups unsweetened almond milk
¼ cup raw honey, plus more for drizzling (optional)
½ cup nonfat plain Greek yogurt
1 teaspoon vanilla extract
½ teaspoon ground cinnamon
¼ teaspoon salt
1½ cups diced peaches, divided, plus more for serving (optional)

1. Preheat the air fryer to 380°F(193°C). Lightly coat the inside of a 6-inch cake pan with olive oil cooking spray. 2. In a large bowl, mix together the oats, almond milk, honey, yogurt, vanilla, cinnamon, and salt until well combined. 3. Fold in ¾ cup of the peaches and then pour the mixture into the prepared cake pan. 4. Sprinkle the remaining peaches across the top of the oatmeal mixture. Bake in the air fryer for 30 minutes. 5. Allow to set and cool for 5 minutes before serving with additional fresh fruit and honey for drizzling, if desired.

Per Serving:
calories: 197 | fat: 3g | protein: 9g | carbs: 36g | fiber: 4g | sodium: 138mg

Mediterranean Omelet

Prep time: 10 minutes | Cook time: 12 minutes | Serves 2

2 teaspoons extra-virgin olive oil, divided
1 garlic clove, minced
½ red bell pepper, thinly sliced
½ yellow bell pepper, thinly sliced
¼ cup thinly sliced red onion
2 tablespoons chopped fresh basil
2 tablespoons chopped fresh parsley, plus extra for garnish
½ teaspoon salt
½ teaspoon freshly ground black pepper
4 large eggs, beaten

1. In a large, heavy skillet, heat 1 teaspoon of the olive oil over medium heat. Add the garlic, peppers, and onion to the pan and sauté, stirring frequently, for 5 minutes. 2. Add the basil, parsley, salt, and pepper, increase the heat to medium-high, and sauté for 2 minutes. Slide the vegetable mixture onto a plate and return the pan to the heat. 3. Heat the remaining 1 teaspoon olive oil in the same pan and pour in the beaten eggs, tilting the pan to coat evenly. Cook the eggs just until the edges are bubbly and all but the center is dry, 3 to 5 minutes. 4. Either flip the omelet or use a spatula to turn it over. 5. Spoon the vegetable mixture onto one-half of the omelet and use a spatula to fold the empty side over the top. Slide the omelet onto a platter or cutting board. 6. To serve, cut the omelet in half and garnish with fresh parsley.

Per Serving:
calories: 218 | fat: 14g | protein: 14g | carbs: 9g | fiber: 1g | sodium: 728mg

Avocado Toast with Smoked Trout

Prep time: 10 minutes | Cook time: 0 minutes | Serves 2

1 avocado, peeled and pitted
2 teaspoons lemon juice, plus more for serving
¾ teaspoon ground cumin
¼ teaspoon kosher salt
¼ teaspoon red pepper flakes, plus more for sprinkling
¼ teaspoon lemon zest
2 pieces whole-wheat bread, toasted
1 (3.75-ounce / 106-g) can smoked trout

1. In a medium bowl, mash together the avocado, lemon juice, cumin, salt, red pepper flakes, and lemon zest. 2. Spread half the avocado mixture on each piece of toast. Top each piece of toast with half the smoked trout. Garnish with a pinch of red pepper flakes (if desired), and/or a sprinkle of lemon juice (if desired).

Per Serving:
calories: 300 | fat: 20g | protein: 11g | carbs: 21g | fiber: 6g | sodium: 390mg

Turkish Egg Bowl

Prep time: 10 minutes | Cook time: 15 minutes | Serves 2

2 tablespoons ghee
½–1 teaspoon red chile flakes
2 tablespoons extra-virgin olive oil
1 cup full-fat goat's or sheep's milk yogurt
1 clove garlic, minced
1 tablespoon fresh lemon juice
Salt and black pepper, to taste
Dash of vinegar
4 large eggs
Optional: pinch of sumac
2 tablespoons chopped fresh cilantro or parsley

1. In a skillet, melt the ghee over low heat. Add the chile flakes and let it infuse while you prepare the eggs. Remove from the heat and mix with the extra-virgin olive oil. Set aside. Combine the yogurt, garlic, lemon juice, salt, and pepper. 2. Poach the eggs. Fill a medium saucepan with water and a dash of vinegar. Bring to a boil over high heat. Crack each egg individually into a ramekin or a cup. Using a spoon, create a gentle whirlpool in the water; this will help the egg white wrap around the egg yolk. Slowly lower the egg into the water in the center of the whirlpool. Turn off the heat and cook for 3 to 4 minutes. Use a slotted spoon to remove the egg from the water and place it on a plate. Repeat for all remaining eggs. 3. To assemble, place the yogurt mixture in a bowl and add the poached eggs. Drizzle with the infused oil, and garnish with cilantro. Add a pinch of sumac, if using. Eat warm.

Per Serving:
calories: 576 | fat: 46g | protein: 27g | carbs: 17g | fiber: 4g | sodium: 150mg

Savory Breakfast Oats

Prep time: 10 minutes | Cook time: 15 minutes | Serves 2

½ cup steel-cut oats
1 cup water
1 large tomato, chopped
1 medium cucumber, chopped
1 tablespoon olive oil
Freshly grated, low-fat Parmesan cheese
Flat-leaf parsley or mint, chopped, for garnish
Sea salt and freshly ground pepper, to taste

1. Put the oats and 1 cup of water in a medium saucepan and bring to a boil on high heat. 2. Stir continuously until water is absorbed, about 15 minutes. 3. To serve, divide the oatmeal between 2 bowls and top with the tomatoes and cucumber. 4. Drizzle with olive oil, then top with the Parmesan cheese and parsley or mint. 5. Season to taste. 6. Serve immediately.

Per Serving:
calories: 240 | fat: 10g | protein: 8g | carbs: 32g | fiber: 6g | sodium: 10mg

Oat and Fruit Parfait

Prep time: 5 minutes | Cook time: 12 minutes | Serves 2

½ cup whole-grain rolled or quickcooking oats (not instant)
½ cup walnut pieces
1 teaspoon honey
1 cup sliced fresh strawberries
1½ cups vanilla low-fat Greek yogurt
Fresh mint leaves for garnish

1. Preheat the oven to 300°F(150°C). 2. Spread the oats and walnuts in a single layer on a baking sheet. 3. Toast the oats and nuts just until you begin to smell the nuts, 10 to 12 minutes. Remove the pan from the oven and set aside. 4. In a small microwave-safe bowl, heat the honey just until warm, about 30 seconds. Add the strawberries and stir to coat. 5. Place 1 tablespoon of the strawberries in the bottom of each of 2 dessert dishes or 8-ounce glasses. Add a portion of yogurt and then a portion of oats and repeat the layers until the containers are full, ending with the berries. Serve immediately or chill until ready to eat.

Per Serving:
calories: 541 | fat: 25g | protein: 21g | carbs: 66g | fiber: 8g | sodium: 124mg

Mediterranean Fruit Bulgur Breakfast Bowl

Prep time: 5 minutes |Cook time: 15 minutes| Serves: 6

1½ cups uncooked bulgur
2 cups 2% milk
1 cup water
½ teaspoon ground cinnamon
2 cups frozen (or fresh, pitted) dark sweet cherries
8 dried (or fresh) figs, chopped
½ cup chopped almonds
¼ cup loosely packed fresh mint, chopped
Warm 2% milk, for serving (optional)

1. In a medium saucepan, combine the bulgur, milk, water, and cinnamon. Stir once, then bring just to a boil. Cover, reduce the heat to medium-low, and simmer for 10 minutes or until the liquid is absorbed. 2. Turn off the heat, but keep the pan on the stove, and stir in the frozen cherries (no need to thaw), figs, and almonds. Stir well, cover for 1 minute, and let the hot bulgur thaw the cherries and partially hydrate the figs. Stir in the mint. 3. Scoop into serving bowls. Serve with warm milk, if desired. You can also serve it chilled.

Per Serving:
calories: 273 | fat: 7g | protein: 10g | carbs: 48g | fiber: 8g | sodium: 46mg

Grilled Halloumi with Whole-Wheat Pita Bread

Prep time: 5 minutes | Cook time: 10 minutes | Serves 4

2 teaspoons olive oil
8 (½-inch-thick) slices of halloumi cheese
4 whole-wheat pita rounds
1 Persian cucumber, thinly sliced
1 large tomato, sliced
½ cup pitted Kalamata olives

1. Brush a bit of olive oil on a grill pan and heat it over medium-high heat. 2. Brush the cheese slices all over with olive oil. Add the cheese slices in a single layer and cook until grill marks appear on the bottom, about 3 minutes. Flip the slices over and grill until grill marks appear on the second side, about 2 to 3 minutes more. 3. While the cheese is cooking, heat the pita bread, either in a skillet or in a toaster. 4. Serve the cheese inside of the pita pockets with the sliced cucumber, tomato, and olives.

Per Serving:
calories: 358 | fat: 24g | protein: 17g | carbs: 21g | fiber: 4g | sodium: 612mg

Mediterranean Breakfast Pita Sandwiches

Prep time: 5 minutes | Cook time: 7 minutes | Serves 2

2 eggs
1 small avocado, peeled, halved, and pitted
¼ teaspoon fresh lemon juice
Pinch of salt
¼ teaspoon freshly ground black pepper
1(8-inch) whole-wheat pocket pita bread, halved
12 (¼-inch) thick cucumber slices
6 oil-packed sun-dried tomatoes, rinsed, patted dry, and cut in half
2 tablespoons crumbled feta
½ teaspoon extra virgin olive oil

1. Fill a small saucepan with water and place it over medium heat. When the water is boiling, use a slotted spoon to carefully lower the eggs into the water. Gently boil for 7 minutes, then remove the pan from the heat and transfer the eggs to a bowl of cold water. Set aside. 2. In a small bowl, mash the avocado with a fork and then add the lemon juice and salt. Mash to combine. 3. Peel and slice the eggs, then sprinkle the black pepper over the egg slices. 4. Spread half of the avocado mixture over one side of the pita half. Top the pita half with 1 sliced egg, 6 cucumber slices, and 6 sun-dried tomato pieces. 5. Sprinkle 1 tablespoon crumbled feta over the top and drizzle ¼ teaspoon olive oil over the feta. Repeat with the other pita half. Serve promptly.

Per Serving:
calories: 427 | fat: 28g | protein: 14g | carbs: 36g | fiber: 12g | sodium: 398mg

South of the Coast Sweet Potato Toast

Prep time: 5 minutes | Cook time: 15 minutes | Serves 4

2 plum tomatoes, halved
6 tablespoons extra-virgin olive oil, divided
Salt
Freshly ground black pepper
2 large sweet potatoes, sliced lengthwise
1 cup fresh spinach
8 medium asparagus, trimmed
4 large cooked eggs or egg substitute (poached, scrambled, or fried)
1 cup arugula
4 tablespoons pesto
4 tablespoons shredded Asiago cheese

1. Preheat the oven to 450°F(235ºC). 2. On a baking sheet, brush the plum tomato halves with 2 tablespoons of olive oil and season with salt and pepper. Roast the tomatoes in the oven for approximately 15 minutes, then remove from the oven and allow to rest. 3. Put the sweet potato slices on a separate baking sheet and brush about 2 tablespoons of oil on each side and season with salt and pepper. Bake the sweet potato slices for about 15 minutes, flipping once after 5 to 7 minutes, until just tender. Remove from the oven and set aside. 4. In a sauté pan or skillet, heat the remaining 2 tablespoons of olive oil over medium heat and sauté the fresh spinach until just wilted. Remove from the pan and rest on a paper-towel-lined dish. In the same pan, add the asparagus and sauté, turning throughout. Transfer to a paper towel-lined dish. 5. Place the slices of grilled sweet potato on serving plates and divide the spinach and asparagus evenly among the slices. Place a prepared egg on top of the spinach and asparagus. Top this with ¼ cup of arugula. 6. Finish by drizzling with 1 tablespoon of pesto and sprinkle with 1 tablespoon of cheese. Serve with 1 roasted plum tomato.

Per Serving:
calories: 441 | fat: 35g | protein: 13g | carbs: 23g | fiber: 4g | sodium: 481mg

Spinach Pie

Prep time: 10 minutes | Cook time: 25 minutes | Serves 8

Nonstick cooking spray
2 tablespoons extra-virgin olive oil
1 onion, chopped
1 pound (454 g) frozen spinach, thawed
¼ teaspoon garlic salt
¼ teaspoon freshly ground black pepper
¼ teaspoon ground nutmeg
4 large eggs, divided
1 cup grated Parmesan cheese, divided
2 puff pastry doughs, (organic, if available), at room temperature
4 hard-boiled eggs, halved

1. Preheat the oven to 350°F(180ºC). Spray a baking sheet with nonstick cooking spray and set aside. 2. Heat a large sauté pan or skillet over medium-high heat. Put in the oil and onion and cook for about 5 minutes, until translucent. 3. Squeeze the excess water from the spinach, then add to the pan and cook, uncovered, so that any excess water from the spinach can evaporate. Add the garlic salt, pepper, and nutmeg. Remove from heat and set aside to cool. 4. In a small bowl, crack 3 eggs and mix well. Add the eggs and ½ cup Parmesan cheese to the cooled spinach mix. 5. On the prepared baking sheet, roll out the pastry dough. Layer the spinach mix on top of dough, leaving 2 inches around each edge. 6. Once the spinach is spread onto the pastry dough, place hard-boiled egg halves evenly throughout the pie, then cover with the second pastry dough. Pinch the edges closed. 7. Crack the remaining egg in a small bowl and mix well. Brush the egg wash over the pastry dough. 8. Bake for 15 to 20 minutes, until golden brown and warmed through.

Per Serving:
calories: 417 | fat: 28g | protein: 17g | carbs: 25g | fiber: 3g | sodium: 490mg

Egg Salad with Red Pepper and Dill

Prep time: 5 minutes | Cook time: 10 minutes | Serves 6

6 large eggs
1 cup water
1 tablespoon olive oil
1 medium red bell pepper, seeded and chopped
¼ teaspoon salt
¼ teaspoon ground black pepper
½ cup low-fat plain Greek yogurt
2 tablespoons chopped fresh dill

1. Have ready a large bowl of ice water. Place rack or egg holder into bottom of the Instant Pot®. 2. Arrange eggs on rack or holder and add water to the Instant Pot®. Close lid, set steam release to Sealing, press the Manual button, and set time to 5 minutes. 3. When the timer beeps, let pressure release naturally for 5 minutes, then quick-release the remaining pressure until the float valve drops. Press the Cancel button and open lid. Carefully transfer eggs to the bowl of ice water. Let stand in ice water for 10 minutes, then peel, chop, and add eggs to a medium bowl. 4. Clean out pot, dry well, and return to machine. Press the Sauté button and heat oil. Add bell pepper, salt, and black pepper. Cook, stirring often, until bell pepper is tender, about 5 minutes. Transfer to bowl with eggs. 5. Add yogurt and dill to bowl, and fold to combine. Cover and chill for 1 hour before serving.

Per Serving:
calories: 111 | fat: 8g | protein: 8g | carbs: 3g | fiber: 0g | sodium: 178mg

Oatmeal with Apple and Cardamom

Prep time: 10 minutes | Cook time: 7 minutes | Serves 4

1 tablespoon light olive oil
1 large Granny Smith, Honeycrisp, or Pink Lady apple, peeled, cored, and diced
½ teaspoon ground cardamom
1 cup steel-cut oats
3 cups water
¼ cup maple syrup
½ teaspoon salt

1. Press the Sauté button on the Instant Pot® and heat oil. Add apple and cardamom and cook until apple is just softened, about 2 minutes. Press the Cancel button. 2. Add oats, water, maple syrup, and salt to pot, and stir well. Close lid, set steam release to Sealing, press the Manual button, and set time to 5 minutes. 3. When the timer beeps, let pressure release naturally for 10 minutes, then quick-release the remaining pressure until the float valve drops. Press the Cancel button, open lid, and stir well. Serve hot.

Per Serving:
calories: 249 | fat: 6g | protein: 6g | carbs: 48g | fiber: 5g | sodium: 298mg

Cauliflower Avocado Toast

Prep time: 15 minutes | Cook time: 8 minutes | Serves 2

1 (12-ounce / 340-g) steamer bag cauliflower
1 large egg
½ cup shredded Mozzarella cheese
1 ripe medium avocado
½ teaspoon garlic powder
¼ teaspoon ground black pepper

1. Cook cauliflower according to package instructions. Remove from bag and place into cheesecloth or clean towel to remove excess moisture. 2. Place cauliflower into a large bowl and mix in egg and Mozzarella. Cut a piece of parchment to fit your air fryer basket. Separate the cauliflower mixture into two, and place it on the parchment in two mounds. Press out the cauliflower mounds into a ¼-inch-thick rectangle. Place the parchment into the air fryer basket. 3. Adjust the temperature to 400°F (204°C) and set the timer for 8 minutes. 4. Flip the cauliflower halfway through the cooking time. 5. When the timer beeps, remove the parchment and allow the cauliflower to cool 5 minutes. 6. Cut open the avocado and remove the pit. Scoop out the inside, place it in a medium bowl, and mash it with garlic powder and pepper. Spread onto the cauliflower. Serve immediately.

Per Serving:
calories: 321 | fat: 22g | protein: 16g | carbs: 19g | fiber: 10g | sodium: 99mg

Quickie Honey Nut Granola

Prep time: 10 minutes |Cook time: 20 minutes| Serves: 6

2½ cups regular rolled oats
⅓ cup coarsely chopped almonds
⅛ teaspoon kosher or sea salt
½ teaspoon ground cinnamon
½ cup chopped dried apricots
2 tablespoons ground flaxseed
¼ cup honey
¼ cup extra-virgin olive oil
2 teaspoons vanilla extract

1. Preheat the oven to 325°F(165°C). Line a large, rimmed baking sheet with parchment paper. 2. In a large skillet, combine the oats, almonds, salt, and cinnamon. Turn the heat to medium-high and cook, stirring often, to toast, about 6 minutes. 3. While the oat mixture is toasting, in a microwave-safe bowl, combine the apricots, flaxseed, honey, and oil. Microwave on high for about 1 minute, or until very hot and just beginning to bubble. (Or heat these ingredients in a small saucepan over medium heat for about 3 minutes.) 4. Stir the vanilla into the honey mixture, then pour it over the oat mixture in the skillet. Stir well. 5. Spread out the granola on the prepared baking sheet. Bake for 15 minutes, until lightly browned. Remove from the oven and cool completely. 6. Break the granola into small pieces, and store in an airtight container in the refrigerator for up to 2 weeks (if it lasts that long!).

Per Serving:
calories: 449 | fat: 17g | protein: 13g | carbs: 64g | fiber: 9g | sodium: 56mg

Berry Baked Oatmeal

Prep time: 10 minutes | Cook time: 45 to 50 minutes | Serves 8

2 cups gluten-free rolled oats
2 cups (10-ounce / 283-g bag) frozen mixed berries (blueberries and raspberries work best)
2 cups plain, unsweetened almond milk
1 cup plain Greek yogurt
¼ cup maple syrup
2 tablespoons extra-virgin olive oil
2 teaspoons ground cinnamon
1 teaspoon baking powder
1 teaspoon vanilla extract
½ teaspoon kosher salt
¼ teaspoon ground nutmeg
⅛ teaspoon ground cloves

1. Preheat the oven to 375°F (190°C). 2. Mix all the ingredients together in a large bowl. Pour into a 9-by-13-inch baking dish. Bake for 45 to 50 minutes, or until golden brown.

Per Serving:
calories: 180 | fat: 6g | protein: 6g | carbs: 28g | fiber: 4g | sodium: 180mg

Chapter 4 Beef, Pork, and Lamb

Saucy Beef Fingers

Prep time: 30 minutes | Cook time: 14 minutes | Serves 4

1½ pounds (680 g) sirloin steak
¼ cup red wine
¼ cup fresh lime juice
1 teaspoon garlic powder
1 teaspoon shallot powder
1 teaspoon celery seeds
1 teaspoon mustard seeds
Coarse sea salt and ground black pepper, to taste
1 teaspoon red pepper flakes
2 eggs, lightly whisked
1 cup Parmesan cheese
1 teaspoon paprika

1. Place the steak, red wine, lime juice, garlic powder, shallot powder, celery seeds, mustard seeds, salt, black pepper, and red pepper in a large ceramic bowl; let it marinate for 3 hours. 2. Tenderize the cube steak by pounding with a mallet; cut into 1-inch strips. 3. In a shallow bowl, whisk the eggs. In another bowl, mix the Parmesan cheese and paprika. 4. Dip the beef pieces into the whisked eggs and coat on all sides. Now, dredge the beef pieces in the Parmesan mixture. 5. Cook at 400°F (204°C) for 14 minutes, flipping halfway through the cooking time. 6. Meanwhile, make the sauce by heating the reserved marinade in a saucepan over medium heat; let it simmer until thoroughly warmed. Serve the steak fingers with the sauce on the side. Enjoy!

Per Serving:
calories: 483 | fat: 29g | protein: 49g | carbs: 4g | fiber: 1g | sodium: 141mg

Greek-Inspired Beef Kebabs

Prep timePrep Time: 15 minutes | Cook Time: 15 minutes | Serves 2

6 ounces (170 g) beef sirloin tip, trimmed of fat and cut into 2-inch pieces
3 cups of any mixture of vegetables: mushrooms, zucchini, summer squash, onions, cherry tomatoes, red peppers
½ cup olive oil
¼ cup freshly squeezed lemon juice
2 tablespoons balsamic vinegar
2 teaspoons dried oregano
1 teaspoon garlic powder
1 teaspoon minced fresh rosemary
1 teaspoon salt

1. Place the meat in a large shallow container or in a plastic freezer bag. 2. Cut the vegetables into similar-size pieces and place them in a second shallow container or freezer bag. 3. For the marinade, combine the olive oil, lemon juice, balsamic vinegar, oregano, garlic powder, rosemary, and salt in a measuring cup. Whisk well to combine. Pour half of the marinade over the meat, and the other half over the vegetables. 4. Place the meat and vegetables in the refrigerator to marinate for 4 hours. 5. When you are ready to cook, preheat the grill to medium-high (350–400°F) and grease the grill grate. 6. Thread the meat onto skewers and the vegetables onto separate skewers. 7. Grill the meat for 3 minutes on each side. They should only take 10 to 12 minutes to cook, but it will depend on how thick the meat is. 8. Grill the vegetables for about 3 minutes on each side or until they have grill marks and are softened.

Per Serving:
calories: 285 | fat: 18g | protein: 21g | carbs: 9g | fiber: 4g | sodium: 123mg

Beef Brisket with Onions

Prep time: 10 minutes | Cook time: 6 hours | Serves 6

1 large yellow onion, thinly sliced
2 garlic cloves, smashed and peeled
1 first cut of beef brisket (4 pounds / 1.8 kg), trimmed of excess fat
Coarse sea salt
Black pepper
2 cups chicken broth
2 tablespoons chopped fresh parsley leaves, for serving

1. Combine the onion and garlic in the slow cooker. 2. Season the brisket with salt and pepper, and place, fat-side up, in the slow cooker. 3. Add the broth to the slow cooker. Cover and cook until the brisket is fork-tender, on high for about 6 hours. 4. Remove the brisket to a cutting board and thinly slice across the grain. 5. Serve with the onion and some cooking liquid, sprinkled with parsley.

Per Serving:
calories: 424 | fat: 16g | protein: 67g | carbs: 4g | fiber: 1g | sodium: 277mg

Beef Ragù

Prep time: 15 minutes | Cook time: 4½ hours | Serves 6

1 medium yellow onion, diced small
3 cloves garlic, minced
6 tablespoons tomato paste
3 tablespoons chopped fresh oregano leaves (or 3 teaspoons dried oregano)
1 (4-pound / 1.8-kg) beef chuck roast, halved
Coarse sea salt
Black pepper
2 cups beef stock
2 tablespoons red wine vinegar

1. Combine the onion, garlic, tomato paste, and oregano in the slow cooker. 2. Season the roast halves with salt and pepper and place on top of the onion mixture in the slow cooker. Add the beef stock. 3. Cover and cook until meat is tender and can easily be pulled apart with a fork, on high for 4½ hours, or on low for 9 hours. Let cool 10 minutes. 4. Shred the meat while it is still in the slow cooker using two forks. Stir the vinegar into the sauce. Serve hot, over pasta.

Per Serving:
calories: 482 | fat: 19g | protein: 67g | carbs: 13g | fiber: 1g | sodium: 292mg

Mustard Lamb Chops

Prep time: 5 minutes | Cook time: 14 minutes | Serves 4

Oil, for spraying
1 tablespoon Dijon mustard
2 teaspoons lemon juice
½ teaspoon dried tarragon
¼ teaspoon salt
¼ teaspoon freshly ground black pepper
4 (1¼-inch-thick) loin lamb chops

1. Preheat the air fryer to 390ºF (199ºC). Line the air fryer basket with parchment and spray lightly with oil. 2. In a small bowl, mix together the mustard, lemon juice, tarragon, salt, and black pepper. 3. Pat dry the lamb chops with a paper towel. Brush the chops on both sides with the mustard mixture. 4. Place the chops in the prepared basket. You may need to work in batches, depending on the size of your air fryer. 5. Cook for 8 minutes, flip, and cook for another 6 minutes, or until the internal temperature reaches 125ºF (52ºC) for rare, 145ºF (63ºC) for medium-rare, or 155ºF (68ºC) for medium.

Per Serving:
calories: 96 | fat: 4g | protein: 14g | carbs: 0g | fiber: 0g | sodium: 233mg

One-Pan Greek Pork and Vegetables

Prep time: 10 minutes | Cook time: 40 minutes | Serves 3

1 pound (454 g) pork shoulder, cut into 1-inch cubes
¾ teaspoon fine sea salt, divided
½ teaspoon freshly ground black pepper, divided, plus more for serving
4 tablespoons extra virgin olive oil, divided
1 medium red onion, sliced
1 medium green bell pepper, seeded and sliced
1 medium carrot, peeled and julienned
¼ cup dry red wine
15 cherry tomatoes, halved
2 tablespoons hot water
½ teaspoon dried oregano

1. Scatter the cubed pork onto a cutting board and sprinkle with ¼ teaspoon of sea salt and ¼ teaspoon of black pepper. Flip the pieces over and sprinkle an additional ¼ teaspoon of sea salt and the remaining ¼ teaspoon of black pepper. 2. In a large pan wide enough to hold all the pork in a single layer, heat 3 tablespoons of olive oil over high heat. Once the oil is hot, add the pork pieces and brown for 2 minutes, then flip the pork pieces and brown for 2 more minutes. (Do not stir.) 3. Add the onions and sauté for 2 minutes and then add the bell peppers and carrots and sauté for 2 more minutes, ensuring all vegetables are coated with the oil. Reduce the heat to medium, cover the pan loosely, and cook for 5 minutes, stirring occasionally. 4. Add the wine and continue cooking for about 4 minutes, using a wooden spatula to scrape any browned bits from the bottom of the pan. Add about 20 cherry tomato halves and stir gently, then drizzle with the remaining 1 tablespoon of olive oil and add the hot water. Reduce the heat to low and simmer for 15–20 minutes or until all the liquids are absorbed. Remove the pan from the heat. 5. Sprinkle the oregano over the top. Top with the remaining cherry tomato halves and season to taste with the remaining ¼ teaspoon of sea salt and additional black pepper before serving. Store covered in the refrigerator for up to 3 days.

Per Serving:
calories: 407 | fat: 27g | protein: 30g | carbs: 8g | fiber: 2g | sodium: 700mg

Lamb Stew

Prep time: 20 minutes | Cook time: 2 hours 20 minutes | Serves 6

3 carrots, peeled and sliced
2 onions, minced
2 cups white wine
½ cup flat-leaf parsley, chopped
2 garlic cloves, minced
3 bay leaves
1 teaspoon dried rosemary leaves
¼ teaspoon nutmeg
¼ teaspoon ground cloves
2 pounds (907 g) boneless lamb, cut into 1-inch pieces
¼ cup olive oil
1 package frozen artichoke hearts
Sea salt and freshly ground pepper, to taste

1. Combine the carrots, onion, white wine, parsley, garlic, bay leaves, and seasonings in a plastic bag or shallow dish. 2. Add the lamb and marinate overnight. 3. Drain the lamb, reserving the marinade, and pat dry. 4. Heat the olive oil in a large stew pot. Brown the lamb meat, turning frequently. 5. Pour the marinade into the stew pot, cover, and simmer on low for 2 hours. 6. Add the artichoke hearts and simmer an additional 20 minutes. Season with sea salt and freshly ground pepper.

Per Serving:
calories: 399 | fat: 18g | protein: 33g | carbs: 13g | fiber: 3g | sodium: 167mg

Asian Glazed Meatballs

Prep time: 15 minutes | Cook time: 10 minutes per batch | Serves 4 to 6

1 large shallot, finely chopped
2 cloves garlic, minced
1 tablespoon grated fresh ginger
2 teaspoons fresh thyme, finely chopped
1½ cups brown mushrooms, very finely chopped (a food processor works well here)
2 tablespoons soy sauce
Freshly ground black pepper, to taste
1 pound (454 g) ground beef
½ pound (227 g) ground pork
3 egg yolks
1 cup Thai sweet chili sauce (spring roll sauce)
¼ cup toasted sesame seeds
2 scallions, sliced

1. Combine the shallot, garlic, ginger, thyme, mushrooms, soy sauce, freshly ground black pepper, ground beef and pork, and egg yolks in a bowl and mix the ingredients together. Gently shape the mixture into 24 balls, about the size of a golf ball. 2. Preheat the air fryer to 380ºF (193ºC). 3. Working in batches, air fry the meatballs for 8 minutes, turning the meatballs over halfway through the cooking time. Drizzle some of the Thai sweet chili sauce on top of each meatball and return the basket to the air fryer, air frying for another 2 minutes. Reserve the remaining Thai sweet chili sauce for serving. 4. As soon as the meatballs are done, sprinkle with toasted sesame seeds and transfer them to a serving platter. Scatter the scallions around and serve warm.

Per Serving:
calories: 274 | fat: 11g | protein: 29g | carbs: 14g | fiber: 4g | sodium: 802mg

Tenderloin with Crispy Shallots

Prep time: 30 minutes | Cook time: 18 to 20 minutes | Serves 6

1½ pounds (680 g) beef tenderloin steaks
Sea salt and freshly ground black pepper, to taste
4 medium shallots
1 teaspoon olive oil or avocado oil

1. Season both sides of the steaks with salt and pepper, and let them sit at room temperature for 45 minutes. 2. Set the air fryer to 400ºF (204ºC) and let it preheat for 5 minutes. 3. Working in batches if necessary, place the steaks in the air fryer basket in a single layer and air fry for 5 minutes. Flip and cook for 5 minutes longer, until an instant-read thermometer inserted in the center of the steaks registers 120ºF (49ºC) for medium-rare (or as desired). Remove the steaks and tent with aluminum foil to rest. 4. Set the air fryer to 300ºF (149ºC). In a medium bowl, toss the shallots with the oil. Place the shallots in the basket and air fry for 5 minutes, then give them a toss and cook for 3 to 5 minutes more, until crispy and golden brown. 5. Place the steaks on serving plates and arrange the shallots on top.

Per Serving:
calories: 166 | fat: 8g | protein: 24g | carbs: 1g | fiber: 0g | sodium: 72mg

Spaghetti Zoodles and Meatballs

Prep time: 30 minutes | Cook time: 11 to 13 minutes | Serves 6

1 pound (454 g) ground beef
1½ teaspoons sea salt, plus more for seasoning
1 large egg, beaten
1 teaspoon gelatin
¾ cup Parmesan cheese
2 teaspoons minced garlic
1 teaspoon Italian seasoning
Freshly ground black pepper, to taste
Avocado oil spray
Keto-friendly marinara sauce, for serving
6 ounces (170 g) zucchini noodles, made using a spiralizer or store-bought

1. Place the ground beef in a large bowl, and season with the salt. 2. Place the egg in a separate bowl and sprinkle with the gelatin. Allow to sit for 5 minutes. 3. Stir the gelatin mixture, then pour it over the ground beef. Add the Parmesan, garlic, and Italian seasoning. Season with salt and pepper. 4. Form the mixture into 1½-inch meatballs and place them on a plate; cover with plastic wrap and refrigerate for at least 1 hour or overnight. 5. Spray the meatballs with oil. Set the air fryer to 400ºF (204ºC) and arrange the meatballs in a single layer in the air fryer basket. Air fry for 4 minutes. Flip the meatballs and spray them with more oil. Air fry for 4 minutes more, until an instant-read thermometer reads 160ºF (71ºC). Transfer the meatballs to a plate and allow them to rest. 6. While the meatballs are resting, heat the marinara in a saucepan on the stove over medium heat. 7. Place the zucchini noodles in the air fryer, and cook at 400ºF (204ºC) for 3 to 5 minutes. 8. To serve, place the zucchini noodles in serving bowls. Top with meatballs and warm marinara.

Per Serving:
calories: 176 | fat: 8g | protein: 23g | carbs: 2g | fiber: 0g | sodium: 689mg

Pork Tenderloin with Vegetable Ragu

Prep time: 25 minutes | Cook time: 18 minutes | Serves 6

2 tablespoons light olive oil, divided
1 (1½-pound / 680-g) pork tenderloin
¼ teaspoon salt
¼ teaspoon ground black pepper
1 medium zucchini, trimmed and sliced
1 medium yellow squash, sliced
1 medium onion, peeled and chopped
1 medium carrot, peeled and grated
1 (14½-ounce / 411-g) can diced tomatoes, drained
2 cloves garlic, peeled and minced
¼ teaspoon crushed red pepper flakes
1 tablespoon chopped fresh basil
1 tablespoon chopped fresh oregano
1 sprig fresh thyme
½ cup red wine

1. Press the Sauté button on the Instant Pot® and heat 1 tablespoon oil. Season pork with salt and black pepper. Brown pork lightly on all sides, about 2 minutes per side. Transfer pork to a plate and set aside. 2. Add remaining 1 tablespoon oil to the pot. Add zucchini and squash, and cook until tender, about 5 minutes. Add onion and carrot, and cook until just softened, about 5 minutes. Add tomatoes, garlic, crushed red pepper flakes, basil, oregano, thyme, and red wine to pot, and stir well. Press the Cancel button. 3. Top vegetable mixture with browned pork. Close lid, set steam release to Sealing, press the Manual button, and set time to 3 minutes. When the timer beeps, quick-release the pressure until the float valve drops and open lid. Transfer pork to a cutting board and cut into 1" slices. Pour sauce on a serving platter and arrange pork slices on top. Serve immediately.

Per Serving:
calories: 190 | fat: 7g | protein: 23g | carbs: 9g | fiber: 2g | sodium: 606mg

Pork and Cabbage Egg Roll in a Bowl

Prep time: 10 minutes | Cook time: 10 minutes | Serves 6

1 tablespoon light olive oil
1 pound (454 g) ground pork
1 medium yellow onion, peeled and chopped
1 clove garlic, peeled and minced
2 teaspoons minced fresh ginger
¼ cup low-sodium chicken broth
2 tablespoons soy sauce
2 (10-ounce/ 283-g) bags shredded coleslaw mix
1 teaspoon sesame oil
1 teaspoon garlic chili sauce

1. Press the Sauté button on the Instant Pot® and heat olive oil. Add pork and sauté until cooked through, about 8 minutes. Add onion, garlic, and ginger, and cook until fragrant, about 2 minutes. Stir in chicken broth and soy sauce. Press the Cancel button. 2. Spread coleslaw mix over pork, but do not mix. Close lid, set steam release to Sealing, press the Manual button, and set time to 0 minutes. 3. When the timer beeps, quick-release the pressure until the float valve drops and open lid. Stir in sesame oil and garlic chili sauce. Serve hot.

Per Serving:
calories: 283 | fat: 24g | protein: 12g | carbs: 5g | fiber: 2g | sodium: 507mg

Beef Bourguignon with Egg Noodles

Prep time: 15 minutes | Cook time: 8 hours | Serves 8

2 pounds (907 g) lean beef stew meat
6 tablespoons all-purpose flour
2 large carrots, cut into 1-inch slices
16 ounces (454 g) pearl onions, peeled fresh or frozen, thawed
8 ounces (227 g) mushrooms, stems removed
2 garlic cloves, minced
¾ cup beef stock
½ cup dry red wine
¼ cup tomato paste
1½ teaspoons sea salt
½ teaspoon dried rosemary
¼ teaspoon dried thyme
½ teaspoon black pepper
8 ounces (227 g) uncooked egg noodles
¼ cup chopped fresh thyme leaves

1. Place the beef in a medium bowl, sprinkle with the flour, and toss well to coat. 2. Place the beef mixture, carrots, onions, mushrooms, and garlic in the slow cooker. 3. Combine the stock, wine, tomato paste, salt, rosemary, thyme, and black pepper in a small bowl. Stir into the beef mixture. 4. Cover and cook on low for 8 hours. 5. Cook the noodles according to package directions, omitting any salt. 6. Serve the beef mixture over the noodles, sprinkled with the thyme.

Per Serving:
calories: 397 | fat: 6g | protein: 34g | carbs: 53g | fiber: 6g | sodium: 592mg

Meatballs in Creamy Almond Sauce

Prep time: 15 minutes | Cook time: 35 minutes | Serves 4 to 6

8 ounces (227 g) ground veal or pork
8 ounces (227 g) ground beef
½ cup finely minced onion, divided
1 large egg, beaten
¼ cup almond flour
1½ teaspoons salt, divided
1 teaspoon garlic powder
½ teaspoon freshly ground black pepper
½ teaspoon ground nutmeg
2 teaspoons chopped fresh flat-leaf Italian parsley, plus ¼ cup, divided
½ cup extra-virgin olive oil, divided
¼ cup slivered almonds
1 cup dry white wine or chicken broth
¼ cup unsweetened almond butter

1. In a large bowl, combine the veal, beef, ¼ cup onion, and the egg and mix well with a fork. In a small bowl, whisk together the almond flour, 1 teaspoon salt, garlic powder, pepper, and nutmeg. Add to the meat mixture along with 2 teaspoons chopped parsley and incorporate well. Form the mixture into small meatballs, about 1 inch in diameter, and place on a plate. Let sit for 10 minutes at room temperature. 2. In a large skillet, heat ¼ cup oil over medium-high heat. Add the meatballs to the hot oil and brown on all sides, cooking in batches if necessary, 2 to 3 minutes per side. Remove from skillet and keep warm. 3. In the hot skillet, sauté the remaining ¼ cup minced onion in the remaining ¼ cup olive oil for 5 minutes. Reduce the heat to medium-low and add the slivered almonds. Sauté until the almonds are golden, another 3 to 5 minutes. 4. In a small bowl, whisk together the white wine, almond butter, and remaining ½ teaspoon salt. Add to the skillet and bring to a boil, stirring constantly. Reduce the heat to low, return the meatballs to skillet, and cover. Cook until the meatballs are cooked through, another 8 to 10 minutes. 5. Remove from the heat, stir in the remaining ¼ cup chopped parsley, and serve the meatballs warm and drizzled with almond sauce.

Per Serving:
calories: 447 | fat: 36g | protein: 20g | carbs: 7g | fiber: 2g | sodium: 659mg

Red Curry Flank Steak

Prep time: 30 minutes | Cook time: 12 to 18 minutes | Serves 4

²3 tablespoons red curry paste
¼ cup olive oil
2 teaspoons grated fresh ginger
2 tablespoons soy sauce
2 tablespoons rice wine vinegar
3 scallions, minced
1½ pounds (680 g) flank steak
Fresh cilantro (or parsley) leaves

1. Mix the red curry paste, olive oil, ginger, soy sauce, rice vinegar and scallions together in a bowl. Place the flank steak in a shallow glass dish and pour half the marinade over the steak. Pierce the steak several times with a fork or meat tenderizer to let the marinade penetrate the meat. Turn the steak over, pour the remaining marinade over the top and pierce the steak several times again. Cover and marinate the steak in the refrigerator for 6 to 8 hours. 2. When you are ready to cook, remove the steak from the refrigerator and let it sit at room temperature for 30 minutes. 3. Preheat the air fryer to 400ºF (204ºC). 4. Cut the flank steak in half so that it fits more easily into the air fryer and transfer both pieces to the air fryer basket. Pour the marinade over the steak. Air fry for 12 to 18 minutes, depending on your preferred degree of doneness of the steak (12 minutes = medium rare). Flip the steak over halfway through the cooking time. 5. When your desired degree of doneness has been reached, remove the steak to a cutting board and let it rest for 5 minutes before slicing. Thinly slice the flank steak against the grain of the meat. Transfer the slices to a serving platter, pour any juice from the bottom of the air fryer over the sliced flank steak and sprinkle the fresh cilantro on top.

Per Serving:
calories: 397 | fat: 24g | protein: 38g | carbs: 6g | fiber: 3g | sodium: 216mg

Herb-Roasted Beef Tips with Onions

Prep time: 5 minutes | Cook time: 10 minutes | Serves 4

1 pound (454 g) rib eye steak, cubed
2 garlic cloves, minced
2 tablespoons olive oil
1 tablespoon fresh oregano
1 teaspoon salt
½ teaspoon black pepper
1 yellow onion, thinly sliced

1. Preheat the air fryer to 380ºF (193ºC). 2. In a medium bowl, combine the steak, garlic, olive oil, oregano, salt, pepper, and onion. Mix until all of the beef and onion are well coated. 3. Put the seasoned steak mixture into the air fryer basket. Roast for 5 minutes. Stir and roast for 5 minutes more. 4. Let rest for 5 minutes before serving with some favorite sides.

Per Serving:
calories: 380 | fat: 28g | protein: 28g | carbs: 3g | fiber: 0g | sodium: 646mg

Herbed Lamb Meatballs

Prep time: 10 minutes | Cook time: 6 to 8 hours | Serves 4

1 (28-ounce / 794-g) can no-salt-added diced tomatoes
2 garlic cloves, minced, divided
1 pound (454 g) raw ground lamb
1 small onion, finely diced, or 1 tablespoon dried onion flakes
1 large egg
2 tablespoons bread crumbs
1 teaspoon dried basil
1 teaspoon dried oregano
1 teaspoon dried rosemary
1 teaspoon dried thyme
1 teaspoon sea salt
½ teaspoon freshly ground black pepper

1. In a slow cooker, combine the tomatoes and 1 clove of garlic. Stir to mix well. 2. In a large bowl, mix together the ground lamb, onion, egg, bread crumbs, basil, oregano, rosemary, thyme, salt, pepper, and the remaining 1 garlic clove until all of the ingredients are well-blended. Shape the meat mixture into 10 to 12 (2½-inch) meatballs. Put the meatballs in the slow cooker. 3. Cover the cooker and cook for 6 to 8 hours on Low heat.

Per Serving:
calories: 406 | fat: 28g | protein: 23g | carbs: 16g | fiber: 5g | sodium: 815mg

Greek Lamb Burgers

Prep time: 10 minutes | Cook time: 10 minutes | Serves 4

1 pound (454 g) ground lamb
½ teaspoon salt
½ teaspoon freshly ground black pepper
4 tablespoons feta cheese, crumbled
Buns, toppings, and tzatziki, for serving (optional)

1. Preheat a grill, grill pan, or lightly oiled skillet to high heat. 2. In a large bowl, using your hands, combine the lamb with the salt and pepper. 3. Divide the meat into 4 portions. Divide each portion in half to make a top and a bottom. Flatten each half into a 3-inch circle. Make a dent in the center of one of the halves and place 1 tablespoon of the feta cheese in the center. Place the second half of the patty on top of the feta cheese and press down to close the 2 halves together, making it resemble a round burger. 4. Cook the stuffed patty for 3 minutes on each side, for medium-well. Serve on a bun with your favorite toppings and tzatziki sauce, if desired.

Per Serving:
calories: 345 | fat: 29g | protein: 20g | carbs: 1g | fiber: 0g | sodium: 462mg

Blackened Cajun Pork Roast

Prep time: 20 minutes | Cook time: 33 minutes | Serves 4

2 pounds (907 g) bone-in pork loin roast
2 tablespoons oil
¼ cup Cajun seasoning
½ cup diced onion
½ cup diced celery
½ cup diced green bell pepper
1 tablespoon minced garlic

1. Cut 5 slits across the pork roast. Spritz it with oil, coating it completely. Evenly sprinkle the Cajun seasoning over the pork roast. 2. In a medium bowl, stir together the onion, celery, green bell pepper, and garlic until combined. Set aside. 3. Preheat the air fryer to 360ºF (182ºC). Line the air fryer basket with parchment paper. 4. Place the pork roast on the parchment and spritz with oil. 5. Cook for 5 minutes. Flip the roast and cook for 5 minutes more. Continue to flip and cook in 5-minute increments for a total cook time of 20 minutes. 6. Increase the air fryer temperature to 390ºF (199ºC). 7. Cook the roast for 8 minutes more and flip. Add the vegetable mixture to the basket and cook for a final 5 minutes. Let the roast sit for 5 minutes before serving.

Per Serving:
calories: 400 | fat: 16g | protein: 52g | carbs: 8g | fiber: 2g | sodium: 738mg

Fajita Meatball Lettuce Wraps

Prep time: 10 minutes | Cook time: 10 minutes | Serves 4

1 pound (454 g) ground beef (85% lean)
½ cup salsa, plus more for serving if desired
¼ cup chopped onions
¼ cup diced green or red bell peppers
1 large egg, beaten
1 teaspoon fine sea salt
½ teaspoon chili powder
½ teaspoon ground cumin
1 clove garlic, minced
For Serving (Optional):
8 leaves Boston lettuce
Pico de gallo or salsa
Lime slices

1. Spray the air fryer basket with avocado oil. Preheat the air fryer to 350ºF (177ºC). 2. In a large bowl, mix together all the ingredients until well combined. 3. Shape the meat mixture into eight 1-inch balls. Place the meatballs in the air fryer basket, leaving a little space between them. Air fry for 10 minutes, or until cooked through and no longer pink inside and the internal temperature reaches 145ºF (63ºC). 4. Serve each meatball on a lettuce leaf, topped with pico de gallo or salsa, if desired. Serve with lime slices if desired. 5. Store leftovers in an airtight container in the fridge for 3 days or in the freezer for up to a month. Reheat in a preheated 350ºF (177ºC) air fryer for 4 minutes, or until heated through.

Per Serving:
calories: 289 | fat: 20g | protein: 24g | carbs: 4g | fiber: 1g | sodium: 815mg

Mediterranean Pork with Olives

Prep time: 10 minutes | Cook time: 6 to 8 hours | Serves 4

1 small onion, sliced
4 thick-cut, bone-in pork chops
1 cup low-sodium chicken broth
Juice of 1 lemon
2 garlic cloves, minced
1 teaspoon sea salt
1 teaspoon dried oregano
1 teaspoon dried parsley
½ teaspoon freshly ground black pepper
2 cups whole green olives, pitted
1 pint cherry tomatoes

1. Put the onion in a slow cooker and arrange the pork chops on top. 2. In a small bowl, whisk together the chicken broth, lemon juice, garlic, salt, oregano, parsley, and pepper. Pour the sauce over the pork chops. Top with the olives and tomatoes. 3. Cover the cooker and cook for 6 to 8 hours on Low heat.

Per Serving:
calories: 339 | fat: 14g | protein: 42g | carbs: 6g | fiber: 4g | sodium: 708mg

Beef Whirls

Prep time: 30 minutes | Cook time: 18 minutes | Serves 6

- 3 cube steaks (6 ounces / 170 g each)
- 1 (16-ounce / 454-g) bottle Italian dressing
- 1 cup Italian-style bread crumbs
- ½ cup grated Parmesan cheese
- 1 teaspoon dried basil
- 1 teaspoon dried oregano
- 1 teaspoon dried parsley
- ¼ cup beef broth
- 1 to 2 tablespoons oil

1. In a large resealable bag, combine the steaks and Italian dressing. Seal the bag and refrigerate to marinate for 2 hours. 2. In a medium bowl, whisk the bread crumbs, cheese, basil, oregano, and parsley until blended. Stir in the beef broth. 3. Place the steaks on a cutting board and cut each in half so you have 6 equal pieces. Sprinkle with the bread crumb mixture. Roll up the steaks, jelly roll-style, and secure with toothpicks. 4. Preheat the air fryer to 400°F (204°C). 5. Place 3 roll-ups in the air fryer basket. 6. Cook for 5 minutes. Flip the roll-ups and spritz with oil. Cook for 4 minutes more until the internal temperature reaches 145°F (63°C). Repeat with the remaining roll-ups. Let rest for 5 to 10 minutes before serving.

Per Serving:
calories: 307 | fat: 15g | protein: 24g | carbs: 17g | fiber: 1g | sodium: 236mg

Herb-Crusted Lamb Chops

Prep time: 10 minutes | Cook time: 5 minutes | Serves 2

- 1 large egg
- 2 cloves garlic, minced
- ¼ cup pork dust
- ¼ cup powdered Parmesan cheese
- 1 tablespoon chopped fresh oregano leaves
- 1 tablespoon chopped fresh rosemary leaves
- 1 teaspoon chopped fresh thyme leaves
- ½ teaspoon ground black pepper
- 4 (1-inch-thick) lamb chops
- For Garnish/Serving (Optional):
- Sprigs of fresh oregano
- Sprigs of fresh rosemary
- Sprigs of fresh thyme
- Lavender flowers
- Lemon slices

1. Spray the air fryer basket with avocado oil. Preheat the air fryer to 400°F (204°C). 2. Beat the egg in a shallow bowl, add the garlic, and stir well to combine. In another shallow bowl, mix together the pork dust, Parmesan, herbs, and pepper. 3. One at a time, dip the lamb chops into the egg mixture, shake off the excess egg, and then dredge them in the Parmesan mixture. Use your hands to coat the chops well in the Parmesan mixture and form a nice crust on all sides; if necessary, dip the chops again in both the egg and the Parmesan mixture. 4. Place the lamb chops in the air fryer basket, leaving space between them, and air fry for 5 minutes, or until the internal temperature reaches 145°F (63°C) for medium doneness. Allow to rest for 10 minutes before serving. 5. Garnish with sprigs of oregano, rosemary, and thyme, and lavender flowers, if desired. Serve with lemon slices, if desired. 6. Best served fresh. Store leftovers in an airtight container in the fridge for up to 4 days. Serve chilled over a salad, or reheat in a 350°F (177°C) air fryer for 3 minutes, or until heated through.

Per Serving:
calories: 510 | fat: 42g | protein: 30g | carbs: 3g | fiber: 1g | sodium: 380mg

Pepper Steak

Prep time: 30 minutes | Cook time: 16 to 20 minutes | Serves 4

- 1 pound (454 g) cube steak, cut into 1-inch pieces
- 1 cup Italian dressing
- 1½ cups beef broth
- 1 tablespoon soy sauce
- ½ teaspoon salt
- ¼ teaspoon freshly ground black pepper
- ¼ cup cornstarch
- 1 cup thinly sliced bell pepper, any color
- 1 cup chopped celery
- 1 tablespoon minced garlic
- 1 to 2 tablespoons oil

1. In a large resealable bag, combine the beef and Italian dressing. Seal the bag and refrigerate to marinate for 8 hours. 2. In a small bowl, whisk the beef broth, soy sauce, salt, and pepper until blended. 3. In another small bowl, whisk ¼ cup water and the cornstarch until dissolved. Stir the cornstarch mixture into the beef broth mixture until blended. 4. Preheat the air fryer to 375°F (191°C). 5. Pour the broth mixture into a baking pan. Cook for 4 minutes. Stir and cook for 4 to 5 minutes more. Remove and set aside. 6. Increase the air fryer temperature to 400°F (204°C). Line the air fryer basket with parchment paper. 7. Remove the steak from the marinade and place it in a medium bowl. Discard the marinade. Stir in the bell pepper, celery, and garlic. 8. Place the steak and pepper mixture on the parchment. Spritz with oil. 9. Cook for 4 minutes. Shake the basket and cook for 4 to 7 minutes more, until the vegetables are tender and the meat reaches an internal temperature of 145°F (63°C). Serve with the gravy.

Per Serving:
calories: 302 | fat: 14g | protein: 27g | carbs: 15g | fiber: 1g | sodium: 635mg

Roasted Pork with Apple-Dijon Sauce

Prep time: 15 minutes | Cook time: 40 minutes | Serves 8

- 1½ tablespoons extra-virgin olive oil
- 1 (12-ounce/ 340-g) pork tenderloin
- ¼ teaspoon kosher salt
- ¼ teaspoon freshly ground black pepper
- ¼ cup apple jelly
- ¼ cup apple juice
- 2 to 3 tablespoons Dijon mustard
- ½ tablespoon cornstarch
- ½ tablespoon cream

1. Preheat the oven to 325°F(165°C). 2. In a large sauté pan or skillet, heat the olive oil over medium heat. 3. Add the pork to the skillet, using tongs to turn and sear the pork on all sides. Once seared, sprinkle pork with salt and pepper, and set it on a small baking sheet. 4. In the same skillet, with the juices from the pork, mix the apple jelly, juice, and mustard into the pan juices. Heat thoroughly over low heat, stirring consistently for 5 minutes. Spoon over the pork. 5. Put the pork in the oven and roast for 15 to 17 minutes, or 20 minutes per pound. Every 10 to 15 minutes, baste the pork with the apple-mustard sauce. 6. Once the pork tenderloin is done, remove it from the oven and let it rest for 15 minutes. Then, cut it into 1-inch slices. 7. In a small pot, blend the cornstarch with cream. Heat over low heat. Add the pan juices into the pot, stirring for 2 minutes, until thickened. Serve the sauce over the pork.

Per Serving:
calories: 146 | fat: 7g | protein: 13g | carbs: 8g | fiber: 0g | sodium: 192mg

Bone-in Pork Chops

Prep time: 5 minutes | Cook time: 10 to 12 minutes | Serves 2

1 pound (454 g) bone-in pork chops	½ teaspoon onion powder
1 tablespoon avocado oil	¼ teaspoon cayenne pepper
1 teaspoon smoked paprika	Sea salt and freshly ground black pepper, to taste

1. Brush the pork chops with the avocado oil. In a small dish, mix together the smoked paprika, onion powder, cayenne pepper, and salt and black pepper to taste. Sprinkle the seasonings over both sides of the pork chops. 2. Set the air fryer to 400°F (204°C). Place the chops in the air fryer basket in a single layer, working in batches if necessary. Air fry for 10 to 12 minutes, until an instant-read thermometer reads 145°F (63°C) at the chops' thickest point. 3. Remove the chops from the air fryer and allow them to rest for 5 minutes before serving.

Per Serving:
calories: 356 | fat: 16g | protein: 50g | carbs: 1g | fiber: 1g | sodium: 133mg

Smoky Pork Tenderloin

Prep time: 5 minutes | Cook time: 19 to 22 minutes | Serves 6

1½ pounds (680 g) pork tenderloin	1 teaspoon garlic powder
1 tablespoon avocado oil	1 teaspoon sea salt
1 teaspoon chili powder	1 teaspoon freshly ground black pepper
1 teaspoon smoked paprika	

1. Pierce the tenderloin all over with a fork and rub the oil all over the meat. 2. In a small dish, stir together the chili powder, smoked paprika, garlic powder, salt, and pepper. 3. Rub the spice mixture all over the tenderloin. 4. Set the air fryer to 400°F (204°C). Place the pork in the air fryer basket and air fry for 10 minutes. Flip the tenderloin and cook for 9 to 12 minutes more, until an instant-read thermometer reads at least 145°F (63°C). 5. Allow the tenderloin to rest for 5 minutes, then slice and serve.

Per Serving:
calories: 149 | fat: 5g | protein: 24g | carbs: 1g | fiber: 0g | sodium: 461mg

Parmesan Herb Filet Mignon

Prep time: 20 minutes | Cook time: 13 minutes | Serves 4

1 pound (454 g) filet mignon	1 teaspoon dried rosemary
Sea salt and ground black pepper, to taste	1 teaspoon dried thyme
½ teaspoon cayenne pepper	1 tablespoon sesame oil
1 teaspoon dried basil	1 small-sized egg, well-whisked
	½ cup Parmesan cheese, grated

1. Season the filet mignon with salt, black pepper, cayenne pepper, basil, rosemary, and thyme. Brush with sesame oil. 2. Put the egg in a shallow plate. Now, place the Parmesan cheese in another plate. 3. Coat the filet mignon with the egg; then lay it into the Parmesan cheese. Set the air fryer to 360°F (182°C). 4. Cook for 10 to 13 minutes or until golden. Serve with mixed salad leaves and enjoy!

Per Serving:
calories: 252 | fat: 13g | protein: 32g | carbs: 1g | fiber: 0g | sodium: 96mg

Wedding Soup

Prep time: 15 minutes | Cook time: 17 minutes | Serves 6

3 (1-ounce/ 28-g) slices Italian bread, toasted	oregano
¾ pound (340 g) 90% lean ground beef	1 tablespoon minced fresh basil
1 large egg, beaten	1 teaspoon salt
1 medium onion, peeled and chopped	½ teaspoon ground black pepper
3 cloves garlic, peeled and minced	½ cup grated Parmesan cheese, divided
¼ cup chopped fresh parsley	2 tablespoons olive oil
1 tablespoon minced fresh	8 cups low-sodium chicken broth
	5 ounces (142 g) baby spinach

1. Wet toasted bread with water and then squeeze out all the liquid. Place soaked bread in a large bowl. Add ground beef, egg, onion, garlic, parsley, oregano, basil, salt, pepper, and ¼ cup cheese. Mix well. Form the mixture into 1" balls. 2. Press the Sauté button on the Instant Pot® and heat oil. Brown meatballs in batches on all sides, about 3 minutes per side. Transfer meatballs to a plate. Press the Cancel button. 3. Add broth to pot, stirring well to release any browned bits. Add meatballs and stir well. Close lid, set steam release to Sealing, press the Manual button, and set time to 10 minutes. When the timer beeps, quick-release the pressure until the float valve drops. Open lid. 4. Add spinach and stir until wilted, about 1 minute. Ladle the soup into bowls and sprinkle with remaining ¼ cup cheese.

Per Serving:
calories: 270 | fat: 16g | protein: 24g | carbs: 10g | fiber: 1g | sodium: 590mg

Greek Lamb Chops

Prep time: 10 minutes | Cook time: 6 to 8 hours | Serves 6

3 pounds (1.4 kg) lamb chops	2 garlic cloves, minced
½ cup low-sodium beef broth	1 teaspoon dried oregano
Juice of 1 lemon	1 teaspoon sea salt
1 tablespoon extra-virgin olive oil	½ teaspoon freshly ground black pepper

1. Put the lamb chops in a slow cooker. 2. In a small bowl, whisk together the beef broth, lemon juice, olive oil, garlic, oregano, salt, and pepper until blended. Pour the sauce over the lamb chops. 3. Cover the cooker and cook for 6 to 8 hours on Low heat.

Per Serving:
calories: 325 | fat: 13g | protein: 47g | carbs: 1g | fiber: 0g | sodium: 551mg

Baby Back Ribs

Prep time: 5 minutes | Cook time: 25 minutes | Serves 4

2 pounds (907 g) baby back ribs
2 teaspoons chili powder
1 teaspoon paprika
½ teaspoon onion powder
½ teaspoon garlic powder
¼ teaspoon ground cayenne pepper
½ cup low-carb, sugar-free barbecue sauce

1. Rub ribs with all ingredients except barbecue sauce. Place into the air fryer basket. 2. Adjust the temperature to 400°F (204°C) and roast for 25 minutes. 3. When done, ribs will be dark and charred with an internal temperature of at least 185°F (85°C). Brush ribs with barbecue sauce and serve warm.

Per Serving:
calories: 571 | fat: 36g | protein: 45g | carbs: 17g | fiber: 1g | sodium: 541mg

Lamb and Bean Stew

Prep time: 15 minutes | Cook time: 35 minutes | Serves 4

4 tablespoons olive oil, divided
1 pound (454 g) lamb shoulder, cut into 2-inch cubes
Sea salt
Freshly ground black pepper
2 garlic cloves, minced (optional)
1 large onion, diced
1 cup chopped celery
1 cup chopped tomatoes
1 cup chopped carrots
⅓ cup tomato paste
1 (28-ounce/ 794-g) can white kidney beans, drained and rinsed
2 cups water

1. In a stockpot, heat 1 tablespoon of olive oil over medium-high heat. Season the lamb pieces with salt and pepper and add to the stockpot with the garlic, if desired. Brown the lamb, turning it frequently, for 3 to 4 minutes. Add the remaining 3 tablespoons of olive oil, the onion, celery, tomatoes, and carrots and cook for 4 to 5 minutes. 2. Add the tomato paste and stir to combine, then add the beans and water. Bring the mixture to a boil, reduce the heat to low, cover, and simmer for 25 minutes, or until the lamb is fully cooked. 3. Taste, adjust the seasoning, and serve.

Per Serving:
calories: 521 | fat: 24g | protein: 36g | carbs: 43g | fiber: 12g | sodium: 140mg

Lamb and Vegetable Bake

Prep time: 20 minutes | Cook time: 1 hour 20 minutes | Serves 8

¼ cup olive oil
1 pound (454 g) boneless, lean lamb, cut into ½ -inch pieces
2 large red potatoes, scrubbed and diced
1 large onion, coarsely chopped
2 cloves garlic, minced
1 (28-ounce) can diced tomatoes with liquid (no salt added)
2 medium zucchini, cut into ½ -inch slices
1 red bell pepper, seeded and cut into 1-inch cubes
2 tablespoons flat-leaf parsley, chopped
1 teaspoon dried thyme
1 tablespoon paprika
½ teaspoon ground cinnamon
½ cup red wine
Sea salt and freshly ground pepper, to taste

1. Preheat the oven to 325°F (165°C) degrees. 2. Heat the olive oil in a large stew pot or cast-iron skillet over medium-high heat. 3. Add the lamb and brown the meat, stirring frequently. Transfer the lamb to an ovenproof baking dish. 4. Cook the potatoes, onion, and garlic in the skillet until tender, then transfer them to the baking dish. 5. Pour the tomatoes, zucchini, and pepper into the pan along with the herbs and spices, and simmer for 10 minutes. 6. Cover the lamb, onions, and potatoes with the tomato and pepper sauce and wine. 7. Cover with aluminum foil and bake for 1 hour. Uncover during the last 15 minutes of baking. 8. Season to taste, and serve with a green salad.

Per Serving:
calories: 264 | fat: 12g | protein: 15g | carbs: 24g | fiber: 5g | sodium: 75mg

Braised Short Ribs with Fennel and Pickled Grapes

Prep time: 20 minutes | Cook time: 55 minutes | Serves 4

1½ pounds (680 g) boneless beef short ribs, trimmed and cut into 2-inch pieces
1 teaspoon table salt, divided
1 tablespoon extra-virgin olive oil
1 fennel bulb, 2 tablespoons fronds chopped, stalks discarded, bulb halved, cored, and sliced into 1-inch-thick wedges
1 onion, halved and sliced ½ inch thick
4 garlic cloves, minced
2 teaspoons fennel seeds
½ cup chicken broth
1 sprig fresh rosemary
¼ cup red wine vinegar
1 tablespoon sugar
4 ounces (113 g) seedless red grapes, halved (½ cup)

1. Pat short ribs dry with paper towels and sprinkle with ½ teaspoon salt. Using highest sauté function, heat oil in Instant Pot for 5 minutes (or until just smoking). Brown short ribs on all sides, 6 to 8 minutes; transfer to plate. 2. Add fennel wedges, onion, and ¼ teaspoon salt to fat left in pot and cook, using highest sauté function, until vegetables are softened and lightly browned, about 5 minutes. Stir in garlic and fennel seeds and cook until fragrant, about 30 seconds. Stir in broth and rosemary sprig, scraping up any browned bits. Nestle short ribs into vegetable mixture and add any accumulated juices. Lock lid in place and close pressure release valve. Select high pressure cook function and cook for 35 minutes. 3. Meanwhile, microwave vinegar, sugar, and remaining ¼ teaspoon salt in bowl until simmering, about 1 minute. Add grapes and let sit, stirring occasionally, for 20 minutes. Drain grapes and return to now-empty bowl. (Drained grapes can be refrigerated for up to 1 week.) 4. Turn off Instant Pot and let pressure release naturally for 15 minutes. Quick-release any remaining pressure, then carefully remove lid, allowing steam to escape away from you. Transfer short ribs to serving dish, tent with aluminum foil, and let rest while finishing sauce. 5. Strain braising liquid through fine-mesh strainer into fat separator. Discard rosemary sprig and transfer vegetables to serving dish with beef. Let braising liquid settle for 5 minutes, then pour ¾ cup defatted liquid over short ribs and vegetables; discard remaining liquid. Sprinkle with grapes and fennel fronds. Serve.

Per Serving:
calories: 310 | fat: 17g | protein: 24g | carbs: 15g | fiber: 3g | sodium: 750mg

Lebanese Ground Meat with Rice

Prep time: 10 minutes | Cook time: 35 minutes | Serves 6

- 3 tablespoons olive oil, divided
- 4 ounces (113 g) cremini (baby bella) mushrooms, sliced
- ½ red onion, finely chopped
- 2 garlic cloves, minced
- 1 pound (454 g) lean ground beef
- ¾ teaspoon ground cinnamon
- ¼ teaspoon ground cloves
- ¼ teaspoon ground nutmeg
- Sea salt
- Freshly ground black pepper
- 1½ cups basmati rice
- 2¾ cups chicken broth
- ½ cup pine nuts
- ½ cup coarsely chopped fresh Italian parsley

1. In a sauté pan, heat 2 tablespoons of olive oil over medium-high heat. Add the mushrooms, onion, and garlic and sauté until the mushrooms release their liquid and the onion becomes translucent, about 5 minutes. Add the ground beef, cinnamon, cloves, and nutmeg and season with salt and pepper. Reduce the heat to medium and cook, stirring often, for 5 to 7 minutes, until the meat is cooked through. Remove the beef mixture from the pan with a slotted spoon and set aside in a medium bowl. 2. In the same pan, heat the remaining 1 tablespoon of olive oil over medium-high heat. Add the rice and fry for about 5 minutes. Return the meat mixture to the pan and mix well to combine with the rice. Add the broth and bring to a boil, then reduce the heat to low, cover, and simmer for 15 minutes, or until you can fluff the rice with a fork. 3. Add the pine nuts and mix well. Garnish with the parsley and serve.

Per Serving:
calories: 422 | fat: 19g | protein: 22g | carbs: 43g | fiber: 2g | sodium: 81mg

Greek Meatball Soup

Prep time: 20 minutes | Cook time: 45 minutes | Serves 5

- 1 pound (454 g) ground beef
- ⅓ cup orzo
- 4 large eggs
- 1 onion, finely chopped
- 2 garlic cloves, minced
- 2 tablespoons finely chopped fresh Italian parsley
- Sea salt
- Freshly ground black pepper
- ½ cup all-purpose flour
- 5 to 6 cups chicken broth
- Juice of 2 lemons

1. In a large bowl, combine the ground beef, orzo, 1 egg, the onion, garlic, and parsley and stir until well mixed. Season with salt and pepper and mix again. 2. Place the flour in a small bowl. 3. Roll the meat mixture into a ball about the size of a golf ball and dredge it in the flour to coat, shaking off any excess. Place the meatball in a stockpot and repeat with the remaining meat mixture. 4. Pour enough broth into the pot to cover the meatballs by about 1 inch. Bring the broth to a boil over high heat. Reduce the heat to low, cover, and simmer for 30 to 45 minutes, until the meatballs are cooked through. 5. While the meatballs are simmering, in a small bowl, whisk the 3 remaining eggs until frothy. Add the lemon juice and whisk well. 6. When the meatballs are cooked, while whisking continuously, slowly pour 1½ cups of the hot broth into the egg mixture. Pour the egg mixture back into the pot and mix well. Bring back to a simmer, then remove from the heat and serve.

Per Serving:
calories: 297 | fat: 9g | protein: 27g | carbs: 28g | fiber: 1g | sodium: 155mg

Spiced Lamb Stew with Fennel and Dates

Prep time: 10 minutes | Cook time: 3 hours | Serves 4

- 2 tablespoons olive oil, divided
- 1 fennel bulb, trimmed, cored, and thinly sliced
- 1 red onion, thinly sliced
- 2 cloves garlic, thinly sliced
- 1½ pounds (680 g) lamb shoulder, cut into 1½-inch cubes and dried with paper towels
- 1 teaspoon ground ginger
- 2 teaspoons ground cumin
- 2 teaspoons ground coriander
- ¼ teaspoon cayenne pepper
- 1 teaspoon salt
- 1 cup pitted chopped dates
- 2 cups water, divided
- ¼ cup chopped cilantro, for garnish

1. Heat 1 tablespoon of olive oil in a Dutch oven. Add the fennel, onion, and garlic and cook, stirring frequently, until softened and beginning to brown, about 7 minutes. Transfer the vegetables to a plate. 2. Add the remaining 1 tablespoon of olive oil to the pot and cook the lamb, turning every couple of minutes, until browned on all sides. 3. In a small bowl, combine the ginger, cumin, coriander, cayenne, and salt and mix well. Sprinkle the spice mixture over the meat in the pot and cook, stirring, for 1 minute. 4. Return the vegetables to the pot and add the dates and 1 cup of water. Reduce the heat to medium-low, cover, and cook, stirring occasionally and adding the remaining 1 cup of water as needed, for 2½ hours, until the lamb is very tender and the sauce has thickened. Serve immediately, garnished with cilantro.

Per Serving:
calories: 539 | fat: 20g | protein: 50g | carbs: 52g | fiber: 6g | sodium: 749mg

Smoky Herb Lamb Chops and Lemon-Rosemary Dressing

Prep time: 1 hour 35 minutes | Cook time: 10 minutes | Serves 6

- 4 large cloves garlic
- 1 cup lemon juice
- ⅓ cup fresh rosemary
- 1 cup extra-virgin olive oil
- 1½ teaspoons salt
- 1 teaspoon freshly ground black pepper
- 6 (1-inch-thick) lamb chops

1. In a food processor or blender, blend the garlic, lemon juice, rosemary, olive oil, salt, and black pepper for 15 seconds. Set aside. 2. Put the lamb chops in a large plastic zip-top bag or container. Cover the lamb with two-thirds of the rosemary dressing, making sure that all of the lamb chops are coated with the dressing. Let the lamb marinate in the fridge for 1 hour. 3. When you are almost ready to eat, take the lamb chops out of the fridge and let them sit on the counter-top for 20 minutes. Preheat a grill, grill pan, or lightly oiled skillet to high heat. 4. Cook the lamb chops for 3 minutes on each side. To serve, drizzle the lamb with the remaining dressing.

Per Serving:
calories: 484 | fat: 42g | protein: 24g | carbs: 5g | fiber: 1g | sodium: 655mg

Beef Burger

Prep time: 20 minutes | Cook time: 12 minutes | Serves 4

1¼ pounds (567 g) lean ground beef
1 tablespoon coconut aminos
1 teaspoon Dijon mustard
A few dashes of liquid smoke
1 teaspoon shallot powder
1 clove garlic, minced
½ teaspoon cumin powder
¼ cup scallions, minced
⅓ teaspoon sea salt flakes
⅓ teaspoon freshly cracked mixed peppercorns
1 teaspoon celery seeds
1 teaspoon parsley flakes

1. Mix all of the above ingredients in a bowl; knead until everything is well incorporated. 2. Shape the mixture into four patties. Next, make a shallow dip in the center of each patty to prevent them puffing up during air frying. 3. Spritz the patties on all sides using nonstick cooking spray. Cook approximately 12 minutes at 360°F (182°C). 4. Check for doneness, an instant-read thermometer should read 160°F (71°C). Bon appétit!

Per Serving:
calories: 193 | fat: 7g | protein: 31g | carbs: 1g | fiber: 0g | sodium: 304mg

Pork Souvlaki

Prep time: 1 hour 15 minutes | Cook time: 10 minutes | Serves 4

1 (1½-pound / 680-g) pork loin
2 tablespoons garlic, minced
⅓ cup extra-virgin olive oil
⅓ cup lemon juice
1 tablespoon dried oregano
1 teaspoon salt
Pita bread and tzatziki, for serving (optional)

1. Cut the pork into 1-inch cubes and put them into a bowl or plastic zip-top bag. 2. In a large bowl, mix together the garlic, olive oil, lemon juice, oregano, and salt. 3. Pour the marinade over the pork and let it marinate for at least 1 hour. 4. Preheat a grill, grill pan, or lightly oiled skillet to high heat. Using wood or metal skewers, thread the pork onto the skewers. 5. Cook the skewers for 3 minutes on each side, for 12 minutes in total. 6. Serve with pita bread and tzatziki sauce, if desired.

Per Serving:
calories: 393 | fat: 25g | protein: 38g | carbs: 3g | fiber: 0g | sodium: 666mg

Moroccan Lamb Roast

Prep time: 15 minutes | Cook time: 6 to 8 hours | Serves 6

¼ cup low-sodium beef broth or low-sodium chicken broth
1 teaspoon dried ginger
1 teaspoon dried cumin
1 teaspoon ground turmeric
1 teaspoon paprika
1 teaspoon garlic powder
1 teaspoon red pepper flakes
½ teaspoon ground cinnamon
½ teaspoon ground coriander
½ teaspoon ground nutmeg
½ teaspoon ground cloves
½ teaspoon sea salt
½ teaspoon freshly ground black pepper
1 (3-pound/ 1.4-kg) lamb roast
4 ounces (113 g) carrots, chopped
¼ cup sliced onion
¼ cup chopped fresh mint

1. Pour the broth into a slow cooker. 2. In a small bowl, stir together the ginger, cumin, turmeric, paprika, garlic powder, red pepper flakes, cinnamon, coriander, nutmeg, cloves, salt, and black pepper. Rub the spice mix firmly all over the lamb roast. Put the lamb in the slow cooker and add the carrots and onion. 3. Top everything with the mint. 4. Cover the cooker and cook for 6 to 8 hours on Low heat.

Per Serving:
calories: 601 | fat: 39g | protein: 56g | carbs: 4g | fiber: 1g | sodium: 398mg

Lamb Shanks and Potatoes

Prep time: 10 minutes | Cook time: 8 hours | Serves 6

1 (15-ounce/ 425-g) can crushed tomatoes in purée
3 tablespoons tomato paste
2 tablespoons apricot jam
6 cloves garlic, thinly sliced
3 strips orange zest
¾ teaspoon crushed dried rosemary
½ teaspoon ground ginger
½ teaspoon ground cinnamon
Coarse sea salt
Black pepper
3½ pounds (1.6 kg) lamb shanks, trimmed of excess fat and cut into 1½-inch slices
1¼ pounds (567 g) small new potatoes, halved (or quartered, if large)

1. Stir together the tomatoes and purée, tomato paste, jam, garlic, orange zest, rosemary, ginger, and cinnamon in the slow cooker. Season with salt and pepper. 2. Add the lamb and potatoes, and spoon the tomato mixture over the lamb to coat. 3. Cover and cook until the lamb and potatoes are tender, on low for 8 hours or on high for 5 hours. Season again with salt and pepper, if desired. 4. Serve hot.

Per Serving:
calories: 438 | fat: 10g | protein: 62g | carbs: 26g | fiber: 4g | sodium: 248mg

Southern Chili

Prep time: 20 minutes | Cook time: 25 minutes | Serves 4

1 pound (454 g) ground beef (85% lean)
1 cup minced onion
1 (28-ounce / 794-g) can tomato purée
1 (15-ounce / 425-g) can diced tomatoes with green chilies
1 (15-ounce / 425-g) can light red kidney beans, rinsed and drained
¼ cup Chili seasoning

1. Preheat the air fryer to 400°F (204°C). 2. In a baking pan, mix the ground beef and onion. Place the pan in the air fryer. 3. Cook for 4 minutes. Stir and cook for 4 minutes more until browned. Remove the pan from the fryer. Drain the meat and transfer to a large bowl. 4. Reduce the air fryer temperature to 350°F (177°C). 5. To the bowl with the meat, add in the tomato purée, diced tomatoes and green chilies, kidney beans, and Chili seasoning. Mix well. Pour the mixture into the baking pan. 6. Cook for 25 minutes, stirring every 10 minutes, until thickened.

Per Serving:
calories: 455 | fat: 18g | protein: 32g | carbs: 44g | fiber: 11g | sodium: 815mg

Balsamic Pork Chops with Figs and Pears

Prep time: 15 minutes | Cook time: 13 minutes | Serves 2

- 2 (8-ounce/ 227-g) bone-in pork chops
- ½ teaspoon salt
- 1 teaspoon ground black pepper
- ¼ cup balsamic vinegar
- ¼ cup low-sodium chicken broth
- 1 tablespoon dried mint
- 2 tablespoons olive oil
- 1 medium sweet onion, peeled and sliced
- 3 medium pears, peeled, cored, and chopped
- 5 dried figs, stems removed and halved

1. Pat pork chops dry with a paper towel and season both sides with salt and pepper. Set aside. 2. In a small bowl, whisk together vinegar, broth, and mint. Set aside. 3. Press the Sauté button on the Instant Pot® and heat oil. Brown pork chops for 5 minutes per side. Remove chops and set aside. 4. Add vinegar mixture and scrape any brown bits from sides and bottom of pot. Layer onion slices in the pot, then scatter pears and figs over slices. Place pork chops on top. Press the Cancel button. 5. Close lid, set steam release to Sealing, press the Steam button, and set time to 3 minutes. When the timer beeps, let pressure release naturally for 10 minutes. Quick-release any remaining pressure until the float valve drops and then open lid. 6. Using a slotted spoon, transfer pork, onion, figs, and pears to a serving platter. Serve warm.

Per Serving:
calories: 672 | fat: 32g | protein: 27g | carbs: 68g | fiber: 13g | sodium: 773mg

Moroccan Meatballs

Prep time: 10 minutes | Cook time: 20 minutes | Serves: 4

- ¼ cup finely chopped onion (about ⅛ onion)
- ¼ cup raisins, coarsely chopped
- 1 teaspoon ground cumin
- ½ teaspoon ground cinnamon
- ¼ teaspoon smoked paprika
- 1 large egg
- 1 pound (454 g) ground beef (93% lean) or ground lamb
- ⅓ cup panko bread crumbs
- 1 teaspoon extra-virgin olive oil
- 1 (28-ounce/ 794-g) can low-sodium or no-salt-added crushed tomatoes
- Chopped fresh mint, feta cheese, and/or fresh orange or lemon wedges, for serving (optional)

1. In a large bowl, combine the onion, raisins, cumin, cinnamon, smoked paprika, and egg. Add the ground beef and bread crumbs and mix gently with your hands. Divide the mixture into 20 even portions, then wet your hands and roll each portion into a ball. Wash your hands. 2. In a large skillet over medium-high heat, heat the oil. Add the meatballs and cook for 8 minutes, rolling around every minute or so with tongs or a fork to brown them on most sides. (They won't be cooked through.) Transfer the meatballs to a paper towel–lined plate. Drain the fat out of the pan, and carefully wipe out the hot pan with a paper towel. 3. Return the meatballs to the pan, and pour the tomatoes over the meatballs. Cover and cook on medium-high heat until the sauce begins to bubble. Lower the heat to medium, cover partially, and cook for 7 to 8 more minutes, until the meatballs are cooked through. Garnish with fresh mint, feta cheese, and/or a squeeze of citrus, if desired, and serve.

Per Serving:
calories: 351 | fat: 18g | protein: 28g | carbs: 23g | fiber: 5g | sodium: 170mg

The Best Spaghetti Sauce

Prep time: 10 minutes | Cook time: 1 hour | Serves 4

- 1 tablespoon extra-virgin olive oil
- 1 pound (454 g) ground beef, about 90% lean
- 4 garlic cloves, minced or pressed
- 1 medium to large onion, diced
- 1 green bell pepper, diced
- 1 (15-ounce / 425-g) can tomato sauce
- 1 (6-ounce / 170-g) can tomato paste
- 10 to 15 ounces (283 to 425 g) red wine
- 1 tablespoon sugar
- 1 tablespoon Worcestershire sauce
- 1 tablespoon Italian seasoning
- Salt and freshly ground black pepper, to taste
- 1 (15-ounce / 425-g) can diced tomatoes, drained

1. In a large skillet, heat the olive oil over medium heat. Add the ground beef and cook, breaking it up with a wooden spoon as it cooks, until nearly browned. Add the garlic, onion, and bell pepper and cook, stirring occasionally, until the onion is translucent. Drain any excess liquid from the skillet. 2. Add the tomato sauce and tomato paste and stir them into the beef mixture. Add the wine, sugar, Worcestershire, and Italian seasoning. Season with salt and pepper. Cook over low heat, stirring occasionally, for at least 1 hour, or as long as 4 hours, adding more water as needed to maintain the desired consistency. 3. Ten minutes before serving, stir in the diced tomatoes.

Per Serving:
1 cup: calories: 334 | fat: 14g | protein: 28g | carbs: 24g | fiber: 6g | sodium: 536mg

Kofta with Vegetables in Tomato Sauce

Prep time: 15 minutes | Cook time: 6 to 8 hours | Serves 4

- 1 pound (454 g) raw ground beef
- 1 small white or yellow onion, finely diced
- 2 garlic cloves, minced
- 1 tablespoon dried parsley
- 2 teaspoons ground coriander
- 1 teaspoon ground cumin
- ½ teaspoon sea salt
- ½ teaspoon freshly ground black pepper
- ¼ teaspoon ground nutmeg
- ¼ teaspoon dried mint
- ¼ teaspoon paprika
- 1 (28-ounce/ 794-g) can no-salt-added diced tomatoes
- 2 or 3 zucchini, cut into 1½-inch-thick rounds
- 4 ounces (113 g) mushrooms
- 1 large red onion, chopped
- 1 green bell pepper, seeded and chopped

1. In large bowl, mix together the ground beef, white or yellow onion, garlic, parsley, coriander, cumin, salt, pepper, nutmeg, mint, and paprika until well combined and all of the spices and onion are well blended into the meat. Form the meat mixture into 10 to 12 oval patties. Set aside. 2. In a slow cooker, combine the tomatoes, zucchini, mushrooms, red onion, and bell pepper. Stir to mix well. 3. Place the kofta patties on top of the tomato mixture. 4. Cover the cooker and cook for 6 to 8 hours on Low heat.

Per Serving:
calories: 263 | fat: 9g | protein: 27g | carbs: 23g | fiber: 7g | sodium: 480mg

Seasoned Beef Kebabs

Prep time: 15 minutes | Cook time: 10 minutes | Serves 6

2 pounds beef fillet
1½ teaspoons salt
1 teaspoon freshly ground black pepper
½ teaspoon ground allspice
½ teaspoon ground nutmeg
⅓ cup extra-virgin olive oil
1 large onion, cut into 8 quarters
1 large red bell pepper, cut into 1-inch cubes

1. Preheat a grill, grill pan, or lightly oiled skillet to high heat. 2. Cut the beef into 1-inch cubes and put them in a large bowl. 3. In a small bowl, mix together the salt, black pepper, allspice, and nutmeg. 4. Pour the olive oil over the beef and toss to coat the beef. Then evenly sprinkle the seasoning over the beef and toss to coat all pieces. 5. Skewer the beef, alternating every 1 or 2 pieces with a piece of onion or bell pepper. 6. To cook, place the skewers on the grill or skillet, and turn every 2 to 3 minutes until all sides have cooked to desired doneness, 6 minutes for medium-rare, 8 minutes for well done. Serve warm.

Per Serving:
calories: 326 | fat: 21g | protein: 32g | carbs: 4g | fiber: 1g | sodium: 714mg

Beef Stew with Red Wine

Prep time: 15 minutes | Cook time: 46 minutes | Serves 8

1 pound (454 g) beef stew meat, cut into 1" pieces
2 tablespoons all-purpose flour
¼ teaspoon salt
¼ teaspoon ground black pepper
2 tablespoons olive oil, divided
1 pound (454 g) whole crimini mushrooms
2 cloves garlic, peeled and minced
4 sprigs thyme
2 bay leaves
8 ounces (227 g) baby carrots
8 ounces (227 g) frozen pearl onions, thawed
1 cup red wine
½ cup beef broth
¼ cup chopped fresh parsley

1. In a medium bowl, toss beef with flour, salt, and pepper until thoroughly coated. Set aside. 2. Press the Sauté button on the Instant Pot® and heat 1 tablespoon oil. Add half of the beef pieces in a single layer, leaving space between each piece to prevent steaming, and brown well on all sides, about 3 minutes per side. Transfer beef to a medium bowl and repeat with remaining 1 tablespoon oil and beef. Press the Cancel button. 3. Add mushrooms, garlic, thyme, bay leaves, carrots, onions, wine, and broth to the Instant Pot®. Stir well. Close lid, set steam release to Sealing, press the Stew button, and set time to 40 minutes. When the timer beeps, quick-release the pressure until the float valve drops, open lid, and stir well. Remove and discard thyme and bay leaves. Sprinkle with parsley and serve hot.

Per Serving:
calories: 206 | fat: 13g | protein: 12g | carbs: 6g | fiber: 1g | sodium: 186mg

Pork and Cannellini Bean Stew

Prep time: 15 minutes | Cook time: 1 hour | Serves 6

1 cup dried cannellini beans
¼ cup olive oil
1 medium onion, diced
2 pounds (907 g) pork roast, cut into 1-inch chunks
3 cups water
1 (8-ounce/ 227-g) can tomato paste
¼ cup flat-leaf parsley, chopped
½ teaspoon dried thyme
Sea salt and freshly ground pepper, to taste

1. Rinse and sort the beans. 2. Cover beans with water, and allow to soak overnight. Heat the olive oil in a large stew pot. 3. Add the onion, stirring occasionally, until golden brown. 4. Add the pork chunks and cook 5–8 minutes, stirring frequently, until the pork is browned. Drain and rinse the beans, and add to the pot. 5. Add the water, and bring to a boil. Reduce heat and simmer for 45 minutes, until beans are tender. 6. Add the tomato paste, parsley, and thyme, and simmer an additional 15 minutes, or until the sauce thickens slightly. Season to taste.

Per Serving:
calories: 373 | fat: 16g | protein: 39g | carbs: 19g | fiber: 4g | sodium: 107mg

Chapter 5 Fish and Seafood

Baked Monkfish

Prep time: 20 minutes | Cook time: 12 minutes | Serves 2

2 teaspoons olive oil
1 cup celery, sliced
2 bell peppers, sliced
1 teaspoon dried thyme
½ teaspoon dried marjoram
½ teaspoon dried rosemary
2 monkfish fillets
1 tablespoon coconut aminos
2 tablespoons lime juice
Coarse salt and ground black pepper, to taste
1 teaspoon cayenne pepper
½ cup Kalamata olives, pitted and sliced

1. In a nonstick skillet, heat the olive oil for 1 minute. Once hot, sauté the celery and peppers until tender, about 4 minutes. Sprinkle with thyme, marjoram, and rosemary and set aside. 2. Toss the fish fillets with the coconut aminos, lime juice, salt, black pepper, and cayenne pepper. Place the fish fillets in the lightly greased air fryer basket and bake at 390ºF (199ºC) for 8 minutes. 3. Turn them over, add the olives, and cook an additional 4 minutes. Serve with the sautéed vegetables on the side. Bon appétit!

Per Serving:
calories: 263 | fat: 11g | protein: 27g | carbs: 13g | fiber: 5g | sodium: 332mg

Balsamic Tilapia

Prep time: 5 minutes | Cook time: 15 minutes | Serves 4

4 tilapia fillets, boneless
2 tablespoons balsamic vinegar
1 teaspoon avocado oil
1 teaspoon dried basil

1. Sprinkle the tilapia fillets with balsamic vinegar, avocado oil, and dried basil. 2. Then put the fillets in the air fryer basket and cook at 365ºF (185ºC) for 15 minutes.

Per Serving:
calories: 129 | fat: 3g | protein: 23g | carbs: 1g | fiber: 0g | sodium: 92mg

Cucumber and Salmon Salad

Prep time: 10 minutes | Cook time: 8 to 10 minutes | Serves 2

1 pound (454 g) salmon fillet
1½ tablespoons olive oil, divided
1 tablespoon sherry vinegar
1 tablespoon capers, rinsed and drained
1 seedless cucumber, thinly sliced
¼ Vidalia onion, thinly sliced
2 tablespoons chopped fresh parsley
Salt and freshly ground black pepper, to taste

1. Preheat the air fryer to 400ºF (204ºC). 2. Lightly coat the salmon with ½ tablespoon of the olive oil. Place skin-side down in the air fryer basket and air fry for 8 to 10 minutes until the fish is opaque and flakes easily with a fork. Transfer the salmon to a plate and let cool to room temperature. Remove the skin and carefully flake the fish into bite-size chunks. 3. In a small bowl, whisk the remaining 1 tablespoon olive oil and the vinegar until thoroughly combined. Add the flaked fish, capers, cucumber, onion, and parsley. Season to taste with salt and freshly ground black pepper. Toss gently to coat. Serve immediately or cover and refrigerate for up to 4 hours.

Per Serving:
calories: 399 | fat: 20g | protein: 47g | carbs: 4g | fiber: 1g | sodium: 276mg

Grilled Bluefish

Prep time: 10 minutes | Cook time: 8 minutes | Serves 4

1 cup olive oil
½ cup white wine
¼ cup fresh basil leaves, chopped
Juice and zest of 2 lemons or oranges
2–3 garlic cloves, minced
1 teaspoon ground cumin
1 teaspoon thyme
2 pinches cayenne pepper
4 bluefish or fish fillets
Sea salt and freshly ground pepper, to taste

1. Combine all the ingredients except the fish in a plastic bag or shallow bowl. 2. Divide marinade in half, reserving half in the refrigerator and placing the fish in the other half of the marinade. 3. Refrigerate for at least 1 hour. Heat the grill to medium-high. 4. Brush the grates with olive oil, and grill the fish for 6–8 minutes, turning halfway through the cooking time. 5. Season with sea salt and freshly ground pepper, to taste. Warm the reserved marinade and serve with the fish.

Per Serving:
calories: 713 | fat: 61g | protein: 31g | carbs: 7g | fiber: 0g | sodium: 93mg

Cod with Jalapeño

Prep time: 5 minutes | Cook time: 14 minutes | Serves 4

4 cod fillets, boneless
1 jalapeño, minced
1 tablespoon avocado oil
½ teaspoon minced garlic

1. In the shallow bowl, mix minced jalapeño, avocado oil, and minced garlic. 2. Put the cod fillets in the air fryer basket in one layer and top with minced jalapeño mixture. 3. Cook the fish at 365ºF (185ºC) for 7 minutes per side.

Per Serving:
calories: 222 | fat: 5g | protein: 41g | carbs: 0g | fiber: 0g | sodium: 125mg

Crispy Fish Sticks

Prep time: 15 minutes | Cook time: 10 minutes | Serves 4

1 ounce (28 g) pork rinds, finely ground
¼ cup blanched finely ground almond flour
½ teaspoon Old Bay seasoning
1 tablespoon coconut oil
1 large egg
1 pound (454 g) cod fillet, cut into ¾-inch strips

1. Place ground pork rinds, almond flour, Old Bay seasoning, and coconut oil into a large bowl and mix together. In a medium bowl, whisk egg. 2. Dip each fish stick into the egg and then gently press into the flour mixture, coating as fully and evenly as possible. Place fish sticks into the air fryer basket. 3. Adjust the temperature to 400°F (204°C) and air fry for 10 minutes or until golden. 4. Serve immediately.

Per Serving:
calories: 223 | fat: 14g | protein: 21g | carbs: 2g | fiber: 1g | sodium: 390mg

Tomato-Basil Salmon

Prep time: 10 minutes | Cook time: 4 to 6 hours | Serves 4

1 (15-ounce / 425-g) can no-salt-added crushed tomatoes
½ cup chopped onion
4 teaspoons dried basil
3 garlic cloves, minced
2 pounds (907 g) fresh salmon fillets, skin on or off as preferred
1 teaspoon sea salt
¼ teaspoon freshly ground black pepper
¼ cup chopped fresh basil

1. In a slow cooker, combine the tomatoes, onion, basil, and garlic. Stir to mix well. 2. Season the salmon all over with salt and pepper. Add the salmon to the slow cooker, cutting it into pieces to fit if needed, and spoon some of the tomato mixture on top. 3. Cover the cooker and cook for 4 to 6 hours on Low heat. 4. Garnish with fresh basil for serving.

Per Serving:
calories: 471 | fat: 24g | protein: 58g | carbs: 9g | fiber: 3g | sodium: 733mg

Cod with Parsley Pistou

Prep time: 15 minutes | Cook time: 10 minutes | Serves 4

1 cup packed roughly chopped fresh flat-leaf Italian parsley
1 to 2 small garlic cloves, minced
Zest and juice of 1 lemon
1 teaspoon salt
½ teaspoon freshly ground black pepper
1 cup extra-virgin olive oil, divided
1 pound (454 g) cod fillets, cut into 4 equal-sized pieces

1. In a food processor, combine the parsley, garlic, lemon zest and juice, salt, and pepper. Pulse to chop well. 2. While the food processor is running, slowly stream in ¾ cup olive oil until well combined. Set aside. 3. In a large skillet, heat the remaining ¼ cup olive oil over medium-high heat. Add the cod fillets, cover, and cook 4 to 5 minutes on each side, or until cooked through. Thicker fillets may require a bit more cooking time. Remove from the heat and keep warm. 4. Add the pistou to the skillet and heat over medium-low heat. Return the cooked fish to the skillet, flipping to coat in the sauce. Serve warm, covered with pistou.

Per Serving:
calories: 580 | fat: 55g | protein: 21g | carbs: 2g | fiber: 1g | sodium: 591mg

Stuffed Shrimp

Prep time: 20 minutes | Cook time: 12 minutes per batch | Serves 4

16 tail-on shrimp, peeled and deveined (last tail section intact)
¾ cup crushed panko bread crumbs
Oil for misting or cooking spray
Stuffing:
2 (6-ounce / 170-g) cans lump crab meat
2 tablespoons chopped shallots
2 tablespoons chopped green onions
2 tablespoons chopped celery
2 tablespoons chopped green bell pepper
½ cup crushed saltine crackers
1 teaspoon Old Bay Seasoning
1 teaspoon garlic powder
¼ teaspoon ground thyme
2 teaspoons dried parsley flakes
2 teaspoons fresh lemon juice
2 teaspoons Worcestershire sauce
1 egg, beaten

1. Rinse shrimp. Remove tail section (shell) from 4 shrimp, discard, and chop the meat finely. 2. To prepare the remaining 12 shrimp, cut a deep slit down the back side so that the meat lies open flat. Do not cut all the way through. 3. Preheat the air fryer to 360°F (182°C). 4. Place chopped shrimp in a large bowl with all of the stuffing ingredients and stir to combine. 5. Divide stuffing into 12 portions, about 2 tablespoons each. 6. Place one stuffing portion onto the back of each shrimp and form into a ball or oblong shape. Press firmly so that stuffing sticks together and adheres to shrimp. 7. Gently roll each stuffed shrimp in panko crumbs and mist with oil or cooking spray. 8. Place 6 shrimp in air fryer basket and air fry at 360°F (182°C) for 10 minutes. Mist with oil or spray and cook 2 minutes longer or until stuffing cooks through inside and is crispy outside. 9. Repeat step 8 to cook remaining shrimp.

Per Serving:
calories: 223 | fat: 4g | protein: 24g | carbs: 24g | fiber: 2g | sodium: 758mg

Simple Poached Turbot

Prep time: 10 minutes | Cook time: 50 minutes | Serves 4

1 cup vegetable or chicken stock
½ cup dry white wine
1 yellow onion, sliced
1 lemon, sliced
4 sprigs fresh dill
½ teaspoon sea salt
4 (6-ounce / 170-g) turbot fillets

1. Combine the stock and wine in the slow cooker. Cover and heat on high for 20 to 30 minutes. 2. Add the onion, lemon, dill, salt, and turbot to the slow cooker. Cover and cook on high for about 20 minutes, until the turbot is opaque and cooked through according to taste. Serve hot.

Per Serving:
calories: 210 | fat: 5g | protein: 29g | carbs: 6g | fiber: 1g | sodium: 565mg

Mixed Seafood Soup

Prep time: 15 minutes | Cook time: 22 minutes | Serves 8

2 tablespoons light olive oil
1 medium yellow onion, peeled and diced
1 medium red bell pepper, seeded and diced
3 cloves garlic, peeled and minced
1 tablespoon chopped fresh oregano
½ teaspoon Italian seasoning
½ teaspoon ground black pepper
2 tablespoons tomato paste
½ cup white wine
2 cups seafood stock
1 bay leaf
½ pound (227 g) medium shrimp, peeled and deveined
½ pound (227 g) fresh scallops
½ pound (227 g) fresh calamari rings
1 tablespoon lemon juice

1. Press the Sauté button on the Instant Pot® and heat oil. Add onion and bell pepper and cook until just tender, about 5 minutes. Add garlic, oregano, Italian seasoning, and pepper. Cook until fragrant, about 30 seconds. Add tomato paste and cook for 1 minute, then slowly pour in wine and scrape bottom of pot well. Press the Cancel button. 2. Add stock and bay leaf. Stir well. Close lid and set steam release to Sealing, then press the Manual button and set time to 5 minutes. 3. When the timer beeps, quick-release the pressure until the float valve drops. Open lid and stir in shrimp, scallops, calamari rings, and lemon juice. Press the Cancel button, then press the Sauté button and allow soup to simmer until seafood is cooked through, about 10 minutes. Remove and discard bay leaf. Serve hot.

Per Serving:
calories: 172 | fat: 7g | protein: 15g | carbs: 9g | fiber: 1g | sodium: 481mg

Halibut Fillets with Vegetables

Prep time: 20 minutes | Cook time: 5 minutes | Serves 2

1 cup chopped broccoli
1 large potato, peeled and diced
1 large carrot, peeled and grated
1 small zucchini, trimmed and grated
4 ounces (113 g) mushrooms, sliced
¼ teaspoon dried thyme
¼ teaspoon grated lemon zest
1 (½-pound / 227-g) halibut fillet
½ cup white wine
½ cup lemon juice
1 teaspoon dried parsley
¼ teaspoon salt
¼ teaspoon ground black pepper
⅛ teaspoon ground nutmeg

1. Place the rack and steamer basket in the Instant Pot®. Place broccoli, potato, carrot, zucchini, and mushrooms in layers in the basket. Sprinkle thyme and lemon zest over vegetables. 2. Place fish over vegetables. Pour wine and lemon juice over fish. Sprinkle parsley, salt, and pepper over the fish and vegetables. 3. Close lid, set steam release to Sealing, press the Manual button, and set time to 5 minutes. When the timer beeps, quick-release the pressure until the float valve drops and open lid. Divide fish and vegetables between two plates. Sprinkle nutmeg over each serving.

Per Serving:
calories: 278 | fat: 3g | protein: 31g | carbs: 23g | fiber: 5g | sodium: 409mg

Lemon-Pepper Trout

Prep time: 5 minutes | Cook time: 15 minutes | Serves 4

4 trout fillets
2 tablespoons olive oil
½ teaspoon salt
1 teaspoon black pepper
2 garlic cloves, sliced
1 lemon, sliced, plus additional wedges for serving

1. Preheat the air fryer to 380°F(193°C). 2. Brush each fillet with olive oil on both sides and season with salt and pepper. Place the fillets in an even layer in the air fryer basket. 3. Place the sliced garlic over the tops of the trout fillets, then top the garlic with lemon slices and roast for 12 to 15 minutes, or until it has reached an internal temperature of 145°F(63°C). 4. Serve with fresh lemon wedges.

Per Serving:
calories: 185 | fat: 12g | protein: 17g | carbs: 2g | fiber: 1g | sodium: 333mg

Italian Halibut with Grapes and Olive Oil

Prep time: 15 minutes | Cook time: 20 minutes | Serves 4

¼ cup extra-virgin olive oil
4 boneless halibut fillets, 4 ounces (113 g) each
4 cloves garlic, roughly chopped
1 small red chile pepper, finely chopped
2 cups seedless green grapes
A handful of fresh basil leaves, roughly torn
½ teaspoon unrefined sea salt or salt
Freshly ground black pepper

1. Heat the olive oil in a large, heavy-bottomed skillet over medium-high heat. Add the halibut, followed by the garlic, chile pepper, grapes, basil, and the salt and pepper. Pour in 1¾ cups of water, turn the heat down to medium-low, cover, and cook the fish until opaque, or for 7 minutes on each side. 2. Remove the fish from the pan and place on a large serving dish. Raise the heat, cook the sauce for 30 seconds to concentrate the flavors slightly. Taste and adjust salt and pepper. Pour sauce over the fish.

Per Serving:
calories: 389 | fat: 29g | protein: 17g | carbs: 15g | fiber: 1g | sodium: 384mg

Parmesan Mackerel with Coriander

Prep time: 10 minutes | Cook time: 7 minutes | Serves 2

12 ounces (340 g) mackerel fillet
2 ounces (57 g) Parmesan, grated
1 teaspoon ground coriander
1 tablespoon olive oil

1. Sprinkle the mackerel fillet with olive oil and put it in the air fryer basket. 2. Top the fish with ground coriander and Parmesan. 3. Cook the fish at 390°F (199°C) for 7 minutes.

Per Serving:
calories: 522 | fat: 39g | protein: 42g | carbs: 1g | fiber: 0g | sodium: 544mg

Salmon with Garlicky Broccoli Rabe and White Beans

Prep time: 20 minutes | Cook time: 10 minutes | Serves 4

2 tablespoons extra-virgin olive oil, plus extra for drizzling
4 garlic cloves, sliced thin
½ cup chicken or vegetable broth
¼ teaspoon red pepper flakes
1 lemon, sliced ¼ inch thick, plus lemon wedges for serving
4 (6-ounce / 170-g) skinless salmon fillets, 1½ inches thick
½ teaspoon table salt
¼ teaspoon pepper
1 pound (454 g) broccoli rabe, trimmed and cut into 1-inch pieces
1 (15-ounce / 425-g) can cannellini beans, rinsed

1. Using highest sauté function, cook oil and garlic in Instant Pot until garlic is fragrant and light golden brown, about 3 minutes. Using slotted spoon, transfer garlic to paper towel–lined plate and season with salt to taste; set aside for serving. Turn off Instant Pot, then stir in broth and pepper flakes. 2. Fold sheet of aluminum foil into 16 by 6-inch sling. Arrange lemon slices widthwise in 2 rows across center of sling. Sprinkle flesh side of salmon with salt and pepper, then arrange skinned side down on top of lemon slices. Using sling, lower salmon into Instant Pot; allow narrow edges of sling to rest along sides of insert. Lock lid in place and close pressure release valve. Select high pressure cook function and cook for 3 minutes. 3. Turn off Instant Pot and quick-release pressure. Carefully remove lid, allowing steam to escape away from you. Using sling, transfer salmon to large plate. Tent with foil and let rest while preparing broccoli rabe mixture. 4. Stir broccoli rabe and beans into cooking liquid, partially cover, and cook, using highest sauté function, until broccoli rabe is tender, about 5 minutes. Season with salt and pepper to taste. Gently lift and tilt salmon fillets with spatula to remove lemon slices. Serve salmon with broccoli rabe mixture and lemon wedges, sprinkling individual portions with garlic chips and drizzling with extra oil.

Per Serving:
calories: 510 | fat: 30g | protein: 43g | carbs: 15g | fiber: 6g | sodium: 650mg

Poached Octopus

Prep time: 10 minutes | Cook time: 16 minutes | Serves 8

2 pounds (907 g) potatoes (about 6 medium)
3 teaspoons salt, divided
1 (2-pound / 907-g) frozen octopus, thawed, cleaned, and rinsed
3 cloves garlic, peeled, divided
1 bay leaf
2 teaspoons whole peppercorns
½ cup olive oil
¼ cup white wine vinegar
½ teaspoon ground black pepper
½ cup chopped fresh parsley

1. Place potatoes in the Instant Pot® with 2 teaspoons salt and enough water to just cover the potatoes halfway. Close lid, set steam release to Sealing, press the Manual button, and set time to 6 minutes. When the timer beeps, quick-release the pressure until the float valve drops and open lid. Press the Cancel button. 2. Remove potatoes with tongs (reserve the cooking water), and peel them as soon as you can handle them. Dice potatoes into bite-sized pieces. Set aside. 3. Add octopus to potato cooking water in the pot and add more water to cover if needed. Add 1 garlic clove, bay leaf, and peppercorns. Close lid, set steam release to Sealing, press the Manual button, and set time to 10 minutes. When the timer beeps, quick-release the pressure until the float valve drops and open lid. Remove and discard bay leaf. 4. Check octopus for tenderness by seeing if a fork will sink easily into the thickest part of the flesh. If not, close the top and bring it to pressure for another minute or two and check again. 5. Remove octopus and drain. Chop head and tentacles into small, bite-sized chunks. 6. Crush remaining 2 garlic cloves and place in a small jar or plastic container. Add olive oil, vinegar, remaining 1 teaspoon salt, and pepper. Close the lid and shake well. 7. In a large serving bowl, mix potatoes with octopus, cover with vinaigrette, and sprinkle with parsley.

Per Serving:
calories: 301 | fat: 15g | protein: 15g | carbs: 30g | fiber: 2g | sodium: 883mg

Fried Fresh Sardines

Prep time: 5 minutes | Cook time: 5 minutes | Serves 4

Avocado oil
1½ pounds (680 g) whole fresh sardines, scales removed
1 teaspoon salt
1 teaspoon freshly ground black pepper
2 cups flour

1. Preheat a deep skillet over medium heat. Pour in enough oil so there is about 1 inch of it in the pan. 2. Season the fish with the salt and pepper. 3. Dredge the fish in the flour so it is completely covered. 4. Slowly drop in 1 fish at a time, making sure not to overcrowd the pan. 5. Cook for about 3 minutes on each side or just until the fish begins to brown on all sides. Serve warm.

Per Serving:
calories: 581 | fat: 20g | protein: 48g | carbs: 48g | fiber: 2g | sodium: 583mg

Herbed Shrimp Pita

Prep time: 5 minutes | Cook time: 8 minutes | Serves 4

1 pound (454 g) medium shrimp, peeled and deveined
2 tablespoons olive oil
1 teaspoon dried oregano
½ teaspoon dried thyme
½ teaspoon garlic powder
¼ teaspoon onion powder
½ teaspoon salt
¼ teaspoon black pepper
4 whole wheat pitas
4 ounces (113 g) feta cheese, crumbled
1 cup shredded lettuce
1 tomato, diced
¼ cup black olives, sliced
1 lemon

1. Preheat the oven to 380°F(193°C). 2. In a medium bowl, combine the shrimp with the olive oil, oregano, thyme, garlic powder, onion powder, salt, and black pepper. 3. Pour shrimp in a single layer in the air fryer basket and roast for 6 to 8 minutes, or until cooked through. 4. Remove from the air fryer and divide into warmed pitas with feta, lettuce, tomato, olives, and a squeeze of lemon.

Per Serving:
calories: 320 | fat: 14g | protein: 30g | carbs: 20g | fiber: 3g | sodium: 813mg

Baked Grouper with Tomatoes and Garlic

Prep time: 5 minutes | Cook time: 12 minutes | Serves 4

4 grouper fillets
½ teaspoon salt
3 garlic cloves, minced
1 tomato, sliced
¼ cup sliced Kalamata olives
¼ cup fresh dill, roughly chopped
Juice of 1 lemon
¼ cup olive oil

1. Preheat the air fryer to 380°F(193°C). 2. Season the grouper fillets on all sides with salt, then place into the air fryer basket and top with the minced garlic, tomato slices, olives, and fresh dill. 3. Drizzle the lemon juice and olive oil over the top of the grouper, then bake for 10 to 12 minutes, or until the internal temperature reaches 145°F(63°C).

Per Serving:
calories: 379 | fat: 17g | protein: 51g | carbs: 3g | fiber: 1g | sodium: 492mg

Salmon Croquettes

Prep time: 10 minutes | Cook time: 7 to 8 minutes | Serves 4

1 tablespoon oil
½ cup bread crumbs
1 (14¾-ounce / 418-g) can salmon, drained and all skin and fat removed
1 egg, beaten
⅓ cup coarsely crushed saltine crackers (about 8 crackers)
½ teaspoon Old Bay Seasoning
½ teaspoon onion powder
½ teaspoon Worcestershire sauce

1. Preheat the air fryer to 390°F (199°C). 2. In a shallow dish, mix oil and bread crumbs until crumbly. 3. In a large bowl, combine the salmon, egg, cracker crumbs, Old Bay, onion powder, and Worcestershire. Mix well and shape into 8 small patties about ½-inch thick. 4. Gently dip each patty into bread crumb mixture and turn to coat well on all sides. 5. Cook for 7 to 8 minutes or until outside is crispy and browned.

Per Serving:
calories: 250 | fat: 11g | protein: 25g | carbs: 11g | fiber: 1g | sodium: 244mg

Roasted Sea Bass

Prep time: 5 minutes | Cook time: 15 minutes | Serves 6

¼ cup olive oil
Whole sea bass or fillets
Sea salt and freshly ground pepper, to taste
¼ cup dry white wine
3 teaspoons fresh dill
2 teaspoons fresh thyme
1 garlic clove, minced

1. Preheat the oven to 425°F (220°C). 2. Brush the bottom of a roasting pan with olive oil. Place the fish in the pan and brush the fish with oil. 3. Season fish with sea salt and freshly ground pepper. Combine the remaining ingredients and pour over the fish. Bake for 10–15 minutes, depending on the size of the fish. Sea bass is done when the flesh is firm and opaque.

Per Serving:
calories: 217 | fat: 12g | protein: 24g | carbs: 1g | fiber: 0g | sodium: 88mg

Maple Balsamic Glazed Salmon

Prep time: 5 minutes | Cook time: 10 minutes | Serves 4

4 (6-ounce / 170-g) fillets of salmon
Salt and freshly ground black pepper, to taste
Vegetable oil
¼ cup pure maple syrup
3 tablespoons balsamic vinegar
1 teaspoon Dijon mustard

1. Preheat the air fryer to 400°F (204°C). 2. Season the salmon well with salt and freshly ground black pepper. Spray or brush the bottom of the air fryer basket with vegetable oil and place the salmon fillets inside. Air fry the salmon for 5 minutes. 3. While the salmon is air frying, combine the maple syrup, balsamic vinegar and Dijon mustard in a small saucepan over medium heat and stir to blend well. Let the mixture simmer while the fish is cooking. It should start to thicken slightly, but keep your eye on it so it doesn't burn. 4. Brush the glaze on the salmon fillets and air fry for an additional 5 minutes. The salmon should feel firm to the touch when finished and the glaze should be nicely browned on top. Brush a little more glaze on top before removing and serving with rice and vegetables, or a nice green salad.

Per Serving:
calories: 279 | fat: 8g | protein: 35g | carbs: 15g | fiber: 0g | sodium: 146mg

Quick Seafood Paella

Prep time: 20 minutes | Cook time: 20 minutes | Serves 4

¼ cup plus 1 tablespoon extra-virgin olive oil
1 large onion, finely chopped
2 tomatoes, peeled and chopped
1½ tablespoons garlic powder
1½ cups medium-grain Spanish paella rice or arborio rice
2 carrots, finely diced
Salt
1 tablespoon sweet paprika
8 ounces (227 g) lobster meat or canned crab
½ cup frozen peas
3 cups chicken stock, plus more if needed
1 cup dry white wine
6 jumbo shrimp, unpeeled
⅓ pound calamari rings
1 lemon, halved

1. In a large sauté pan or skillet (16-inch is ideal), heat the oil over medium heat until small bubbles start to escape from oil. Add the onion and cook for about 3 minutes, until fragrant, then add tomatoes and garlic powder. Cook for 5 to 10 minutes, until the tomatoes are reduced by half and the consistency is sticky. 2. Stir in the rice, carrots, salt, paprika, lobster, and peas and mix well. In a pot or microwave-safe bowl, heat the chicken stock to almost boiling, then add it to the rice mixture. Bring to a simmer, then add the wine. 3. Smooth out the rice in the bottom of the pan. Cover and cook on low for 10 minutes, mixing occasionally, to prevent burning. 4. Top the rice with the shrimp, cover, and cook for 5 more minutes. Add additional broth to the pan if the rice looks dried out. 5. Right before removing the skillet from the heat, add the calamari rings. Toss the ingredients frequently. In about 2 minutes, the rings will look opaque. Remove the pan from the heat immediately—you don't want the paella to overcook). Squeeze fresh lemon juice over the dish.

Per Serving:
calories: 613 | fat: 15g | protein: 26g | carbs: 86g | fiber: 7g | sodium: 667mg

Rosemary Salmon

Prep time: 5 minutes | Cook time: 5 minutes | Serves 4

1 cup water
4 (4-ounce / 113-g) salmon fillets
½ teaspoon salt
½ teaspoon ground black pepper
1 sprig rosemary, leaves stripped off and minced
2 tablespoons chopped fresh thyme
2 tablespoons extra-virgin olive oil
4 lemon wedges

1. Add water to the Instant Pot® and place rack inside. 2. Season fish fillets with salt and pepper. Measure out four pieces of foil large enough to wrap around fish fillets. Lay fish fillets on foil. Top with rosemary and thyme, then drizzle each with olive oil. Carefully wrap loosely in foil. 3. Place foil packets on rack. Close lid, set steam release to Sealing, press the Steam button, and set time to 5 minutes. 4. When the timer beeps, quick-release the pressure until the float valve drops. Press the Cancel button and open lid. Carefully remove packets to plates. Serve immediately with lemon wedges.

Per Serving:
calories: 160 | fat: 8g | protein: 24g | carbs: 0g | fiber: 0g | sodium: 445mg

Honey-Balsamic Salmon

Prep time: 5 minutes | Cook time: 8 minutes | Serves 2

Oil, for spraying
2 (6-ounce / 170-g) salmon fillets
¼ cup balsamic vinegar
2 tablespoons honey
2 teaspoons red pepper flakes
2 teaspoons olive oil
½ teaspoon salt
¼ teaspoon freshly ground black pepper

1. Line the air fryer basket with parchment and spray lightly with oil. 2. Place the salmon in the prepared basket. 3. In a small bowl, whisk together the balsamic vinegar, honey, red pepper flakes, olive oil, salt, and black pepper. Brush the mixture over the salmon. 4. Roast at 390°F (199°C) for 7 to 8 minutes, or until the internal temperature reaches 145°F (63°C). Serve immediately.

Per Serving:
calories: 353 | fat: 12g | protein: 35g | carbs: 24g | fiber: 1g | sodium: 590mg

Friday Night Fish Fry

Prep time: 10 minutes | Cook time: 10 minutes | Serves 4

1 large egg
½ cup powdered Parmesan cheese (about 1½ ounces / 43 g)
1 teaspoon smoked paprika
¼ teaspoon celery salt
¼ teaspoon ground black pepper
4 (4-ounce / 113-g) cod fillets
Chopped fresh oregano or parsley, for garnish (optional)
Lemon slices, for serving (optional)

1. Spray the air fryer basket with avocado oil. Preheat the air fryer to 400°F (204°C). 2. Crack the egg in a shallow bowl and beat it lightly with a fork. Combine the Parmesan cheese, paprika, celery salt, and pepper in a separate shallow bowl. 3. One at a time, dip the fillets into the egg, then dredge them in the Parmesan mixture. Using your hands, press the Parmesan onto the fillets to form a nice crust. As you finish, place the fish in the air fryer basket. 4. Air fry the fish in the air fryer for 10 minutes, or until it is cooked through and flakes easily with a fork. Garnish with fresh oregano or parsley and serve with lemon slices, if desired. 5. Store leftovers in an airtight container in the refrigerator for up to 3 days. Reheat in a preheated 400°F (204°C) air fryer for 5 minutes, or until warmed through.

Per Serving:
calories: 165 | fat: 6g | protein: 25g | carbs: 2g | fiber: 0g | sodium: 392mg

Mediterranean Grilled Shrimp

Prep time: 20 minutes | Cook time: 5 minutes | Serves 4 to 6

2 tablespoons garlic, minced
½ cup lemon juice
3 tablespoons fresh Italian parsley, finely chopped
¼ cup extra-virgin olive oil
1 teaspoon salt
2 pounds (907 g) jumbo shrimp (21-25), peeled and deveined

1. In a large bowl, mix the garlic, lemon juice, parsley, olive oil, and salt. 2. Add the shrimp to the bowl and toss to make sure all the pieces are coated with the marinade. Let the shrimp sit for 15 minutes. 3. Preheat a grill, grill pan, or lightly oiled skillet to high heat. While heating, thread about 5 to 6 pieces of shrimp onto each skewer. 4. Place the skewers on the grill, grill pan, or skillet and cook for 2 to 3 minutes on each side until cooked through. Serve warm.

Per Serving:
calories: 217 | fat: 10g | protein: 31g | carbs: 2g | fiber: 0g | sodium: 569mg

Salmon Spring Rolls

Prep time: 20 minutes | Cook time: 8 to 10 minutes | Serves 4

½ pound (227 g) salmon fillet
1 teaspoon toasted sesame oil
1 onion, sliced
8 rice paper wrappers
1 yellow bell pepper, thinly sliced
1 carrot, shredded
⅓ cup chopped fresh flat-leaf parsley
¼ cup chopped fresh basil

1. Put the salmon in the air fryer basket and drizzle with the sesame oil. Add the onion. Air fry at 370°F (188°C) for 8 to 10 minutes, or until the salmon just flakes when tested with a fork and the onion is tender. 2. Meanwhile, fill a small shallow bowl with warm water. One at a time, dip the rice paper wrappers into the water and place on a work surface. 3. Top each wrapper with one-eighth each of the salmon and onion mixture, yellow bell pepper, carrot, parsley, and basil. Roll up the wrapper, folding in the sides, to enclose the ingredients. 4. If you like, bake in the air fryer at 380°F (193°C) for 7 to 9 minutes, until the rolls are crunchy. Cut the rolls in half to serve.

Per Serving:
calories: 197 | fat: 4g | protein: 14g | carbs: 26g | fiber: 2g | sodium: 145mg

Shrimp with Arugula Pesto and Zucchini Noodles

Prep time: 20 minutes | Cook time: 5 minutes | Serves 2

3 cups lightly packed arugula
½ cup lightly packed basil leaves
3 medium garlic cloves
¼ cup walnuts
3 tablespoons olive oil
2 tablespoons grated Parmesan cheese
1 tablespoon freshly squeezed lemon juice
Salt
Freshly ground black pepper
1 (10-ounce / 283-g) package zucchini noodles
8 ounces (227 g) cooked, shelled shrimp
2 Roma tomatoes, diced

1. Combine the arugula, basil, garlic, walnuts, olive oil, Parmesan cheese, and lemon juice in a food processor fitted with the chopping blade. Process until smooth, scraping down the sides as needed. Season with salt and pepper. 2. Heat a sauté pan over medium heat. Add the pesto, zucchini noodles, and shrimp. Toss to combine the sauce over the noodles and shrimp, and cook until warmed through. Don't overcook or the zucchini will become limp. 3. Taste and add additional salt and pepper if needed. Top with the diced tomatoes.

Per Serving:
calories: 434 | fat: 30g | protein: 33g | carbs: 15g | fiber: 5g | sodium: 412mg

Linguine with Clams and White Wine

Prep time: 20 minutes | Cook time: 12 minutes | Serves 4

2 tablespoons olive oil
4 cups sliced mushrooms
1 medium yellow onion, peeled and diced
2 tablespoons chopped fresh oregano
3 cloves garlic, peeled and minced
¼ teaspoon salt
¼ teaspoon ground black pepper
½ cup white wine
1½ cups water
8 ounces (227 g) linguine, broken in half
1 pound (454 g) fresh clams, rinsed and purged
3 tablespoons lemon juice
¼ cup grated Parmesan cheese
2 tablespoons chopped fresh parsley

1. Press the Sauté button on the Instant Pot® and heat oil. Add mushrooms and onion. Cook until tender, about 5 minutes. Add oregano, garlic, salt, and pepper, and cook until very fragrant, about 30 seconds. Add wine, water, and pasta, pushing pasta down until submerged in liquid. Press the Cancel button. 2. Top pasta with clams and sprinkle lemon juice on top. Close lid, set steam release to Sealing, press the Manual button, and set time to 5 minutes. When the timer beeps, quick-release the pressure until the float valve drops and open lid. Transfer to a serving bowl and top with cheese and parsley. Serve immediately.

Per Serving:
calories: 486 | fat: 11g | protein: 39g | carbs: 52g | fiber: 5g | sodium: 301mg

Fish Gratin

Prep time: 30 minutes | Cook time: 17 minutes | Serves 4

1 tablespoon avocado oil
1 pound (454 g) hake fillets
1 teaspoon garlic powder
Sea salt and ground white pepper, to taste
2 tablespoons shallots, chopped
1 bell pepper, seeded and chopped
½ cup Cottage cheese
½ cup sour cream
1 egg, well whisked
1 teaspoon yellow mustard
1 tablespoon lime juice
½ cup Swiss cheese, shredded

1. Brush the bottom and sides of a casserole dish with avocado oil. Add the hake fillets to the casserole dish and sprinkle with garlic powder, salt, and pepper. 2. Add the chopped shallots and bell peppers. 3. In a mixing bowl, thoroughly combine the Cottage cheese, sour cream, egg, mustard, and lime juice. Pour the mixture over fish and spread evenly. 4. Cook in the preheated air fryer at 370°F (188°C) for 10 minutes. 5. Top with the Swiss cheese and cook an additional 7 minutes. Let it rest for 10 minutes before slicing and serving. Bon appétit!

Per Serving:
calories: 256 | fat: 12g | protein: 28g | carbs: 8g | fiber: 1g | sodium: 523mg

Mediterranean Spice-Crusted Salmon over White Beans

Prep time: 10 minutes | Cook time: 25 minutes | Serves 6

¼ cup olive oil, divided
1 large bulb fennel, cored and thinly sliced
1 yellow onion, diced
2 cloves garlic, minced
½ cup white wine
3 cans (15 ounces / 425 g each) no-salt-added cannellini beans, drained and rinsed
1 (14½-ounce / 411-g) can diced fire-roasted tomatoes
1 teaspoon Dijon mustard
⅛ teaspoon red-pepper flakes
1 tablespoon fennel seeds
2 teaspoons ground black pepper
1 teaspoon kosher salt
6 wild salmon fillets (6 ounces / 170 g each)
¼ cup thinly sliced basil

1. In a large skillet over medium heat, warm 2 tablespoons of the oil until shimmering. Cook the sliced fennel, onion, and garlic, stirring, until tender, about 8 minutes. Stir in the wine and cook until reduced by half, about 5 minutes. Add the beans and tomatoes and cook, stirring occasionally, to meld all the flavors, about 10 minutes. Stir in the mustard and pepper flakes. 2. Meanwhile, in a small bowl, combine the fennel seeds, black pepper, and salt. Sprinkle all over the salmon fillets. 3. In a large nonstick skillet over medium heat, warm the remaining 2 tablespoons oil. Cook the salmon, skin side up, until golden brown, about 5 minutes. Flip and cook until your desired doneness, about 3 minutes for medium. 4. Stir the basil into the bean mixture just before serving, divide among 6 shallow bowls, and top each with a salmon fillet.

Per Serving:
calories: 488 | fat: 22g | protein: 42g | carbs: 30g | fiber: 9g | sodium: 745mg

Catfish in Creole Sauce

Prep time: 10 minutes | Cook time: 5 minutes | Serves 4

1 (1½-pound / 680-g) catfish fillet, rinsed in cold water, patted dry, cut into bite-sized pieces	1 teaspoon hot paprika
	¼ teaspoon dried tarragon
	1 medium green bell pepper, seeded and diced
1 (14½-ounce / 411-g) can diced tomatoes	1 stalk celery, finely diced
2 teaspoons dried minced onion	¼ teaspoon sugar
¼ teaspoon onion powder	½ cup chili sauce
1 teaspoon dried minced garlic	½ teaspoon salt
¼ teaspoon garlic powder	½ teaspoon ground black pepper

1. Add all ingredients to the Instant Pot® and stir to mix. 2. Close lid, set steam release to Sealing, press the Manual button, and set time to 5 minutes. When the timer beeps, quick-release the pressure until the float valve drops and open lid. Gently stir and serve.

Per Serving:
calories: 284 | fat: 9g | protein: 31g | carbs: 7g | fiber: 3g | sodium: 696mg

Apple Cider Mussels

Prep time: 10 minutes | Cook time: 2 minutes | Serves 5

2 pounds (907 g) mussels, cleaned, peeled	1 teaspoon ground cumin
	1 tablespoon avocado oil
1 teaspoon onion powder	¼ cup apple cider vinegar

1. Mix mussels with onion powder, ground cumin, avocado oil, and apple cider vinegar. 2. Put the mussels in the air fryer and cook at 395°F (202°C) for 2 minutes.

Per Serving:
calories: 187 | fat: 7g | protein: 22g | carbs: 7g | fiber: 0g | sodium: 521mg

Mediterranean Cod Stew

Prep time: 10 minutes | Cook time: 20 minutes | Serves: 6

2 tablespoons extra-virgin olive oil	chopped
2 cups chopped onion (about 1 medium onion)	1 cup sliced olives, green or black
2 garlic cloves, minced (about 1 teaspoon)	⅓ cup dry red wine
¾ teaspoon smoked paprika	¼ teaspoon freshly ground black pepper
1 (14½-ounce / 411-g) can diced tomatoes, undrained	¼ teaspoon kosher or sea salt
	1½ pounds (680 g) cod fillets, cut into 1-inch pieces
1 (12-ounce / 340-g) jar roasted red peppers, drained and	3 cups sliced mushrooms (about 8 ounces / 227 g)

1. In a large stockpot over medium heat, heat the oil. Add the onion and cook for 4 minutes, stirring occasionally. Add the garlic and smoked paprika and cook for 1 minute, stirring often. 2. Mix in the tomatoes with their juices, roasted peppers, olives, wine, pepper, and salt, and turn the heat up to medium-high. Bring to a boil. Add the cod and mushrooms, and reduce the heat to medium. 3. Cover and cook for about 10 minutes, stirring a few times, until the cod is cooked through and flakes easily, and serve.

Per Serving:
calories: 209 | fat: 8g | protein: 23g | carbs: 12g | fiber: 4g | sodium: 334mg

Paprika-Spiced Fish

Prep time: 5 minutes | Cook time: 10 minutes | Serves 4

4 (5-ounce / 142-g) sea bass fillets	1 tablespoon smoked paprika
	3 tablespoons unsalted butter
½ teaspoon salt	Lemon wedges

1. Season the fish on both sides with the salt. Repeat with the paprika. 2. Preheat a skillet over high heat. Melt the butter. 3. Once the butter is melted, add the fish and cook for 4 minutes on each side. 4. Once the fish is done cooking, move to a serving dish and squeeze lemon over the top.

Per Serving:
calories: 257 | fat: 34g | protein: 34g | carbs: 1g | fiber: 1g | sodium: 416mg

Baked Salmon with Tomatoes and Olives

Prep time: 5 minutes | Cook time: 8 minutes | Serves 4

2 tablespoons olive oil	1 teaspoon chopped fresh dill
4 (1½-inch-thick) salmon fillets	2 Roma tomatoes, diced
½ teaspoon salt	¼ cup sliced Kalamata olives
¼ teaspoon cayenne	4 lemon slices

1. Preheat the air fryer to 380°F (193°C). 2. Brush the olive oil on both sides of the salmon fillets, and then season them lightly with salt, cayenne, and dill. 3. Place the fillets in a single layer in the basket of the air fryer, then layer the tomatoes and olives over the top. Top each fillet with a lemon slice. 4. Bake for 8 minutes, or until the salmon has reached an internal temperature of 145°F (63°C).

Per Serving:
calories: 483 | fat: 22g | protein: 66g | carbs: 3g | fiber: 1g | sodium: 593mg

Salmon with Cauliflower

Prep time: 10 minutes | Cook time: 25 minutes | Serves 4

1 pound (454 g) salmon fillet, diced	1 tablespoon coconut oil, melted
1 cup cauliflower, shredded	1 teaspoon ground turmeric
1 tablespoon dried cilantro	¼ cup coconut cream

1. Mix salmon with cauliflower, dried cilantro, ground turmeric, coconut cream, and coconut oil. 2. Transfer the salmon mixture into the air fryer and cook the meal at 350°F (177°C) for 25 minutes. Stir the meal every 5 minutes to avoid the burning.

Per Serving:
calories: 232 | fat: 14g | protein: 24g | carbs: 3g | fiber: 1g | sodium: 94mg

Snapper with Shallot and Tomato

Prep time: 20 minutes | Cook time: 15 minutes | Serves 2

2 snapper fillets	1 tablespoon olive oil
1 shallot, peeled and sliced	¼ teaspoon freshly ground black pepper
2 garlic cloves, halved	½ teaspoon paprika
1 bell pepper, sliced	Sea salt, to taste
1 small-sized serrano pepper, sliced	2 bay leaves
1 tomato, sliced	

1. Place two parchment sheets on a working surface. Place the fish in the center of one side of the parchment paper. 2. Top with the shallot, garlic, peppers, and tomato. Drizzle olive oil over the fish and vegetables. Season with black pepper, paprika, and salt. Add the bay leaves. 3. Fold over the other half of the parchment. Now, fold the paper around the edges tightly and create a half moon shape, sealing the fish inside. 4. Cook in the preheated air fryer at 390°F (199°C) for 15 minutes. Serve warm.

Per Serving:
calories: 325 | fat: 10g | protein: 47g | carbs: 11g | fiber: 2g | sodium: 146mg

Herbed Tuna Steaks

Prep time: 10 minutes | Cook time: 4 to 6 hours | Serves 4

Nonstick cooking spray	black pepper
4 (1-inch-thick) fresh tuna steaks (about 2 pounds / 907 g total)	2 teaspoons extra-virgin olive oil
1 teaspoon sea salt	2 teaspoons dried thyme
¼ teaspoon freshly ground	2 teaspoons dried rosemary

1. Coat a slow-cooker insert with cooking spray, or line the bottom and sides with parchment paper or aluminum foil. 2. Season the tuna steaks all over with salt and pepper and place them in the prepared slow cooker in a single layer. Drizzle with the olive oil and sprinkle with the thyme and rosemary. 3. Cover the cooker and cook for 4 to 6 hours on Low heat.

Per Serving:
calories: 339 | fat: 5g | protein: 68g | carbs: 1g | fiber: 1g | sodium: 689mg

Lemon Salmon with Dill

Prep time: 10 minutes | Cook time: 3 minutes | Serves 4

1 cup water	¼ cup chopped fresh dill
4 (4-ounce / 113-g) skin-on salmon fillets	1 small lemon, thinly sliced
½ teaspoon salt	2 tablespoons extra-virgin olive oil
½ teaspoon ground black pepper	1 tablespoon chopped fresh parsley

1. Add water to the Instant Pot® and place rack inside. 2. Season fish fillets with salt and pepper. Place fillets on rack. Top each fillet with dill and two or three lemon slices. Close lid, set steam release to Sealing, press the Steam button, and set time to 3 minutes. 3. When the timer beeps, quick-release the pressure until the float valve drops. Press the Cancel button and open lid. Place fillets on a serving platter, drizzle with olive oil, and garnish with parsley. Serve immediately.

Per Serving:
calories: 160 | fat: 9g | protein: 19g | carbs: 0g | fiber: 0g | sodium: 545mg

Tuna and Fruit Kebabs

Prep time: 15 minutes | Cook time: 8 to 12 minutes | Serves 4

1 pound (454 g) tuna steaks, cut into 1-inch cubes	1 tablespoon honey
½ cup canned pineapple chunks, drained, juice reserved	2 teaspoons grated fresh ginger
½ cup large red grapes	1 teaspoon olive oil
	Pinch cayenne pepper

1. Thread the tuna, pineapple, and grapes on 8 bamboo or 4 metal skewers that fit in the air fryer. 2. In a small bowl, whisk the honey, 1 tablespoon of reserved pineapple juice, the ginger, olive oil, and cayenne. Brush this mixture over the kebabs. Let them stand for 10 minutes. 3. Air fry the kebabs at 370°F (188°C) for 8 to 12 minutes, or until the tuna reaches an internal temperature of at least 145°F (63°C) on a meat thermometer, and the fruit is tender and glazed, brushing once with the remaining sauce. Discard any remaining marinade. Serve immediately.

Per Serving:
calories: 213 | fat: 7g | protein: 27g | carbs: 11g | fiber: 1g | sodium: 45mg

Lemon-Dill Salmon Burgers

Prep time: 10 minutes | Cook time: 8 minutes | Serves 4

2 (6-ounce / 170-g) fillets of salmon, finely chopped by hand or in a food processor	1 teaspoon salt
	Freshly ground black pepper, to taste
1 cup fine bread crumbs	2 eggs, lightly beaten
1 teaspoon freshly grated lemon zest	4 brioche or hamburger buns
2 tablespoons chopped fresh dill weed	Lettuce, tomato, red onion, avocado, mayonnaise or mustard, for serving

1. Preheat the air fryer to 400°F (204°C). 2. Combine all the ingredients in a bowl. Mix together well and divide into four balls. Flatten the balls into patties, making an indentation in the center of each patty with your thumb (this will help the burger stay flat as it cooks) and flattening the sides of the burgers so that they fit nicely into the air fryer basket. 3. Transfer the burgers to the air fryer basket and air fry for 4 minutes. Flip the burgers over and air fry for another 3 to 4 minutes, until nicely browned and firm to the touch. 4. Serve on soft brioche buns with your choice of topping: lettuce, tomato, red onion, avocado, mayonnaise or mustard

Per Serving:
calories: 367 | fat: 9g | protein: 28g | carbs: 42g | fiber: 2g | sodium: 585mg

Shrimp and Fish Chowder

Prep time: 20 minutes | Cook time: 4 to 6 hours | Serves 4

3 cups low-sodium vegetable broth
1 (28-ounce / 794-g) can no-salt-added crushed tomatoes
1 large bell pepper, any color, seeded and diced
1 large onion, diced
2 zucchini, chopped
3 garlic cloves, minced
1 teaspoon dried thyme
1 teaspoon dried basil
½ teaspoon sea salt
¼ teaspoon freshly ground black pepper
¼ teaspoon red pepper flakes
8 ounces (227 g) whole raw medium shrimp, peeled and deveined
8 ounces (227 g) fresh cod fillets, cut into 1-inch pieces

1. In a slow cooker, combine the vegetable broth, tomatoes, bell pepper, onion, zucchini, garlic, thyme, basil, salt, black pepper, and red pepper flakes. Stir to mix well. 2. Cover the cooker and cook for 4 to 6 hours on Low heat. 3. Stir in the shrimp and cod. Replace the cover on the cooker and cook for 15 to 30 minutes on Low heat, or until the shrimp have turned pink and the cod is firm and flaky.

Per Serving:
calories: 201 | fat: 1g | protein: 26g | carbs: 24g | fiber: 7g | sodium: 598mg

Southern-Style Catfish

Prep time: 10 minutes | Cook time: 12 minutes | Serves 4

4 (7-ounce / 198-g) catfish fillets
⅓ cup heavy whipping cream
1 tablespoon lemon juice
1 cup blanched finely ground almond flour
2 teaspoons Old Bay seasoning
½ teaspoon salt
¼ teaspoon ground black pepper

1. Place catfish fillets into a large bowl with cream and pour in lemon juice. Stir to coat. 2. In a separate large bowl, mix flour and Old Bay seasoning. 3. Remove each fillet and gently shake off excess cream. Sprinkle with salt and pepper. Press each fillet gently into flour mixture on both sides to coat. 4. Place fillets into ungreased air fryer basket. Adjust the temperature to 400°F (204°C) and air fry for 12 minutes, turning fillets halfway through cooking. Catfish will be golden brown and have an internal temperature of at least 145°F (63°C) when done. Serve warm.

Per Serving:
calories: 438 | fat: 28g | protein: 41g | carbs: 7g | fiber: 4g | sodium: 387mg

Shrimp over Black Bean Linguine

Prep time: 10 minutes | Cook time: 15 minutes | Serves 4

1 pound (454 g) black bean linguine or spaghetti
1 pound (454 g) fresh shrimp, peeled and deveined
4 tablespoons extra-virgin olive oil
1 onion, finely chopped
3 garlic cloves, minced
¼ cup basil, cut into strips

1. Bring a large pot of water to a boil and cook the pasta according to the package instructions. 2. In the last 5 minutes of cooking the pasta, add the shrimp to the hot water and allow them to cook for 3 to 5 minutes. Once they turn pink, take them out of the hot water, and, if you think you may have overcooked them, run them under cool water. Set aside. 3. Reserve 1 cup of the pasta cooking water and drain the noodles. In the same pan, heat the oil over medium-high heat and cook the onion and garlic for 7 to 10 minutes. Once the onion is translucent, add the pasta back in and toss well. 4. Plate the pasta, then top with shrimp and garnish with basil.

Per Serving:
calories: 668 | fat: 19g | protein: 57g | carbs: 73g | fiber: 31g | sodium: 615mg

Wild Cod Oreganata

Prep time: 10 minutes | Cook time: 20 minutes | Serves 2

10 ounces (283 g) wild cod (1 large piece or 2 smaller ones)
⅓ cup panko bread crumbs
1 tablespoon dried oregano
Zest of 1 lemon
½ teaspoon salt
Pinch freshly ground black pepper
1 tablespoon olive oil
2 tablespoons freshly squeezed lemon juice
2 tablespoons white wine
1 tablespoon minced fresh parsley

1. Preheat the oven to 350°F (180°C). Place the cod in a baking dish and pat it dry with a paper towel. 2. In a small bowl, combine the panko, oregano, lemon zest, salt, pepper, and olive oil and mix well. Pat the panko mixture onto the fish. 3. Combine the lemon juice and wine in a small bowl and pour it around the fish. 4. Bake the fish for 20 minutes, or until it flakes apart easily and reaches an internal temperature of 145°F (63°C). 5. Garnish with fresh minced parsley.

Per Serving:
calories: 203 | fat: 8g | protein: 23g | carbs: 9g | fiber: 2g | sodium: 149mg

Tuna Steaks with Olive Tapenade

Prep time: 10 minutes | Cook time: 10 minutes | Serves 4

4 (6-ounce / 170-g) ahi tuna steaks
1 tablespoon olive oil
Salt and freshly ground black pepper, to taste
½ lemon, sliced into 4 wedges
Olive Tapenade:
½ cup pitted kalamata olives
1 tablespoon olive oil
1 tablespoon chopped fresh parsley
1 clove garlic
2 teaspoons red wine vinegar
1 teaspoon capers, drained

1. Preheat the air fryer to 400°F (204°C). 2. Drizzle the tuna steaks with the olive oil and sprinkle with salt and black pepper. Arrange the tuna steaks in a single layer in the air fryer basket. Pausing to turn the steaks halfway through the cooking time, air fry for 10 minutes until the fish is firm. 3. To make the tapenade: In a food processor fitted with a metal blade, combine the olives, olive oil, parsley, garlic, vinegar, and capers. Pulse until the mixture is finely chopped, pausing to scrape down the sides of the bowl if necessary. Spoon the tapenade over the top of the tuna steaks and serve with lemon wedges.

Per Serving:
calories: 269 | fat: 9g | protein: 42g | carbs: 2g | fiber: 1g | sodium: 252mg

Salmon Cakes with Bell Pepper and Lemon Yogurt

Prep time: 15 minutes | Cook time: 15 minutes | Serves 4

¼ cup whole-wheat bread crumbs
¼ cup mayonnaise
1 large egg, beaten
1 tablespoon chives, chopped
1 tablespoon fresh parsley, chopped
Zest of 1 lemon
¾ teaspoon kosher salt, divided
¼ teaspoon freshly ground black pepper
2 (5- to 6-ounce / 142- to 170-g) cans no-salt boneless/skinless salmon, drained and finely flaked
½ bell pepper, diced small
2 tablespoons extra-virgin olive oil, divided
1 cup plain Greek yogurt
Juice of 1 lemon

1. In a large bowl, combine the bread crumbs, mayonnaise, egg, chives, parsley, lemon zest, ½ teaspoon of the salt, and black pepper and mix well. Add the salmon and the bell pepper and stir gently until well combined. Shape the mixture into 8 patties. 2. Heat 1 tablespoon of the olive oil in a large skillet over medium-high heat. Cook half the cakes until the bottoms are golden brown, 4 to 5 minutes. Adjust the heat to medium if the bottoms start to burn. Flip the cakes and cook until golden brown, an additional 4 to 5 minutes. Repeat with the remaining 1 tablespoon olive oil and the rest of the cakes. 3. In a small bowl, combine the yogurt, lemon juice, and the remaining ¼ teaspoon salt and mix well. Serve with the salmon cakes.

Per Serving:
calories: 330 | fat: 23g | protein: 21g | carbs: 9g | fiber: 1g | sodium: 385mg

Chapter 6 Poultry

Chicken Chili Verde over Rice

Prep time: 15 minutes | Cook time: 6 hours | Serves 2

1 cup diced tomatillos
1 onion, halved and sliced thin
2 garlic cloves, minced
1 jalapeño pepper, seeds and membranes removed, minced
1 teaspoon ground cumin
1 teaspoon ground coriander
1 teaspoon extra-virgin olive oil
½ cup long-grain brown rice
1 cup low-sodium chicken broth
2 boneless, skinless chicken breasts, about 8 ounces (227 g) each, cut into 4-inch tenders
¼ cup fresh cilantro

1. Combine the tomatillos, onion, garlic, jalapeño, cumin, and coriander in a food processor. Pulse until it has a sauce-like consistency but is still slightly chunky. 2. Grease the inside of the slow cooker with the olive oil. 3. Add the rice to the slow cooker and pour in the chicken broth. Gently stir to make sure the rice grains are fully submerged. 4. Place the chicken on top of the rice and pour the tomatillo salsa over the top. 5. Cover and cook on low for 6 hours.

Per Serving:
calories: 536 | fat: 11g | protein: 59g | carbs: 48g | net carbs: 44g | sugars: 6g | fiber: 4g | sodium: 148mg | cholesterol: 166mg

Classic Chicken Kebab

Prep time: 35 minutes | Cook time: 25 minutes | Serves 4

¼ cup olive oil
1 teaspoon garlic powder
1 teaspoon onion powder
1 teaspoon ground cumin
½ teaspoon dried oregano
½ teaspoon dried basil
¼ cup lemon juice
1 tablespoon apple cider vinegar
Olive oil cooking spray
1 pound (454 g) boneless skinless chicken thighs, cut into 1-inch pieces
1 red bell pepper, cut into 1-inch pieces
1 red onion, cut into 1-inch pieces
1 zucchini, cut into 1-inch pieces
12 cherry tomatoes

1. In a large bowl, mix together the olive oil, garlic powder, onion powder, cumin, oregano, basil, lemon juice, and apple cider vinegar. 2. Spray six skewers with olive oil cooking spray. 3. On each skewer, slide on a piece of chicken, then a piece of bell pepper, onion, zucchini, and finally a tomato and then repeat. Each skewer should have at least two pieces of each item. 4. Once all of the skewers are prepared, place them in a 9-by-13-inch baking dish and pour the olive oil marinade over the top of the skewers. Turn each skewer so that all sides of the chicken and vegetables are coated. 5. Cover the dish with plastic wrap and place it in the refrigerator for 30 minutes. 6. After 30 minutes, preheat the air fryer to 380°F (193°C). (If using a grill attachment, make sure it is inside the air fryer during preheating.) 7. Remove the skewers from the marinade and lay them in a single layer in the air fryer basket. If the air fryer has a grill attachment, you can also lay them on this instead. 8. Cook for 10 minutes. Rotate the kebabs, then cook them for 15 minutes more. 9. Remove the skewers from the air fryer and let them rest for 5 minutes before serving.

Per Serving:
calories: 306 | fat: 19g | protein: 24g | carbs: 10g | fiber: 3g | sodium: 119mg

Blackened Cajun Chicken Tenders

Prep time: 10 minutes | Cook time: 17 minutes | Serves 4

2 teaspoons paprika
1 teaspoon chili powder
½ teaspoon garlic powder
½ teaspoon dried thyme
¼ teaspoon onion powder
⅛ teaspoon ground cayenne pepper
2 tablespoons coconut oil
1 pound (454 g) boneless, skinless chicken tenders
¼ cup full-fat ranch dressing

1. In a small bowl, combine all seasonings. 2. Drizzle oil over chicken tenders and then generously coat each tender in the spice mixture. Place tenders into the air fryer basket. 3. Adjust the temperature to 375°F (191°C) and air fry for 17 minutes. 4. Tenders will be 165°F (74°C) internally when fully cooked. Serve with ranch dressing for dipping.

Per Serving:
calories: 266 | fat: 17g | protein: 26g | carbs: 2g | fiber: 1g | sodium: 207mg

Buffalo Chicken Cheese Sticks

Prep time: 5 minutes | Cook time: 8 minutes | Serves 2

1 cup shredded cooked chicken
¼ cup buffalo sauce
1 cup shredded Mozzarella cheese
1 large egg
¼ cup crumbled feta

1. In a large bowl, mix all ingredients except the feta. Cut a piece of parchment to fit your air fryer basket and press the mixture into a ½-inch-thick circle. 2. Sprinkle the mixture with feta and place into the air fryer basket. 3. Adjust the temperature to 400°F (204°C) and air fry for 8 minutes. 4. After 5 minutes, flip over the cheese mixture. 5. Allow to cool 5 minutes before cutting into sticks. Serve warm.

Per Serving:
calories: 413 | fat: 25g | protein: 43g | carbs: 3g | fiber: 0g | sodium: 453mg

Cilantro Chicken Kebabs

Prep time: 30 minutes | Cook time: 10 minutes | Serves 4

Chutney:
½ cup unsweetened shredded coconut
½ cup hot water
2 cups fresh cilantro leaves, roughly chopped
¼ cup fresh mint leaves, roughly chopped
6 cloves garlic, roughly chopped
1 jalapeño, seeded and roughly chopped
¼ to ¾ cup water, as needed
Juice of 1 lemon
Chicken:
1 pound (454 g) boneless, skinless chicken thighs, cut crosswise into thirds
Olive oil spray

1. For the chutney: In a blender or food processor, combine the coconut and hot water; set aside to soak for 5 minutes. 2. To the processor, add the cilantro, mint, garlic, and jalapeño, along with ¼ cup water. Blend at low speed, stopping occasionally to scrape down the sides. Add the lemon juice. With the blender or processor running, add only enough additional water to keep the contents moving. Turn the blender to high once the contents are moving freely and blend until the mixture is puréed. 3. For the chicken: Place the chicken pieces in a large bowl. Add ¼ cup of the chutney and mix well to coat. Set aside the remaining chutney to use as a dip. Marinate the chicken for 15 minutes at room temperature. 4. Spray the air fryer basket with olive oil spray. Arrange the chicken in the air fryer basket. Set the air fryer to 350°F (177°C) for 10 minutes. Use a meat thermometer to ensure that the chicken has reached an internal temperature of 165°F (74°C). 5. Serve the chicken with the remaining chutney.

Per Serving:
calories: 184 | fat: 8g | protein: 23g | carbs: 4g | fiber: 1g | sodium: 115mg

Chicken and Chickpea Skillet with Berbere Spice

Prep time: 15 minutes | Cook time: 45 minutes | Serves 6

2 tablespoons olive oil
1 (3-to 4-pound / 1.4-to 1.8-kg) whole chicken, cut into 8 pieces
3 teaspoons Berbere or baharat spice blend
1 large onion, preferably Spanish, thinly sliced into half-moons
2 garlic cloves, minced
2 cups 1-inch cubes peeled butternut squash, or 1 (12-ounce / 340-g) bag pre-cut squash
1 (15-ounce / 425-g) can no-salt-added chickpeas, undrained
½ cup golden raisins
Hot cooked rice, for serving

1. In a 12-inch skillet, heat 1 tablespoon olive oil over medium-high heat. Sprinkle the chicken with 2 teaspoons of the Berbere spice. Add half the chicken to the skillet and cook until browned, 4 to 6 minutes per side. Transfer the chicken to a plate and repeat to brown the remaining chicken. Set aside. 2. In the same skillet, heat the remaining 1 tablespoon olive oil. Add the onion and cook, stirring, until softened, about 5 minutes. Add the remaining 1 teaspoon Berbere spice, the garlic, squash, chickpeas, and raisins and stir to combine. Return the chicken to skillet, pushing the pieces between the vegetables, and bring to a boil. Reduce the heat to maintain a simmer, cover tightly, and cook for 20 to 25 minutes, until the chicken is cooked through and an instant-read thermometer inserted into the thickest part registers 165°F (74°C), and the squash is tender. 3. Serve over hot cooked rice.

Per Serving:
1 cup: calories: 507 | fat: 26g | protein: 42g | carbs: 33g | fiber: 9g | sodium: 218mg

Chicken Legs with Leeks

Prep time: 30 minutes | Cook time: 18 minutes | Serves 6

2 leeks, sliced
2 large-sized tomatoes, chopped
3 cloves garlic, minced
½ teaspoon dried oregano
6 chicken legs, boneless and skinless
½ teaspoon smoked cayenne pepper
2 tablespoons olive oil
A freshly ground nutmeg

1. In a mixing dish, thoroughly combine all ingredients, minus the leeks. Place in the refrigerator and let it marinate overnight. 2. Lay the leeks onto the bottom of the air fryer basket. Top with the chicken legs. 3. Roast chicken legs at 375°F (191°C) for 18 minutes, turning halfway through. Serve with hoisin sauce.

Per Serving:
calories: 390 | fat: 16g | protein: 52g | carbs: 7g | fiber: 1g | sodium: 264mg

One-Pan Parsley Chicken and Potatoes

Prep time: 5 minutes | Cook time: 25 minutes | Serves: 6

1½ pounds (680 g) boneless, skinless chicken thighs, cut into 1-inch cubes
1 tablespoon extra-virgin olive oil
1½ pounds (680 g) Yukon Gold potatoes, unpeeled, cut into ½-inch cubes (about 6 small potatoes)
2 garlic cloves, minced (about 1 teaspoon)
¼ cup dry white wine or apple cider vinegar
1 cup low-sodium or no-salt-added chicken broth
1 tablespoon Dijon mustard
¼ teaspoon kosher or sea salt
¼ teaspoon freshly ground black pepper
1 cup chopped fresh flat-leaf (Italian) parsley, including stems
1 tablespoon freshly squeezed lemon juice (½ small lemon)

1. Pat the chicken dry with a few paper towels. In a large skillet over medium-high heat, heat the oil. Add the chicken and cook for 5 minutes, stirring only after the chicken has browned on one side. Remove the chicken from the pan with a slotted spoon, and put it on a plate; it will not yet be fully cooked. Leave the skillet on the stove. 2. Add the potatoes to the skillet and cook for 5 minutes, stirring only after the potatoes have become golden and crispy on one side. Push the potatoes to the side of the skillet, add the garlic, and cook, stirring constantly, for 1 minute. Add the wine and cook for 1 minute, until nearly evaporated. Add the chicken broth, mustard, salt, pepper, and reserved chicken pieces. Turn the heat up to high, and bring to a boil. 3. Once boiling, cover the skillet, reduce the heat to medium-low, and cook for 10 to 12 minutes, until the potatoes are tender and the internal temperature of the chicken measures 165°F (74°C) on a meat thermometer and any juices run clear. 4. During the last minute of cooking, stir in the parsley. Remove from the heat, stir in the lemon juice, and serve.

Per Serving:
calories: 266 | fat: 7g | protein: 26g | carbs: 22g | fiber: 3g | sodium: 258mg

South Indian Pepper Chicken

Prep time: 30 minutes | Cook time: 15 minutes | Serves 4

Spice Mix:
1 dried red chile, or ½ teaspoon dried red pepper flakes
1-inch piece cinnamon or cassia bark
1½ teaspoons coriander seeds
1 teaspoon fennel seeds
1 teaspoon cumin seeds
1 teaspoon black peppercorns
½ teaspoon cardamom seeds
¼ teaspoon ground turmeric
1 teaspoon kosher salt
Chicken:
1 pound (454 g) boneless, skinless chicken thighs, cut crosswise into thirds
2 medium onions, cut into ½-inch-thick slices
¼ cup olive oil
Cauliflower rice, steamed rice, or naan bread, for serving

1. For the spice mix: Combine the dried chile, cinnamon, coriander, fennel, cumin, peppercorns, and cardamom in a clean coffee or spice grinder. Grind, shaking the grinder lightly so all the seeds and bits get into the blades, until the mixture is broken down to a fine powder. Stir in the turmeric and salt. 2. For the chicken: Place the chicken and onions in resealable plastic bag. Add the oil and 1½ tablespoons of the spice mix. Seal the bag and massage until the chicken is well coated. Marinate at room temperature for 30 minutes or in the refrigerator for up to 24 hours. 3. Place the chicken and onions in the air fryer basket. Set the air fryer to 350ºF (177ºC) for 10 minutes, stirring once halfway through the cooking time. Increase the temperature to 400ºF (204ºC) for 5 minutes. Use a meat thermometer to ensure the chicken has reached an internal temperature of 165ºF (74ºC). 4. Serve with steamed rice, cauliflower rice, or naan.

Per Serving:
calories: 295 | fat: 19g | protein: 24g | carbs: 9g | fiber: 3g | sodium: 694mg

Catalonian Chicken with Spiced Lemon Rice

Prep time: 10 minutes | Cook time: 4 hours 10 minutes | Serves 4

3 tablespoons all-purpose flour
2 tablespoons paprika
1 tablespoon garlic powder
Sea salt
Black pepper
6 chicken thighs
¼ cup olive oil
1 (15-ounce / 425-g) can diced tomatoes, with the juice
2 green bell peppers, diced into 2-inch pieces
1 large yellow onion, sliced into thick pieces
2 tablespoons tomato paste
4 cups chicken stock
1 cup uncooked brown rice
½ teaspoon red pepper flakes
Zest and juice from 1 lemon
½ cup pitted green olives

1. In a large resealable bag, mix together the flour, paprika, and garlic powder and season with salt and pepper. Add the chicken, reseal the bag, and toss to coat. 2. In a large skillet over medium heat, heat the olive oil. Add the chicken and brown on both sides, 3 to 4 minutes per side. 3. While the chicken is cooking, add the tomatoes, bell peppers, and onion to the slow cooker. 4. Place the browned chicken thighs in the slow cooker. 5. In same skillet used to brown the chicken, add the tomato paste and cook for 1 minute, stirring constantly. 6. Add 2 cups of the chicken stock to the skillet and bring to a simmer, stirring with a wooden spoon to scrape up the flavorful browned bits off the bottom of the pan. Pour over the top of the chicken in the slow cooker. 7. Cook on low for 4 hours, or until the chicken is extremely tender. 8. In a heavy medium saucepan over medium-high heat, combine the remaining 2 cups stock, the rice, red pepper flakes, lemon zest, and juice of one-half of the lemon, and season with salt. Bring to a boil, reduce the heat to low, and simmer, covered, until the rice is tender and has absorbed all the liquid, about 25 minutes. 9. To serve, spoon the rice onto plates and ladle the Catalonian chicken and vegetables over the top. Garnish with the olives and squeeze the juice from the remaining one-half lemon over the dish.

Per Serving:
calories: 791 | fat: 31g | protein: 69g | carbs: 60g | fiber: 8g | sodium: 497mg

Ginger Turmeric Chicken Thighs

Prep time: 5 minutes | Cook time: 25 minutes | Serves 4

4 (4-ounce / 113-g) boneless, skin-on chicken thighs
2 tablespoons coconut oil, melted
½ teaspoon ground turmeric
½ teaspoon salt
½ teaspoon garlic powder
½ teaspoon ground ginger
¼ teaspoon ground black pepper

1. Place chicken thighs in a large bowl and drizzle with coconut oil. Sprinkle with remaining ingredients and toss to coat both sides of thighs. 2. Place thighs skin side up into ungreased air fryer basket. Adjust the temperature to 400ºF (204ºC) and air fry for 25 minutes. After 10 minutes, turn thighs. When 5 minutes remain, flip thighs once more. Chicken will be done when skin is golden brown and the internal temperature is at least 165ºF (74ºC). Serve warm.

Per Serving:
calories: 392 | fat: 31g | protein: 25g | carbs: 1g | fiber: 0g | sodium: 412mg

Garlic Chicken (Shish Tawook)

Prep time: 15 minutes | Cook time: 15 minutes | Serves 4 to 6

2 tablespoons garlic, minced
2 tablespoons tomato paste
1 teaspoon smoked paprika
½ cup lemon juice
½ cup extra-virgin olive oil
1½ teaspoons salt
½ teaspoon freshly ground black pepper
2 pounds (907 g) boneless and skinless chicken (breasts or thighs)
Rice, tzatziki, or hummus, for serving (optional)

1. In a large bowl, add the garlic, tomato paste, paprika, lemon juice, olive oil, salt, and pepper and whisk to combine. 2. Cut the chicken into ½-inch cubes and put them into the bowl; toss to coat with the marinade. Set aside for at least 10 minutes. 3. To grill, preheat the grill on high. Thread the chicken onto skewers and cook for 3 minutes per side, for a total of 9 minutes. 4. To cook in a pan, preheat the pan on high heat, add the chicken, and cook for 9 minutes, turning over the chicken using tongs. 5. Serve the chicken with rice, tzatziki, or hummus, if desired.

Per Serving:
calories: 350 | fat: 22g | protein: 34g | carbs: 3g | fiber: 0g | sodium: 586mg

Chicken Piccata with Mushrooms

Prep time: 25 minutes | Cook time: 25 minutes | Serves 4

1 pound (454 g) thinly sliced chicken breasts	2 cups sliced mushrooms
1½ teaspoons salt, divided	½ cup dry white wine or chicken stock
½ teaspoon freshly ground black pepper	¼ cup freshly squeezed lemon juice
¼ cup ground flaxseed	¼ cup roughly chopped capers
2 tablespoons almond flour	Zucchini noodles, for serving
8 tablespoons extra-virgin olive oil, divided	¼ cup chopped fresh flat-leaf Italian parsley, for garnish
4 tablespoons butter, divided	

1. Season the chicken with 1 teaspoon salt and the pepper. On a plate, combine the ground flaxseed and almond flour and dredge each chicken breast in the mixture. Set aside. 2. In a large skillet, heat 4 tablespoons olive oil and 1 tablespoon butter over medium-high heat. Working in batches if necessary, brown the chicken, 3 to 4 minutes per side. Remove from the skillet and keep warm. 3. Add the remaining 4 tablespoons olive oil and 1 tablespoon butter to the skillet along with mushrooms and sauté over medium heat until just tender, 6 to 8 minutes. 4. Add the white wine, lemon juice, capers, and remaining ½ teaspoon salt to the skillet and bring to a boil, whisking to incorporate any little browned bits that have stuck to the bottom of the skillet. Reduce the heat to low and whisk in the final 2 tablespoons butter. 5. Return the browned chicken to skillet, cover, and simmer over low heat until the chicken is cooked through and the sauce has thickened, 5 to 6 more minutes. 6. Serve chicken and mushrooms warm over zucchini noodles, spooning the mushroom sauce over top and garnishing with chopped parsley.

Per Serving:
calories: 596 | fat: 48g | protein: 30g | carbs: 8g | fiber: 4g | sodium: 862mg

Chicken Jalfrezi

Prep time: 15 minutes | Cook time: 15 minutes | Serves 4

Chicken:	½ to 1 teaspoon cayenne pepper
1 pound (454 g) boneless, skinless chicken thighs, cut into 2 or 3 pieces each	Sauce:
	¼ cup tomato sauce
1 medium onion, chopped	1 tablespoon water
1 large green bell pepper, stemmed, seeded, and chopped	1 teaspoon garam masala
	½ teaspoon kosher salt
2 tablespoons olive oil	½ teaspoon cayenne pepper
1 teaspoon ground turmeric	Side salad, rice, or naan bread, for serving
1 teaspoon garam masala	
1 teaspoon kosher salt	

1. For the chicken: In a large bowl, combine the chicken, onion, bell pepper, oil, turmeric, garam masala, salt, and cayenne. Stir and toss until well combined. 2. Place the chicken and vegetables in the air fryer basket. Set the air fryer to 350°F (177°C) for 15 minutes, stirring and tossing halfway through the cooking time. Use a meat thermometer to ensure the chicken has reached an internal temperature of 165°F (74°C). 3. Meanwhile, for the sauce: In a small microwave-safe bowl, combine the tomato sauce, water, garam masala, salt, and cayenne. Microwave on high for 1 minute. Remove and stir. Microwave for another minute; set aside. 4. When the chicken is cooked, remove and place chicken and vegetables in a large bowl. Pour the sauce over all. Stir and toss to coat the chicken and vegetables evenly. 5. Serve with rice, naan, or a side salad.

Per Serving:
calories: 224 | fat: 12g | protein: 23g | carbs: 6g | fiber: 2g | sodium: 827mg

Apricot Chicken

Prep time: 15 minutes | Cook time: 10 to 12 minutes | Serves 4

⅔ cup apricot preserves	¾ cup panko bread crumbs
2 tablespoons freshly squeezed lemon juice	2 whole boneless, skinless chicken breasts (1 pound / 454 g each), halved
1 teaspoon soy sauce	1 to 2 tablespoons oil
¼ teaspoon salt	

1. In a shallow bowl, stir together the apricot preserves, lemon juice, soy sauce, and salt. Place the bread crumbs in a second shallow bowl. 2. Roll the chicken in the preserves mixture and then the bread crumbs, coating thoroughly. 3. Preheat the air fryer to 350°F (177°C). Line the air fryer basket with parchment paper. 4. Place the coated chicken on the parchment and spritz with oil. 5. Cook for 5 minutes. Flip the chicken, spritz it with oil, and cook for 5 to 7 minutes more until the internal temperature reaches 165°F (74°C) and the chicken is no longer pink inside. Let sit for 5 minutes.

Per Serving:
calories: 304 | fat: 8g | protein: 29g | carbs: 29g | fiber: 3g | sodium: 367mg

Calabrian Chicken with Potatoes and Vegetables

Prep time: 10 minutes | Cook time: 45 minutes | Serves 4

4 chicken drumsticks	strips
4 bone-in, skin-on chicken thighs	1 large sweet onion, cut into ½' wedges
1 pint cherry tomatoes, halved	¼ cup olive oil
1 pound (454 g) potatoes, scrubbed and cut into ½' wedges	4 cloves garlic, minced
	1 teaspoon dried oregano
	1 teaspoon sweet paprika
3 red, orange, or yellow bell peppers, seeded and cut into ½'	1 teaspoon kosher salt
	¼ teaspoon red-pepper flakes

1. Preheat the oven to 400°F (205°C). 2. On a large rimmed baking sheet, combine the chicken, tomatoes, potatoes, bell peppers, onion, oil, garlic, oregano, paprika, salt, and pepper flakes, tossing to combine and rubbing the chicken with the spices. 3. Arrange the vegetables underneath the chicken pieces. Roast until the vegetables are tender and a thermometer inserted in the thickest part of the chicken, but not touching bone, registers 165°F (74°C), about 45 minutes, turning the chicken and tossing the vegetables halfway through.

Per Serving:
calories: 571 | fat: 23g | protein: 56g | carbs: 34g | fiber: 6g | sodium: 755mg

Harissa Yogurt Chicken Thighs

Prep time: 5 minutes | Cook time: 25 minutes | Serves 4

½ cup plain Greek yogurt
2 tablespoons harissa
1 tablespoon lemon juice
½ teaspoon kosher salt
¼ teaspoon freshly ground black pepper
1½ pounds (680 g) boneless, skinless chicken thighs

1. In a bowl, combine the yogurt, harissa, lemon juice, salt, and black pepper. Add the chicken and mix together. Marinate for at least 15 minutes, and up to 4 hours in the refrigerator. 2. Preheat the oven to 425°F (220°C). Line a baking sheet with parchment paper or foil. Remove the chicken thighs from the marinade and arrange in a single layer on the baking sheet. Roast for 20 minutes, turning the chicken over halfway. 3. Change the oven temperature to broil. Broil the chicken until golden brown in spots, 2 to 3 minutes.

Per Serving:
calories: 190 | fat: 10g | protein: 24g | carbs: 1g | fiber: 0g | sodium: 230mg

Skillet Creamy Tarragon Chicken and Mushrooms

Prep time: 10 minutes | Cook time: 20 minutes | Serves 2

2 tablespoons olive oil, divided
½ medium onion, minced
4 ounces (113 g) baby bella (cremini) mushrooms, sliced
2 small garlic cloves, minced
8 ounces (227 g) chicken cutlets
2 teaspoons tomato paste
2 teaspoons dried tarragon
2 cups low-sodium chicken stock
6 ounces (170 g) pappardelle pasta
¼ cup plain full-fat Greek yogurt
Salt
Freshly ground black pepper

1. Heat 1 tablespoon of the olive oil in a sauté pan over medium-high heat. Add the onion and mushrooms and sauté for 5 minutes. Add the garlic and cook for 1 minute more. 2. Move the vegetables to the edges of the pan and add the remaining 1 tablespoon of olive oil to the center of the pan. Place the cutlets in the center and let them cook for about 3 minutes, or until they lift up easily and are golden brown on the bottom. 3. Flip the chicken and cook for another 3 minutes. 4. Mix in the tomato paste and tarragon. Add the chicken stock and stir well to combine everything. Bring the stock to a boil. 5. Add the pappardelle. Break up the pasta if needed to fit into the pan. Stir the noodles so they don't stick to the bottom of the pan. 6. Cover the sauté pan and reduce the heat to medium-low. Let the chicken and noodles simmer for 15 minutes, stirring occasionally, until the pasta is cooked and the liquid is mostly absorbed. If the liquid absorbs too quickly and the pasta isn't cooked, add more water or chicken stock, about ¼ cup at a time as needed. 7. Remove the pan from the heat. 8. Stir 2 tablespoons of the hot liquid from the pan into the yogurt. Pour the tempered yogurt into the pan and stir well to mix it into the sauce. Season with salt and pepper. 9. The sauce will tighten up as it cools, so if it seems too thick, add a few tablespoons of water.

Per Serving:
calories: 556 | fat: 18g | protein: 42g | carbs: 56g | fiber: 2g | sodium: 190mg

Taco Chicken

Prep time: 10 minutes | Cook time: 23 minutes | Serves 4

2 large eggs
1 tablespoon water
Fine sea salt and ground black pepper, to taste
1 cup pork dust
1 teaspoon ground cumin
1 teaspoon smoked paprika
4 (5-ounce / 142-g) boneless, skinless chicken breasts or thighs, pounded to ¼ inch thick
1 cup salsa
1 cup shredded Monterey Jack cheese (about 4 ounces / 113 g) (omit for dairy-free)
Sprig of fresh cilantro, for garnish (optional)

1. Spray the air fryer basket with avocado oil. Preheat the air fryer to 400°F (204°C). 2. Crack the eggs into a shallow baking dish, add the water and a pinch each of salt and pepper, and whisk to combine. In another shallow baking dish, stir together the pork dust, cumin, and paprika until well combined. 3. Season the chicken breasts well on both sides with salt and pepper. Dip 1 chicken breast in the eggs and let any excess drip off, then dredge both sides of the chicken breast in the pork dust mixture. Spray the breast with avocado oil and place it in the air fryer basket. Repeat with the remaining 3 chicken breasts. 4. Air fry the chicken in the air fryer for 20 minutes, or until the internal temperature reaches 165°F (74°C) and the breading is golden brown, flipping halfway through. 5. Dollop each chicken breast with ¼ cup of the salsa and top with ¼ cup of the cheese. Return the breasts to the air fryer and cook for 3 minutes, or until the cheese is melted. Garnish with cilantro before serving, if desired. 6. Store leftovers in an airtight container in the refrigerator for up to 4 days. Reheat in a preheated 400°F (204°C) air fryer for 5 minutes, or until warmed through.

Per Serving:
calories: 360 | fat: 15g | protein: 20g | carbs: 4g | fiber: 1g | sodium: 490mg

Jerk Chicken Kebabs

Prep time: 10 minutes | Cook time: 14 minutes | Serves 4

8 ounces (227 g) boneless, skinless chicken thighs, cut into 1-inch cubes
2 tablespoons jerk seasoning
2 tablespoons coconut oil
½ medium red bell pepper, seeded and cut into 1-inch pieces
¼ medium red onion, peeled and cut into 1-inch pieces
½ teaspoon salt

1. Place chicken in a medium bowl and sprinkle with jerk seasoning and coconut oil. Toss to coat on all sides. 2. Using eight (6-inch) skewers, build skewers by alternating chicken, pepper, and onion pieces, about three repetitions per skewer. 3. Sprinkle salt over skewers and place into ungreased air fryer basket. Adjust the temperature to 370°F (188°C) and air fry for 14 minutes, turning skewers halfway through cooking. Chicken will be golden and have an internal temperature of at least 165°F (74°C) when done. Serve warm.

Per Serving:
calories: 142 | fat: 9g | protein: 12g | carbs: 4g | fiber: 1g | sodium: 348mg

Classic Whole Chicken

Prep time: 5 minutes | Cook time: 50 minutes | Serves 4

Oil, for spraying
1 (4-pound / 1.8-kg) whole chicken, giblets removed
1 tablespoon olive oil
1 teaspoon paprika
½ teaspoon granulated garlic
½ teaspoon salt
½ teaspoon freshly ground black pepper
¼ teaspoon finely chopped fresh parsley, for garnish

1. Line the air fryer basket with parchment and spray lightly with oil. 2. Pat the chicken dry with paper towels. Rub it with the olive oil until evenly coated. 3. In a small bowl, mix together the paprika, garlic, salt, and black pepper and sprinkle it evenly over the chicken. 4. Place the chicken in the prepared basket, breast-side down. 5. Air fry at 360°F (182°C) for 30 minutes, flip, and cook for another 20 minutes, or until the internal temperature reaches 165°F (74°C) and the juices run clear. 6. Sprinkle with the parsley before serving.

Per Serving:
calories: 549 | fat: 11g | protein: 105g | carbs: 0g | fiber: 0g | sodium: 523mg

Honey-Glazed Chicken Thighs

Prep time: 5 minutes | Cook time: 14 minutes | Serves 4

Oil, for spraying
4 boneless, skinless chicken thighs, fat trimmed
3 tablespoons soy sauce
1 tablespoon balsamic vinegar
2 teaspoons honey
2 teaspoons minced garlic
1 teaspoon ground ginger

1. Preheat the air fryer to 400°F (204°C). Line the air fryer basket with parchment and spray lightly with oil. 2. Place the chicken in the prepared basket. 3. Cook for 7 minutes, flip, and cook for another 7 minutes, or until the internal temperature reaches 165°F (74°C) and the juices run clear. 4. In a small saucepan, combine the soy sauce, balsamic vinegar, honey, garlic, and ginger and cook over low heat for 1 to 2 minutes, until warmed through. 5. Transfer the chicken to a serving plate and drizzle with the sauce just before serving.

Per Serving:
calories: 286 | fat: 10g | protein: 39g | carbs: 7g | fiber: 0g | sodium: 365mg

Brazilian Tempero Baiano Chicken Drumsticks

Prep time: 30 minutes | Cook time: 20 minutes | Serves 4

1 teaspoon cumin seeds
1 teaspoon dried oregano
1 teaspoon dried parsley
1 teaspoon ground turmeric
½ teaspoon coriander seeds
1 teaspoon kosher salt
½ teaspoon black peppercorns
½ teaspoon cayenne pepper
¼ cup fresh lime juice
2 tablespoons olive oil
1½ pounds (680 g) chicken drumsticks

1. In a clean coffee grinder or spice mill, combine the cumin, oregano, parsley, turmeric, coriander seeds, salt, peppercorns, and cayenne. Process until finely ground. 2. In a small bowl, combine the ground spices with the lime juice and oil. Place the chicken in a resealable plastic bag. Add the marinade, seal, and massage until the chicken is well coated. Marinate at room temperature for 30 minutes or in the refrigerator for up to 24 hours. 3. When you are ready to cook, place the drumsticks skin side up in the air fryer basket. Set the air fryer to 400°F (204°C) for 20 to 25 minutes, turning the legs halfway through the cooking time. Use a meat thermometer to ensure that the chicken has reached an internal temperature of 165°F (74°C). 4. Serve with plenty of napkins.

Per Serving:
calories: 267 | fat: 13g | protein: 33g | carbs: 2g | fiber: 1g | sodium: 777mg

Hoisin Turkey Burgers

Prep time: 30 minutes | Cook time: 20 minutes | Serves 4

Olive oil
1 pound (454 g) lean ground turkey
¼ cup whole-wheat bread crumbs
¼ cup hoisin sauce
2 tablespoons soy sauce
4 whole-wheat buns

1. Spray the air fryer basket lightly with olive oil. 2. In a large bowl, mix together the turkey, bread crumbs, hoisin sauce, and soy sauce. 3. Form the mixture into 4 equal patties. Cover with plastic wrap and refrigerate the patties for 30 minutes. 4. Place the patties in the air fryer basket in a single layer. Spray the patties lightly with olive oil. 5. Air fry at 370°F (188°C) for 10 minutes. Flip the patties over, lightly spray with olive oil, and cook until golden brown, an additional 5 to 10 minutes. 6. Place the patties on buns and top with your choice of low-calorie burger toppings like sliced tomatoes, onions, and cabbage slaw.

Per Serving:
calories: 330 | fat: 13g | protein: 26g | carbs: 29g | fiber: 3g | sodium: 631mg

Chicken Marsala

Prep time: 10 minutes | Cook time: 30 minutes | Serves 4

¼ cup olive oil
4 boneless, skinless chicken breasts, pounded thin
Sea salt and freshly ground pepper, to taste
¼ cup whole-wheat flour
½ pound (227 g) mushrooms, sliced
1 cup Marsala wine
1 cup chicken broth
¼ cup flat-leaf parsley, chopped

1. Heat the olive oil in a large skillet on medium-high heat. 2. Season the chicken breasts with sea salt and freshly ground pepper, then dredge them in flour. 3. Sauté them in the olive oil until golden brown. 4. Transfer to an oven-safe plate, and keep warm in the oven on low. Sauté the mushrooms in the same pan. Add the wine and chicken broth and bring to a simmer. 5. Simmer for 10 minutes, or until the sauce is reduced and thickened slightly. Return the chicken to the pan, and cook it in the sauce for 10 minutes. Transfer to a serving dish and sprinkle with the parsley.

Per Serving:
calories: 543 | fat: 21g | protein: 65g | carbs: 10g | fiber: 2g | sodium: 146mg

Chicken Caprese Casserole

Prep time: 10 minutes | Cook time: 6 to 8 hours | Serves 4

2 pounds (907 g) boneless, skinless chicken thighs, cut into 1-inch cubes
1 (15-ounce / 425-g) can no-salt-added diced tomatoes
2 cups fresh basil leaves (about 1 large bunch)
¼ cup extra-virgin olive oil
2½ tablespoons balsamic vinegar
½ teaspoon sea salt
⅛ teaspoon freshly ground black pepper
2 cups shredded mozzarella cheese

1. In a slow cooker, layer the chicken, tomatoes, and basil. 2. In a small bowl, whisk together the olive oil, vinegar, salt, and pepper until blended. Pour the dressing into the slow cooker. Stir to mix well. 3. Cover the cooker and cook for 6 to 8 hours on Low heat. 4. Sprinkle the mozzarella cheese on top. Replace the cover on the cooker and cook for 10 to 20 minutes on Low heat, or until the cheese melts.

Per Serving:
calories: 805 | fat: 61g | protein: 54g | carbs: 8g | fiber: 2g | sodium: 497mg

Whole Tandoori-Style Braised Chicken

Prep time: 10 minutes | Cook time: 4 to 8 hours | Serves 6

1 tablespoon freshly grated ginger
5 garlic cloves, minced
2 fresh green chiles, finely chopped
⅔ cup Greek yogurt
2 tablespoons mustard oil
1 tablespoon Kashmiri chili powder
1 tablespoon dried fenugreek leaves
1 tablespoon gram flour
2 teaspoons garam masala
1 teaspoon sea salt
1 teaspoon ground cumin
Juice of 1 large lemon
1 whole chicken, about 3⅓ pounds (1½ kg)
Handful fresh coriander leaves, chopped

1. Put the ginger, garlic, and green chiles in a spice grinder and grind to a paste. Empty into a large bowl and stir in all the other ingredients, except for the chicken and the coriander leaves. 2. Skin the chicken. Then, using a sharp knife, slash the chicken breasts and legs to allow the marinade to penetrate. 3. Marinate in the refrigerator for as long as you can leave it. (Overnight is fine.) 4. Preheat the slow cooker on high. My cooker has a stand I can sit meat on, but if you don't have one, scrunch up some foil and put it in the bottom of the cooker. Pour a few tablespoons of water in the bottom of the cooker and place the chicken on the foil. 5. Cook on high for 4 hours, or on low for 6 to 8 hours. 6. Remove the chicken from the cooker and cut it into pieces. Sprinkle the chopped coriander leaves over the chicken and serve.

Per Serving:
calories: 634 | fat: 45g | protein: 50g | carbs: 5g | net carbs: 4g | sugars: 1g | fiber: 1g | sodium: 615mg | cholesterol: 198mg

Grilled Chicken and Vegetables with Lemon-Walnut Sauce

Prep time: 20 minutes | Cook time: 16 minutes | Serves 4

1 cup chopped walnuts, toasted
1 small shallot, very finely chopped
½ cup olive oil, plus more for brushing
Juice and zest of 1 lemon
4 boneless, skinless chicken breasts
Sea salt and freshly ground pepper, to taste
2 zucchini, sliced diagonally ¼-inch thick
½ pound (227 g) asparagus
1 red onion, sliced ⅓-inch thick
1 teaspoon Italian seasoning

1. Preheat a grill to medium-high. 2. Put the walnuts, shallots, olive oil, lemon juice, and zest in a food processor and process until smooth and creamy. 3. Season the chicken with sea salt and freshly ground pepper, and grill on an oiled grate until cooked through, about 7–8 minutes a side or until an instant-read thermometer reaches 180°F (82°C) in the thickest part. 4. When the chicken is halfway done, put the vegetables on the grill. Sprinkle Italian seasoning over the chicken and vegetables to taste. 5. To serve, lay the grilled veggies on a plate, place the chicken breast on the grilled vegetables, and spoon the lemon-walnut sauce over the chicken and vegetables.

Per Serving:
calories: 800 | fat: 54g | protein: 68g | carbs: 13g | fiber: 5g | sodium: 134mg

Lebanese Garlic Chicken Flatbreads

Prep time: 5 minutes | Cook time: 20 minutes | Serves 6

8 cloves garlic
½ teaspoon kosher salt
¼ cup olive oil
2 tablespoons fresh lemon juice
½ teaspoon ground sumac
1 pound (454 g) boneless, skinless chicken thighs
1 cup thinly sliced cucumber
6 whole wheat flatbreads

1. In a medium bowl, muddle the garlic and salt together using the end of a wooden spoon, or use a mortar and pestle if you have one. Add the oil, lemon juice, and sumac and stir into a thick paste. 2. Place the chicken thighs in a gallon-size resealable plastic bag and pour the garlic mixture over the top. Massage the marinade into the chicken and place in the fridge for 6 hours or overnight. 3. Coat a grill rack or grill pan with olive oil and prepare to medium-high heat. 4. Remove the chicken from the marinade and discard the marinade. Grill the chicken until grill marks form and a thermometer inserted in the thickest part reaches 165°F(74°C), about 10 minutes per side. 5. Slice the chicken into bite-size pieces and distribute, along with the cucumber slices, among 6 flatbreads. Roll the flatbreads around the chicken and serve.

Per Serving:
calories: 407 | fat: 13g | protein: 37g | carbs:379g | fiber: 5g | sodium: 154mg

Hot Goan-Style Coconut Chicken

Prep time: 20 minutes | Cook time: 4 to 6 hours | Serves 6

Spice Paste:
8 dried Kashmiri chiles, broken into pieces
2 tablespoons coriander seeds
2-inch piece cassia bark, broken into pieces
1 teaspoon black peppercorns
1 teaspoon cumin seeds
1 teaspoon fennel seeds
4 cloves
2 star anise
1 tablespoon poppy seeds
1 cup freshly grated coconut, or desiccated coconut shreds
6 garlic cloves
⅓ cup water
Chicken:
12 chicken thigh and drumstick pieces, on the bone, skinless
1 teaspoon salt (or to taste)
1 teaspoon turmeric
2 tablespoons coconut oil
2 medium onions, finely sliced
⅓ cup water
½ teaspoon ground nutmeg
2 teaspoons tamarind paste
Handful fresh coriander leaves, chopped for garnish
1 or 2 fresh red chiles, for garnish

Make the Spice Paste: 1. In a dry frying pan, roast the Kashmiri chiles, coriander seeds, cassia bark, peppercorns, cumin seeds, fennel seeds, cloves, and star anise until fragrant, about 1 minute. Add the poppy seeds and continue roasting for a few minutes. Then remove from the heat and leave to cool. 2. Once cooled, grind the toasted spices in your spice grinder and set aside. 3. In the same pan, add the dried coconut and toast it for 5 to 7 minutes, until it just starts to turn golden. 4. Transfer to a blender with the garlic, and add the water. Blend to make a thick, wet paste. 5. Add the ground spices and blend again to mix together. Make the Chicken: 6. In a large bowl, toss the chicken with the salt and turmeric. Marinate for 15 to 20 minutes. In the meantime, heat the slow cooker to high. 7. Heat the oil in a frying pan (or in the slow cooker if you have a sear setting). Cook the sliced onions for 10 minutes, and then add the spice and coconut paste. Cook until it becomes fragrant. 8. Transfer everything to the slow cooker. Add the chicken, then the water. Cover and cook on low for 6 hours, or on high for 4 hours. 9. Sprinkle in the nutmeg and stir in the tamarind paste. Cover and cook for another 5 minutes. 10. Garnish with fresh coriander leaves and whole red chiles to serve.

Per Serving:
calories: 583 | fat: 26g | protein: 77g | carbs: 7g | net carbs: 4g | sugars: 2g | fiber: 3g | sodium: 762mg | cholesterol: 363mg

Chapter 7 Beans and Grains

Spanakorizo (Greek Spinach and Rice)

Prep time: 5 minutes | Cook time: 27 minutes | Serves 2

3½ tbsp extra virgin olive oil, divided
1lb (450g) fresh spinach, rinsed and torn into large pieces
2 tbsp fresh lemon juice plus juice of ½ lemon, for serving
1 medium red onion, chopped
1 tsp dried mint
2 tbsp chopped fresh dill
⅓ cup uncooked medium-grain rice
⅔ cup hot water
½ tsp fine sea salt
¼ tsp freshly ground black pepper

1. Add 1½ teaspoons of olive oil to a deep pan over medium heat. When the oils starts to shimmer, add the spinach and 2 tablespoons lemon juice. Using tongs, toss the spinach until it's wilted and develops a bright green color, about 2–3 minutes, then transfer to a colander and set aside to drain. 2. In a separate large pot placed over medium heat, combine the onions with 2 tablespoons of the olive oil. Sauté until the onions are soft, about 3 minutes. 3. Add the cooked spinach, mint, dill, and rice to the pot and then stir to coat the spinach and rice in the olive oil. Continue sautéing for 1 minute, then add the hot water, sea salt, and black pepper. Stir, then increase the heat slightly and bring the mixture to a boil. 4. Once the mixture comes to a boil, reduce the heat to low and simmer for 20 minutes or until the rice is soft, adding more warm water as needed if the rice becomes too dry. 5. Serve warm or at room temperature with a squeeze of lemon juice and 1½ teaspoons of the olive oil drizzled over each serving. Store covered in the refrigerator for up to 3 days.

Per Serving:
Calories 431 Total fat 25g Saturated fat 4g Carbohydrate 42g Protein 10g

Sweet Potato Black Bean Burgers

Prep time: 10 minutes | Cook time: 10 minutes | Serves 4

1 (15-ounce/ 425-g) can black beans, drained and rinsed
1 cup mashed sweet potato
½ teaspoon dried oregano
¼ teaspoon dried thyme
¼ teaspoon dried marjoram
1 garlic clove, minced
¼ teaspoon salt
¼ teaspoon black pepper
1 tablespoon lemon juice
1 cup cooked brown rice
¼ to ½ cup whole wheat bread crumbs
1 tablespoon olive oil
For serving:
Whole wheat buns or whole wheat pitas
Plain Greek yogurt
Avocado
Lettuce
Tomato
Red onion

1. Preheat the air fryer to 380°F(193°C). 2. In a large bowl, use the back of a fork to mash the black beans until there are no large pieces left. 3. Add the mashed sweet potato, oregano, thyme, marjoram, garlic, salt, pepper, and lemon juice, and mix until well combined. 4. Stir in the cooked rice. 5. Add in ¼ cup of the whole wheat bread crumbs and stir. Check to see if the mixture is dry enough to form patties. If it seems too wet and loose, add an additional ¼ cup bread crumbs and stir. 6. Form the dough into 4 patties. Place them into the air fryer basket in a single layer, making sure that they don't touch each other. 7. Brush half of the olive oil onto the patties and bake for 5 minutes. 8. Flip the patties over, brush the other side with the remaining oil, and bake for an additional 4 to 5 minutes. 9. Serve on toasted whole wheat buns or whole wheat pitas with a spoonful of yogurt and avocado, lettuce, tomato, and red onion as desired.

Per Serving:
calories: 112 | fat: 4.3g | protein: 2.8g | carbs: 17g | fiber: 3g | sodium: 161mg

Barley Salad with Lemon-Tahini Dressing

Prep time: 15 minutes | Cook time: 10 minutes | Serves 4 to 6

1½ cups pearl barley
5 tablespoons extra-virgin olive oil, divided
1½ teaspoons table salt, for cooking barley
¼ cup tahini
1 teaspoon grated lemon zest plus ¼ cup juice (2 lemons)
1 tablespoon sumac, divided
1 garlic clove, minced
¾ teaspoon table salt
1 English cucumber, cut into ½-inch pieces
1 carrot, peeled and shredded
1 red bell pepper, stemmed, seeded, and chopped
4 scallions, sliced thin
2 tablespoons finely chopped jarred hot cherry peppers
¼ cup coarsely chopped fresh mint

1. Combine 6 cups water, barley, 1 tablespoon oil, and 1½ teaspoons salt in Instant Pot. Lock lid in place and close pressure release valve. Select high pressure cook function and cook for 8 minutes. Turn off Instant Pot and let pressure release naturally for 15 minutes. Quick-release any remaining pressure, then carefully remove lid, allowing steam to escape away from you. Drain barley, spread onto rimmed baking sheet, and let cool completely, about 15 minutes. 2. Meanwhile, whisk remaining ¼ cup oil, tahini, 2 tablespoons water, lemon zest and juice, 1 teaspoon sumac, garlic, and ¾ teaspoon salt in large bowl until combined; let sit for 15 minutes. 3. Measure out and reserve ½ cup dressing for serving. Add barley, cucumber, carrot, bell pepper, scallions, and cherry peppers to bowl with dressing and gently toss to combine. Season with salt and pepper to taste. Transfer salad to serving dish and sprinkle with mint and remaining 2 teaspoons sumac. Serve, passing reserved dressing separately.

Per Serving:
calories: 370 | fat: 18g | protein: 8g | carbs: 47g | fiber: 10g | sodium: 510mg

Creamy Lima Bean Soup

Prep time: 10 minutes | Cook time: 17 minutes | Serves 6

1 tablespoon olive oil
1 small onion, peeled and diced
1 clove garlic, peeled and minced
2 cups vegetable stock
½ cup water
2 cups dried lima beans, soaked overnight and drained
½ teaspoon salt
½ teaspoon ground black pepper
2 tablespoons thinly sliced chives

1. Press the Sauté button on the Instant Pot® and heat oil. Add onion and cook until golden brown, about 10 minutes. Add garlic and cook until fragrant, about 30 seconds. Press the Cancel button. 2. Add stock, water, and lima beans. Close lid, set steam release to Sealing, press the Manual button, and set time to 6 minutes. When the timer beeps, let pressure release naturally, about 20 minutes. 3. Open lid and purée soup with an immersion blender or in batches in a blender. Season with salt and pepper, then sprinkle with chives before serving.

Per Serving:
calories: 67 | fat: 2g | protein: 2g | carbs: 9g | fiber: 2g | sodium: 394mg

Greek Chickpeas with Coriander and Sage

Prep time: 20 minutes | Cook time: 22 minutes | Serves 6 to 8

1½ tablespoons table salt, for brining
1 pound (454 g) dried chickpeas, picked over and rinsed
2 tablespoons extra-virgin olive oil, plus extra for drizzling
2 onions, halved and sliced thin
¼ teaspoon table salt
1 tablespoon coriander seeds, cracked
¼–½ teaspoon red pepper flakes
2½ cups chicken broth
¼ cup fresh sage leaves
2 bay leaves
1½ teaspoons grated lemon zest plus 2 teaspoons juice
2 tablespoons minced fresh parsley

1. Dissolve 1½ tablespoons salt in 2 quarts cold water in large container. Add chickpeas and soak at room temperature for at least 8 hours or up to 24 hours. Drain and rinse well. 2. Using highest sauté function, heat oil in Instant Pot until shimmering. Add onions and ¼ teaspoon salt and cook until onions are softened and well browned, 10 to 12 minutes. Stir in coriander and pepper flakes and cook until fragrant, about 30 seconds. Stir in broth, scraping up any browned bits, then stir in chickpeas, sage, and bay leaves. 3. Lock lid in place and close pressure release valve. Select low pressure cook function and cook for 10 minutes. Turn off Instant Pot and let pressure release naturally for 15 minutes. Quick-release any remaining pressure, then carefully remove lid, allowing steam to escape away from you. 4. Discard bay leaves. Stir lemon zest and juice into chickpeas and season with salt and pepper to taste. Sprinkle with parsley. Serve, drizzling individual portions with extra oil.

Per Serving:
calories: 190 | fat: 6g | protein: 11g | carbs: 40g | fiber: 1g | sodium: 360mg

Quinoa with Artichokes

Prep time: 10 minutes | Cook time: 26 minutes | Serves 4

2 tablespoons light olive oil
1 medium yellow onion, peeled and diced
2 cloves garlic, peeled and minced
½ teaspoon salt
½ teaspoon ground black pepper
1 cup quinoa, rinsed and drained
2 cups vegetable broth
1 cup roughly chopped marinated artichoke hearts
½ cup sliced green olives
½ cup minced fresh flat-leaf parsley
2 tablespoons lemon juice

1. Press the Sauté button on the Instant Pot® and heat oil. Add onion and cook until tender, about 5 minutes. Add garlic, salt, and pepper, and cook until fragrant, about 30 seconds. Press the Cancel button. 2. Stir in quinoa and broth. Close lid, set steam release to Sealing, press the Manual button, and set time to 20 minutes. When the timer beeps, let pressure release naturally, about 20 minutes, then open lid. Fluff quinoa with a fork, then stir in remaining ingredients. Serve immediately.

Per Serving:
calories: 270 | fat: 13g | protein: 6g | carbs: 33g | fiber: 4g | sodium: 718mg

Vegetable Barley Soup

Prep time: 30 minutes | Cook time: 26 minutes | Serves 8

2 tablespoons olive oil
½ medium yellow onion, peeled and chopped
1 medium carrot, peeled and chopped
1 stalk celery, chopped
2 cups sliced button mushrooms
2 cloves garlic, peeled and minced
½ teaspoon dried thyme
½ teaspoon ground black pepper
1 large russet potato, peeled and cut into ½" pieces
1 (14½-ounce / 411-g) can fire-roasted diced tomatoes, undrained
½ cup medium pearl barley, rinsed and drained
4 cups vegetable broth
2 cups water
1 (15-ounce / 425-g) can corn, drained
1 (15-ounce / 425-g) can cut green beans, drained
1 (15-ounce / 425-g) can Great Northern beans, drained and rinsed
½ teaspoon salt

1. Press the Sauté button on the Instant Pot® and heat oil. Add onion, carrot, celery, and mushrooms. Cook until just tender, about 5 minutes. Add garlic, thyme, and pepper. Cook 30 seconds. Press the Cancel button. 2. Add potato, tomatoes, barley, broth, and water to pot. Close lid, set steam release to Sealing, press the Soup button, and cook for the default time of 20 minutes. 3. When the timer beeps, let pressure release naturally, about 15 minutes. Open lid and stir soup, then add corn, green beans, and Great Northern beans. Close lid and let stand on the Keep Warm setting for 10 minutes. Stir in salt. Serve hot.

Per Serving:
calories: 190 | fat: 4g | protein: 7g | carbs: 34g | fiber: 8g | sodium: 548mg

Chili-Spiced Beans

Prep time: 10 minutes | Cook time: 30 minutes | Serves 8

1 pound (454 g) dried pinto beans, soaked overnight and drained
1 medium onion, peeled and chopped
¼ cup chopped fresh cilantro
1 (15-ounce / 425-g) can tomato sauce
¼ cup chili powder
2 tablespoons smoked paprika
1 teaspoon ground cumin
1 teaspoon ground coriander
½ teaspoon ground black pepper
2 cups vegetable broth
1 cup water

1. Place all ingredients in the Instant Pot® and stir to combine. 2. Close lid, set steam release to Sealing, press the Chili button, and cook for the default time of 30 minutes. When the timer beeps, quick-release the pressure until the float valve drops, open lid, and stir well. If beans are too thin, press the Cancel button, then press the Sauté button and let beans simmer, uncovered, until desired thickness is reached. Serve warm.

Per Serving:
calories: 86 | fat: 0g | protein: 5g | carbs: 17g | fiber: 4g | sodium: 323mg

White Beans with Kale

Prep time: 15 minutes | Cook time: 7½ hours | Serves 2

1 onion, chopped
1 leek, white part only, sliced
2 celery stalks, sliced
2 garlic cloves, minced
1 cup dried white lima beans or cannellini beans, sorted and rinsed
2 cups vegetable broth
½ teaspoon salt
½ teaspoon dried thyme leaves
⅛ teaspoon freshly ground black pepper
3 cups torn kale

1. In the slow cooker, combine all the ingredients except the kale. 2. Cover and cook on low for 7 hours, or until the beans are tender. 3. Add the kale and stir. 4. Cover and cook on high for 30 minutes, or until the kale is tender but still firm, and serve.

Per Serving:
calories: 176 | fat: 1g | protein: 9g | carbs: 36g | net carbs: 27g | sugars: 7g | fiber: 9g | sodium: 616mg | cholesterol: 0mg

Garlic-Asparagus Israeli Couscous

Prep time: 5 minutes |Cook time: 25 minutes| Serves: 6

1 cup garlic-and-herb goat cheese (about 4 ounces/ 113 g)
1½ pounds (680 g) asparagus spears, ends trimmed and stalks chopped into 1-inch pieces (about 2¾ to 3 cups chopped)
1 tablespoon extra-virgin olive oil
1 garlic clove, minced (about ½ teaspoon)
¼ teaspoon freshly ground black pepper
1¾ cups water
1 (8-ounce/ 227-g) box uncooked whole-wheat or regular Israeli couscous (about 1⅓ cups)
¼ teaspoon kosher or sea salt

1. Preheat the oven to 425°F (220°C). Put the goat cheese on the counter to bring to room temperature. 2. In a large bowl, mix together the asparagus, oil, garlic, and pepper. Spread the asparagus on a large, rimmed baking sheet and roast for 10 minutes, stirring a few times. Remove the pan from the oven, and spoon the asparagus into a large serving bowl. 3. While the asparagus is roasting, in a medium saucepan, bring the water to a boil. Add the couscous and salt. Reduce the heat to medium-low, cover, and cook for 12 minutes, or until the water is absorbed. 4. Pour the hot couscous into the bowl with the asparagus. Add the goat cheese, mix thoroughly until completely melted, and serve.

Per Serving:
calories: 98 | fat: 1.3g | protein: 10.2g | carbs: 13.5g | fiber:3.67g | sodium: 262mg

Bulgur with Chickpeas, Spinach, and Za'atar

Prep time: 15 minutes | Cook time: 7 minutes | Serves 4 to 6

3 tablespoons extra-virgin olive oil, divided
1 onion, chopped fine
½ teaspoon table salt
3 garlic cloves, minced
2 tablespoons za'atar, divided
1 cup medium-grind bulgur, rinsed
1 (15-ounce/ 425-g) can chickpeas, rinsed
1½ cups water
5 ounces (142 g) baby spinach, chopped
1 tablespoon lemon juice, plus lemon wedges for serving

1. Using highest sauté function, heat 2 tablespoons oil in Instant Pot until shimmering. Add onion and salt and cook until onion is softened, about 5 minutes. Stir in garlic and 1 tablespoon za'atar and cook until fragrant, about 30 seconds. Stir in bulgur, chickpeas, and water. 2. Lock lid in place and close pressure release valve. Select high pressure cook function and cook for 1 minute. Turn off Instant Pot and quick-release pressure. Carefully remove lid, allowing steam to escape away from you. 3. Gently fluff bulgur with fork. Lay clean dish towel over pot, replace lid, and let sit for 5 minutes. Add spinach, lemon juice, remaining 1 tablespoon za'atar, and remaining 1 tablespoon oil and gently toss to combine. Season with salt and pepper to taste. Serve with lemon wedges.

Per Serving:
calories: 200 | fat: 8g | protein: 6g | carbs: 28g | fiber: 6g | sodium: 320mg

Wheat Berry Pilaf

Prep time: 15 minutes | Cook time: 7 hours | Makes 7 cups

1 cup wheat berries
1 onion, chopped
1 leek, white part only, chopped
1 cup sliced cremini mushrooms
3 cups vegetable broth
1 tablespoon freshly squeezed lemon juice
½ teaspoon dried thyme leaves
½ teaspoon salt
⅛ teaspoon freshly ground black pepper

1. Rinse the wheat berries well, and drain. 2. In the slow cooker, combine all the ingredients, and stir. 3. Cover and cook on low for 7 hours, or until the wheat berries and vegetables are tender.

Per Serving:
calories: 90 | fat: 0g | protein: 3g | carbs: 20g | net carbs: 17g | sugars: 2g | fiber: 3g | sodium: 173mg | cholesterol: 0mg

Creamy Thyme Polenta

Prep time: 5 minutes | Cook time: 10 minutes | Serves 6

3½ cups water
½ cup coarse polenta
½ cup fine cornmeal
1 cup corn kernels
1 teaspoon dried thyme
1 teaspoon salt

1. Add all ingredients to the Instant Pot® and stir. 2. Close lid, set steam release to Sealing, press the Manual button, and set time to 10 minutes. When the timer beeps, quick-release the pressure until the float valve drops and open lid. Serve immediately.

Per Serving:
calories: 74 | fat: 1g | protein: 2g | carbs: 14g | fiber: 2g | sodium: 401mg

Rice with Blackened Fish

Prep time: 10 minutes | Cook time: 2 to 4 hours | Serves 4

1 teaspoon ground cumin
1 teaspoon ground coriander
1 teaspoon garlic powder
1 teaspoon paprika
½ teaspoon sea salt
½ teaspoon freshly ground black pepper
½ teaspoon onion powder
1 pound (454 g) fresh salmon fillets
1 cup raw long-grain brown rice, rinsed
2½ cups low-sodium chicken broth
¼ cup diced tomato

1. In a small bowl, stir together the cumin, coriander, garlic powder, paprika, salt, pepper, and onion powder. Generously season the salmon fillets with the blackening seasoning. 2. In a slow cooker, combine the rice, chicken broth, and tomato. Stir to mix well. 3. Place the seasoned salmon on top of the rice mixture. 4. Cover the cooker and cook for 2 to 4 hours on Low heat.

Per Serving:
calories: 318 | fat: 6g | protein: 29g | carbs: 38g | fiber: 3g | sodium: 337mg

Revithosoupa (Chickpea Soup)

Prep time: 10 minutes | Cook time: 30 minutes | Serves 8

1 pound (454 g) dried chickpeas
4 cups water
¾ teaspoon salt
½ teaspoon ground black pepper
10 strands saffron
2 medium onions, peeled and diced
1 cup extra-virgin olive oil
1 teaspoon dried oregano
3 tablespoons lemon juice
2 tablespoons chopped fresh parsley

1. Add chickpeas, water, salt, pepper, saffron, onions, oil, and oregano to the Instant Pot® and stir well. Close lid, set steam release to Sealing, press the Bean button, and cook for the default time of 30 minutes. 2. When the timer beeps, let pressure release naturally, about 25 minutes. Open lid. Serve hot or cold, sprinkled with lemon juice. Garnish with chopped parsley.

Per Serving:
calories: 464 | fat: 30g | protein: 12g | carbs: 38g | fiber: 10g | sodium: 236mg

Quinoa Salad with Tomatoes

Prep time: 10 minutes | Cook time: 22 minutes | Serves 4

2 tablespoons olive oil
2 cloves garlic, peeled and minced
1 cup diced fresh tomatoes
¼ cup chopped fresh Italian flat-leaf parsley
1 tablespoon lemon juice
1 cup quinoa, rinsed and drained
2 cups water
1 teaspoon salt

1. Press the Sauté button on the Instant Pot® and heat oil. Add garlic and cook 30 seconds, then add tomatoes, parsley, and lemon juice. Cook an additional 1 minute. Transfer mixture to a small bowl and set aside. Press the Cancel button. 2. Add quinoa and water to the Instant Pot®. Close lid, set steam release to Sealing, press the Multigrain button, and set time to 20 minutes. 3. When timer beeps, let pressure release naturally, about 20 minutes, then open lid. Fluff with a fork and stir in tomato mixture and salt. Serve immediately.

Per Serving:
calories: 223 | fat: 10g | protein: 6g | carbs: 29g | fiber: 3g | sodium: 586mg

Vegetable Risotto with Beet Greens

Prep time: 30 minutes | Cook time: 10 minutes | Serves 6

¼ cup light olive oil
1 clove garlic, peeled and minced
1 small Asian eggplant, sliced
1 small zucchini, trimmed and sliced
1 large red bell pepper, seeded and cut in quarters
1 large portobello mushroom, gills and stem removed, cap sliced
1 medium onion, peeled and thickly sliced
½ teaspoon salt
½ teaspoon ground black pepper
1 cup Arborio rice
½ cup dry white wine
2 cups low-sodium chicken broth
2 cups sliced young beet greens
¼ cup sliced fresh basil
½ cup grated Parmesan cheese

1. Combine oil and garlic in a small bowl. Stir to mix and set aside 10 minutes to infuse. 2. Preheat a grill or a grill pan over medium-high heat. 3. Brush all sides of eggplant slices, zucchini slices, bell pepper quarters, mushroom slices, and onion slices with garlic-infused oil, making sure to reserve 1 tablespoon of the oil. 4. Place vegetables on the grill rack or in the grill pan. Sprinkle with salt and black pepper. 5. Grill vegetables for several minutes on each side or until softened and slightly charred, about 1 minute per side. Set aside to cool, and then coarsely chop. 6. Press the Sauté button on the Instant Pot® and heat reserved 1 tablespoon garlic-infused oil. Add rice and stir it to coat it in oil. Stir in wine and broth. Press the Cancel button. 7. Close lid, set steam release to Sealing, press the Manual button, and set time to 7 minutes. When the timer beeps, quick-release the pressure until the float valve drops and open the lid. 8. Add chopped grilled vegetables, beet greens, and basil. Cover the Instant Pot® (but do not lock the lid into place). Set aside for 5 minutes or until greens are wilted. Stir in cheese and serve hot.

Per Serving:
calories: 261 | fat: 12g | protein: 9g | carbs: 30g | fiber: 5g | sodium: 544mg

Couscous with Apricots

Prep time: 10 minutes | Cook time: 15 minutes | Serves 4

2 tablespoons olive oil
1 small onion, diced
1 cup whole-wheat couscous
2 cups water or broth
½ cup dried apricots, soaked in water overnight
½ cup slivered almonds or pistachios
½ teaspoon dried mint
½ teaspoon dried thyme

1. Heat the olive oil in a large skillet over medium-high heat. Add the onion and cook until translucent and soft. 2. Stir in the couscous and cook for 2–3 minutes. 3. Add the water or broth, cover, and cook for 8–10 minutes until the water is mostly absorbed. 4. Remove from the heat and let stand for a few minutes. 5. Fluff with a fork and fold in the apricots, nuts, mint, and thyme.

Per Serving:
calories: 294 | fat: 15g | protein: 8g | carbs: 38g | fiber: 6g | sodium: 6mg

Amaranth Salad

Prep time: 5 minutes | Cook time: 6 minutes | Serves 4

2 cups water
1 cup amaranth
1 teaspoon dried Greek oregano
½ teaspoon salt
½ teaspoon ground black pepper
1 tablespoon extra-virgin olive oil
2 teaspoons red wine vinegar

1. Add water and amaranth to the Instant Pot®. Close lid, set steam release to Sealing, press the Manual button, and set time to 6 minutes. When the timer beeps, quick-release the pressure until the float valve drops. 2. Open lid and fluff amaranth with a fork. Add oregano, salt, and pepper. Mix well. Drizzle with olive oil and wine vinegar. Serve hot.

Per Serving:
calories: 93 | fat: 5g | protein: 3g | carbs: 12g | fiber: 3g | sodium: 299mg

Puréed Red Lentil Soup

Prep time: 15 minutes | Cook time: 21 minutes | Serves 6

2 tablespoons olive oil
1 medium yellow onion, peeled and chopped
1 medium carrot, peeled and chopped
1 medium red bell pepper, seeded and chopped
1 clove garlic, peeled and minced
1 bay leaf
½ teaspoon ground black pepper
¼ teaspoon salt
1 (15-ounce / 425-g) can diced tomatoes, drained
2 cups dried red lentils, rinsed and drained
6 cups low-sodium chicken broth

1. Press the Sauté button on the Instant Pot® and heat oil. Add onion, carrot, and bell pepper. Cook until just tender, about 5 minutes. Add garlic, bay leaf, black pepper, and salt, and cook until fragrant, about 30 seconds. Press the Cancel button. 2. Add tomatoes, lentils, and broth, then close lid, set steam release to Sealing, press the Manual button, and set time to 15 minutes. When the timer beeps, let pressure release naturally, about 15 minutes. Open lid, remove and discard bay leaf, and purée with an immersion blender or in batches in a blender. Serve warm.

Per Serving:
calories: 289 | fat: 6g | protein: 18g | carbs: 39g | fiber: 8g | sodium: 438mg

Barley Risotto

Prep time: 10 minutes | Cook time: 30 minutes | Serves 6

2 tablespoons olive oil
1 large onion, peeled and diced
1 clove garlic, peeled and minced
1 stalk celery, finely minced
1½ cups pearl barley, rinsed and drained
⅓ cup dried mushrooms
4 cups low-sodium chicken broth
2¼ cups water
1 cup grated Parmesan cheese
2 tablespoons minced fresh parsley
¼ teaspoon salt

1. Press the Sauté button on the Instant Pot® and heat oil. Add onion and sauté 5 minutes. Add garlic and cook 30 seconds. Stir in celery, barley, mushrooms, broth, and water. Press the Cancel button. 2. Close lid, set steam release to Sealing, press the Manual button, and set time to 18 minutes. When the timer beeps, quick-release the pressure until the float valve drops and open the lid. 3. Drain off excess liquid, leaving enough to leave the risotto slightly soupy. Press the Cancel button, then press the Sauté button and cook until thickened, about 5 minutes. Stir in cheese, parsley, and salt. Serve immediately.

Per Serving:
calories: 175 | fat: 9g | protein: 10g | carbs: 13g | fiber: 2g | sodium: 447mg

Greek-Style Black-Eyed Pea Soup

Prep time: 10 minutes | Cook time: 26 minutes | Serves 8

2 tablespoons light olive oil
2 stalks celery, chopped
1 medium white onion, peeled and chopped
2 cloves garlic, peeled and minced
2 tablespoons chopped fresh oregano
1 teaspoon fresh thyme leaves
1 pound (454 g) dried black-eyed peas, soaked overnight and drained
¼ teaspoon salt
1 teaspoon ground black pepper
4 cups water
1 (15-ounce / 425-g) can diced tomatoes

1. Press the Sauté button on the Instant Pot® and heat oil. Add celery and onion, and cook until just tender, about 5 minutes. Add garlic, oregano, and thyme, and cook until fragrant, about 30 seconds. Press the Cancel button. 2. Add black-eyed peas, salt, pepper, water, and tomatoes to the Instant Pot® and stir well. Close lid, set steam release to Sealing, press the Manual button, and set time to 20 minutes. When the timer beeps, let pressure release naturally, about 20 minutes. 3. Open lid and stir well. Serve hot.

Per Serving:
calories: 153 | fat: 3g | protein: 8g | carbs: 25g | fiber: 5g | sodium: 189mg

Rice with Pork Chops

Prep time: 10 minutes | Cook time: 3 to 5 hours | Serves 4

- 1 cup raw long-grain brown rice, rinsed
- 2½ cups low-sodium chicken broth
- 1 cup sliced tomato
- 8 ounces (227 g) fresh spinach, chopped
- 1 small onion, chopped
- 2 garlic cloves, minced
- 2 teaspoons dried oregano
- 2 teaspoons dried basil
- 1 teaspoon sea salt
- ½ teaspoon freshly ground black pepper
- 4 thick-cut pork chops
- ¼ cup grated Parmesan cheese

1. In a slow cooker, combine the rice, chicken broth, tomato, spinach, onion, garlic, oregano, basil, salt, and pepper. Stir to mix well. 2. Place the pork chops on top of the rice mixture. 3. Cover the cooker and cook for 3 to 5 hours on Low heat. 4. Top with the Parmesan cheese for serving.

Per Serving:
calories: 482 | fat: 11g | protein: 51g | carbs: 44g | fiber: 4g | sodium: 785mg

Apple Couscous with Curry

Prep time: 10 minutes | Cook time: 10 minutes | Serves 4

- 2 teaspoons olive oil
- 2 leeks, white parts only, sliced
- 1 Granny Smith apple, diced
- 2 cups cooked whole-wheat couscous
- 2 tablespoons curry powder
- ½ cup chopped pecans

1. Heat the olive oil in a large skillet on medium heat and add leeks. Cook until soft and tender, about 5 minutes. 2. Add diced apple and cook until soft. 3. Add couscous and curry powder, then stir to combine. Remove from heat, mix in nuts, and serve.

Per Serving:
calories: 255 | fat: 12g | protein: 5g | carbs: 34g | fiber: 6g | sodium: 15mg

Lentils with Artichoke, Tomato, and Feta

Prep time: 10 minutes | Cook time: 12 minutes | Serves 6

- 2 cups dried red lentils, rinsed and drained
- ½ teaspoon salt
- 4 cups water
- 1 (12-ounce / 340-g) jar marinated artichokes, drained and chopped
- 2 medium vine-ripe tomatoes, chopped
- ½ medium red onion, peeled and diced
- ½ large English cucumber, diced
- ½ cup crumbled feta cheese
- ¼ cup chopped fresh flat-leaf parsley
- 3 tablespoons extra-virgin olive oil
- 2 tablespoons balsamic vinegar
- ½ teaspoon ground black pepper

1. Add lentils, salt, and water to the Instant Pot®. Close lid, set steam release to Sealing, press the Manual button, and set time to 12 minutes. When the timer beeps, quick-release the pressure until the float valve drops. Open lid and drain off any excess liquid. Let lentils cool to room temperature, about 30 minutes. 2. Add artichokes, tomatoes, onion, cucumber, feta, parsley, oil, vinegar, and pepper, and toss to mix. Transfer to a serving bowl. Serve at room temperature or refrigerate for at least 2 hours.

Per Serving:
calories: 332 | fat: 13g | protein: 17g | carbs: 40g | fiber: 6g | sodium: 552mg

Lemon Farro Bowl with Avocado

Prep time: 5 minutes | Cook time: 25 minutes | Serves: 6

- 1 tablespoon plus 2 teaspoons extra-virgin olive oil, divided
- 1 cup chopped onion (about ½ medium onion)
- 2 garlic cloves, minced (about 1 teaspoon)
- 1 carrot, shredded (about 1 cup)
- 2 cups low-sodium or no-salt-added vegetable broth
- 1 cup (6 ounces) uncooked pearled or 10-minute farro
- 2 avocados, peeled, pitted, and sliced
- 1 small lemon
- ¼ teaspoon kosher or sea salt

1. In a medium saucepan over medium-high heat, heat 1 tablespoon of oil. Add the onion and cook for 5 minutes, stirring occasionally. Add the garlic and carrot and cook for 1 minute, stirring frequently. Add the broth and farro, and bring to a boil over high heat. Lower the heat to medium-low, cover, and simmer for about 20 minutes or until the farro is plump and slightly chewy (al dente). 2. Pour the farro into a serving bowl, and add the avocado slices. Using a Microplane or citrus zester, zest the peel of the lemon directly into the bowl of farro. Halve the lemon, and squeeze the juice out of both halves using a citrus juicer or your hands. Drizzle the remaining 2 teaspoons of oil over the bowl, and sprinkle with salt. Gently mix all the ingredients and serve.

Per Serving:
calories: 212 | fat: 11.2g | protein: 3.4g | carbs: 28.7g | fiber: 7g | sodium: 147mg

Lentils with Spinach

Prep time: 10 minutes | Cook time: 20 minutes | Serves 4

- 1 cup dried yellow lentils, rinsed and drained
- 4 cups water
- 1 tablespoon olive oil
- ½ medium yellow onion, peeled and chopped
- 1 clove garlic, peeled and minced
- ½ teaspoon smoked paprika
- ½ teaspoon ground black pepper
- 1 (15-ounce / 425-g) can diced tomatoes, drained
- 10 ounces (283 g) baby spinach leaves
- ½ cup crumbled feta cheese

1. Add lentils and water to the Instant Pot®. Close lid, set steam release to Sealing, press the Manual button, and set time to 6 minutes. When the timer beeps, quick-release the pressure. Press the Cancel button and open lid. Drain lentils and set aside. Clean pot. 2. Press the Sauté button and heat oil. Add onion and cook until just tender, about 3 minutes. Add garlic, smoked paprika, and pepper, and cook for an additional 30 seconds. Stir in tomatoes, spinach, and lentils. Simmer for 10 minutes. Top with feta and serve.

Per Serving:
calories: 289 | fat: 8g | protein: 21g | carbs: 31g | fiber: 10g | sodium: 623mg

Lentil and Zucchini Boats

Prep time: 15 minutes | Cook time: 50 minutes | Serves 4

1 cup dried green lentils, rinsed and drained
¼ teaspoon salt
2 cups water
1 tablespoon olive oil
½ medium red onion, peeled and diced
1 clove garlic, peeled and minced
1 cup marinara sauce
¼ teaspoon crushed red pepper flakes
4 medium zucchini, trimmed and cut lengthwise
½ cup shredded part-skim mozzarella cheese
¼ cup chopped fresh flat-leaf parsley

1. Add lentils, salt, and water to the Instant Pot®. Close lid, set steam release to Sealing, press the Manual button, and set time to 12 minutes. When the timer beeps, quick-release the pressure until the float valve drops. Press the Cancel button. Open lid and drain off any excess liquid. Transfer lentils to a medium bowl. Set aside. 2. Press the Sauté button and heat oil. Add onion and cook until tender, about 3 minutes. Add garlic and cook until fragrant, about 30 seconds. Add marinara sauce and crushed red pepper flakes and stir to combine. Press the Cancel button. Stir in lentils. 3. Preheat oven to 350°F (180°C) and spray a 9" × 13" baking dish with nonstick cooking spray. 4. Using a teaspoon, hollow out each zucchini half. Lay zucchini in prepared baking dish. Divide lentil mixture among prepared zucchini. Top with cheese. Bake for 30–35 minutes, or until zucchini are tender and cheese is melted and browned. Top with parsley and serve hot.

Per Serving:
calories: 326 | fat: 10g | protein: 22g | carbs: 39g | fiber: 16g | sodium: 568mg

Lentils and Bulgur with Caramelized Onions

Prep time: 10 minutes | Cook time: 50 minutes | Serves 6

½ cup extra-virgin olive oil
4 large onions, chopped
2 teaspoons salt, divided
6 cups water
2 cups brown lentils, picked over and rinsed
1 teaspoon freshly ground black pepper
1 cup bulgur wheat

1. In a medium pot over medium heat, cook the olive oil and onions for 7 to 10 minutes until the edges are browned. 2. Turn the heat to high, add the water, cumin, and salt, and bring this mixture to a boil, boiling for about 3 minutes. 3. Add the lentils and turn the heat to medium-low. Cover the pot and cook for 20 minutes, stirring occasionally. 4. Stir in the rice and cover; cook for an additional 20 minutes. 5. Fluff the rice with a fork and serve 1.In a large pot over medium heat, cook and stir the olive oil, onions, and 1 teaspoon of salt for 12 to 15 minutes, until the onions are a medium brown/golden color. 2. Put half of the cooked onions in a bowl. 3. Add the water, remaining 1 teaspoon of salt, and lentils to the remaining onions. Stir. Cover and cook for 30 minutes. 4. Stir in the black pepper and bulgur, cover, and cook for 5 minutes. Fluff with a fork, cover, and let stand for another 5 minutes. 5. Spoon the lentils and bulgur onto a serving plate and top with the reserved onions. Serve warm.

Per Serving:
calories: 479 | fat: 20g | protein: 20g | carbs: 60g | fiber: 24g | sodium: 789mg

Black Beans with Corn and Tomato Relish

Prep time: 20 minutes | Cook time: 30 minutes | Serves 6

½ pound (227 g) dried black beans, soaked overnight and drained
1 medium white onion, peeled and sliced in half
2 cloves garlic, peeled and lightly crushed
8 cups water
1 cup corn kernels
1 large tomato, seeded and chopped
½ medium red onion, peeled and chopped
¼ cup minced fresh cilantro
½ teaspoon ground cumin
¼ teaspoon smoked paprika
¼ teaspoon ground black pepper
¼ teaspoon salt
3 tablespoons extra-virgin olive oil
3 tablespoons lime juice

1. Add beans, white onion, garlic, and water to the Instant Pot®. Close lid, set steam release to Sealing, press the Bean button, and cook for the default time of 30 minutes. When the timer beeps, let pressure release naturally, about 20 minutes. 2. Open lid and remove and discard onion and garlic. Drain beans well and transfer to a medium bowl. Cool to room temperature, about 30 minutes. 3. In a separate small bowl, combine corn, tomato, red onion, cilantro, cumin, paprika, pepper, and salt. Toss to combine. Add to black beans and gently fold to mix. Whisk together olive oil and lime juice in a small bowl and pour over black bean mixture. Gently toss to coat. Serve at room temperature or refrigerate for at least 2 hours.

Per Serving:
calories: 216 | fat: 7g | protein: 8g | carbs: 28g | fiber: 6g | sodium: 192mg

Lentil Pâté

Prep time: 10 minutes | Cook time: 34 minutes | Serves 12

2 tablespoons olive oil, divided
1 cup diced yellow onion
3 cloves garlic, peeled and minced
1 teaspoon red wine vinegar
2 cups dried green lentils, rinsed and drained
4 cups water
1 teaspoon salt
¼ teaspoon ground black pepper

1. Press the Sauté button on the Instant Pot® and heat 1 tablespoon oil. Add onion and cook until translucent, about 3 minutes. Add garlic and vinegar, and cook for 30 seconds. Add lentils, water, remaining 1 tablespoon oil, and salt to pot and stir to combine. Press the Cancel button. 2. Close lid, set steam release to Sealing, press the Bean button, and allow to cook for default time of 30 minutes. When the timer beeps, let pressure release naturally for 10 minutes. Quick-release any remaining pressure until the float valve drops, then open lid. 3. Transfer lentil mixture to a food processor or blender, and blend until smooth. Season with pepper and serve warm.

Per Serving:
calories: 138 | fat: 3g | protein: 8g | carbs: 20g | fiber: 10g | sodium: 196mg

Herbed Barley

Prep time: 10 minutes | Cook time: 30 minutes | Serves 4

- 2 tablespoons olive oil
- ½ cup diced onion
- ½ cup diced celery
- 1 carrot, peeled and diced
- 3 cups water or chicken broth
- 1 cup barley
- 1 bay leaf
- ½ teaspoon thyme
- ½ teaspoon rosemary
- ¼ cup walnuts or pine nuts
- Sea salt and freshly ground pepper, to taste

1. Heat the olive oil in a medium saucepan over medium-high heat. Sauté the onion, celery, and carrot over medium heat until they are tender. 2. Add the water or chicken broth, barley, and seasonings, and bring to a boil. Reduce the heat and simmer for 25 minutes, or until tender. 3. Stir in the nuts and season to taste.

Per Serving:
calories: 283 | fat: 11g | protein: 6g | carbs: 43g | fiber: 9g | sodium: 26mg

Wild Mushroom Farrotto

Prep time: 15 minutes | Cook time: 20 minutes | Serves 4 to 6

- 1½ cups whole farro
- 3 tablespoons extra-virgin olive oil, divided, plus extra for drizzling
- 12 ounces (340 g) cremini or white mushrooms, trimmed and sliced thin
- ½ onion, chopped fine
- ½ teaspoon table salt
- ¼ teaspoon pepper
- 1 garlic clove, minced
- ¼ ounce dried porcini mushrooms, rinsed and chopped fine
- 2 teaspoons minced fresh thyme or ½ teaspoon dried
- ¼ cup dry white wine
- 2½ cups chicken or vegetable broth, plus extra as needed
- 2 ounces (57 g) Parmesan cheese, grated (1 cup), plus extra for serving
- 2 teaspoons lemon juice
- ½ cup chopped fresh parsley

1. Pulse farro in blender until about half of grains are broken into smaller pieces, about 6 pulses. 2. Using highest sauté function, heat 2 tablespoons oil in Instant Pot until shimmering. Add cremini mushrooms, onion, salt, and pepper, partially cover, and cook until mushrooms are softened and have released their liquid, about 5 minutes. Stir in farro, garlic, porcini mushrooms, and thyme and cook until fragrant, about 1 minute. Stir in wine and cook until nearly evaporated, about 30 seconds. Stir in broth. 3. Lock lid in place and close pressure release valve. Select high pressure cook function and cook for 12 minutes. Turn off Instant Pot and quick-release pressure. Carefully remove lid, allowing steam to escape away from you. 4. If necessary adjust consistency with extra hot broth, or continue to cook farrotto, using highest sauté function, stirring frequently, until proper consistency is achieved. (Farrotto should be slightly thickened, and spoon dragged along bottom of multicooker should leave trail that quickly fills in.) Add Parmesan and remaining 1 tablespoon oil and stir vigorously until farrotto becomes creamy. Stir in lemon juice and season with salt and pepper to taste. Sprinkle individual portions with parsley and extra Parmesan, and drizzle with extra oil before serving.

Per Serving:
calories: 280 | fat: 10g | protein: 13g | carbs: 35g | fiber: 4g | sodium: 630mg

Lentil Chili

Prep time: 15 minutes | Cook time: 30 minutes | Serves 6

- 2 tablespoons olive oil
- 1 medium yellow onion, peeled and chopped
- 1 large poblano pepper, seeded and chopped
- ¼ cup chopped fresh cilantro
- 2 cloves garlic, peeled and minced
- 1 tablespoon chili powder
- ½ teaspoon ground cumin
- ½ teaspoon ground black pepper
- ¼ teaspoon salt
- 2 cups dried red lentils, rinsed and drained
- 6 cups vegetable broth
- 1 (10-ounce / 283-g) can tomatoes with green chilies, drained
- 1 (15-ounce / 425-g) can kidney beans, drained and rinsed
- 1 tablespoon lime juice

1. Press the Sauté button on the Instant Pot® and heat oil. Add onion and poblano pepper, and cook until just tender, about 3 minutes. Add cilantro, garlic, chili powder, cumin, black pepper, and salt, and cook until fragrant, about 30 seconds. Press the Cancel button. 2. Add lentils and broth, close lid, set steam release to Sealing, press the Manual button, and set time to 25 minutes. When the timer beeps, let pressure release naturally, about 15 minutes. 3. Open lid and stir in tomatoes, beans, and lime juice. Let stand uncovered on the Keep Warm setting for 10 minutes. Serve warm.

Per Serving:
calories: 261 | fat: 6g | protein: 15g | carbs: 42g | fiber: 9g | sodium: 781mg

Baked Mushroom-Barley Pilaf

Prep time: 5 minutes | Cook time: 37 minutes | Serves 4

- Olive oil cooking spray
- 2 tablespoons olive oil
- 8 ounces (227 g) button mushrooms, diced
- ½ yellow onion, diced
- 2 garlic cloves, minced
- 1 cup pearl barley
- 2 cups vegetable broth
- 1 tablespoon fresh thyme, chopped
- ½ teaspoon salt
- ¼ teaspoon smoked paprika
- Fresh parsley, for garnish

1. Preheat the air fryer to 380°F(193°C). Lightly coat the inside of a 5-cup capacity casserole dish with olive oil cooking spray. (The shape of the casserole dish will depend upon the size of the air fryer, but it needs to be able to hold at least 5 cups.) 2. In a large skillet, heat the olive oil over medium heat. Add the mushrooms and onion and cook, stirring occasionally, for 5 minutes, or until the mushrooms begin to brown. 3. Add the garlic and cook for an additional 2 minutes. Transfer the vegetables to a large bowl. 4. Add the barley, broth, thyme, salt, and paprika. 5. Pour the barley-and-vegetable mixture into the prepared casserole dish, and place the dish into the air fryer. Bake for 15 minutes. 6. Stir the barley mixture. Reduce the heat to 360°F(182°C), then return the barley to the air fryer and bake for 15 minutes more. 7. Remove from the air fryer and let sit for 5 minutes before fluffing with a fork and topping with fresh parsley.

Per Serving:
calories: 428 | fat: 9.2g | protein: 10.7g | carbs: 84.7g | fiber: 9.2g | sodium: 775mg

Rice with Olives and Basil

Prep time: 10 minutes | Cook time: 32 minutes | Serves 8

2 tablespoons extra-virgin olive oil
1 medium yellow onion, peeled and chopped
2 cloves garlic, peeled and minced
2 cups brown rice
2¼ cups water
1 cup pitted Kalamata olives
½ cup torn basil
1 tablespoon lemon juice
2 teaspoons grated lemon zest
½ teaspoon ground black pepper

1. Press the Sauté button on the Instant Pot® and heat oil. Add onion and cook until soft, about 6 minutes. Add garlic and cook until fragrant, about 30 seconds. Add rice and cook, stirring constantly, until well coated and starting to toast, about 3 minutes. Press the Cancel button. 2. Stir in water. Close lid, set steam release to Sealing, press the Manual button, and set time to 22 minutes. When the timer beeps, let pressure release naturally for 10 minutes, then quick-release the remaining pressure until the float valve drops. Open lid and fluff rice with a fork. Fold in olives, basil, lemon juice, lemon zest, and pepper. Serve warm.

Per Serving:
calories: 182 | fat: 11g | protein: 1g | carbs: 18g | fiber: 1g | sodium: 355mg

Lemon Orzo with Fresh Herbs

Prep time: 10 minutes | Cook time: 10 minutes | Serves 4

2 cups orzo
½ cup fresh parsley, finely chopped
½ cup fresh basil, finely chopped
2 tablespoons lemon zest
½ cup extra-virgin olive oil
⅓ cup lemon juice
1 teaspoon salt
½ teaspoon freshly ground black pepper

1. Bring a large pot of water to a boil. Add the orzo and cook for 7 minutes. Drain and rinse with cold water. Let the orzo sit in a strainer to completely drain and cool. 2. Once the orzo has cooled, put it in a large bowl and add the parsley, basil, and lemon zest. 3. In a small bowl, whisk together the olive oil, lemon juice, salt, and pepper. Add the dressing to the pasta and toss everything together. Serve at room temperature or chilled.

Per Serving:
calories: 568 | fat: 29g | protein: 11g | carbs: 65g | fiber: 4g | sodium: 586mg

Garlicky Split Chickpea Curry

Prep time: 10 minutes | Cook time: 4 to 6 hours | Serves 6

1½ cups split gram
1 onion, finely chopped
2 tomatoes, chopped
1 tablespoon freshly grated ginger
1 teaspoon cumin seeds, ground or crushed with a mortar and pestle
2 teaspoons turmeric
2 garlic cloves, crushed
1 hot green Thai or other fresh chile, thinly sliced
3 cups hot water
1 teaspoon salt
2 tablespoons rapeseed oil
1 teaspoon cumin seeds, crushed
1 garlic clove, sliced
1 fresh green chile, sliced

1. Heat the slow cooker to high. Add the split gram, onion, tomatoes, ginger, crushed cumin seeds, turmeric, crushed garlic, hot chile, water, and salt, and then stir. 2. Cover and cook on high for 4 hours, or on low for 6 hours, until the split gram is tender. 3. Just before serving, heat the oil in a saucepan. When the oil is hot, add the cumin seeds with the sliced garlic. Cook until the garlic is golden brown, and then pour it over the dhal. 4. To serve, top with the sliced green chile.

Per Serving:
calories: 119 | fat: 5g | protein: 4g | carbs: 15g | net carbs: 12g | sugars: 7g | fiber: 3g | sodium: 503mg | cholesterol: 1mg

Lentil Bowl

Prep time: 10 minutes | Cook time: 6 to 8 hours | Serves 6

1 cup dried lentils, any color, rinsed well under cold water and picked over to remove debris
3 cups low-sodium vegetable broth
1 (15-ounce/ 425-g) can no-salt-added diced tomatoes
1 small onion, chopped
3 celery stalks, chopped
3 carrots, chopped
3 garlic cloves, minced
2 tablespoons Italian seasoning
1 teaspoon sea salt
½ teaspoon freshly ground black pepper
2 bay leaves
1 tablespoon freshly squeezed lemon juice

1. In a slow cooker, combine the lentils, vegetable broth, tomatoes, onion, celery, carrots, garlic, Italian seasoning, salt, pepper, and bay leaves. Stir to mix well. 2. Cover the cooker and cook for 6 to 8 hours on Low heat. 3. Stir in the lemon juice before serving.

Per Serving:
calories: 152 | fat: 1g | protein: 10g | carbs: 29g | fiber: 13g | sodium: 529mg

Garbanzo and Pita No-Bake Casserole

Prep time: 10 minutes | Cook time: 10 minutes | Serves 4

4 cups Greek yogurt
3 cloves garlic, minced
1 teaspoon salt
2 (16-ounce/ 454-g) cans garbanzo beans, rinsed and drained
2 cups water
4 cups pita chips
5 tablespoons unsalted butter

1. In a large bowl, whisk together the yogurt, garlic, and salt. Set aside. 2. Put the garbanzo beans and water in a medium pot. Bring to a boil; let beans boil for about 5 minutes. 3. Pour the garbanzo beans and the liquid into a large casserole dish. 4. Top the beans with pita chips. Pour the yogurt sauce over the pita chip layer. 5. In a small saucepan, melt and brown the butter, about 3 minutes. Pour the brown butter over the yogurt sauce.

Per Serving:
calories: 772 | fat: 36g | protein: 39g | carbs: 73g | fiber: 13g | sodium: 1,003mg

Herbed Lima Beans

Prep time: 10 minutes | Cook time: 6 minutes | Serves 6

1 pound (454 g) frozen baby lima beans, thawed
2 cloves garlic, peeled and minced
2 thyme sprigs
1 bay leaf
2 tablespoons extra-virgin olive oil
3 cups water
1 tablespoon chopped fresh dill
1 tablespoon chopped fresh tarragon
1 tablespoon chopped fresh mint

1. Add lima beans, garlic, thyme, bay leaf, oil, and water to the Instant Pot®. Close lid, set steam release to Sealing, press the Manual button, and set time to 6 minutes. When the timer beeps, quick-release the pressure until the float valve drops. Open lid, remove and discard thyme and bay leaf, and stir well. 2. Stir in dill, tarragon, and mint, and let stand for 10 minutes on the Keep Warm setting before serving.

Per Serving:
calories: 134 | fat: 5g | protein: 5g | carbs: 17g | fiber: 4g | sodium: 206mg

Za'atar Chickpeas and Chicken

Prep time: 10 minutes | Cook time: 4 to 6 hours | Serves 4

2 pounds (907 g) bone-in chicken thighs or legs
1 (15-ounce/ 425-g) can reduced-sodium chickpeas, drained and rinsed
½ cup low-sodium chicken broth
Juice of 1 lemon
1 tablespoon extra-virgin olive oil
2 teaspoons white vinegar
2 tablespoons za'atar
1 garlic clove, minced
½ teaspoon sea salt
¼ teaspoon freshly ground black pepper

1. In a slow cooker, combine the chicken and chickpeas. Stir to mix well. 2. In a small bowl, whisk together the chicken broth, lemon juice, olive oil, vinegar, za'atar, garlic, salt, and pepper until combined. Pour the mixture over the chicken and chickpeas. 3. Cover the cooker and cook for 4 to 6 hours on Low heat.

Per Serving:
calories: 647 | fat: 41g | protein: 46g | carbs: 23g | fiber: 7g | sodium: 590mg

Moroccan Date Pilaf

Prep time: 10 minutes | Cook time: 30 minutes | Serves 4

3 tablespoons olive oil
1 onion, chopped
3 garlic cloves, minced
1 cup uncooked long-grain rice
½ to 1 tablespoon harissa
5 or 6 Medjool dates (or another variety), pitted and chopped
¼ cup dried cranberries
¼ teaspoon ground cinnamon
½ teaspoon ground turmeric
¼ teaspoon sea salt
¼ teaspoon freshly ground black pepper
2 cups chicken broth
¼ cup shelled whole pistachios, for garnish

1. In a large stockpot, heat the olive oil over medium heat. Add the onion and garlic and sauté for 3 to 5 minutes, until the onion is soft. Add the rice and cook for 3 minutes, until the grains start to turn opaque. Add the harissa, dates, cranberries, cinnamon, turmeric, salt, and pepper and cook for 30 seconds. Add the broth and bring to a boil, then reduce the heat to low, cover, and simmer for 20 minutes, or until the liquid has been absorbed. 2. Remove the rice from the heat and stir in the nuts. Let stand for 10 minutes before serving.

Per Serving:
calories: 368 | fat: 15g | protein: 6g | carbs: 54g | fiber: 4g | sodium: 83mg

White Beans with Garlic and Tomatoes

Prep time: 10 minutes | Cook time: 40 minutes | Serves 6

1 cup dried cannellini beans, soaked overnight and drained
4 cups water
4 cups vegetable stock
1 tablespoon olive oil
1 teaspoon salt
2 cloves garlic, peeled and minced
½ cup diced tomato
½ teaspoon dried sage
½ teaspoon ground black pepper

1. Add beans and water to the Instant Pot®. Close lid, set steam release to Sealing, press the Bean button, and cook for default time of 30 minutes. When timer beeps, quick-release the pressure until the float valve drops. 2. Press the Cancel button, open lid, drain and rinse beans, and return to pot along with stock. Soak for 1 hour. 3. Add olive oil, salt, garlic, tomato, sage, and pepper to beans. Close lid, set steam release to Sealing, press the Manual button, and set time to 10 minutes. When the timer beeps, quick-release the pressure until the float valve drops and open lid. Serve hot.

Per Serving:
calories: 128 | fat: 2g | protein: 7g | carbs: 20g | fiber: 4g | sodium: 809mg

Quinoa with Kale, Carrots, and Walnuts

Prep time: 10 minutes | Cook time: 20 minutes | Serves 4

1 cup quinoa, rinsed and drained
2 cups water
¼ cup olive oil
2 tablespoons apple cider vinegar
1 clove garlic, peeled and minced
½ teaspoon ground black pepper
½ teaspoon salt
2 cups chopped kale
1 cup shredded carrot
1 cup toasted walnut pieces
½ cup crumbled feta cheese

1. Add quinoa and water to the Instant Pot® and stir well. Close lid, set steam release to Sealing, press the Manual button, and set time to 20 minutes. When the timer beeps, let pressure release naturally, about 20 minutes, then open lid. Fluff quinoa with a fork, then transfer to a medium bowl and set aside to cool to room temperature, about 40 minutes. 2. Add oil, vinegar, garlic, pepper, salt, kale, carrot, walnuts, and feta to quinoa and toss well. Refrigerate for 4 hours before serving.

Per Serving:
calories: 625 | fat: 39g | protein: 19g | carbs: 47g | fiber: 10g | sodium: 738mg

Simple Herbed Rice

Prep time: 10 minutes | Cook time: 32 minutes | Serves 8

2 tablespoons extra-virgin olive oil
½ medium yellow onion, peeled and chopped
4 cloves garlic, peeled and minced
¼ teaspoon salt
½ teaspoon ground black pepper
2¼ cups brown rice
2 cups water
¼ cup chopped fresh flat-leaf parsley
¼ cup chopped fresh basil
2 tablespoons chopped fresh oregano
2 teaspoons fresh thyme leaves

1. Press the Sauté button on the Instant Pot® and heat oil. Add onion and cook until soft, about 6 minutes. Add garlic, salt, and pepper and cook until fragrant, about 30 seconds. Add rice and cook, stirring constantly, until well-coated and starting to toast, about 3 minutes. Press the Cancel button. 2. Stir in water. Close lid, set steam release to Sealing, press the Manual button, and set time to 22 minutes. When the timer beeps, let pressure release naturally for 10 minutes, then quick-release the remaining pressure. Open lid and fold in parsley, basil, oregano, and thyme. Serve warm.

Per Serving:
calories: 102 | fat: 4g | protein: 2g | carbs: 15g | fiber: 1g | sodium: 96mg

Mediterranean Lentils and Rice

Prep time: 5 minutes |Cook time: 25 minutes| Serves: 4

2¼ cups low-sodium or no-salt-added vegetable broth
½ cup uncooked brown or green lentils
½ cup uncooked instant brown rice
½ cup diced carrots (about 1 carrot)
½ cup diced celery (about 1 stalk)
1 (2¼-ounce / 64-g) can sliced olives, drained (about ½ cup)
¼ cup diced red onion (about ⅛ onion)
¼ cup chopped fresh curly-leaf parsley
1½ tablespoons extra-virgin olive oil
1 tablespoon freshly squeezed lemon juice (from about ½ small lemon)
1 garlic clove, minced (about ½ teaspoon)
¼ teaspoon kosher or sea salt
¼ teaspoon freshly ground black pepper

1. In a medium saucepan over high heat, bring the broth and lentils to a boil, cover, and lower the heat to medium-low. Cook for 8 minutes. 2. Raise the heat to medium, and stir in the rice. Cover the pot and cook the mixture for 15 minutes, or until the liquid is absorbed. Remove the pot from the heat and let it sit, covered, for 1 minute, then stir. 3. While the lentils and rice are cooking, mix together the carrots, celery, olives, onion, and parsley in a large serving bowl. 4. In a small bowl, whisk together the oil, lemon juice, garlic, salt, and pepper. Set aside. 5. When the lentils and rice are cooked, add them to the serving bowl. Pour the dressing on top, and mix everything together. Serve warm or cold, or store in a sealed container in the refrigerator for up to 7 days.

Per Serving:
calories: 183 | fat: 6g | protein: 4.9g | carbs: 29.5g | fiber: 3.3g | sodium: 552mg

Moroccan-Style Rice and Chickpea Bake

Prep time: 10 minutes | Cook time: 45 minutes | Serves 6

Olive oil cooking spray
1 cup long-grain brown rice
2¼ cups chicken stock
1 (15½-ounce/ 439-g) can chickpeas, drained and rinsed
½ cup diced carrot
½ cup green peas
1 teaspoon ground cumin
½ teaspoon ground turmeric
½ teaspoon ground ginger
½ teaspoon onion powder
½ teaspoon salt
¼ teaspoon ground cinnamon
¼ teaspoon garlic powder
¼ teaspoon black pepper
Fresh parsley, for garnish

1. Preheat the air fryer to 380°F(193°C). Lightly coat the inside of a 5-cup capacity casserole dish with olive oil cooking spray. (The shape of the casserole dish will depend upon the size of the air fryer, but it needs to be able to hold at least 5 cups.) 2. In the casserole dish, combine the rice, stock, chickpeas, carrot, peas, cumin, turmeric, ginger, onion powder, salt, cinnamon, garlic powder, and black pepper. Stir well to combine. 3. Cover loosely with aluminum foil. 4. Place the covered casserole dish into the air fryer and bake for 20 minutes. Remove from the air fryer and stir well. 5. Place the casserole back into the air fryer, uncovered, and bake for 25 minutes more. 6. Fluff with a spoon and sprinkle with fresh chopped parsley before serving.

Per Serving:
calories: 223 | fat: 3.3g | protein: 8.6g | carbs: 40.1g | fiber: 5g | sodium: 462mg

Lebanese Rice and Broken Noodles with Cabbage

Prep time: 5 minutes |Cook time: 25 minutes| Serves: 6

1 tablespoon extra-virgin olive oil
1 cup (about 3 ounces / 85 g) uncooked vermicelli or thin spaghetti, broken into 1- to 1½-inch pieces
3 cups shredded cabbage (about half a 14-ounce package of coleslaw mix or half a small head of cabbage)
3 cups low-sodium or no-salt-added vegetable broth
½ cup water
1 cup instant brown rice
2 garlic cloves
¼ teaspoon kosher or sea salt
⅛ to ¼ teaspoon crushed red pepper
½ cup loosely packed, coarsely chopped cilantro
Fresh lemon slices, for serving (optional)

1. In a large saucepan over medium-high heat, heat the oil. Add the pasta and cook for 3 minutes to toast, stirring often. Add the cabbage and cook for 4 minutes, stirring often. Add the broth, water, rice, garlic, salt, and crushed red pepper, and bring to a boil over high heat. Stir, cover, and reduce the heat to medium-low. Simmer for 10 minutes. 2. Remove the pan from the heat, but do not lift the lid. Let sit for 5 minutes. Fish out the garlic cloves, mash them with a fork, then stir the garlic back into the rice. Stir in the cilantro. Serve with the lemon slices (if using).

Per Serving:
calories: 150 | fat: 3.6g | protein: 3g | carbs: 27g | fiber: 2.8g | sodium: 664mg

Black Lentil Dhal

Prep time: 10 minutes | Cook time: 8 to 10 hours | Serves 6

2 cups dry whole black lentils
1 medium onion, finely chopped
1 heaped tablespoon freshly grated ginger
3 garlic cloves, chopped
3 fresh tomatoes, puréed, or 7 to 8 ounces (198 to 227 g) canned tomatoes, blended
2 fresh green chiles, chopped
2 tablespoons ghee
½ teaspoon turmeric
1 teaspoon chili powder
2 teaspoons coriander seeds, ground
1 teaspoon cumin seeds, ground
1 teaspoon sea salt
6⅓ cups water
1 to 2 tablespoons butter (optional)
1 teaspoon garam masala
1 teaspoon dried fenugreek leaves
Handful fresh coriander leaves, chopped

1. Preheat the slow cooker on high. 2. Clean and wash the black lentils. 3. Put the lentils, onion, ginger, garlic, tomatoes, chiles, ghee, turmeric, chili powder, coriander seeds, cumin seeds, salt, and water into the slow cooker. Cover and cook for 10 hours on low or for 8 hours on high. 4. When the lentils are cooked and creamy, stir in the butter (if using), garam masala, and fenugreek leaves to make the dhal rich and delicious. Garnish with a sprinkle of fresh coriander leaves and serve.

Per Serving:
calories: 271 | fat: 3g | protein: 17g | carbs: 47g | net carbs: 38g | sugars: 4g | fiber: 9g | sodium: 415mg | cholesterol: 5mg

Chapter 8 Pasta

Tahini Soup

Prep time: 5 minutes | Cook time: 4 minutes | Serves 6

2 cups orzo
8 cups water
1 tablespoon olive oil
1 teaspoon salt
½ teaspoon ground black pepper
½ cup tahini
¼ cup lemon juice

1. Add pasta, water, oil, salt, and pepper to the Instant Pot®. Close lid, set steam release to Sealing, press the Manual button, and set time to 4 minutes. When the timer beeps, quick-release the pressure until the float valve drops, and open lid. Set aside. 2. Add tahini to a small mixing bowl and slowly add lemon juice while whisking constantly. Once lemon juice has been incorporated, take about ½ cup hot broth from the pot and slowly add to tahini mixture while whisking, until creamy smooth. 3. Pour mixture into the soup and mix well. Serve immediately.

Per Serving:
calories: 338 | fat: 13g | protein: 12g | carbs: 49g | fiber: 5g | sodium: 389mg

Puglia-Style Pasta with Broccoli Sauce

Prep time: 15 minutes | Cook time: 25 minutes | Serves 3

1 pound (454 g) fresh broccoli, washed and cut into small florets
7 ounces (198 g) uncooked rigatoni pasta
2 tablespoons extra virgin olive oil, plus 1½ tablespoons for serving
3 garlic cloves, thinly sliced
2 tablespoons pine nuts
4 canned packed-in-oil anchovies
½ teaspoon kosher salt
3 teaspoons fresh lemon juice
3 ounces (85 g) grated or shaved Parmesan cheese, divided
½ teaspoon freshly ground black pepper

1. Place the broccoli in a large pot filled with enough water to cover the broccoli. Bring the pot to a boil and cook for 12 minutes or until the stems can be easily pierced with a fork. Use a slotted spoon to transfer the broccoli to a plate, but do not discard the cooking water. Set the broccoli aside. 2. Add the pasta to the pot with the broccoli water and cook according to package instructions. 3. About 3 minutes before the pasta is ready, place a large, deep pan over medium heat and add 2 tablespoons of the olive oil. When the olive oil is shimmering, add the garlic and sauté for 1 minute, stirring continuously, until the garlic is golden, then add the pine nuts and continue sautéing for 1 more minute. 4. Stir in the anchovies, using a wooden spoon to break them into smaller pieces, then add the broccoli. Continue cooking for 1 additional minute, stirring continuously and using the spoon to break the broccoli into smaller pieces. 5. When the pasta is ready, remove the pot from the heat and drain, reserving ¼ cup of the cooking water. 6. Add the pasta and 2 tablespoons of the cooking water to the pan, stirring until all the ingredients are well combined. Cook for 1 minute, then remove the pan from the heat. 7. Promptly divide the pasta among three plates. Top each serving with a pinch of kosher salt, 1 teaspoon of the lemon juice, 1 ounce (28 g) of the Parmesan, 1½ teaspoons of the remaining olive oil, and a pinch of fresh ground pepper. Store covered in the refrigerator for up to 3 days.

Per Serving:
calories: 610 | fat: 31g | protein: 24g | carbs: 66g | fiber: 12g | sodium: 654mg

Pine Nut and Currant Couscous with Butternut Squash

Prep time: 10 minutes | Cook time: 50 minutes | Serves 4

3 tablespoons olive oil
1 medium onion, chopped
3 cloves garlic, minced
6 canned plum tomatoes, crushed
1 cinnamon stick
1 teaspoon ground coriander
1 teaspoon ground cumin
1 teaspoon salt, divided
¼ teaspoon red pepper flakes
1½ pounds (680 g) diced butternut squash
1 (16-ounce / 454-g) can chickpeas, drained and rinsed
4½ cups vegetable broth, divided
1-inch strip lemon zest
½ cup currants
4 cups (about 5 ounces / 142 g) chopped spinach
Juice of ½ lemon
¼ teaspoon pepper
1 cup whole-wheat couscous
¼ cup toasted pine nuts

1. Heat the olive oil in a medium saucepan set over medium heat. Add the onion and cook, stirring frequently, until softened and lightly browned, about 10 minutes. Stir in the garlic, tomatoes, cinnamon stick, coriander, cumin, ½ teaspoon of the salt, and the red pepper flakes and cook for about 3 minutes more, until the tomatoes begin to break down. Stir in the butternut squash, chickpeas, 3 cups broth, lemon zest, and currants and bring to a simmer. 2. Partially cover the pan and cook for about 25 minutes, until the squash is tender. Add the spinach and cook, stirring, for 2 or 3 more minutes, until the spinach is wilted. Stir in the lemon juice. 3. While the vegetables are cooking, prepare the couscous. Combine the remaining 1½ cups broth, the remaining ½ teaspoon of salt, and the pepper in a small saucepan and bring to a boil. Remove the pan from the heat and stir in the couscous. Cover immediately and let sit for about 5 minutes, until the liquid has been fully absorbed. Fluff with a fork. 4. Spoon the couscous into serving bowls, top with the vegetable and chickpea mixture, and sprinkle some of the pine nuts over the top of each bowl. Serve immediately.

Per Serving:
calories: 549 | fat: 19g | protein: 16g | carbs: 84g | fiber: 14g | sodium: 774mg

Mixed Vegetable Couscous

Prep time: 20 minutes | Cook time: 10 minutes | Serves 8

- 1 tablespoon light olive oil
- 1 medium zucchini, trimmed and chopped
- 1 medium yellow squash, chopped
- 1 large red bell pepper, seeded and chopped
- 1 large orange bell pepper, seeded and chopped
- 2 tablespoons chopped fresh oregano
- 2 cups Israeli couscous
- 3 cups vegetable broth
- ½ cup crumbled feta cheese
- ¼ cup red wine vinegar
- ¼ cup extra-virgin olive oil
- ½ teaspoon ground black pepper
- ¼ cup chopped fresh basil

1. Press the Sauté button on the Instant Pot® and heat light olive oil. Add zucchini, squash, bell peppers, and oregano, and sauté 8 minutes. Press the Cancel button. Transfer to a serving bowl and set aside to cool. 2. Add couscous and broth to the Instant Pot® and stir well. Close lid, set steam release to Sealing, press the Manual button, and set time to 2 minutes. When the timer beeps, let pressure release naturally for 5 minutes, then quick-release the remaining pressure and open lid. 3. Fluff with a fork and stir in cooked vegetables, cheese, vinegar, extra-virgin olive oil, black pepper, and basil. Serve warm.

Per Serving:
calories: 355 | fat: 9g | protein: 14g | carbs: 61g | fiber: 7g | sodium: 588mg

Rotini with Spinach, Cherry Tomatoes, and Feta

Prep time: 5 minutes | Cook time: 30 minutes | Serves 2

- 6 ounces (170 g) uncooked rotini pasta (penne pasta will also work)
- 1 garlic clove, minced
- 3 tablespoons extra virgin olive oil, divided
- 1½ cups cherry tomatoes, halved and divided
- 9 ounces (255 g) baby leaf spinach, washed and chopped
- 1½ ounces (43 g) crumbled feta, divided
- Kosher salt, to taste
- Freshly ground black pepper, to taste

1. Cook the pasta according to the package instructions, reserving ½ cup of the cooking water. Drain and set aside. 2. While the pasta is cooking, combine the garlic with 2 tablespoons of the olive oil in a small bowl. Set aside. 3. Add the remaining tablespoon of olive oil to a medium pan placed over medium heat and then add 1 cup of the tomatoes. Cook for 2–3 minutes, then use a fork to mash lightly. 4. Add the spinach to the pan and continue cooking, stirring occasionally, until the spinach is wilted and the liquid is absorbed, about 4–5 minutes. 5. Transfer the cooked pasta to the pan with the spinach and tomatoes. Add 3 tablespoons of the pasta water, the garlic and olive oil mixture, and 1 ounce (28 g) of the crumbled feta. Increase the heat to high and cook for 1 minute. 6. Top with the remaining cherry tomatoes and feta, and season to taste with kosher salt and black pepper. Store covered in the refrigerator for up to 2 days.

Per Serving:
calories: 602 | fat: 27g | protein: 19g | carbs: 74g | fiber: 7g | sodium: 307mg

Rotini with Walnut Pesto, Peas, and Cherry Tomatoes

Prep time: 10 minutes | Cook time: 4 minutes | Serves 8

- 1 cup packed fresh basil leaves
- ⅓ cup chopped walnuts
- ¼ cup grated Parmesan cheese
- ¼ cup plus 1 tablespoon extra-virgin olive oil, divided
- 1 clove garlic, peeled
- 1 tablespoon lemon juice
- ¼ teaspoon salt
- 1 pound (454 g) whole-wheat rotini pasta
- 4 cups water
- 1 pint cherry tomatoes
- 1 cup fresh or frozen green peas
- ½ teaspoon ground black pepper

1. In a food processor, add basil and walnuts. Pulse until finely chopped, about 12 pulses. Add cheese, ¼ cup oil, garlic, lemon juice, and salt, and pulse until a rough paste forms, about 10 pulses. Refrigerate until ready to use. 2. Add pasta, water, and remaining 1 tablespoon oil to the Instant Pot®. Close lid, set steam release to Sealing, press the Manual button, and set time to 4 minutes. 3. When the timer beeps, quick-release the pressure until the float valve drops and open lid. Drain off any excess liquid. Allow pasta to cool to room temperature, about 30 minutes. Stir in basil mixture until pasta is well coated. Add tomatoes, peas, and pepper and toss to coat. Refrigerate for 2 hours. Stir well before serving.

Per Serving:
calories: 371 | fat: 15g | protein: 12g | carbs: 47g | fiber: 7g | sodium: 205mg

Creamy Spring Vegetable Linguine

Prep time: 10 minutes | Cook time: 10 minutes | Serves 4 to 6

- 1 pound (454 g) linguine
- 5 cups water, plus extra as needed
- 1 tablespoon extra-virgin olive oil
- 1 teaspoon table salt
- 1 cup jarred whole baby artichokes packed in water, quartered
- 1 cup frozen peas, thawed
- 4 ounces (113 g) finely grated Pecorino Romano (2 cups), plus extra for serving
- ½ teaspoon pepper
- 2 teaspoons grated lemon zest
- 2 tablespoons chopped fresh tarragon

1. Loosely wrap half of pasta in dish towel, then press bundle against corner of counter to break noodles into 6-inch lengths; repeat with remaining pasta. 2. Add pasta, water, oil, and salt to Instant Pot, making sure pasta is completely submerged. Lock lid in place and close pressure release valve. Select high pressure cook function and cook for 4 minutes. Turn off Instant Pot and quick-release pressure. Carefully remove lid, allowing steam to escape away from you. 3. Stir artichokes and peas into pasta, cover, and let sit until heated through, about 3 minutes. Gently stir in Pecorino and pepper until cheese is melted and fully combined, 1 to 2 minutes. Adjust consistency with extra hot water as needed. Stir in lemon zest and tarragon, and season with salt and pepper to taste. Serve, passing extra Pecorino separately.

Per Serving:
calories: 390 | fat: 8g | protein: 17g | carbs: 59g | fiber: 4g | sodium: 680mg

Orzo with Feta and Marinated Peppers

Prep time: 1 hour 25 minutes | Cook time: 37 minutes | Serves 2

- 2 medium red bell peppers
- ¼ cup extra virgin olive oil
- 1 tablespoon balsamic vinegar plus 1 teaspoon for serving
- ¼ teaspoon ground cumin
- Pinch of ground cinnamon
- Pinch of ground cloves
- ¼ teaspoon fine sea salt plus a pinch for the orzo
- 1 cup uncooked orzo
- 3 ounces (85 g) crumbled feta
- 1 tablespoon chopped fresh basil
- ¼ teaspoon freshly ground black pepper

1. Preheat the oven at 350°F (180°C). Place the peppers on a baking pan and roast in the oven for 25 minutes or until they're soft and can be pierced with a fork. Set aside to cool for 10 minutes. 2. While the peppers are roasting, combine the olive oil, 1 tablespoon of the balsamic vinegar, cumin, cinnamon, cloves, and ¼ teaspoon of the sea salt. Stir to combine, then set aside. 3. Peel the cooled peppers, remove the seeds, and then chop into large pieces. Place the peppers in the olive oil and vinegar mixture and then toss to coat, ensuring the peppers are covered in the marinade. Cover and place in the refrigerator to marinate for 20 minutes. 4. While the peppers are marinating, prepare the orzo by bringing 3 cups of water and a pinch of salt to a boil in a large pot over high heat. When the water is boiling, add the orzo, reduce the heat to medium, and cook, stirring occasionally, for 10–12 minutes or until soft, then drain and transfer to a serving bowl. 5. Add the peppers and marinade to the orzo, mixing well, then place in the refrigerator and to cool for at least 1 hour. 6. To serve, top with the feta, basil, black pepper, and 1 teaspoon of the balsamic vinegar. Mix well, and serve promptly. Store covered in the refrigerator for up to 3 days.

Per Serving:
calories: 600 | fat: 37g | protein: 15g | carbs: 51g | fiber: 4g | sodium: 690mg

Couscous with Tomatoes and Olives

Prep time: 5 minutes | Cook time: 3 minutes | Serves 4

- 1 tablespoon tomato paste
- 2 cups vegetable broth
- 1 cup couscous
- 1 cup halved cherry tomatoes
- ½ cup halved mixed olives
- ¼ cup minced fresh flat-leaf parsley
- 2 tablespoons minced fresh oregano
- 2 tablespoons minced fresh chives
- 1 tablespoon extra-virgin olive oil
- 1 tablespoon red wine vinegar
- ½ teaspoon ground black pepper

1. Pour tomato paste and broth into the Instant Pot® and stir until completely dissolved. Stir in couscous. Close lid, set steam release to Sealing, press the Manual button, and set time to 3 minutes. When the timer beeps, let pressure release naturally for 10 minutes, then quick-release the remaining pressure and open lid. 2. Fluff couscous with a fork. Add tomatoes, olives, parsley, oregano, chives, oil, vinegar, and pepper, and stir until combined. Serve warm or at room temperature.

Per Serving:
calories: 232 | fat: 5g | protein: 7g | carbs: 37g | fiber: 2g | sodium: 513mg

Penne with Roasted Vegetables

Prep time: 20 minutes | Cook time: 25 to 30 minutes | Serves 6

- 1 large butternut squash, peeled and diced
- 1 large zucchini, diced
- 1 large yellow onion, chopped
- 2 tablespoons extra-virgin olive oil
- ½ teaspoon salt
- ½ teaspoon freshly ground black pepper
- 1 teaspoon paprika
- ½ teaspoon garlic powder
- 1 pound (454 g) whole-grain penne
- ½ cup dry white wine or chicken stock
- 2 tablespoons grated Parmesan cheese

1. Preheat the oven to 400°F (205°C). Line a baking sheet with aluminum foil. 2. In a large bowl, toss the vegetables with the olive oil, then spread them out on the baking sheet. Sprinkle the vegetables with the salt, pepper, paprika, and garlic powder and bake just until fork-tender, 25 to 30 minutes. 3. Meanwhile, bring a large stockpot of water to a boil over high heat and cook the penne according to the package instructions until al dente (still slightly firm). Drain but do not rinse. 4. Place ½ cup of the roasted vegetables and the wine or stock in a blender or food processor and blend until smooth. 5. Place the purée in a large skillet and heat over medium-high heat. Add the pasta and cook, stirring, just until heated through. 6. Serve the pasta and sauce topped with the roasted vegetables. Sprinkle with Parmesan cheese.

Per Serving:
calories: 456 | fat: 7g | protein: 9g | carbs: 92g | fiber: 14g | sodium: 241mg

Quick Shrimp Fettuccine

Prep time: 10 minutes | Cook time: 10 minutes | Serves 4 to 6

- 8 ounces (227 g) fettuccine pasta
- ¼ cup extra-virgin olive oil
- 3 tablespoons garlic, minced
- 1 pound (454 g) large shrimp (21-25), peeled and deveined
- ⅓ cup lemon juice
- 1 tablespoon lemon zest
- ½ teaspoon salt
- ½ teaspoon freshly ground black pepper

1. Bring a large pot of salted water to a boil. Add the fettuccine and cook for 8 minutes. 2. In a large saucepan over medium heat, cook the olive oil and garlic for 1 minute. 3. Add the shrimp to the saucepan and cook for 3 minutes on each side. Remove the shrimp from the pan and set aside. 4. Add the lemon juice and lemon zest to the saucepan, along with the salt and pepper. 5. Reserve ½ cup of the pasta water and drain the pasta. 6. Add the pasta water to the saucepan with the lemon juice and zest and stir everything together. Add the pasta and toss together to evenly coat the pasta. Transfer the pasta to a serving dish and top with the cooked shrimp. Serve warm.

Per Serving:
calories: 615 | fat: 17g | protein: 33g | carbs: 89g | fiber: 4g | sodium: 407mg

Penne with Tuna and Green Olives

Prep time: 5 minutes | Cook time: 5 minutes | Serves 4

2 tablespoons olive oil	olive oil (don't drain off the oil)
3 garlic cloves, minced	½ teaspoon wine vinegar
½ cup green olives	12 ounces (340 g) penne pasta, cooked according to package directions
½ teaspoon salt	
¼ teaspoon freshly ground black pepper	
2 (6-ounce / 170-g) cans tuna in	2 tablespoons chopped flat-leaf parsley

1. Heat the olive oil in a medium skillet over medium heat. Add the garlic and cook, stirring, 2 to 3 minutes, just until the garlic begins to brown. Add the olives, salt, pepper, and the tuna along with its oil. Cook, stirring, for a minute or two to heat the ingredients through. Remove from the heat and stir in the vinegar. 2. Add the cooked pasta to the skillet and toss to combine the pasta with the sauce. Serve immediately, garnished with the parsley.

Per Serving:
calories: 511 | fat: 22g | protein: 31g | carbs: 52g | fiber: 1g | sodium: 826mg

Linguine with Avocado Pesto

Prep time: 10 minutes | Cook time: 10 minutes | Serves 4

1 pound (454 g) dried linguine	1 tablespoon packed sun-dried tomatoes
2 avocados, coarsely chopped	
½ cup olive oil	⅛ teaspoon Italian seasoning
½ cup packed fresh basil	⅛ teaspoon red pepper flakes
½ cup pine nuts	Sea salt
Juice of 1 lemon	Freshly ground black pepper
3 garlic cloves	

1. Fill a large stockpot three-quarters full with water and bring to a boil over high heat. Add the pasta and cook according to the package instructions until al dente, about 15 minutes. 2. While the pasta is cooking, in a food processor, combine the avocados, olive oil, basil, pine nuts, lemon juice, garlic, sun-dried tomatoes, Italian seasoning, and red pepper flakes and process until a paste forms. Taste and season with salt and black pepper. 3. When the pasta is done, drain it and return it to the pot. Add half the pesto and mix. Add more pesto as desired and serve.

Per Serving:
calories: 694 | fat: 29g | protein: 17g | carbs: 93g | fiber: 8g | sodium: 11mg

Whole-Wheat Spaghetti à la Puttanesca

Prep time: 5 minutes | Cook time: 20 minutes | Serves 6

1 pound (454 g) dried whole-wheat spaghetti	black pepper
⅓ cup olive oil	1 (28-ounce / 794-g) can tomato purée
5 garlic cloves, minced or pressed	1 pint cherry tomatoes, halved
4 anchovy fillets, chopped	½ cup pitted green olives, halved
½ teaspoon red pepper flakes	2 tablespoons drained capers
1 teaspoon salt	¾ cup coarsely chopped basil
½ teaspoon freshly ground	

1. Cook the pasta according to the package instructions. 2. Meanwhile, heat the oil in a large skillet over medium-high heat. Add the garlic, anchovies, red pepper flakes, salt, and pepper. Cook, stirring frequently, until the garlic just begins to turn golden brown, 2 to 3 minutes. Add the tomato purée, olives, cherry tomatoes, and capers and let the mixture simmer, reducing the heat if necessary, and stirring occasionally, until the pasta is done, about 10 minutes. 3. Drain the pasta in a colander and then add it to the sauce, tossing with tongs until the pasta is well coated. Serve hot, garnished with the basil.

Per Serving:
calories: 464 | fat: 17g | protein: 12g | carbs: 70g | fiber: 12g | sodium: 707mg

Whole-Wheat Capellini with Sardines, Olives, and Manchego

Prep time: 5 minutes | Cook time: 15 minutes | Serves 4

1 (7-ounce / 198-g) jar Spanish sardines in olive oil, chopped (reserve the oil)	wheat capellini pasta, cooked according to package instructions
1 medium onion, diced	1 cup pitted, chopped cured black olives, such as Kalamata
4 cloves garlic, minced	
2 medium tomatoes, sliced	3 ounces (85 g) freshly grated manchego cheese
1 pound (454 g) whole-	

1. Heat the olive oil from the sardines in a large skillet over medium-high heat. Add the onion and garlic and cook, stirring frequently, until softened, about 5 minutes. Add the tomatoes and sardines and cook, stirring, 2 minutes more. 2. Add the cooked and drained pasta to the skillet with the sauce and toss to combine. 3. Stir in the olives and serve immediately, topped with the grated cheese.

Per Serving:
calories: 307 | fat: 11g | protein: 8g | carbs: 38g | fiber: 6g | sodium: 433mg

Bowtie Pesto Pasta Salad

Prep time: 5 minutes | Cook time: 4 minutes | Serves 8

1 pound (454 g) whole-wheat bowtie pasta	2 cups baby spinach
	½ cup chopped fresh basil
4 cups water	½ cup prepared pesto
1 tablespoon extra-virgin olive oil	½ teaspoon ground black pepper
2 cups halved cherry tomatoes	½ cup grated Parmesan cheese

1. Add pasta, water, and olive oil to the Instant Pot®. Close lid, set steam release to Sealing, press the Manual button, and set time to 4 minutes. 2. When the timer beeps, quick-release the pressure until the float valve drops and open lid. Drain off any excess liquid. Allow pasta to cool to room temperature, about 30 minutes. Stir in tomatoes, spinach, basil, pesto, pepper, and cheese. Refrigerate for 2 hours. Stir well before serving.

Per Serving:
calories: 360 | fat: 13g | protein: 16g | carbs: 44g | fiber: 7g | sodium: 372mg

Meaty Baked Penne

Prep time: 10 minutes | Cook time: 40 minutes | Serves 8

1 pound (454 g) penne pasta	1 (1-pound / 454-g) bag baby spinach, washed
1 pound (454 g) ground beef	
1 teaspoon salt	3 cups shredded mozzarella cheese, divided
1 (25-ounce / 709-g) jar marinara sauce	

1. Bring a large pot of salted water to a boil, add the penne, and cook for 7 minutes. Reserve 2 cups of the pasta water and drain the pasta. 2. Preheat the oven to 350°F(180ºC). 3. In a large saucepan over medium heat, cook the ground beef and salt. Brown the ground beef for about 5 minutes. 4. Stir in marinara sauce, and 2 cups of pasta water. Let simmer for 5 minutes. 5. Add a handful of spinach at a time into the sauce, and cook for another 3 minutes. 6. To assemble, in a 9-by-13-inch baking dish, add the pasta and pour the pasta sauce over it. Stir in 1½ cups of the mozzarella cheese. Cover the dish with foil and bake for 20 minutes. 7. After 20 minutes, remove the foil, top with the rest of the mozzarella, and bake for another 10 minutes. Serve warm.

Per Serving:
calories: 454 | fat: 13g | protein: 31g | carbs: 55g | fiber: 9g | sodium: 408mg

Chilled Pearl Couscous Salad

Prep time: 15 minutes | Cook time: 10 minutes | Serves 6

3 tablespoons olive oil, divided	¼ cup slivered almonds
1 cup pearl couscous	¼ cup chopped fresh mint leaves
1 cup water	
1 cup orange juice	2 tablespoons lemon juice
1 small cucumber, seeded and diced	1 teaspoon grated lemon zest
	¼ cup crumbled feta cheese
1 small yellow bell pepper, seeded and diced	¼ teaspoon fine sea salt
	1 teaspoon smoked paprika
2 small Roma tomatoes, seeded and diced	1 teaspoon garlic powder

1. Press the Sauté button and heat 1 tablespoon oil. Add couscous and cook for 2–4 minutes until couscous is slightly browned. Add water and orange juice. Press the Cancel button. 2. Close lid, set steam release to Sealing, press the Manual button, and set time to 5 minutes. When the timer beeps, let pressure release naturally for 5 minutes. Quick-release any remaining pressure until the float valve drops and open lid. Drain any liquid and set aside to cool for 20 minutes. 3. Combine remaining 2 tablespoons oil, cucumber, bell pepper, tomatoes, almonds, mint, lemon juice, lemon zest, cheese, salt, paprika, and garlic powder in a medium bowl. Add couscous and toss ingredients together. Cover and refrigerate overnight before serving.

Per Serving:
calories: 177 | fat: 11g | protein: 5g | carbs: 12g | fiber: 1g | sodium: 319mg

Zucchini with Bow Ties

Prep time: 5 minutes |Cook time: 25 minutes| Serves: 4

3 tablespoons extra-virgin olive oil	¼ teaspoon ground nutmeg
	8 ounces (227 g) uncooked farfalle (bow ties) or other small pasta shape
2 garlic cloves, minced (about 1 teaspoon)	
3 large or 4 medium zucchini, diced (about 4 cups)	½ cup grated Parmesan or Romano cheese (about 2 ounces / 57 g)
½ teaspoon freshly ground black pepper	
	1 tablespoon freshly squeezed lemon juice (from ½ medium lemon)
¼ teaspoon kosher or sea salt	
½ cup 2% milk	

1. In a large skillet over medium heat, heat the oil. Add the garlic and cook for 1 minute, stirring frequently. Add the zucchini, pepper, and salt. Stir well, cover, and cook for 15 minutes, stirring once or twice. 2. In a small, microwave-safe bowl, warm the milk in the microwave on high for 30 seconds. Stir the milk and nutmeg into the skillet and cook uncovered for another 5 minutes, stirring occasionally. 3. While the zucchini is cooking, in a large stockpot, cook the pasta according to the package directions. 4. Drain the pasta in a colander, saving about 2 tablespoons of pasta water. Add the pasta and pasta water to the skillet. Mix everything together and remove from the heat. Stir in the cheese and lemon juice and serve.

Per Serving:
calories: 405 | fat: 16g | protein: 12g | carbs: 57g | fiber: 9g | sodium: 407mg

Couscous with Crab and Lemon

Prep time: 10 minutes | Cook time: 7 minutes | Serves 4

1 cup couscous	1 tablespoon minced fresh dill
1 clove garlic, peeled and minced	8 ounces (227 g) jumbo lump crabmeat
2 cups water	3 tablespoons lemon juice
3 tablespoons extra-virgin olive oil, divided	½ teaspoon ground black pepper
¼ cup minced fresh flat-leaf parsley	¼ cup grated Parmesan cheese

1. Place couscous, garlic, water, and 1 tablespoon oil in the Instant Pot® and stir well. Close lid, set steam release to Sealing, press the Manual button, and set time to 7 minutes. When the timer beeps, let pressure release naturally for 10 minutes, then quick-release the remaining pressure and open lid. 2. Fluff couscous with a fork. Add parsley, dill, crabmeat, lemon juice, pepper, and remaining 2 tablespoons oil, and stir until combined. Top with cheese and serve immediately.

Per Serving:
calories: 360 | fat: 15g | protein: 22g | carbs: 34g | fiber: 2g | sodium: 388mg

Chapter 9 Pizzas, Wraps, and Sandwiches

Classic Margherita Pizza

Prep time: 10 minutes | Cook time: 10 minutes | Serves 4

All-purpose flour, for dusting
1 pound (454 g) premade pizza dough
1 (15-ounce / 425-g) can crushed San Marzano tomatoes, with their juices
2 garlic cloves
1 teaspoon Italian seasoning
Pinch sea salt, plus more as needed
1½ teaspoons olive oil, for drizzling
10 slices mozzarella cheese
12 to 15 fresh basil leaves

1. Preheat the oven to 475°F (245°C). 2. On a floured surface, roll out the dough to a 12-inch round and place it on a lightly floured pizza pan or baking sheet. 3. In a food processor, combine the tomatoes with their juices, garlic, Italian seasoning, and salt and process until smooth. Taste and adjust the seasoning. 4. Drizzle the olive oil over the pizza dough, then spoon the pizza sauce over the dough and spread it out evenly with the back of the spoon, leaving a 1-inch border. Evenly distribute the mozzarella over the pizza. 5. Bake until the crust is cooked through and golden, 8 to 10 minutes. Remove from the oven and let sit for 1 to 2 minutes. Top with the basil right before serving.

Per Serving:
calories: 570 | fat: 21g | protein: 28g | carbs: 66g | fiber: 4g | sodium: 570mg

Grilled Chicken Salad Pita

Prep time: 15 minutes | Cook time: 16 minutes | Serves 1

1 boneless, skinless chicken breast
Sea salt and freshly ground pepper, to taste
1 cup baby spinach
1 roasted red pepper, sliced
1 tomato, chopped
½ small red onion, thinly sliced
½ small cucumber, chopped
1 tablespoon olive oil
Juice of 1 lemon
1 whole-wheat pita pocket
2 tablespoons crumbled feta cheese

1. Preheat a gas or charcoal grill to medium-high heat. 2. Season the chicken breast with sea salt and freshly ground pepper, and grill until cooked through, about 7–8 minutes per side. 3. Allow chicken to rest for 5 minutes before slicing into strips. 4. While the chicken is cooking, put all the chopped vegetables into a medium-mixing bowl and season with sea salt and freshly ground pepper. 5. Chop the chicken into cubes and add to salad. Add the olive oil and lemon juice and toss well. 6. Stuff the mixture onto a pita pocket and top with the feta cheese. Serve immediately.

Per Serving:
calories: 653 | fat: 26g | protein: 71g | carbs: 34g | fiber: 6g | sodium: 464mg

Grilled Eggplant and Feta Sandwiches

Prep time: 10 minutes | Cook time: 8 minutes | Serves 2

1 medium eggplant, sliced into ½-inch-thick slices
2 tablespoons olive oil
Sea salt and freshly ground pepper, to taste
5 to 6 tablespoons hummus
4 slices whole-wheat bread, toasted
1 cup baby spinach leaves
2 ounces (57 g) feta cheese, softened

1. Preheat a gas or charcoal grill to medium-high heat. 2. Salt both sides of the sliced eggplant, and let sit for 20 minutes to draw out the bitter juices. 3. Rinse the eggplant and pat dry with a paper towel. 4. Brush the eggplant slices with olive oil and season with sea salt and freshly ground pepper. 5. Grill the eggplant until lightly charred on both sides but still slightly firm in the middle, about 3–4 minutes a side. 6. Spread the hummus on the bread and top with the spinach leaves, feta, and eggplant. Top with the other slice of bread and serve warm.

Per Serving:
calories: 516 | fat: 27g | protein: 14g | carbs: 59g | fiber: 14g | sodium: 597mg

Dill Salmon Salad Wraps

Prep time: 10 minutes |Cook time: 10 minutes| Serves:6

1 pound (454 g) salmon filet, cooked and flaked, or 3 (5-ounce / 142-g) cans salmon
½ cup diced carrots (about 1 carrot)
½ cup diced celery (about 1 celery stalk)
3 tablespoons chopped fresh dill
3 tablespoons diced red onion (a little less than ⅛ onion)
2 tablespoons capers
1½ tablespoons extra-virgin olive oil
1 tablespoon aged balsamic vinegar
½ teaspoon freshly ground black pepper
¼ teaspoon kosher or sea salt
4 whole-wheat flatbread wraps or soft whole-wheat tortillas

1. In a large bowl, mix together the salmon, carrots, celery, dill, red onion, capers, oil, vinegar, pepper, and salt. 2. Divide the salmon salad among the flatbreads. Fold up the bottom of the flatbread, then roll up the wrap and serve.

Per Serving:
calories: 185 | fat: 8g | protein: 17g | carbs: 12g | fiber: 2g | sodium: 237mg

Beans and Greens Pizza

Prep time: 11 minutes | Cook time: 14 to 19 minutes | Serves 4

- ¾ cup whole-wheat pastry flour
- ½ teaspoon low-sodium baking powder
- 1 tablespoon olive oil, divided
- 1 cup chopped kale
- 2 cups chopped fresh baby spinach
- 1 cup canned no-salt-added cannellini beans, rinsed and drained
- ½ teaspoon dried thyme
- 1 piece low-sodium string cheese, torn into pieces

1. In a small bowl, mix the pastry flour and baking powder until well combined. 2. Add ¼ cup of water and 2 teaspoons of olive oil. Mix until a dough forms. 3. On a floured surface, press or roll the dough into a 7-inch round. Set aside while you cook the greens. 4. In a baking pan, mix the kale, spinach, and remaining teaspoon of the olive oil. Air fry at 350°F (177°C) for 3 to 5 minutes, until the greens are wilted. Drain well. 5. Put the pizza dough into the air fryer basket. Top with the greens, cannellini beans, thyme, and string cheese. Air fry for 11 to 14 minutes, or until the crust is golden brown and the cheese is melted. Cut into quarters to serve.

Per Serving:
calories: 181 | fat: 6g | protein: 8g | carbs: 27g | fiber: 6g | sodium: 103mg

Moroccan Lamb Wrap with Harissa

Prep time: 10 minutes | Cook time: 10 minutes | Serves 4

- 1 clove garlic, minced
- 2 teaspoons ground cumin
- 2 teaspoons chopped fresh thyme
- ¼ cup olive oil, divided
- 1 lamb leg steak, about 12 ounces (340 g)
- 4 (8-inch) pocketless pita rounds or naan, preferably whole-wheat
- 1 medium eggplant, sliced ½-inch thick
- 1 medium zucchini, sliced lengthwise into 4 slices
- 1 bell pepper (any color), roasted and skinned
- 6 to 8 Kalamata olives, sliced
- Juice of 1 lemon
- 2 to 4 tablespoons harissa
- 2 cups arugula

1. In a large bowl, combine the garlic, cumin, thyme, and 1 tablespoon of the olive oil. Add the lamb, turn to coat, cover, refrigerate, and marinate for at least an hour. 2. Preheat the oven to 400°F (205°C). 3. Heat a grill or grill pan to high heat. Remove the lamb from the marinade and grill for about 4 minutes per side, until medium-rare. Transfer to a plate and let rest for about 10 minutes before slicing thinly across the grain. 4. While the meat is resting, wrap the bread rounds in aluminum foil and heat in the oven for about 10 minutes. 5. Meanwhile, brush the eggplant and zucchini slices with the remaining olive oil and grill until tender, about 3 minutes. Dice them and the bell pepper. Toss in a large bowl with the olives and lemon juice. 6. Spread some of the harissa onto each warm flatbread round and top each evenly with roasted vegetables, a few slices of lamb, and a handful of the arugula. 7. Roll up the wraps, cut each in half crosswise, and serve immediately.

Per Serving:
calories: 553 | fat: 24g | protein: 33g | carbs: 53g | fiber: 11g | sodium: 531mg

Roasted Vegetable Bocadillo with Romesco Sauce

Prep time: 10 minutes | Cook time: 20 minutes | Serves 4

- 2 small yellow squash, sliced lengthwise
- 2 small zucchini, sliced lengthwise
- 1 medium red onion, thinly sliced
- 4 large button mushrooms, sliced
- 2 tablespoons olive oil
- 1 teaspoon salt, divided
- ½ teaspoon freshly ground black pepper, divided
- 2 roasted red peppers from a jar, drained
- 2 tablespoons blanched almonds
- 1 tablespoon sherry vinegar
- 1 small clove garlic
- 4 crusty multigrain rolls
- 4 ounces (113 g) goat cheese, at room temperature
- 1 tablespoon chopped fresh basil

1. Preheat the oven to 400°F (205°C). 2. In a medium bowl, toss the yellow squash, zucchini, onion, and mushrooms with the olive oil, ½ teaspoon salt, and ¼ teaspoon pepper. Spread on a large baking sheet. Roast the vegetables in the oven for about 20 minutes, until softened. 3. Meanwhile, in a food processor, combine the roasted peppers, almonds, vinegar, garlic, the remaining ½ teaspoon salt, and the remaining ¼ teaspoon pepper and process until smooth. 4. Split the rolls and spread ¼ of the goat cheese on the bottom of each. Place the roasted vegetables on top of the cheese, dividing equally. Top with chopped basil. Spread the top halves of the rolls with the roasted red pepper sauce and serve immediately.

Per Serving:
calories: 379 | fat: 21g | protein: 17g | carbs: 32g | fiber: 4g | sodium: 592mg

Greek Salad Wraps

Prep time: 15 minutes | Cook time: 0 minutes | Serves: 4

- 1½ cups seedless cucumber, peeled and chopped (about 1 large cucumber)
- 1 cup chopped tomato (about 1 large tomato)
- ½ cup finely chopped fresh mint
- 1 (2¼-ounce / 64-g) can sliced black olives (about ½ cup), drained
- ¼ cup diced red onion (about ¼ onion)
- 2 tablespoons extra-virgin olive oil
- 1 tablespoon red wine vinegar
- ¼ teaspoon freshly ground black pepper
- ¼ teaspoon kosher or sea salt
- ½ cup crumbled goat cheese (about 2 ounces / 57 g)
- 4 whole-wheat flatbread wraps or soft whole-wheat tortillas

1. In a large bowl, mix together the cucumber, tomato, mint, olives, and onion until well combined. 2. In a small bowl, whisk together the oil, vinegar, pepper, and salt. Drizzle the dressing over the salad, and mix gently. 3. With a knife, spread the goat cheese evenly over the four wraps. Spoon a quarter of the salad filling down the middle of each wrap. 4. Fold up each wrap: Start by folding up the bottom, then fold one side over and fold the other side over the top. Repeat with the remaining wraps and serve.

Per Serving:
calories: 217 | fat: 14g | protein: 7g | carbs: 17g | fiber: 3g | sodium: 329mg

Sautéed Mushroom, Onion, and Pecorino Romano Panini

Prep time: 10 minutes | Cook time: 20 minutes | Serves 4

3 tablespoons olive oil, divided
1 small onion, diced
10 ounces (283 g) button or cremini mushrooms, sliced
½ teaspoon salt
¼ teaspoon freshly ground black pepper
4 crusty Italian sandwich rolls
4 ounces (113 g) freshly grated Pecorino Romano

1. Heat 1 tablespoon of the olive oil in a skillet over medium-high heat. Add the onion and cook, stirring, until it begins to soften, about 3 minutes. Add the mushrooms, season with salt and pepper, and cook, stirring, until they soften and the liquid they release evaporates, about 7 minutes. 2. To make the panini, heat a skillet or grill pan over high heat and brush with 1 tablespoon olive oil. Brush the inside of the rolls with the remaining 1 tablespoon olive oil. Divide the mushroom mixture evenly among the rolls and top each with ¼ of the grated cheese. 3. Place the sandwiches in the hot pan and place another heavy pan, such as a cast-iron skillet, on top to weigh them down. Cook for about 3 to 4 minutes, until crisp and golden on the bottom, and then flip over and repeat on the second side, cooking for an additional 3 to 4 minutes until golden and crisp. Slice each sandwich in half and serve hot.

Per Serving:
calories: 348 | fat: 20g | protein: 14g | carbs: 30g | fiber: 2g | sodium: 506mg

Turkey and Provolone Panini with Roasted Peppers and Onions

Prep time: 15 minutes | Cook time: 1 hour 5 minutes | Serves 4

For the peppers and onions
2 red bell pepper, seeded and quartered
2 red onions, peeled and quartered
2 tablespoons olive oil
½ teaspoon salt
½ teaspoon freshly ground black pepper
For the panini
2 tablespoons olive oil
8 slices whole-wheat bread
8 ounces (227 g) thinly sliced provolone cheese
8 ounces (227 g) sliced roasted turkey or chicken breast

1. Preheat the oven to 375°F(190ºC). 2. To roast the peppers and onions, toss them together with the olive oil, salt, and pepper on a large, rimmed baking sheet. Spread them out in a single layer and then bake in the preheated oven for 45 to 60 minutes, turning occasionally, until they are tender and beginning to brown. Remove the peppers and onions from the oven and let them cool for a few minutes until they are cool enough to handle. Skin the peppers and thinly slice them. Thinly slice the onions. 3. Preheat a skillet or grill pan over medium-high heat. 4. To make the panini, brush one side of each of the 8 slices of bread with olive oil. Place 4 of the bread slices, oiled side down, on your work surface. Top each with ¼ of the cheese and ¼ of the turkey, and top with some of the roasted peppers and onions. Place the remaining 4 bread slices on top of the sandwiches, oiled side up. 5. Place the sandwiches in the skillet or grill pan (you may have to cook them in two batches), cover the pan, and cook until the bottoms have golden brown grill marks and the cheese is beginning to melt, about 2 minutes. Turn the sandwiches over and cook, covered, until the second side is golden brown and the cheese is melted, another 2 minutes or so. Cut each sandwich in half and serve immediately.

Per Serving:
calories: 603 | fat: 32g | protein: 41g | carbs: 37g | fiber: 6g | sodium: 792mg

Jerk Chicken Wraps

Prep time: 30 minutes | Cook time: 15 minutes | Serves 4

1 pound (454 g) boneless, skinless chicken tenderloins
1 cup jerk marinade
Olive oil
4 large low-carb tortillas
1 cup julienned carrots
1 cup peeled cucumber ribbons
1 cup shredded lettuce
1 cup mango or pineapple chunks

1. In a medium bowl, coat the chicken with the jerk marinade, cover, and refrigerate for 1 hour. 2. Spray the air fryer basket lightly with olive oil. 3. Place the chicken in the air fryer basket in a single layer and spray lightly with olive oil. You may need to cook the chicken in batches. Reserve any leftover marinade. 4. Air fry at 375ºF (191ºC) for 8 minutes. Turn the chicken over and brush with some of the remaining marinade. Cook until the chicken reaches an internal temperature of at least 165ºF (74ºC), an additional 5 to 7 minutes. 5. To assemble the wraps, fill each tortilla with ¼ cup carrots, ¼ cup cucumber, ¼ cup lettuce, and ¼ cup mango. Place one quarter of the chicken tenderloins on top and roll up the tortilla. These are great served warm or cold.

Per Serving:
calories: 241 | fat: 4g | protein: 28g | carbs: 23g | fiber: 4g | sodium: 85mg

Vegetable Pita Sandwiches

Prep time: 15 minutes | Cook time: 9 to 12 minutes | Serves 4

1 baby eggplant, peeled and chopped
1 red bell pepper, sliced
½ cup diced red onion
½ cup shredded carrot
1 teaspoon olive oil
⅓ cup low-fat Greek yogurt
½ teaspoon dried tarragon
2 low-sodium whole-wheat pita breads, halved crosswise

1. In a baking pan, stir together the eggplant, red bell pepper, red onion, carrot, and olive oil. Put the vegetable mixture into the air fryer basket and roast at 390ºF (199ºC) for 7 to 9 minutes, stirring once, until the vegetables are tender. Drain if necessary. 2. In a small bowl, thoroughly mix the yogurt and tarragon until well combined. 3. Stir the yogurt mixture into the vegetables. Stuff one-fourth of this mixture into each pita pocket. 4. Place the sandwiches in the air fryer and cook for 2 to 3 minutes, or until the bread is toasted. Serve immediately.

Per Serving:
calories: 115 | fat: 2g | protein: 4g | carbs: 22g | fiber: 6g | sodium: 90mg

Cucumber Basil Sandwiches

Prep time: 10 minutes | Cook time: 0 minutes | Serves 2

Cucumber Basil Sandwiches
Prep time: 10 minutes | Cook time: 0 minutes | Serves 2
4 slices whole-grain bread
¼ cup hummus
1 large cucumber, thinly sliced
4 whole basil leaves

1. Spread the hummus on 2 slices of bread, and layer the cucumbers onto it. Top with the basil leaves and close the sandwiches. 2. Press down lightly and serve immediately.

Per Serving:
calories: 209 | fat: 5g | protein: 9g | carbs: 32g | fiber: 6g | sodium: 275mg

Greek Salad Pita

Prep time: 15 minutes | Cook time: 0 minutes | Serves 4

1 cup chopped romaine lettuce
1 tomato, chopped and seeded
½ cup baby spinach leaves
½ small red onion, thinly sliced
½ small cucumber, chopped and deseeded
2 tablespoons olive oil
1 tablespoon crumbled feta cheese
½ tablespoon red wine vinegar
1 teaspoon Dijon mustard
Sea salt and freshly ground pepper, to taste
1 whole-wheat pita

1. Combine everything except the sea salt, freshly ground pepper, and pita bread in a medium bowl. 2. Toss until the salad is well combined. 3. Season with sea salt and freshly ground pepper to taste. Fill the pita with the salad mixture, serve, and enjoy!

Per Serving:
calories: 123 | fat: 8g | protein: 3g | carbs: 12g | fiber: 2g | sodium: 125mg

Turkey Burgers with Feta and Dill

Prep time: 5 minutes | Cook time: 15 minutes | Serves 4

1 pound (454 g) ground turkey breast
1 small red onion, ½ finely chopped, ½ sliced
½ cup crumbled feta cheese
¼ cup chopped fresh dill
1 clove garlic, minced
½ teaspoon kosher salt
¼ teaspoon ground black pepper
4 whole grain hamburger rolls
4 thick slices tomato
4 leaves lettuce

1. Coat a grill rack or grill pan with olive oil and prepare to medium-high heat. 2. In a large bowl, use your hands to combine the turkey, chopped onion, cheese, dill, garlic, salt, and pepper. Do not overmix. Divide into 4 patties, 4' in diameter. 3. Grill the patties, covered, until a thermometer inserted in the center registers 165°F(74°C), 5 to 6 minutes per side. 4. Serve each patty on a roll with the sliced onion, 1 slice of the tomato, and 1 leaf of the lettuce.

Per Serving:
calories: 305 | fat: 7g | protein: 35g | carbs: 26g | fiber: 3g | sodium: 708mg

Open-Faced Eggplant Parmesan Sandwich

Prep time: 10 minutes | Cook time: 10 minutes | Serves 2

1 small eggplant, sliced into ¼-inch rounds
Pinch sea salt
2 tablespoons olive oil
Sea salt and freshly ground pepper, to taste
2 slices whole-grain bread, thickly cut and toasted
1 cup marinara sauce (no added sugar)
¼ cup freshly grated, low-fat Parmesan cheese

1. Preheat broiler to high heat. 2. Salt both sides of the sliced eggplant, and let sit for 20 minutes to draw out the bitter juices. 3. Rinse the eggplant and pat dry with a paper towel. 4. Brush the eggplant with the olive oil, and season with sea salt and freshly ground pepper. 5. Lay the eggplant on a sheet pan, and broil until crisp, about 4 minutes. Flip over and crisp the other side. 6. Lay the toasted bread on a sheet pan. Spoon some marinara sauce on each slice of bread, and layer the eggplant on top. 7. Sprinkle half of the cheese on top of the eggplant and top with more marinara sauce. 8. Sprinkle with remaining cheese. 9. Put the sandwiches under the broiler until the cheese has melted, about 2 minutes. 10. Using a spatula, transfer the sandwiches to plates and serve.

Per Serving:
calories: 355 | fat: 19g | protein: 10g | carbs: 38g | fiber: 13g | sodium: 334mg

Margherita Open-Face Sandwiches

Prep time: 10 minutes |Cook time: 5 minutes| Serves: 4

2 (6- to 7-inch) whole-wheat submarine or hoagie rolls, sliced open horizontally
1 tablespoon extra-virgin olive oil
1 garlic clove, halved
1 large ripe tomato, cut into 8 slices
¼ teaspoon dried oregano
1 cup fresh mozzarella (about 4 ounces / 113 g), patted dry and sliced
¼ cup lightly packed fresh basil leaves, torn into small pieces
¼ teaspoon freshly ground black pepper

1. Preheat the broiler to high with the rack 4 inches under the heating element. 2. Place the sliced bread on a large, rimmed baking sheet. Place under the broiler for 1 minute, until the bread is just lightly toasted. Remove from the oven. 3. Brush each piece of the toasted bread with the oil, and rub a garlic half over each piece. 4. Place the toasted bread back on the baking sheet. Evenly distribute the tomato slices on each piece, sprinkle with the oregano, and layer the cheese on top. 5. Place the baking sheet under the broiler. Set the timer for 1½ minutes, but check after 1 minute. When the cheese is melted and the edges are just starting to get dark brown, remove the sandwiches from the oven (this can take anywhere from 1½ to 2 minutes). 6. Top each sandwich with the fresh basil and pepper.

Per Serving:
calories: 176 | fat: 9g | protein: 10g | carbs: 14g | fiber: 2g | sodium: 119mg

Herbed Focaccia Panini with Anchovies and Burrata

Prep time: 5 minutes | Cook time: 8 minutes | Serves 4

8 ounces (227 g) burrata cheese, chilled and sliced
1 pound (454 g) whole-wheat herbed focaccia, cut crosswise into 4 rectangles and split horizontally
1 can anchovy fillets packed in oil, drained
8 slices tomato, sliced
2 cups arugula
1 tablespoon olive oil

1. Divide the cheese evenly among the bottom halves of the focaccia rectangles. Top each with 3 or 4 anchovy fillets, 2 slices of tomato, and ½ cup arugula. Place the top halves of the focaccia on top of the sandwiches. 2. To make the panini, heat a skillet or grill pan over high heat and brush with the olive oil. 3. Place the sandwiches in the hot pan and place another heavy pan, such as a cast-iron skillet, on top to weigh them down. Cook for about 3 to 4 minutes, until crisp and golden on the bottom, and then flip over and repeat on the second side, cooking for an additional 3 to 4 minutes until golden and crisp. Slice each sandwich in half and serve hot.

Per Serving:
calories: 596 | fat: 30g | protein: 27g | carbs: 58g | fiber: 5g | sodium: 626mg

Mediterranean-Pita Wraps

Prep time: 5 minutes | Cook time: 14 minutes | Serves 4

1 pound (454 g) mackerel fish fillets
2 tablespoons olive oil
1 tablespoon Mediterranean seasoning mix
½ teaspoon chili powder
Sea salt and freshly ground black pepper, to taste
2 ounces (57 g) feta cheese, crumbled
4 tortillas

1. Toss the fish fillets with the olive oil; place them in the lightly oiled air fryer basket. 2. Air fry the fish fillets at 400°F (204°C) for about 14 minutes, turning them over halfway through the cooking time. 3. Assemble your pitas with the chopped fish and remaining ingredients and serve warm.

Per Serving:
calories: 275 | fat: 13g | protein: 27g | carbs: 13g | fiber: 2g | sodium: 322mg

Mexican Pizza

Prep time: 10 minutes | Cook time: 7 to 9 minutes | Serves 4

¾ cup refried beans (from a 16-ounce / 454-g can)
½ cup salsa
10 frozen precooked beef meatballs, thawed and sliced
1 jalapeño pepper, sliced
4 whole-wheat pita breads
1 cup shredded pepper Jack cheese
½ cup shredded Colby cheese
⅓ cup sour cream

1. In a medium bowl, combine the refried beans, salsa, meatballs, and jalapeño pepper. 2. Preheat the air fryer for 3 to 4 minutes or until hot. 3. Top the pitas with the refried bean mixture and sprinkle with the cheeses. 4. Bake at 370°F (188°C) for 7 to 9 minutes or until the pizza is crisp and the cheese is melted and starts to brown. 5. Top each pizza with a dollop of sour cream and serve warm.

Per Serving:
calories: 484 | fat: 30g | protein: 24g | carbs: 32g | fiber: 7g | sodium: 612mg

Chapter 10 Snacks and Appetizers

Domatosalata (Sweet-and-Spicy Tomato Sauce)

Prep time: 10 minutes | Cook time: 50 minutes | Serves 8

2 tablespoons olive oil	½ teaspoon freshly ground black pepper
1 large onion, finely chopped	⅛ teaspoon cayenne pepper
2 (28-ounce / 794-g) cans no-salt added diced tomatoes, with their juices	½ teaspoon kosher salt, or to taste
2 tablespoons tomato paste	2 tablespoons honey
1½ teaspoons ground cinnamon	2 tablespoons red wine vinegar
1 garlic clove, minced	

1. In a large, heavy skillet, heat the olive oil over medium heat. Add the onion and sauté until soft, about 8 minutes. Add the diced tomatoes and their juices, tomato paste, cinnamon, garlic, black pepper, cayenne, and salt. Cook, stirring occasionally, for 30 minutes, or until most of the liquid has evaporated. The tomato mixture should have thickened to a jam-like consistency. 2. Add the honey, reduce the heat to give a slow simmer, and cook, stirring occasionally, for 8 to 10 minutes more, until slightly syrupy. Do not let it burn. 3. Remove from the heat; stir in the vinegar. 4. Serve warm or at room temperature.

Per Serving:
1 cup: calories: 75 | fat: 4g | protein: 2g | carbs: 11g | fiber: 3g | sodium: 159mg

Vegetable Pot Stickers

Prep time: 12 minutes | Cook time: 11 to 18 minutes | Makes 12 pot stickers

1 cup shredded red cabbage	2 garlic cloves, minced
¼ cup chopped button mushrooms	2 teaspoons grated fresh ginger
¼ cup grated carrot	12 gyoza/pot sticker wrappers
2 tablespoons minced onion	2½ teaspoons olive oil, divided

1. In a baking pan, combine the red cabbage, mushrooms, carrot, onion, garlic, and ginger. Add 1 tablespoon of water. Place in the air fryer and air fry at 370°F (188°C) for 3 to 6 minutes, until the vegetables are crisp-tender. Drain and set aside. 2. Working one at a time, place the pot sticker wrappers on a work surface. Top each wrapper with a scant 1 tablespoon of the filling. Fold half of the wrapper over the other half to form a half circle. Dab one edge with water and press both edges together. 3. To another pan, add 1¼ teaspoons of olive oil. Put half of the pot stickers, seam-side up, in the pan. Air fry for 5 minutes, or until the bottoms are light golden brown. Add 1 tablespoon of water and return the pan to the air fryer. 4. Air fry for 4 to 6 minutes more, or until hot. Repeat with the remaining pot stickers, remaining 1¼ teaspoons of oil, and another tablespoon of water. Serve immediately.

Per Serving:
1 pot stickers: calories: 36 | fat: 1g | protein: 1g | carbs: 6g | fiber: 0g | sodium: 49mg

Black Olive and Lentil Pesto

Prep time: 10 minutes | Cook time: 20 minutes | Serves 10 to 12

¾ cup green lentils, rinsed	2 garlic cloves, minced
¼ teaspoon salt	2 tablespoons coarsely chopped fresh parsley
½ cup pitted Kalamata olives	3 tablespoons fresh lemon juice
2 tablespoons fresh Greek oregano	5 tablespoons olive oil

1. Place the lentils in a large saucepan and add cold water to cover by 1 inch. Bring the water to a boil; cover and simmer for 20 minutes, or until the lentils are soft but not disintegrating. Drain and let cool. 2. Shake the colander a few times to remove any excess water, then transfer the lentils to a blender or food processor. Add the salt, olives, oregano, garlic, and parsley. With the machine running, add the lemon juice, then the olive oil, and blend until smooth. 3. Serve with pita chips, pita bread, or as a dip for fresh vegetables.

Per Serving:
1 cup: calories: 70 | fat: 7g | protein: 1g | carbs: 2g | fiber: 1g | sodium: 99mg

Burrata Caprese Stack

Prep time: 5 minutes | Cook time: 0 minutes | Serves 4

1 large organic tomato, preferably heirloom	8 fresh basil leaves, thinly sliced
½ teaspoon salt	2 tablespoons extra-virgin olive oil
¼ teaspoon freshly ground black pepper	1 tablespoon red wine or balsamic vinegar
1 (4-ounce / 113-g) ball burrata cheese	

1. Slice the tomato into 4 thick slices, removing any tough center core and sprinkle with salt and pepper. Place the tomatoes, seasoned-side up, on a plate. 2. On a separate rimmed plate, slice the burrata into 4 thick slices and place one slice on top of each tomato slice. Top each with one-quarter of the basil and pour any reserved burrata cream from the rimmed plate over top. 3. Drizzle with olive oil and vinegar and serve with a fork and knife.

Per Serving:
calories: 109 | fat: 7g | protein: 9g | carbs: 3g | fiber: 1g | sodium: 504mg

Black-Eyed Pea "Caviar"

Prep time: 10 minutes | Cook time: 30 minutes | Makes 5 cups

1 cup dried black-eyed peas
4 cups water
1 pound (454 g) cooked corn kernels
½ medium red onion, peeled and diced
½ medium green bell pepper, seeded and diced
2 tablespoons minced pickled jalapeño pepper
1 medium tomato, diced
2 tablespoons chopped fresh cilantro
¼ cup red wine vinegar
2 tablespoons extra-virgin olive oil
1 teaspoon salt
½ teaspoon ground black pepper
½ teaspoon ground cumin

1. Add black-eyed peas and water to the Instant Pot®. Close lid, set steam release to Sealing, press the Manual button, and set time to 30 minutes. 2. When the timer beeps, let pressure release naturally, about 25 minutes, and open lid. Drain peas and transfer to a large mixing bowl. Add all remaining ingredients and stir until thoroughly combined. Cover and refrigerate for 2 hours before serving.

Per Serving:
½ cup: calories: 28 | fat: 1g | protein: 1g | carbs: 4 | fiber: 1g | sodium: 51mg

Apple Chips with Chocolate Tahini

Prep time: 10 minutes | Cook time: 0 minutes | Serves 2

2 tablespoons tahini
1 tablespoon maple syrup
1 tablespoon unsweetened cocoa powder
1 to 2 tablespoons warm water
(or more if needed)
2 medium apples
1 tablespoon roasted, salted sunflower seeds

1. In a small bowl, mix together the tahini, maple syrup, and cocoa powder. Add warm water, a little at a time, until thin enough to drizzle. Do not microwave it to thin it—it won't work. 2. Slice the apples crosswise into round slices, and then cut each piece in half to make a chip. 3. Lay the apple chips out on a plate and drizzle them with the chocolate tahini sauce. 4. Sprinkle sunflower seeds over the apple chips.

Per Serving:
calories: 261 | fat: 11g | protein: 5g | carbs: 43g | fiber: 8g | sodium: 21mg

Crunchy Orange-Thyme Chickpeas

Prep time: 5 minutes |Cook time: 20 minutes| Serves: 4

1 (15-ounce / 425-g) can chickpeas, drained and rinsed
2 teaspoons extra-virgin olive oil
¼ teaspoon dried thyme or ½ teaspoon chopped fresh thyme leaves
⅛ teaspoon kosher or sea salt
Zest of ½ orange (about ½ teaspoon)

1. Preheat the oven to 450°F (235°C). 2. Spread the chickpeas on a clean kitchen towel, and rub gently until dry. 3. Spread the chickpeas on a large, rimmed baking sheet. Drizzle with the oil, and sprinkle with the thyme and salt. Using a Microplane or citrus zester, zest about half of the orange over the chickpeas. Mix well using your hands. 4. Bake for 10 minutes, then open the oven door and, using an oven mitt, give the baking sheet a quick shake. (Do not remove the sheet from the oven.) Bake for 10 minutes more. Taste the chickpeas (carefully!). If they are golden but you think they could be a bit crunchier, bake for 3 minutes more before serving.

Per Serving:
calories: 167 | fat: 5g | protein: 7g | carbs: 24g | fiber: 7g | sodium: 303mg

Garlic-Lemon Hummus

Prep time: 15 minutes | Cook time: 0 minutes | Serves 6

1 (15-ounce / 425-g) can chickpeas, drained and rinsed
4 to 5 tablespoons tahini (sesame seed paste)
4 tablespoons extra-virgin olive oil, divided
2 lemons, juice
1 lemon, zested, divided
1 tablespoon minced garlic
Pinch salt

1. In a food processor, combine the chickpeas, tahini, 2 tablespoons of olive oil, lemon juice, half of the lemon zest, and garlic and blend for up to 1 minute. After 30 seconds of blending, stop and scrape the sides down with a spatula, before blending for another 30 seconds. At this point, you've made hummus! Taste and add salt as desired. Feel free to add 1 teaspoon of water at a time to help thin the hummus to a better consistency. 2. Scoop the hummus into a bowl, then drizzle with the remaining 2 tablespoons of olive oil and remaining lemon zest.

Per Serving:
calories: 216 | fat: 15g | protein: 5g | carbs: 17g | fiber: 5g | sodium: 12mg

Feta and Quinoa Stuffed Mushrooms

Prep time: 5 minutes | Cook time: 8 minutes | Serves 6

2 tablespoons finely diced red bell pepper
1 garlic clove, minced
¼ cup cooked quinoa
⅛ teaspoon salt
¼ teaspoon dried oregano
24 button mushrooms, stemmed
2 ounces (57 g) crumbled feta
3 tablespoons whole wheat bread crumbs
Olive oil cooking spray

1. Preheat the air fryer to 360°F (182°C). 2. In a small bowl, combine the bell pepper, garlic, quinoa, salt, and oregano. 3. Spoon the quinoa stuffing into the mushroom caps until just filled. 4. Add a small piece of feta to the top of each mushroom. 5. Sprinkle a pinch bread crumbs over the feta on each mushroom. 6. Spray the basket of the air fryer with olive oil cooking spray, then gently place the mushrooms into the basket, making sure that they don't touch each other. (Depending on the size of the air fryer, you may have to cook them in two batches.) 7. Place the basket into the air fryer and bake for 8 minutes. 8. Remove from the air fryer and serve.

Per Serving:
calories: 65 | fat: 3g | protein: 4g | carbs: 7g | fiber: 1g | sodium: 167mg

Grilled Halloumi with Watermelon, Cherry Tomatoes, Olives, and Herb Oil

Prep time: 5 minutes | Cook time: 5 minutes | Serves 4

½ cup coarsely chopped fresh basil
3 tablespoons coarsely chopped fresh mint leaves, plus thinly sliced mint for garnish
1 clove garlic, coarsely chopped
½ cup olive oil, plus more for brushing
½ teaspoon salt, plus a pinch
½ teaspoon freshly ground black pepper, plus a pinch
¾ pound (340 g) cherry tomatoes
8 ounces (227 g) Halloumi cheese, cut crosswise into 8 slices
2 cups thinly sliced watermelon, rind removed
¼ cup sliced, pitted Kalamata olives

1. Heat a grill or grill pan to high. 2. In a food processor or blender, combine the basil, chopped mint, and garlic and pulse to chop. While the machine is running, add the olive oil in a thin stream. Strain the oil through a fine-meshed sieve and discard the solids. Stir in ½ teaspoon of salt and ½ teaspoon of pepper. 3. Brush the grill rack with olive oil. Drizzle 2 tablespoons of the herb oil over the tomatoes and cheese and season them with pinches of salt and pepper. Place the tomatoes on the grill and cook, turning occasionally, until their skins become blistered and begin to burst, about 4 minutes. Place the cheese on the grill and cook until grill marks appear and the cheese begins to get melty, about 1 minute per side. 4. Arrange the watermelon on a serving platter. Arrange the grilled cheese and tomatoes on top of the melon. Drizzle the herb oil over the top and garnish with the olives and sliced mint. Serve immediately.

Per Serving:
calories: 535 | fat: 50g | protein: 14g | carbs: 12g | fiber: 2g | sodium: 663mg

Fig-Pecan Energy Bites

Prep time: 20 minutes |Cook time: 0 minutes| Serves: 6

¾ cup diced dried figs (6 to 8)
½ cup chopped pecans
¼ cup rolled oats (old-fashioned or quick oats)
2 tablespoons ground flaxseed
or wheat germ (flaxseed for gluten-free)
2 tablespoons powdered or regular peanut butter
2 tablespoons honey

1. In a medium bowl, mix together the figs, pecans, oats, flaxseed, and peanut butter. Drizzle with the honey, and mix everything together. A wooden spoon works well to press the figs and nuts into the honey and powdery ingredients. (If you're using regular peanut butter instead of powdered, the dough will be stickier to handle, so freeze the dough for 5 minutes before making the bites.) 2. Divide the dough evenly into four sections in the bowl. Dampen your hands with water—but don't get them too wet or the dough will stick to them. Using your hands, roll three bites out of each of the four sections of dough, making 12 total energy bites. 3. Enjoy immediately or chill in the freezer for 5 minutes to firm up the bites before serving. The bites can be stored in a sealed container in the refrigerator for up to 1 week.

Per Serving:
calories: 196 | fat: 10g | protein: 4g | carbs: 26g | fiber: 4g | sodium: 13mg

Homemade Sweet Potato Chips

Prep time: 5 minutes | Cook time: 15 minutes | Serves 2

1 large sweet potato, sliced thin
⅛ teaspoon salt
2 tablespoons olive oil

1. Preheat the air fryer to 380°F(193°C). 2. In a small bowl, toss the sweet potatoes, salt, and olive oil together until the potatoes are well coated. 3. Put the sweet potato slices into the air fryer and spread them out in a single layer. 4. Fry for 10 minutes. Stir, then air fry for 3 to 5 minutes more, or until the chips reach the preferred level of crispiness.

Per Serving:
calories: 175 | fat: 14g | protein: 1g | carbs: 13g | fiber: 2g | sodium: 191mg

Baked Italian Spinach and Ricotta Balls

Prep time: 15 minutes | Cook time: 2 minutes | Serves 4

1½ tablespoons extra virgin olive oil
1 garlic clove
9 ounces (255 g) fresh baby leaf spinach, washed
3 spring onions (white parts only), thinly sliced
9 ounces (255 g) ricotta, drained
1¾ ounces (50 g) grated Parmesan cheese
2 tablespoons chopped fresh basil
¾ teaspoon salt, divided
¼ teaspoon plus a pinch of freshly ground black pepper, divided
4½ tablespoons plus ⅓ cup unseasoned breadcrumbs, divided
1 egg

1. Preheat the oven to 400°F (205°C). Line a large baking pan with parchment paper. 2. Add the olive oil and garlic clove to a large pan over medium heat. When the oil begins to shimmer, add the spinach and sauté, tossing continuously, until the spinach starts to wilt, then add the spring onions. Continue tossing and sautéing until most of the liquid has evaporated, about 6 minutes, then transfer the spinach and onion mixture to a colander to drain and cool for 10 minutes. 3. When the spinach mixture has cooled, discard the garlic clove and squeeze the spinach to remove as much of the liquid as possible. Transfer the spinach mixture to a cutting board and finely chop. 4. Combine the ricotta, Parmesan, basil, ½ teaspoon of the salt, and ¼ teaspoon of the black pepper in a large bowl. Use a fork to mash the ingredients together, then add the spinach and continue mixing until the ingredients are combined. Add 4½ tablespoons of the breadcrumbs and mix until all ingredients are well combined. 5. In a small bowl, whisk the egg with the remaining ¼ teaspoon salt and a pinch of the black pepper. Place the remaining ⅓ cup of breadcrumbs on a small plate. Scoop out 1 tablespoon of the spinach mixture and roll it into a smooth ball, then dip it in the egg mixture and then roll it in the breadcrumbs. Place the ball on the prepared baking pan and continue the process with the remaining spinach mixture. 6. Bake for 16–20 minutes or until the balls turn a light golden brown. Remove the balls from the oven and serve promptly. Store covered in the refrigerator for up to 1 day. (Reheat before serving.)

Per Serving:
calories: 311 | fat: 19g | protein: 18g | carbs: 18g | fiber: 3g | sodium: 684mg

Eggplant Fries

Prep time: 10 minutes | Cook time: 7 to 8 minutes per batch | Serves 4

1 medium eggplant	1 cup crushed panko bread crumbs
1 teaspoon ground coriander	1 large egg
1 teaspoon cumin	2 tablespoons water
1 teaspoon garlic powder	Oil for misting or cooking spray
½ teaspoon salt	

1. Peel and cut the eggplant into fat fries, ⅜- to ½-inch thick. 2. Preheat the air fryer to 390°F (199°C). 3. In a small cup, mix together the coriander, cumin, garlic, and salt. 4. Combine 1 teaspoon of the seasoning mix and panko crumbs in a shallow dish. 5. Place eggplant fries in a large bowl, sprinkle with remaining seasoning, and stir well to combine. 6. Beat eggs and water together and pour over eggplant fries. Stir to coat. 7. Remove eggplant from egg wash, shaking off excess, and roll in panko crumbs. 8. Spray with oil. 9. Place half of the fries in air fryer basket. You should have only a single layer, but it's fine if they overlap a little. 10. Cook for 5 minutes. Shake basket, mist lightly with oil, and cook 2 to 3 minutes longer, until browned and crispy. 11. Repeat step 10 to cook remaining eggplant.

Per Serving:
calories: 163 | fat: 3g | protein: 7g | carbs: 28g | fiber: 6g | sodium: 510mg

Baked Spanakopita Dip

Prep time: 10 minutes | Cook time: 15 minutes | Serves 2

Olive oil cooking spray	divided
3 tablespoons olive oil, divided	Zest of 1 lemon
2 tablespoons minced white onion	¼ teaspoon ground nutmeg
2 garlic cloves, minced	1 teaspoon dried dill
4 cups fresh spinach	½ teaspoon salt
4 ounces (113 g) cream cheese, softened	Pita chips, carrot sticks, or sliced bread for serving (optional)
4 ounces (113 g) feta cheese,	

1. Preheat the air fryer to 360°F(182°C). Coat the inside of a 6-inch ramekin or baking dish with olive oil cooking spray. 2. In a large skillet over medium heat, heat 1 tablespoon of the olive oil. Add the onion, then cook for 1 minute. 3. Add in the garlic and cook, stirring for 1 minute more. 4. Reduce the heat to low and mix in the spinach and water. Let this cook for 2 to 3 minutes, or until the spinach has wilted. Remove the skillet from the heat. 5. In a medium bowl, combine the cream cheese, 2 ounces (57 g) of the feta, and the remaining 2 tablespoons of olive oil, along with the lemon zest, nutmeg, dill, and salt. Mix until just combined. 6. Add the vegetables to the cheese base and stir until combined. 7. Pour the dip mixture into the prepared ramekin and top with the remaining 2 ounces (57 g) of feta cheese. 8. Place the dip into the air fryer basket and cook for 10 minutes, or until heated through and bubbling. 9. Serve with pita chips, carrot sticks, or sliced bread.

Per Serving:
calories: 376 | fat: 32g | protein: 14g | carbs: 11g | fiber: 2g | sodium: 737mg

Sweet Potato Fries

Prep time: 15 minutes | Cook time: 40 minutes | Serves 4

4 large sweet potatoes, peeled and cut into finger-like strips	½ teaspoon salt
2 tablespoons extra-virgin olive oil	½ teaspoon freshly ground black pepper

1. Preheat the oven to 350°F(180°C). Line a baking sheet with aluminum foil. Toss the potatoes in a large bowl with the olive oil, salt, and pepper. 2. Arrange the potatoes in a single layer on the baking sheet and bake until brown at the edges, about 40 minutes. Serve piping hot.

Per Serving:
calories: 171 | fat: 7g | protein: 2g | carbs: 26g | fiber: 4g | sodium: 362mg

Herbed Labneh Vegetable Parfaits

Prep time: 15 minutes | Cook time: 0 minutes | Serves 2

For the Labneh:	Pinch lemon zest
8 ounces (227 g) plain Greek yogurt (full-fat works best)	For the Parfaits:
Generous pinch salt	½ cup peeled, chopped cucumber
1 teaspoon za'atar seasoning	½ cup grated carrots
1 teaspoon freshly squeezed lemon juice	½ cup cherry tomatoes, halved

Make the Labneh: 1. Line a strainer with cheesecloth and place it over a bowl. 2. Stir together the Greek yogurt and salt and place in the cheesecloth. Wrap it up and let it sit for 24 hours in the refrigerator. 3. When ready, unwrap the labneh and place it into a clean bowl. Stir in the za'atar, lemon juice, and lemon zest. Make the Parfaits: 1. Divide the cucumber between two clear glasses. 2. Top each portion of cucumber with about 3 tablespoons of labneh. 3. Divide the carrots between the glasses. 4. Top with another 3 tablespoons of the labneh. 5. Top parfaits with the cherry tomatoes.

Per Serving:
calories: 143 | fat: 7g | protein: 5g | carbs: 16g | fiber: 2g | sodium: 187mg

Citrus-Kissed Melon

Prep time: 5 minutes | Cook time: 0 minutes | Serves 4

2 cups cubed melon, such as Crenshaw, Sharlyn, or honeydew	juice
	¼ cup freshly squeezed lime juice
2 cups cubed cantaloupe	1 tablespoon orange zest
½ cup freshly squeezed orange	

1. In a large bowl, combine the melon cubes. In a small bowl, whisk together the orange juice, lime juice, and orange zest and pour over the fruit. 2. Cover and refrigerate for at least 4 hours, stirring occasionally. Serve chilled.

Per Serving:
calories: 80 | fat: 0g | protein: 2g | carbs: 20g | fiber: 2g | sodium: 30mg

Smoky Baba Ghanoush

Prep time: 50 minutes | Cook time: 40 minutes | Serves 6

2 large eggplants, washed
¼ cup lemon juice
1 teaspoon garlic, minced
1 teaspoon salt
½ cup tahini paste
3 tablespoons extra-virgin olive oil

1. Grill the whole eggplants over a low flame using a gas stovetop or grill. Rotate the eggplant every 5 minutes to make sure that all sides are cooked evenly. Continue to do this for 40 minutes. 2. Remove the eggplants from the stove or grill and put them onto a plate or into a bowl; cover with plastic wrap. Let sit for 5 to 10 minutes. 3. Using your fingers, peel away and discard the charred skin of the eggplants. Cut off the stem. 4. Put the eggplants into a food processor fitted with a chopping blade. Add the lemon juice, garlic, salt, and tahini paste, and pulse the mixture 5 to 7 times. 5. Pour the eggplant mixture onto a serving plate. Drizzle with the olive oil. Serve chilled or at room temperature.

Per Serving:
calories: 230 | fat: 18g | protein: 5g | carbs: 16g | fiber: 7g | sodium: 416mg

Salmon Niçoise Salad with Dijon-Chive Dressing

Prep time: 10 minutes | Cook time: 20 minutes | Serves 4

1 pound (454 g) baby or fingerling potatoes
½ pound (227 g) green beans
6 tablespoons olive oil
4 (4-ounce / 113-g) salmon fillets
¼ teaspoon freshly ground black pepper
2 teaspoons Dijon mustard
3 tablespoons red wine vinegar
1 tablespoon, plus 1 teaspoon finely chopped fresh chives
1 head romaine lettuce, sliced cross-wise
2 hard-boiled eggs, quartered
¼ cup Niçoise or other small black olives
1 cup cherry tomatoes, quartered

1. Put potatoes in a large saucepan and add cold water to cover. Bring the water to a boil, then reduce the heat to maintain a simmer and cook for 12 to 15 minutes, until fork-tender. Drain and set aside until cool enough to handle, then cut into cubes. Set aside. 2. Meanwhile, bring a medium saucepan of water to a boil. Add the green beans and cook for 3 minutes. Drain and rinse with cold water to stop the cooking. Set aside. 3. In a large skillet, heat 1 tablespoon of the olive oil over medium-high heat. Season the salmon with pepper. Add the salmon to the pan and cook for 4 to 5 minutes on each side. Transfer to a platter; keep warm. 4. In a small bowl, whisk together the mustard, vinegar, 1 tablespoon of chives, and remaining 5 tablespoons olive oil. 5. Divide the lettuce evenly among four plates. Add 1 salmon fillet to each plate. Divide the potatoes, green beans, eggs, olives, and tomatoes among the plates and drizzle with the dressing. 6.Sprinkle with the remaining 1 teaspoon chives and serve.

Per Serving:
1 cup: calories: 398 | fat: 25g | protein: 15g | carbs: 30g | fiber: 8g | sodium: 173mg

Garlic-Parmesan Croutons

Prep time: 3 minutes | Cook time: 12 minutes | Serves 4

Oil, for spraying
4 cups cubed French bread
1 tablespoon grated Parmesan cheese
3 tablespoons olive oil
1 tablespoon granulated garlic
½ teaspoon unsalted salt

1. Line the air fryer basket with parchment and spray lightly with oil. 2. In a large bowl, mix together the bread, Parmesan cheese, olive oil, garlic, and salt, tossing with your hands to evenly distribute the seasonings. Transfer the coated bread cubes to the prepared basket. 3. Air fry at 350°F (177°C) for 10 to 12 minutes, stirring once after 5 minutes, or until crisp and golden brown.

Per Serving:
calories: 220 | fat: 12g | protein: 5g | carbs: 23g | fiber: 1g | sodium: 285mg

Air Fryer Popcorn with Garlic Salt

Prep time: 3 minutes | Cook time: 10 minutes | Serves 2

2 tablespoons olive oil
¼ cup popcorn kernels
1 teaspoon garlic salt

1. Preheat the air fryer to 380°F(193°C). 2. Tear a square of aluminum foil the size of the bottom of the air fryer and place into the air fryer. 3. Drizzle olive oil over the top of the foil, and then pour in the popcorn kernels. 4. Roast for 8 to 10 minutes, or until the popcorn stops popping. 5. Transfer the popcorn to a large bowl and sprinkle with garlic salt before serving.

Per Serving:
calories: 134 | fat: 14g | protein: 0g | carbs: 3g | fiber: 1g | sodium: 620mg

Greek Yogurt Deviled Eggs

Prep time: 15 minutes | Cook time: 15 minutes | Serves 4

4 eggs
¼ cup nonfat plain Greek yogurt
1 teaspoon chopped fresh dill
⅛ teaspoon salt
⅛ teaspoon paprika
⅛ teaspoon garlic powder
Chopped fresh parsley, for garnish

1. Preheat the air fryer to 260°F(127°C). 2. Place the eggs in a single layer in the air fryer basket and cook for 15 minutes. 3. Quickly remove the eggs from the air fryer and place them into a cold water bath. Let the eggs cool in the water for 10 minutes before removing and peeling them. 4. After peeling the eggs, cut them in half. 5. Spoon the yolk into a small bowl. Add the yogurt, dill, salt, paprika, and garlic powder and mix until smooth. 6. Spoon or pipe the yolk mixture into the halved egg whites. Serve with a sprinkle of fresh parsley on top.

Per Serving:
calories: 74 | fat: 4g | protein: 7g | carbs: 2g | fiber: 0g | sodium: 152mg

Sea Salt Potato Chips

Prep time: 30 minutes | Cook time: 27 minutes | Serves 4

Oil, for spraying
4 medium yellow potatoes
1 tablespoon oil
⅛ to ¼ teaspoon fine sea salt

1. Line the air fryer basket with parchment and spray lightly with oil. 2. Using a mandoline or a very sharp knife, cut the potatoes into very thin slices. 3. Place the slices in a bowl of cold water and let soak for about 20 minutes. 4. Drain the potatoes, transfer them to a plate lined with paper towels, and pat dry. 5. Drizzle the oil over the potatoes, sprinkle with the salt, and toss to combine. Transfer to the prepared basket. 6. Air fry at 200°F (93°C) for 20 minutes. Toss the chips, increase the heat to 400°F (204°C), and cook for another 5 to 7 minutes, until crispy.

Per Serving:
calories: 194 | fat: 4g | protein: 4g | carbs: 37g | fiber: 5g | sodium: 90mg

Stuffed Fried Mushrooms

Prep time: 20 minutes | Cook time: 10 to 11 minutes | Serves 10

½ cup panko bread crumbs
½ teaspoon freshly ground black pepper
½ teaspoon onion powder
½ teaspoon cayenne pepper
1 (8-ounce / 227-g) package cream cheese, at room temperature
20 cremini or button mushrooms, stemmed
1 to 2 tablespoons oil

1. In a medium bowl, whisk the bread crumbs, black pepper, onion powder, and cayenne until blended. 2. Add the cream cheese and mix until well blended. Fill each mushroom top with 1 teaspoon of the cream cheese mixture 3. Preheat the air fryer to 360°F (182°C). Line the air fryer basket with a piece of parchment paper. 4. Place the mushrooms on the parchment and spritz with oil. 5. Cook for 5 minutes. Shake the basket and cook for 5 to 6 minutes more until the filling is firm and the mushrooms are soft.

Per Serving:
calories: 120 | fat: 9g | protein: 3g | carbs: 7g | fiber: 1g | sodium: 125mg

Bravas-Style Potatoes

Prep time: 15 minutes | Cook time: 50 minutes | Serves 8

4 large russet potatoes (about 2½ pounds / 1.1 kg), scrubbed and cut into 1' cubes
1 teaspoon kosher salt, divided
½ teaspoon ground black pepper
¼ teaspoon red-pepper flakes
½ small yellow onion, chopped
1 large tomato, chopped
1 tablespoon sherry vinegar
1 teaspoon hot paprika
1 tablespoon chopped fresh flat-leaf parsley Hot sauce (optional)

1. Preheat the oven to 450°F (235°C). Bring a large pot of well-salted water to a boil. 2. Boil the potatoes until just barely tender, 5 to 8 minutes. Drain and transfer the potatoes to a large rimmed baking sheet. Add 1 tablespoon of the oil, ½ teaspoon of the salt, the black pepper, and pepper flakes. With 2 large spoons, toss very well to coat the potatoes in the oil. Spread the potatoes out on the baking sheet. Roast until the bottoms are starting to brown and crisp, 20 minutes. Carefully flip the potatoes and roast until the other side is golden and crisp, 15 to 20 minutes. 3. Meanwhile, in a small skillet over medium heat, warm the remaining 1 teaspoon oil. Cook the onion until softened, 3 to 4 minutes. Add the tomato and cook until it's broken down and saucy, 5 minutes. Stir in the vinegar, paprika, and the remaining ½ teaspoon salt. Cook for 30 seconds, remove from the heat, and cover to keep warm. 4. Transfer the potatoes to a large serving bowl. Drizzle the tomato mixture over the potatoes. Sprinkle with the parsley. Serve with hot sauce, if using.

Per Serving:
calories: 173 | fat: 2g | protein: 4g | carbs: 35g | fiber: 3g | sodium: 251mg

Roasted Rosemary Olives

Prep time: 5 minutes | Cook time: 25 minutes | Serves 4

1 cup mixed variety olives, pitted and rinsed
2 tablespoons lemon juice
1 tablespoon extra-virgin olive oil
6 garlic cloves, peeled
4 rosemary sprigs

1. Preheat the oven to 400°F (205°C). Line the baking sheet with parchment paper or foil. 2. Combine the olives, lemon juice, olive oil, and garlic in a medium bowl and mix together. Spread in a single layer on the prepared baking sheet. Sprinkle on the rosemary. Roast for 25 minutes, tossing halfway through. 3. Remove the rosemary leaves from the stem and place in a serving bowl. Add the olives and mix before serving.

Per Serving:
calories: 100 | fat: 9g | protein: 0g | carbs: 4g | fiber: 0g | sodium: 260mg

Marinated Olives and Mushrooms

Prep time: 10 minutes | Cook time: 0 minutes | Serves 8

1 pound (454 g) white button mushrooms
1 pound (454 g) mixed, high-quality olives
2 tablespoons fresh thyme leaves
1 tablespoon white wine vinegar
½ tablespoon crushed fennel seeds
Pinch chili flakes
Olive oil, to cover
Sea salt and freshly ground pepper, to taste

1. Clean and rinse mushrooms under cold water and pat dry. 2. Combine all ingredients in a glass jar or other airtight container. Cover with olive oil and season with sea salt and freshly ground pepper. 3. Shake to distribute the ingredients. Allow to marinate for at least 1 hour. Serve at room temperature.

Per Serving:
calories: 61 | fat: 4g | protein: 2g | carbs: 5g | fiber: 2g | sodium: 420mg

Quick Garlic Mushrooms

Prep time: 10 minutes | Cook time: 10 minutes | Serves 4 to 6

2 pounds (907 g) cremini mushrooms, cleaned
3 tablespoons unsalted butter
2 tablespoons garlic, minced
½ teaspoon salt
½ teaspoon freshly ground black pepper

1. Cut each mushroom in half, stem to top, and put them into a bowl. 2. Preheat a large sauté pan or skillet over medium heat. 3. Cook the butter and garlic in the pan for 2 minutes, stirring occasionally. 4. Add the mushrooms and salt to the pan and toss together with the garlic butter mixture. Cook for 7 to 8 minutes, stirring every 2 minutes. 5. Remove the mushrooms from the pan and pour into a serving dish. Top with black pepper.

Per Serving:
calories: 183 | fat: 9g | protein: 9g | carbs: 10g | fiber: 3g | sodium: 334mg

Lemon-Pepper Chicken Drumsticks

Prep time: 30 minutes | Cook time: 30 minutes | Serves 2

2 teaspoons freshly ground coarse black pepper
1 teaspoon baking powder
½ teaspoon garlic powder
4 chicken drumsticks (4 ounces / 113 g each)
Kosher salt, to taste
1 lemon

1. In a small bowl, stir together the pepper, baking powder, and garlic powder. Place the drumsticks on a plate and sprinkle evenly with the baking powder mixture, turning the drumsticks so they're well coated. Let the drumsticks stand in the refrigerator for at least 1 hour or up to overnight. 2. Sprinkle the drumsticks with salt, then transfer them to the air fryer, standing them bone-end up and leaning against the wall of the air fryer basket. Air fry at 375°F (191°C) until cooked through and crisp on the outside, about 30 minutes. 3. Transfer the drumsticks to a serving platter and finely grate the zest of the lemon over them while they're hot. Cut the lemon into wedges and serve with the warm drumsticks.

Per Serving:
calories: 438 | fat: 24g | protein: 48g | carbs: 6g | fiber: 2g | sodium: 279mg

Crispy Spiced Chickpeas

Prep time: 5 minutes | Cook time: 25 minutes | Serves 6

3 cans (15 ounces / 425 g each) chickpeas, drained and rinsed
1 cup olive oil
1 teaspoon paprika
½ teaspoon ground cumin
½ teaspoon kosher salt
¼ teaspoon ground cinnamon
¼ teaspoon ground black pepper

1. Spread the chickpeas on paper towels and pat dry. 2. In a large saucepan over medium-high heat, warm the oil until shimmering. Add 1 chickpea; if it sizzles right away, the oil is hot enough to proceed. 3. Add enough chickpeas to form a single layer in the saucepan. Cook, occasionally gently shaking the saucepan until golden brown, about 8 minutes. With a slotted spoon, transfer to a paper towel–lined plate to drain. Repeat with the remaining chickpeas until all the chickpeas are fried. Transfer to a large bowl. 4. In a small bowl, combine the paprika, cumin, salt, cinnamon, and pepper. Sprinkle all over the fried chickpeas and toss to coat. The chickpeas will crisp as they cool.

Per Serving:
calories: 175 | fat: 9g | protein: 6g | carbs: 20g | fiber: 5g | sodium: 509mg

Spicy Roasted Potatoes

Prep time: 20 minutes | Cook time: 25 minutes | Serves 5

1½ pounds (680 g) red potatoes or gold potatoes
3 tablespoons garlic, minced
1½ teaspoons salt
¼ cup extra-virgin olive oil
½ cup fresh cilantro, chopped
½ teaspoon freshly ground black pepper
¼ teaspoon cayenne pepper
3 tablespoons lemon juice

1. Preheat the oven to 450°F (235°C). 2. Scrub the potatoes and pat dry. 3. Cut the potatoes into ½-inch pieces and put them into a bowl. 4. Add the garlic, salt, and olive oil and toss everything together to evenly coat. 5. Pour the potato mixture onto a baking sheet, spread the potatoes out evenly, and put them into the oven, roasting for 25 minutes. Halfway through roasting, turn the potatoes with a spatula; continue roasting for the remainder of time until the potato edges start to brown. 6. Remove the potatoes from the oven and let them cool on the baking sheet for 5 minutes. 7. Using a spatula, remove the potatoes from the pan and put them into a bowl. 8. Add the cilantro, black pepper, cayenne, and lemon juice to the potatoes and toss until well mixed. 9. Serve warm.

Per Serving:
calories: 203 | fat: 11g | protein: 3g | carbs: 24g | fiber: 3g | sodium: 728mg

Dark Chocolate and Cranberry Granola Bars

Prep time: 5 minutes | Cook time: 15 minutes | Serves 6

2 cups certified gluten-free quick oats
2 tablespoons sugar-free dark chocolate chunks
2 tablespoons unsweetened dried cranberries
3 tablespoons unsweetened shredded coconut
½ cup raw honey
1 teaspoon ground cinnamon
⅛ teaspoon salt
2 tablespoons olive oil

1. Preheat the air fryer to 360°F (182°C). Line an 8-by-8-inch baking dish with parchment paper that comes up the side so you can lift it out after cooking. 2. In a large bowl, mix together all of the ingredients until well combined. 3. Press the oat mixture into the pan in an even layer. 4. Place the pan into the air fryer basket and bake for 15 minutes. 5. Remove the pan from the air fryer, and lift the granola cake out of the pan using the edges of the parchment paper. 6. Allow to cool for 5 minutes before slicing into 6 equal bars. 7. Serve immediately, or wrap in plastic wrap and store at room temperature for up to 1 week.

Per Serving:
calories: 272 | fat: 10g | protein: 5g | carbs: 44g | fiber: 7g | sodium: 56mg

Goat Cheese–Mackerel Pâté

Prep time: 10 minutes | Cook time: 0 minutes | Serves 4

4 ounces (113 g) olive oil-packed wild-caught mackerel	1 tablespoon extra-virgin olive oil
2 ounces (57 g) goat cheese	2 teaspoons chopped capers
Zest and juice of 1 lemon	1 to 2 teaspoons fresh horseradish (optional)
2 tablespoons chopped fresh parsley	Crackers, cucumber rounds, endive spears, or celery, for serving (optional)
2 tablespoons chopped fresh arugula	

1. In a food processor, blender, or large bowl with immersion blender, combine the mackerel, goat cheese, lemon zest and juice, parsley, arugula, olive oil, capers, and horseradish (if using). Process or blend until smooth and creamy. 2. Serve with crackers, cucumber rounds, endive spears, or celery. 3. Store covered in the refrigerator for up to 1 week.

Per Serving:
calories: 142 | fat: 10g | protein: 11g | carbs: 1g | fiber: 0g | sodium: 203mg

Mini Lettuce Wraps

Prep time: 10 minutes | Cook time: 0 minutes | Makes about 1 dozen wraps

1 tomato, diced	1 tablespoon olive oil
1 cucumber, diced	Sea salt and freshly ground pepper, to taste
1 red onion, sliced	12 small, intact iceberg lettuce leaves
1 ounce (28 g) low-fat feta cheese, crumbled	
Juice of 1 lemon	

1. Combine the tomato, cucumber, onion, and feta in a bowl with the lemon juice and olive oil. 2. Season with sea salt and freshly ground pepper. 3. Without tearing the leaves, gently fill each leaf with a tablespoon of the veggie mixture. 4. Roll them as tightly as you can, and lay them seam-side-down on a serving platter.

Per Serving:
1 wrap: calories: 26 | fat: 2g | protein: 1g | carbs: 2g | fiber: 1g | sodium: 20mg

Whole Wheat Pitas

Prep time: 5 minutes | Cook time: 30 minutes | Makes 8 pitas

2 cups whole wheat flour	110°F)
1¼ cups all-purpose flour	1 (¼-ounce / 7-g) package active dry yeast (2½ teaspoons)
1¼ teaspoons table salt	1 teaspoon olive oil
1¼ cup warm water (105°–	

1. In the bowl of an electric stand mixer (or a large bowl), whisk together the flours and salt. In a small bowl or glass measuring cup, whisk together the water and yeast until the yeast is dissolved. Let sit until foamy, about 5 minutes. Add the yeast mixture to the flour mixture. Fit the mixer with the dough hook and mix on low (or stir) until it forms a shaggy dough. 2. Increase the speed to medium and knead until the dough is smooth and elastic, 2 to 3 minutes. If kneading by hand, turn the dough out onto a lightly floured work surface and knead about 10 minutes. 3. Form the dough into a ball and return it to the bowl. Pour in the oil, turning the dough to coat. Cover the bowl with a kitchen towel and let the dough rise until doubled in size, about 1 hour. 4. Preheat the oven to 475°F(245°C). Place a baking sheet on the lowest rack of the oven. 5. When the dough has risen, take it out of the bowl and give it a few gentle kneads. Divide the dough into 8 equal portions and shape into balls. Place on a lightly floured surface and cover with the kitchen towel. 6. Roll out each dough ball to form a 6" circle. Place on the heated baking sheet. Bake until puffed up and beginning to turn color, 6 to 7 minutes. Remove with a metal spatula or tongs and place in a bread basket or on a serving platter. Repeat with the remaining dough balls. 7. To make a pocket in the pita, allow it to cool. Slice off ¼ of the pita from 1 edge, and then carefully insert the knife into the pita to cut the pocket. Gently pull the sides apart to make the pocket larger.

Per Serving:
calories: 181 | fat: 2g | protein: 6g | carbs: 37g | fiber: 4g | sodium: 366mg

Pesto Cucumber Boats

Prep time: 10 minutes | Cook time: 0 minutes | Serves 4 to 6

3 medium cucumbers	¼ cup walnut pieces
¼ teaspoon salt	¼ cup grated Parmesan cheese
1 packed cup fresh basil leaves	¼ cup extra-virgin olive oil
1 garlic clove, minced	½ teaspoon paprika

1. Cut each cucumber in half lengthwise and again in half crosswise to make 4 stocky pieces. Use a spoon to remove the seeds and hollow out a shallow trough in each piece. Lightly salt each piece and set aside on a platter. 2. In a blender or food processor, combine the basil, garlic, walnuts, Parmesan cheese, and olive oil and blend until smooth. 3. Use a spoon to spread pesto into each cucumber "boat" and sprinkle each with paprika. Serve.

Per Serving:
calories: 143 | fat: 14g | protein: 3g | carbs: 4g | fiber: 1g | sodium: 175mg

Crispy Chili Chickpeas

Prep time: 5 minutes | Cook time: 15 minutes | Serves 4

1 (15-ounce / 425-g) can cooked chickpeas, drained and rinsed	¼ teaspoon salt
	⅛ teaspoon chili powder
	⅛ teaspoon garlic powder
1 tablespoon olive oil	⅛ teaspoon paprika

1. Preheat the air fryer to 380°F(193°C). 2. In a medium bowl, toss all of the ingredients together until the chickpeas are well coated. 3. Pour the chickpeas into the air fryer and spread them out in a single layer. 4. Roast for 15 minutes, stirring once halfway through the cook time.

Per Serving:
calories: 177 | fat: 6g | protein: 8g | carbs: 24g | fiber: 7g | sodium: 374mg

Red Pepper Tapenade

Prep time: 5 minutes | Cook time: 5 minutes | Serves 4

1 large red bell pepper	and roughly chopped
2 tablespoons plus 1 teaspoon olive oil, divided	1 garlic clove, minced
½ cup Kalamata olives, pitted	½ teaspoon dried oregano
	1 tablespoon lemon juice

1. Preheat the air fryer to 380°F(193°C). 2. Brush the outside of a whole red pepper with 1 teaspoon olive oil and place it inside the air fryer basket. Roast for 5 minutes. 3. Meanwhile, in a medium bowl combine the remaining 2 tablespoons of olive oil with the olives, garlic, oregano, and lemon juice. 4. Remove the red pepper from the air fryer, then gently slice off the stem and remove the seeds. Roughly chop the roasted pepper into small pieces. 5. Add the red pepper to the olive mixture and stir all together until combined. 6. Serve with pita chips, crackers, or crusty bread.

Per Serving:
calories: 94 | fat: 9g | protein: 1g | carbs: 4g | fiber: 2g | sodium: 125mg

Cheese-Stuffed Dates

Prep time: 10 minutes | Cook time: 10 minutes | Serves 4

2 ounces (57 g) low-fat cream cheese, at room temperature	¼ teaspoon kosher salt
2 tablespoons sweet pickle relish	⅛ teaspoon ground black pepper
1 tablespoon low-fat plain Greek yogurt	Dash of hot sauce
1 teaspoon finely chopped fresh chives	2 tablespoons pistachios, chopped
	8 Medjool dates, pitted and halved

1. In a small bowl, stir together the cream cheese, relish, yogurt, chives, salt, pepper, and hot sauce. 2. Put the pistachios on a clean plate. Put the cream cheese mixture into a resealable plastic bag, and snip off 1 corner of the bag. Pipe the cream cheese mixture into the date halves and press the tops into the pistachios to coat.

Per Serving:
calories: 196 | fat: 4g | protein: 3g | carbs: 41g | fiber: 4g | sodium: 294mg

Tuna Croquettes

Prep time: 40 minutes | Cook time: 25 minutes | Makes 36 croquettes

6 tablespoons extra-virgin olive oil, plus 1 to 2 cups	2 teaspoons minced capers
5 tablespoons almond flour, plus 1 cup, divided	½ teaspoon dried dill
1¼ cups heavy cream	¼ teaspoon freshly ground black pepper
1 (4-ounce / 113-g) can olive oil-packed yellowfin tuna	2 large eggs
1 tablespoon chopped red onion	1 cup panko breadcrumbs (or a gluten-free version)

1. In a large skillet, heat 6 tablespoons olive oil over medium-low heat. Add 5 tablespoons almond flour and cook, stirring constantly, until a smooth paste forms and the flour browns slightly, 2 to 3 minutes. 2. Increase the heat to medium-high and gradually add the heavy cream, whisking constantly until completely smooth and thickened, another 4 to 5 minutes. 3. Remove from the heat and stir in the tuna, red onion, capers, dill, and pepper. 4. Transfer the mixture to an 8-inch square baking dish that is well coated with olive oil and allow to cool to room temperature. Cover and refrigerate until chilled, at least 4 hours or up to overnight. 5. To form the croquettes, set out three bowls. In one, beat together the eggs. In another, add the remaining almond flour. In the third, add the panko. Line a baking sheet with parchment paper. 6. Using a spoon, place about a tablespoon of cold prepared dough into the flour mixture and roll to coat. Shake off excess and, using your hands, roll into an oval. 7. Dip the croquette into the beaten egg, then lightly coat in panko. Set on lined baking sheet and repeat with the remaining dough. 8. In a small saucepan, heat the remaining 1 to 2 cups of olive oil, so that the oil is about 1 inch deep, over medium-high heat. The smaller the pan, the less oil you will need, but you will need more for each batch. 9. Test if the oil is ready by throwing a pinch of panko into pot. If it sizzles, the oil is ready for frying. If it sinks, it's not quite ready. Once the oil is heated, fry the croquettes 3 or 4 at a time, depending on the size of your pan, removing with a slotted spoon when golden brown. You will need to adjust the temperature of the oil occasionally to prevent burning. If the croquettes get dark brown very quickly, lower the temperature.

Per Serving:
2 croquettes: calories: 271 | fat: 26g | protein: 5g | carbs: 6g | fiber: 1g | sodium: 89mg

Buffalo Bites

Prep time: 15 minutes | Cook time: 11 to 12 minutes per batch | Makes 16 meatballs

1½ cups cooked jasmine or sushi rice	sauce
¼ teaspoon salt	2 ounces (57 g) Gruyère cheese, cut into 16 cubes
1 pound (454 g) ground chicken	1 tablespoon maple syrup
8 tablespoons buffalo wing	

1. Mix 4 tablespoons buffalo wing sauce into all the ground chicken. 2. Shape chicken into a log and divide into 16 equal portions. 3. With slightly damp hands, mold each chicken portion around a cube of cheese and shape into a firm ball. When you have shaped 8 meatballs, place them in air fryer basket. 4. Air fry at 390°F (199°C) for approximately 5 minutes. Shake basket, reduce temperature to 360°F (182°C), and cook for 5 to 6 minutes longer. 5. While the first batch is cooking, shape remaining chicken and cheese into 8 more meatballs. 6. Repeat step 4 to cook second batch of meatballs. 7. In a medium bowl, mix the remaining 4 tablespoons of buffalo wing sauce with the maple syrup. Add all the cooked meatballs and toss to coat. 8. Place meatballs back into air fryer basket and air fry at 390°F (199°C) for 2 to 3 minutes to set the glaze. Skewer each with a toothpick and serve.

Per Serving:
calories: 85 | fat: 4g | protein: 7g | carbs: 6g | fiber: 0g | sodium: 236mg

Citrus-Marinated Olives

Prep time: 10 minutes | Cook time: 0 minutes | Makes 2 cups

2 cups mixed green olives with pits
¼ cup red wine vinegar
¼ cup extra-virgin olive oil
4 garlic cloves, finely minced
Zest and juice of 2 clementines or 1 large orange
1 teaspoon red pepper flakes
2 bay leaves
½ teaspoon ground cumin
½ teaspoon ground allspice

1. In a large glass bowl or jar, combine the olives, vinegar, oil, garlic, orange zest and juice, red pepper flakes, bay leaves, cumin, and allspice and mix well. Cover and refrigerate for at least 4 hours or up to a week to allow the olives to marinate, tossing again before serving.

Per Serving:
¼ cup: calories: 112 | fat: 10g | protein: 1g | carbs: 5g | fiber: 2g | sodium: 248mg

Marinated Feta and Artichokes

Prep time: 10 minutes | Cook time: 0 minutes | Makes 1½ cups

4 ounces (113 g) traditional Greek feta, cut into ½-inch cubes
4 ounces (113 g) drained artichoke hearts, quartered lengthwise
⅓ cup extra-virgin olive oil
Zest and juice of 1 lemon
2 tablespoons roughly chopped fresh rosemary
2 tablespoons roughly chopped fresh parsley
½ teaspoon black peppercorns

1. In a glass bowl or large glass jar, combine the feta and artichoke hearts. Add the olive oil, lemon zest and juice, rosemary, parsley, and peppercorns and toss gently to coat, being sure not to crumble the feta. 2. Cover and refrigerate for at least 4 hours, or up to 4 days. Pull out of the refrigerator 30 minutes before serving.

Per Serving:
calories: 108 | fat: 9g | protein: 3g | carbs: 4g | fiber: 1g | sodium: 294mg

Mexican Potato Skins

Prep time: 10 minutes | Cook time: 55 minutes | Serves 6

Olive oil
6 medium russet potatoes, scrubbed
Salt and freshly ground black pepper, to taste
1 cup fat-free refried black beans
1 tablespoon taco seasoning
½ cup salsa
¾ cup reduced-fat shredded Cheddar cheese

1. Spray the air fryer basket lightly with olive oil. 2. Spray the potatoes lightly with oil and season with salt and pepper. Pierce each potato a few times with a fork. 3. Place the potatoes in the air fryer basket. Air fry at 400ºF (204ºC) until fork-tender, 30 to 40 minutes. The cooking time will depend on the size of the potatoes. You can cook the potatoes in the microwave or a standard oven, but they won't get the same lovely crispy skin they will get in the air fryer. 4. While the potatoes are cooking, in a small bowl, mix together the beans and taco seasoning. Set aside until the potatoes are cool enough to handle. 5. Cut each potato in half lengthwise. Scoop out most of the insides, leaving about ¼ inch in the skins so the potato skins hold their shape. 6. Season the insides of the potato skins with salt and black pepper. Lightly spray the insides of the potato skins with oil. You may need to cook them in batches. 7. Place them into the air fryer basket, skin-side down, and air fry until crisp and golden, 8 to 10 minutes. 8. Transfer the skins to a work surface and spoon ½ tablespoon of seasoned refried black beans into each one. Top each with 2 teaspoons salsa and 1 tablespoon shredded Cheddar cheese. 9. Place filled potato skins in the air fryer basket in a single layer. Lightly spray with oil. 10. Air fry until the cheese is melted and bubbly, 2 to 3 minutes.

Per Serving:
calories: 239 | fat: 2g | protein: 10g | carbs: 46g | fiber: 5g | sodium: 492mg

Roasted Mushrooms with Garlic

Prep time: 3 minutes | Cook time: 22 to 27 minutes | Serves 4

16 garlic cloves, peeled
2 teaspoons olive oil, divided
16 button mushrooms
½ teaspoon dried marjoram
⅛ teaspoon freshly ground black pepper
1 tablespoon white wine or low-sodium vegetable broth

1. In a baking pan, mix the garlic with 1 teaspoon of olive oil. Roast in the air fryer at 350ºF (177ºC) for 12 minutes. 2. Add the mushrooms, marjoram, and pepper. Stir to coat. Drizzle with the remaining 1 teaspoon of olive oil and the white wine. 3. Return to the air fryer and roast for 10 to 15 minutes more, or until the mushrooms and garlic cloves are tender. Serve.

Per Serving:
calories: 57 | fat: 3g | protein: 3g | carbs: 7g | fiber: 1g | sodium: 6mg

Red Lentils with Sumac

Prep time: 5 minutes | Cook time: 20 minutes | Serves 6 to 8

1 cup red lentils, picked through and rinsed
1 teaspoon ground sumac
½ teaspoon salt
Pita chips, warm pita bread, or raw vegetables, for serving

1. In a medium saucepan, combine the lentils, sumac, and 2 cups water. Bring the water to a boil. Reduce the heat to maintain a simmer and cook for 15 minutes, or until the lentils are softened and most of the water has been absorbed. Stir in the salt and cook until the lentils have absorbed all the water, about 5 minutes more. 2. Serve with pita chips, warm pita bread, or as a dip for raw vegetables.

Per Serving:
1 cup: calories: 162 | fat: 1g | protein: 11g | carbs: 30g | fiber: 9g | sodium: 219mg

Spanish Home Fries with Spicy Tomato Sauce

Prep time: 5 minutes | Cook time: 1 hour | Serves 6

4 russet potatoes, peeled, cut into large dice
¼ cup olive oil plus 1 tablespoon, divided
½ cup crushed tomatoes
1½ teaspoons red wine
1 teaspoon hot smoked paprika
1 serrano chile, seeded and chopped
½ teaspoon salt
¼ teaspoon freshly ground black pepper

1. Preheat the oven to 425°F(220°C). 2. Toss the potatoes with ¼ cup of olive oil and spread on a large baking sheet. Season with salt and pepper and roast in the preheated oven for about 50 to 60 minutes, turning once in the middle, until the potatoes are golden brown and crisp. 3. Meanwhile, make the sauce by combining the tomatoes, the remaining 1 tablespoon olive oil, wine, paprika, chile, salt, and pepper in a food processor or blender and process until smooth. 4. Serve the potatoes hot with the sauce on the side for dipping or spooned over the top.

Per Serving:
calories: 201 | fat: 11g | protein: 3g | carbs: 25g | fiber: 4g | sodium: 243mg

Five-Ingredient Falafel with Garlic-Yogurt Sauce

Prep time: 5 minutes | Cook time: 15 minutes | Serves 4

Falafel:
1 (15-ounce / 425-g) can chickpeas, drained and rinsed
½ cup fresh parsley
2 garlic cloves, minced
½ tablespoon ground cumin
1 tablespoon whole wheat flour
Salt
Garlic-Yogurt Sauce:
1 cup nonfat plain Greek yogurt
1 garlic clove, minced
1 tablespoon chopped fresh dill
2 tablespoons lemon juice

Make the Falafel: 1. Preheat the air fryer to 360°F(182°C). 2. Put the chickpeas into a food processor. Pulse until mostly chopped, then add the parsley, garlic, and cumin and pulse for another 1 to 2 minutes, or until the ingredients are combined and turning into a dough. 3. Add the flour. Pulse a few more times until combined. The dough will have texture, but the chickpeas should be pulsed into small bits. 4. Using clean hands, roll the dough into 8 balls of equal size, then pat the balls down a bit so they are about ½-thick disks. 5. Spray the basket of the air fryer with olive oil cooking spray, then place the falafel patties in the basket in a single layer, making sure they don't touch each other. 6. Fry in the air fryer for 15 minutes. Make the garlic-yogurt sauce 7. In a small bowl, combine the yogurt, garlic, dill, and lemon juice. 8. Once the falafel are done cooking and nicely browned on all sides, remove them from the air fryer and season with salt. 9. Serve hot with a side of dipping sauce.

Per Serving:
calories: 150 | fat: 3g | protein: 10g | carbs: 23g | fiber: 6g | sodium: 194mg

Steamed Artichokes with Herbs and Olive Oil

Prep time: 10 minutes | Cook time: 10 minutes | Serves 6

3 medium artichokes with stems cut off
1 medium lemon, halved
1 cup water
¼ cup lemon juice
⅓ cup extra-virgin olive oil
1 clove garlic, peeled and minced
¼ teaspoon salt
1 teaspoon chopped fresh oregano
1 teaspoon chopped fresh rosemary
1 teaspoon chopped fresh flat-leaf parsley
1 teaspoon fresh thyme leaves

1. Run artichokes under running water, making sure water runs between leaves to flush out any debris. Slice off top ⅓ of artichoke and pull away any tough outer leaves. Rub all cut surfaces with lemon. 2. Add water and lemon juice to the Instant Pot®, then add rack. Place artichokes upside down on rack. Close lid, set steam release to Sealing, press the Manual button, and set time to 10 minutes. When the timer beeps, let pressure release naturally, about 20 minutes. 3. Press the Cancel button and open lid. Remove artichokes, transfer to a cutting board, and slice in half. Place halves on a serving platter. 4. In a small bowl, combine oil, garlic, salt, oregano, rosemary, parsley, and thyme. Drizzle half of mixture over artichokes, then serve remaining mixture in a small bowl for dipping. Serve warm.

Per Serving:
calories: 137 | fat: 13g | protein: 2g | carbs: 7g | fiber: 4g | sodium: 158mg

Chapter 11 Vegetarian Mains

One-Pan Mushroom Pasta with Mascarpone

Prep time: 10 minutes | Cook time: 20 minutes | Serves 2

2 tablespoons olive oil
1 large shallot, minced
8 ounces (227 g) baby bella (cremini) mushrooms, sliced
¼ cup dry sherry
1 teaspoon dried thyme
2 cups low-sodium vegetable stock
6 ounces (170 g) dry pappardelle pasta
2 tablespoons mascarpone cheese
Salt
Freshly ground black pepper

1. Heat olive oil in a large sauté pan over medium-high heat. Add the shallot and mushrooms and sauté for 10 minutes, or until the mushrooms have given up much of their liquid. 2. Add the sherry, thyme, and vegetable stock. Bring the mixture to a boil. 3. Add the pasta, breaking it up as needed so it fits into the pan and is covered by the liquid. Return the mixture to a boil. Cover, and reduce the heat to medium-low. Let the pasta cook for 10 minutes, or until al dente. Stir it occasionally so it doesn't stick. If the sauce gets too dry, add some water or additional chicken stock. 4. When the pasta is tender, stir in the mascarpone cheese and season with salt and pepper. 5. The sauce will thicken up a bit when it's off the heat.

Per Serving:
calories: 517 | fat: 18g | protein: 16g | carbs: 69g | fiber: 3g | sodium: 141mg

Eggs Poached in Moroccan Tomato Sauce

Prep time: 10 minutes | Cook time: 35 minutes | Serves 4

1 tablespoon olive oil
1 medium yellow onion, diced
2 red bell peppers, seeded and diced
1¾ teaspoons sweet paprika
1 teaspoon ras al hanout
½ teaspoon cayenne pepper
1 teaspoon salt
¼ cup tomato paste
1 (28-ounce / 794-g) can diced tomatoes, drained
8 eggs
¼ cup chopped cilantro

1. Heat the olive oil in a skillet over medium-high heat. Add the onion and bell peppers and cook, stirring frequently, until softened, about 5 minutes. Stir in the paprika, ras al hanout, cayenne, salt, and tomato paste and cook, stirring occasionally, for 5 minutes. 2. Stir in the diced tomatoes, reduce the heat to medium-low, and simmer for about 15 minutes, until the tomatoes break down and the sauce thickens. 3. Make 8 wells in the sauce and drop one egg into each. Cover the pan and cook for about 10 minutes, until the whites are fully set, but the yolks are still runny. 4. Spoon the sauce and eggs into serving bowls and serve hot, garnished with cilantro.

Per Serving:
calories: 238 | fat: 13g | protein: 15g | carbs: 18g | fiber: 5g | sodium: 735mg

Stuffed Pepper Stew

Prep time: 20 minutes | Cook time: 50 minutes | Serves 2

2 tablespoons olive oil
2 sweet peppers, diced (about 2 cups)
½ large onion, minced
1 garlic clove, minced
1 teaspoon oregano
1 tablespoon gluten-free vegetarian Worcestershire sauce
1 cup low-sodium vegetable stock
1 cup low-sodium tomato juice
¼ cup brown lentils
¼ cup brown rice
Salt

1. Heat olive oil in a Dutch oven over medium-high heat. Add the sweet peppers and onion and sauté for 10 minutes, or until the peppers are wilted and the onion starts to turn golden. 2. Add the garlic, oregano, and Worcestershire sauce, and cook for another 30 seconds. Add the vegetable stock, tomato juice, lentils, and rice. 3. Bring the mixture to a boil. Cover, and reduce the heat to medium-low. Simmer for 45 minutes, or until the rice is cooked and the lentils are softened. Season with salt.

Per Serving:
calories: 379 | fat: 16g | protein: 11g | carbs: 53g | fiber: 7g | sodium: 392mg

Cauliflower Steaks with Olive Citrus Sauce

Prep time: 15 minutes | Cook time: 30 minutes | Serves 4

1 or 2 large heads cauliflower (at least 2 pounds / 907 g, enough for 4 portions)
⅓ cup extra-virgin olive oil
¼ teaspoon kosher salt
⅛ teaspoon ground black pepper
Juice of 1 orange
Zest of 1 orange
¼ cup black olives, pitted and chopped
1 tablespoon Dijon or grainy mustard
1 tablespoon red wine vinegar
½ teaspoon ground coriander

1. Preheat the oven to 400ºF (205ºC). Line a baking sheet with parchment paper or foil. 2. Cut off the stem of the cauliflower so it will sit upright. Slice it vertically into four thick slabs. Place the cauliflower on the prepared baking sheet. Drizzle with the olive oil, salt, and black pepper. Bake for about 30 minutes, turning over once, until tender and golden brown. 3. In a medium bowl, combine the orange juice, orange zest, olives, mustard, vinegar, and coriander; mix well. 4. Serve the cauliflower warm or at room temperature with the sauce.

Per Serving:
calories: 265 | fat: 21g | protein: 5g | carbs: 19g | fiber: 4g | sodium: 310mg

Tangy Asparagus and Broccoli

Prep time: 25 minutes | Cook time: 22 minutes | Serves 4

½ pound (227 g) asparagus, cut into 1½-inch pieces
½ pound (227 g) broccoli, cut into 1½-inch pieces
2 tablespoons olive oil
Salt and white pepper, to taste
½ cup vegetable broth
2 tablespoons apple cider vinegar

1. Place the vegetables in a single layer in the lightly greased air fryer basket. Drizzle the olive oil over the vegetables. 2. Sprinkle with salt and white pepper. 3. Cook at 380ºF (193ºC) for 15 minutes, shaking the basket halfway through the cooking time. 4. Add ½ cup of vegetable broth to a saucepan; bring to a rapid boil and add the vinegar. Cook for 5 to 7 minutes or until the sauce has reduced by half. 5. Spoon the sauce over the warm vegetables and serve immediately. Bon appétit!

Per Serving:
calories: 93 | fat: 7g | protein: 3g | carbs: 6g | fiber: 3g | sodium: 89mg

Moroccan Red Lentil and Pumpkin Stew

Prep time: 10 minutes | Cook time: 30 minutes | Serves 4

2 tablespoons olive oil
1 teaspoon ground cumin
1 teaspoon ground turmeric
1 tablespoon curry powder
1 large onion, diced
1 teaspoon salt
2 tablespoons minced fresh ginger
4 cloves garlic, minced
1 pound (454 g) pumpkin, peeled, seeded, and cut into 1-inch dice
1 red bell pepper, seeded and diced
1½ cups red lentils, rinsed
6 cups vegetable broth
¼ cup chopped cilantro, for garnish

1. Heat the olive oil in a stockpot over medium heat. Add the cumin, turmeric, and curry powder and cook, stirring, for 1 minute, until fragrant. Add the onion and salt and cook, stirring frequently, until softened, about 5 minutes. Add the ginger and garlic and cook, stirring frequently, for 2 more minutes. Stir in the pumpkin and bell pepper, and then the lentils and broth and bring to a boil. 2. Reduce the heat to low and simmer, uncovered, for about 20 minutes, until the lentils are very tender. Serve hot, garnished with cilantro.

Per Serving:
calories: 405 | fat: 9g | protein: 20g | carbs: 66g | fiber: 11g | sodium: 594mg

Linguine and Brussels Sprouts

Prep time: 10 minutes | Cook time: 25 minutes | Serves 4

8 ounces (227 g) whole-wheat linguine
⅓ cup, plus 2 tablespoons extra-virgin olive oil, divided
1 medium sweet onion, diced
2 to 3 garlic cloves, smashed
8 ounces (227 g) Brussels sprouts, chopped
½ cup chicken stock, as needed
⅓ cup dry white wine
½ cup shredded Parmesan cheese
1 lemon, cut in quarters

1. Bring a large pot of water to a boil and cook the pasta according to package directions. Drain, reserving 1 cup of the pasta water. Mix the cooked pasta with 2 tablespoons of olive oil, then set aside. 2. In a large sauté pan or skillet, heat the remaining ⅓ cup of olive oil on medium heat. Add the onion to the pan and cook for about 5 minutes, until softened. Add the smashed garlic cloves and cook for 1 minute, until fragrant. 3. Add the Brussels sprouts and cook covered for 15 minutes. Add chicken stock as needed to prevent burning. Once Brussels sprouts have wilted and are fork-tender, add white wine and cook down for about 7 minutes, until reduced. 4. Add the pasta to the skillet and add the pasta water as needed. 5. Serve with the Parmesan cheese and lemon for squeezing over the dish right before eating.

Per Serving:
calories: 502 | fat: 31g | protein: 15g | carbs: 50g | fiber: 9g | sodium: 246mg

Zucchini Lasagna

Prep time: 15 minutes | Cook time: 1 hour | Serves 8

½ cup extra-virgin olive oil, divided
4 to 5 medium zucchini squash
1 teaspoon salt
8 ounces (227 g) frozen spinach, thawed and well drained (about 1 cup)
2 cups whole-milk ricotta cheese
¼ cup chopped fresh basil or 2 teaspoons dried basil
1 teaspoon garlic powder
½ teaspoon freshly ground black pepper
2 cups shredded fresh whole-milk mozzarella cheese
1¾ cups shredded Parmesan cheese
½ (24-ounce / 680-g) jar low-sugar marinara sauce (less than 5 grams sugar)

1. Preheat the oven to 425ºF (220ºC). 2. Line two baking sheets with parchment paper or aluminum foil and drizzle each with 2 tablespoons olive oil, spreading evenly. 3. Slice the zucchini lengthwise into ¼-inch-thick long slices and place on the prepared baking sheet in a single layer. Sprinkle with ½ teaspoon salt per sheet. Bake until softened, but not mushy, 15 to 18 minutes. Remove from the oven and allow to cool slightly before assembling the lasagna. 4. Reduce the oven temperature to 375ºF (190ºC). 5. While the zucchini cooks, prep the filling. In a large bowl, combine the spinach, ricotta, basil, garlic powder, and pepper. In a small bowl, mix together the mozzarella and Parmesan cheeses. In a medium bowl, combine the marinara sauce and remaining ¼ cup olive oil and stir to fully incorporate the oil into sauce. 6. To assemble the lasagna, spoon a third of the marinara sauce mixture into the bottom of a 9-by-13-inch glass baking dish and spread evenly. Place 1 layer of softened zucchini slices to fully cover the sauce, then add a third of the ricotta-spinach mixture and spread evenly on top of the zucchini. Sprinkle a third of the mozzarella-Parmesan mixture on top of the ricotta. Repeat with 2 more cycles of these layers: marinara, zucchini, ricotta-spinach, then cheese blend. 7. Bake until the cheese is bubbly and melted, 30 to 35 minutes. Turn the broiler to low and broil until the top is golden brown, about 5 minutes. Remove from the oven and allow to cool slightly before slicing.

Per Serving:
calories: 473 | fat: 36g | protein: 23g | carbs: 17g | fiber: 3g | sodium: 868mg

Balsamic Marinated Tofu with Basil and Oregano

Prep time: 10 minutes | Cook time: 30 minutes | Serves 4

¼ cup extra-virgin olive oil
¼ cup balsamic vinegar
2 tablespoons low-sodium soy sauce or gluten-free tamari
3 garlic cloves, grated
2 teaspoons pure maple syrup
Zest of 1 lemon
1 teaspoon dried basil
1 teaspoon dried oregano
½ teaspoon dried thyme
½ teaspoon dried sage
¼ teaspoon kosher salt
¼ teaspoon freshly ground black pepper
¼ teaspoon red pepper flakes (optional)
1 (16-ounce / 454-g) block extra firm tofu, drained and patted dry, cut into ½-inch or 1-inch cubes

1. In a bowl or gallon zip-top bag, mix together the olive oil, vinegar, soy sauce, garlic, maple syrup, lemon zest, basil, oregano, thyme, sage, salt, black pepper, and red pepper flakes, if desired. Add the tofu and mix gently. Put in the refrigerator and marinate for 30 minutes, or up to overnight if you desire. 2. Preheat the oven to 425°F (220°C). Line a baking sheet with parchment paper or foil. Arrange the marinated tofu in a single layer on the prepared baking sheet. Bake for 20 to 30 minutes, turning over halfway through, until slightly crispy on the outside and tender on the inside.

Per Serving:
calories: 225 | fat: 16g | protein: 13g | carbs: 9g | fiber: 2g | sodium: 265mg

Moroccan Vegetable Tagine

Prep time: 20 minutes | Cook time: 1 hour | Serves 6

½ cup extra-virgin olive oil
2 medium yellow onions, sliced
6 celery stalks, sliced into ¼-inch crescents
6 garlic cloves, minced
1 teaspoon ground cumin
1 teaspoon ginger powder
1 teaspoon salt
½ teaspoon paprika
½ teaspoon ground cinnamon
¼ teaspoon freshly ground black pepper
2 cups vegetable stock
1 medium eggplant, cut into 1-inch cubes
2 medium zucchini, cut into ½-inch-thick semicircles
2 cups cauliflower florets
1 (13¾-ounce / 390-g) can artichoke hearts, drained and quartered
1 cup halved and pitted green olives
½ cup chopped fresh flat-leaf parsley, for garnish
½ cup chopped fresh cilantro leaves, for garnish
Greek yogurt, for garnish (optional)

1. In a large, thick soup pot or Dutch oven, heat the olive oil over medium-high heat. Add the onion and celery and sauté until softened, 6 to 8 minutes. Add the garlic, cumin, ginger, salt, paprika, cinnamon, and pepper and sauté for another 2 minutes. 2. Add the stock and bring to a boil. Reduce the heat to low and add the eggplant, zucchini, and cauliflower. Simmer on low heat, covered, until the vegetables are tender, 30 to 35 minutes. Add the artichoke hearts and olives, cover, and simmer for another 15 minutes. 3. Serve garnished with parsley, cilantro, and Greek yogurt (if using).

Per Serving:
calories: 265 | fat: 21g | protein: 5g | carbs: 19g | fiber: 9g | sodium: 858mg

Quinoa Lentil "Meatballs" with Quick Tomato Sauce

Prep time: 25 minutes | Cook time: 45 minutes | Serves 4

For the Meatballs:
Olive oil cooking spray
2 large eggs, beaten
1 tablespoon no-salt-added tomato paste
½ teaspoon kosher salt
½ cup grated Parmesan cheese
½ onion, roughly chopped
¼ cup fresh parsley
1 garlic clove, peeled
1½ cups cooked lentils
1 cup cooked quinoa

For the Tomato Sauce:
1 tablespoon extra-virgin olive oil
1 onion, minced
½ teaspoon dried oregano
½ teaspoon kosher salt
2 garlic cloves, minced
1 (28-ounce / 794-g) can no-salt-added crushed tomatoes
½ teaspoon honey
¼ cup fresh basil, chopped

Make the Meatballs: 1. Preheat the oven to 400°F (205°C). Lightly grease a 12-cup muffin pan with olive oil cooking spray. 2. In a large bowl, whisk together the eggs, tomato paste, and salt until fully combined. Mix in the Parmesan cheese. 3. In a food processor, add the onion, parsley, and garlic. Process until minced. Add to the egg mixture and stir together. Add the lentils to the food processor and process until puréed into a thick paste. Add to the large bowl and mix together. Add the quinoa and mix well. 4. Form balls, slightly larger than a golf ball, with ¼ cup of the quinoa mixture. Place each ball in a muffin pan cup. Note: The mixture will be somewhat soft but should hold together. 5. Bake 25 to 30 minutes, until golden brown. Make the Tomato Sauce: 6. Heat the olive oil in a large saucepan over medium heat. Add the onion, oregano, and salt and sauté until light golden brown, about 5 minutes. Add the garlic and cook for 30 seconds. 7. Stir in the tomatoes and honey. Increase the heat to high and cook, stirring often, until simmering, then decrease the heat to medium-low and cook for 10 minutes. Remove from the heat and stir in the basil. Serve with the meatballs.

Per Serving:
3 meatballs: calories: 360 | fat: 10g | protein: 20g | carbs: 48g | fiber: 14g | sodium: 520mg

Roasted Veggie Bowl

Prep time: 10 minutes | Cook time: 15 minutes | Serves 2

1 cup broccoli florets
1 cup quartered Brussels sprouts
½ cup cauliflower florets
¼ medium white onion, peeled and sliced ¼ inch thick
½ medium green bell pepper, seeded and sliced ¼ inch thick
1 tablespoon coconut oil
2 teaspoons chili powder
½ teaspoon garlic powder
½ teaspoon cumin

1. Toss all ingredients together in a large bowl until vegetables are fully coated with oil and seasoning. 2. Pour vegetables into the air fryer basket. 3. Adjust the temperature to 360°F (182°C) and roast for 15 minutes. 4. Shake two or three times during cooking. Serve warm.

Per Serving:
calories: 112 | fat: 7.68g | protein: 3.64g | carbs: 10.67g | sugars: 3.08g | fiber: 4.6g | sodium: 106mg

Vegetable Burgers

Prep time: 10 minutes | Cook time: 12 minutes | Serves 4

8 ounces (227 g) cremini mushrooms
2 large egg yolks
½ medium zucchini, trimmed and chopped
¼ cup peeled and chopped yellow onion
1 clove garlic, peeled and finely minced
½ teaspoon salt
¼ teaspoon ground black pepper

1. Place all ingredients into a food processor and pulse twenty times until finely chopped and combined. 2. Separate mixture into four equal sections and press each into a burger shape. Place burgers into ungreased air fryer basket. Adjust the temperature to 375ºF (191ºC) and air fry for 12 minutes, turning burgers halfway through cooking. Burgers will be browned and firm when done. 3. Place burgers on a large plate and let cool 5 minutes before serving.

Per Serving:
calories: 50 | fat: 3g | protein: 3g | carbs: 4g | fiber: 1g | sodium: 299mg

Eggplants Stuffed with Walnuts and Feta

Prep time: 10 minutes | Cook time: 55 minutes | Serves 6

3 medium eggplants, halved lengthwise
2 teaspoons salt, divided
¼ cup olive oil, plus 2 tablespoons, divided
2 medium onions, diced
1½ pints cherry or grape tomatoes, halved
¾ cup roughly chopped walnut pieces
2¼ teaspoons ground cinnamon
1½ teaspoons dried oregano
½ teaspoon freshly ground black pepper
¼ cup whole-wheat breadcrumbs
⅔ cup (about 3 ounces / 85 g) crumbled feta cheese

1. Scoop out the flesh of the eggplants, leaving a ½-inch thick border of flesh in the skins. Dice the flesh that you removed and place it in a colander set over the sink. Sprinkle 1½ teaspoons of salt over the diced eggplant and inside the eggplant shells and let stand for 30 minutes. Rinse the shells and the pieces and pat dry with paper towels. 2. Heat ¼ cup of olive oil in a large skillet over medium heat. Add the eggplant shells, skin-side down, and cook for about 4 minutes, until browned and softened. Turn over and cook on the cut side until golden brown and soft, about 4 minutes more. Transfer to a plate lined with paper towel to drain. 3. Drain off all but about 1 to 2 tablespoons of the oil in the skillet and heat over medium-high heat. Add the onions and cook, stirring, until beginning to soften, about 3 minutes. Add the diced eggplant, tomatoes, walnuts, cinnamon, oregano, ¼ cup water, the remaining ½ teaspoon of salt, and the pepper. Cook, stirring occasionally, until the vegetables are golden brown and softened, about 8 minutes. 4. Preheat the broiler to high. 5. In a small bowl, toss together the breadcrumbs and 1 tablespoon olive oil. 6. Arrange the eggplant shells cut-side up on a large, rimmed baking sheet. Brush each shell with about ½ teaspoon of olive oil. Cook under the broiler until tender and just starting to turn golden brown, about 5 minutes. Remove the eggplants from the broiler and reduce the heat of the oven to 375ºF (190ºC). 7. Spoon the sautéed vegetable mixture into the eggplant shells, dividing equally. Sprinkle the breadcrumbs over the tops of the filled eggplants, dividing equally. Sprinkle the cheese on top, again dividing equally. Bake in the oven until the filling and shells are heated through and the topping is nicely browned and crisp, about 35 minutes.

Per Serving:
calories: 274 | fat: 15g | protein: 7g | carbs: 34g | fiber: 13g | sodium: 973mg

Pistachio Mint Pesto Pasta

Prep time: 10 minutes | Cook time: 10 minutes | Serves 4

8 ounces (227 g) whole-wheat pasta
1 cup fresh mint
½ cup fresh basil
⅓ cup unsalted pistachios, shelled
1 garlic clove, peeled
½ teaspoon kosher salt
Juice of ½ lime
⅓ cup extra-virgin olive oil

1. Cook the pasta according to the package directions. Drain, reserving ½ cup of the pasta water, and set aside. 2. In a food processor, add the mint, basil, pistachios, garlic, salt, and lime juice. Process until the pistachios are coarsely ground. Add the olive oil in a slow, steady stream and process until incorporated. 3. In a large bowl, mix the pasta with the pistachio pesto; toss well to incorporate. If a thinner, more saucy consistency is desired, add some of the reserved pasta water and toss well.

Per Serving:
calories: 420 | fat: 3g | protein: 11g | carbs: 48g | fiber: 2g | sodium: 150mg

Creamy Chickpea Sauce with Whole-Wheat Fusilli

Prep time: 15 minutes | Cook time: 20 minutes | Serves 4

¼ cup extra-virgin olive oil
½ large shallot, chopped
5 garlic cloves, thinly sliced
1 (15-ounce / 425-g) can chickpeas, drained and rinsed, reserving ½ cup canning liquid
Pinch red pepper flakes
1 cup whole-grain fusilli pasta
¼ teaspoon salt
⅛ teaspoon freshly ground black pepper
¼ cup shaved fresh Parmesan cheese
¼ cup chopped fresh basil
2 teaspoons dried parsley
1 teaspoon dried oregano
Red pepper flakes

1. In a medium pan, heat the oil over medium heat, and sauté the shallot and garlic for 3 to 5 minutes, until the garlic is golden. Add ¾ of the chickpeas plus 2 tablespoons of liquid from the can, and bring to a simmer. 2. Remove from the heat, transfer into a standard blender, and blend until smooth. At this point, add the remaining chickpeas. Add more reserved chickpea liquid if it becomes thick. 3. Bring a large pot of salted water to a boil and cook pasta until al dente, about 8 minutes. Reserve ½ cup of the pasta water, drain the pasta, and return it to the pot. 4. Add the chickpea sauce to the hot pasta and add up to ¼ cup of the pasta water. You may need to add more pasta water to reach your desired consistency. 5. Place the pasta pot over medium heat and mix occasionally until the sauce thickens. Season with salt and pepper. 6. Serve, garnished with Parmesan, basil, parsley, oregano, and red pepper flakes.

Per Serving:
1 cup pasta: calories: 310 | fat: 17g | protein: 10g | carbs: 33g | fiber: 7g | sodium: 243mg

Parmesan Artichokes

Prep time: 10 minutes | Cook time: 10 minutes | Serves 4

2 medium artichokes, trimmed and quartered, center removed
2 tablespoons coconut oil
1 large egg, beaten
½ cup grated vegetarian Parmesan cheese
¼ cup blanched finely ground almond flour
½ teaspoon crushed red pepper flakes

1. In a large bowl, toss artichokes in coconut oil and then dip each piece into the egg. 2. Mix the Parmesan and almond flour in a large bowl. Add artichoke pieces and toss to cover as completely as possible, sprinkle with pepper flakes. Place into the air fryer basket. 3. Adjust the temperature to 400ºF (204ºC) and air fry for 10 minutes. 4. Toss the basket two times during cooking. Serve warm.

Per Serving:
calories: 207 | fat: 13g | protein: 10g | carbs: 15g | fiber: 5g | sodium: 211mg

Freekeh, Chickpea, and Herb Salad

Prep time: 15 minutes | Cook time: 10 minutes | Serves 4 to 6

1 (15-ounce / 425-g) can chickpeas, rinsed and drained
1 cup cooked freekeh
1 cup thinly sliced celery
1 bunch scallions, both white and green parts, finely chopped
½ cup chopped fresh flat-leaf parsley
¼ cup chopped fresh mint
3 tablespoons chopped celery leaves
½ teaspoon kosher salt
⅓ cup extra-virgin olive oil
¼ cup freshly squeezed lemon juice
¼ teaspoon cumin seeds
1 teaspoon garlic powder

1. In a large bowl, combine the chickpeas, freekeh, celery, scallions, parsley, mint, celery leaves, and salt and toss lightly. 2. In a small bowl, whisk together the olive oil, lemon juice, cumin seeds, and garlic powder. Once combined, add to freekeh salad.

Per Serving:
calories: 350 | fat: 19g | protein: 9g | carbs: 38g | fiber: 9g | sodium: 329mg

Mozzarella and Sun-Dried Portobello Mushroom Pizza

Prep time: 10 minutes | Cook time: 10 minutes | Serves 4

4 large portobello mushroom caps
3 tablespoons extra-virgin olive oil
Salt
Freshly ground black pepper
4 sun-dried tomatoes
1 cup mozzarella cheese, divided
½ to ¾ cup low-sodium tomato sauce

1. Preheat the broiler on high. 2. On a baking sheet, drizzle the mushroom caps with the olive oil and season with salt and pepper. Broil the portobello mushrooms for 5 minutes on each side, flipping once, until tender. 3. Fill each mushroom cap with 1 sun-dried tomato, 2 tablespoons of cheese, and 2 to 3 tablespoons of sauce. Top each with 2 tablespoons of cheese. Place the caps back under the broiler for a final 2 to 3 minutes, then quarter the mushrooms and serve.

Per Serving:
calories: 218| fat: 16g | protein: 11g | carbs: 12g | fiber: 2g | sodium: 244mg

Crispy Cabbage Steaks

Prep time: 5 minutes | Cook time: 10 minutes | Serves 4

1 small head green cabbage, cored and cut into ½-inch-thick slices
¼ teaspoon salt
¼ teaspoon ground black pepper
2 tablespoons olive oil
1 clove garlic, peeled and finely minced
½ teaspoon dried thyme
½ teaspoon dried parsley

1. Sprinkle each side of cabbage with salt and pepper, then place into ungreased air fryer basket, working in batches if needed. 2. Drizzle each side of cabbage with olive oil, then sprinkle with remaining ingredients on both sides. Adjust the temperature to 350ºF (177ºC) and air fry for 10 minutes, turning "steaks" halfway through cooking. 3.Cabbage will be browned at the edges and tender when done. Serve warm.

Per Serving:
calories: 63 | fat: 7g | protein: 0g | carbs: 1g | fiber: 0g | sodium: 155mg

Root Vegetable Soup with Garlic Aioli

Prep time: 10 minutes | Cook time 25 minutes | Serves 4

For the Soup:
8 cups vegetable broth
½ teaspoon salt
1 medium leek, cut into thick rounds
1 pound (454 g) carrots, peeled and diced
1 pound (454 g) potatoes, peeled and diced
1 pound (454 g) turnips, peeled and cut into 1-inch cubes
1 red bell pepper, cut into strips
2 tablespoons fresh oregano
For the Aioli:
5 garlic cloves, minced
¼ teaspoon salt
⅔ cup olive oil
1 drop lemon juice

1. Bring the broth and salt to a boil and add the vegetables one at a time, letting the water return to a boil after each addition. Add the carrots first, then the leeks, potatoes, turnips, and finally the red bell peppers. Let the vegetables cook for about 3 minutes after adding the green beans and bringing to a boil. The process will take about 20 minutes in total. 2. Meanwhile, make the aioli. In a mortar and pestle, grind the garlic to a paste with the salt. Using a whisk and whisking constantly, add the olive oil in a thin stream. Continue whisking until the mixture thickens to the consistency of mayonnaise. Add the lemon juice. 3. Serve the vegetables in the broth, dolloped with the aioli and garnished with the fresh oregano.

Per Serving:
calories: 538 | fat: 37g | protein: 5g | carbs: 50g | fiber: 9g | sodium: 773mg

Provençal Ratatouille with Herbed Breadcrumbs and Goat Cheese

Prep time: 10 minutes | Cook time: 1 hour 5 minutes | Serves 4

6 tablespoons olive oil, divided	tomatoes, drained
2 medium onions, diced	1 teaspoon salt
2 cloves garlic, minced	½ teaspoon freshly ground black pepper
2 medium eggplants, halved lengthwise and cut into ¾-inch thick half rounds	8 ounces (227 g) fresh breadcrumbs
3 medium zucchini, halved lengthwise and cut into ¾-inch thick half rounds	1 tablespoon chopped fresh parsley
2 red bell peppers, seeded and cut into 1½-inch pieces	1 tablespoon chopped fresh basil
1 green bell pepper, seeded and cut into 1½-inch pieces	1 tablespoon chopped fresh chives
1 (14-ounce / 397-g) can diced	6 ounces (170 g) soft, fresh goat cheese

1. Preheat the oven to 375°F(190°C). 2. Heat 5 tablespoons of the olive oil in a large skillet over medium heat. Add the onions and garlic and cook, stirring frequently, until the onions are soft and beginning to turn golden, about 8 minutes. Add the eggplant, zucchini, and bell peppers and cook, turning the vegetables occasionally, for another 10 minutes. Stir in the tomatoes, salt, and pepper and let simmer for 15 minutes. 3. While the vegetables are simmering, stir together the breadcrumbs, the remaining tablespoon of olive oil, the parsley, basil, and chives. 4. Transfer the vegetable mixture to a large baking dish, spreading it out into an even layer. Crumble the goat cheese over the top, then sprinkle the breadcrumb mixture evenly over the top. Bake in the preheated oven for about 30 minutes, until the topping is golden brown and crisp. Serve hot.

Per Serving:
calories: 644 | fat: 37g | protein: 21g | carbs: 63g | fiber: 16g | sodium: 861mg

Baked Tofu with Sun-Dried Tomatoes and Artichokes

Prep time: 15 minutes | Cook time: 30 minutes | Serves 4

1 (16-ounce / 454-g) package extra-firm tofu, drained and patted dry, cut into 1-inch cubes	1 (14-ounce / 397-g) can artichoke hearts, drained
2 tablespoons extra-virgin olive oil, divided	8 sun-dried tomato halves packed in oil, drained and chopped
2 tablespoons lemon juice, divided	¼ teaspoon freshly ground black pepper
1 tablespoon low-sodium soy sauce or gluten-free tamari	1 tablespoon white wine vinegar
1 onion, diced	Zest of 1 lemon
½ teaspoon kosher salt	¼ cup fresh parsley, chopped
2 garlic cloves, minced	

1. Preheat the oven to 400°F (205°C). Line a baking sheet with foil or parchment paper. 2. In a bowl, combine the tofu, 1 tablespoon of the olive oil, 1 tablespoon of the lemon juice, and the soy sauce. Allow to sit and marinate for 15 to 30 minutes. Arrange the tofu in a single layer on the prepared baking sheet and bake for 20 minutes, turning once, until light golden brown. 3. Heat the remaining 1 tablespoon olive oil in a large skillet or sauté pan over medium heat. Add the onion and salt; sauté until translucent, 5 to 6 minutes. Add the garlic and sauté for 30 seconds. Add the artichoke hearts, sun-dried tomatoes, and black pepper and sauté for 5 minutes. Add the white wine vinegar and the remaining 1 tablespoon lemon juice and deglaze the pan, scraping up any brown bits. Remove the pan from the heat and stir in the lemon zest and parsley. Gently mix in the baked tofu.

Per Serving:
calories: 230 | fat: 14g | protein: 14g | carbs: 13g | fiber: 5g | sodium: 500mg

Crustless Spinach Cheese Pie

Prep time: 10 minutes | Cook time: 20 minutes | Serves 4

6 large eggs	1 cup shredded sharp Cheddar cheese
¼ cup heavy whipping cream	
1 cup frozen chopped spinach, drained	¼ cup diced yellow onion

1. In a medium bowl, whisk eggs and add cream. Add remaining ingredients to bowl. 2. Pour into a round baking dish. Place into the air fryer basket. 3. Adjust the temperature to 320ºF (160ºC) and bake for 20 minutes. 4. Eggs will be firm and slightly browned when cooked. Serve immediately.

Per Serving:
calories: 263 | fat: 20g | protein: 18g | carbs: 4g | fiber: 1g | sodium: 321mg

Grilled Eggplant Stacks

Prep time: 20 minutes | Cook time: 10 minutes | Serves 2

1 medium eggplant, cut crosswise into 8 slices	2 tablespoons olive oil
¼ teaspoon salt	1 large tomato, cut into 4 slices
1 teaspoon Italian herb seasoning mix	4 (1-ounce / 28-g) slices of buffalo mozzarella
	Fresh basil, for garnish

1. Place the eggplant slices in a colander set in the sink or over a bowl. Sprinkle both sides with the salt. Let the eggplant sit for 15 minutes. 2. While the eggplant is resting, heat the grill to medium-high heat (about 350ºF / 180ºC). 3. Pat the eggplant dry with paper towels and place it in a mixing bowl. Sprinkle it with the Italian herb seasoning mix and olive oil. Toss well to coat. 4. Grill the eggplant for 5 minutes, or until it has grill marks and is lightly charred. Flip each eggplant slice over, and grill on the second side for another 5 minutes. 5. Flip the eggplant slices back over and top four of the slices with a slice of tomato and a slice of mozzarella. Top each stack with one of the remaining four slices of eggplant. 6. Turn the grill down to low and cover it to let the cheese melt. Check after 30 seconds and remove when the cheese is soft and mostly melted. 7. Sprinkle with fresh basil slices.

Per Serving:
calories: 354 | fat: 29g | protein: 13g | carbs: 19g | fiber: 9g | sodium: 340mg

Cauliflower Rice-Stuffed Peppers

Prep time: 10 minutes | Cook time: 15 minutes | Serves 4

- 2 cups uncooked cauliflower rice
- ¾ cup drained canned petite diced tomatoes
- 2 tablespoons olive oil
- 1 cup shredded Mozzarella cheese
- ¼ teaspoon salt
- ¼ teaspoon ground black pepper
- 4 medium green bell peppers, tops removed, seeded

1. In a large bowl, mix all ingredients except bell peppers. Scoop mixture evenly into peppers. 2. Place peppers into ungreased air fryer basket. Adjust the temperature to 350°F (177°C) and air fry for 15 minutes. Peppers will be tender and cheese will be melted when done. Serve warm.

Per Serving:
calories: 144 | fat: 7g | protein: 11g | carbs: 11g | fiber: 5g | sodium: 380mg

Farro with Roasted Tomatoes and Mushrooms

Prep time: 20 minutes | Cook time: 1 hour | Serves 4

- For the Tomatoes:
- 2 pints cherry tomatoes
- 1 teaspoon extra-virgin olive oil
- ¼ teaspoon kosher salt
- For the Farro:
- 3 to 4 cups water
- ½ cup farro
- ¼ teaspoon kosher salt
- For the Mushrooms:
- 2 tablespoons extra-virgin olive oil
- 1 onion, julienned
- ½ teaspoon kosher salt
- ¼ teaspoon freshly ground black pepper
- 10 ounces (283 g) baby bella (crimini) mushrooms, stemmed and thinly sliced
- ½ cup no-salt-added vegetable stock
- 1 (15-ounce / 425-g) can no-salt-added or low-sodium cannellini beans, drained and rinsed
- 1 cup baby spinach
- 2 tablespoons fresh basil, cut into ribbons
- ¼ cup pine nuts, toasted
- Aged balsamic vinegar (optional)

Make the Tomatoes: Preheat the oven to 400°F (205°C). Line a baking sheet with parchment paper or foil. Toss the tomatoes, olive oil, and salt together on the baking sheet and roast for 30 minutes. Make the Farro: Bring the water, farro, and salt to a boil in a medium saucepan or pot over high heat. Cover, reduce the heat to low, and simmer, and cook for 30 minutes, or until the farro is al dente. Drain and set aside. Make the Mushrooms: 1. Heat the olive oil in a large skillet or sauté pan over medium-low heat. Add the onions, salt, and black pepper and sauté until golden brown and starting to caramelize, about 15 minutes. Add the mushrooms, increase the heat to medium, and sauté until the liquid has evaporated and the mushrooms brown, about 10 minutes. Add the vegetable stock and deglaze the pan, scraping up any brown bits, and reduce the liquid for about 5 minutes. Add the beans and warm through, about 3 minutes. 2. Remove from the heat and mix in the spinach, basil, pine nuts, roasted tomatoes, and farro. Garnish with a drizzle of balsamic vinegar, if desired.

Per Serving:
calories: 375 | fat: 15g | protein: 14g | carbs: 48g | fiber: 10g | sodium: 305mg

Crispy Tofu

Prep time: 30 minutes | Cook time: 15 to 20 minutes | Serves 4

- 1 (16-ounce / 454-g) block extra-firm tofu
- 2 tablespoons coconut aminos
- 1 tablespoon toasted sesame oil
- 1 tablespoon olive oil
- 1 tablespoon chili-garlic sauce
- 1½ teaspoons black sesame seeds
- 1 scallion, thinly sliced

1. Press the tofu for at least 15 minutes by wrapping it in paper towels and setting a heavy pan on top so that the moisture drains. 2. Slice the tofu into bite-size cubes and transfer to a bowl. Drizzle with the coconut aminos, sesame oil, olive oil, and chili-garlic sauce. Cover and refrigerate for 1 hour or up to overnight. 3. Preheat the air fryer to 400°F (204°C). 4. Arrange the tofu in a single layer in the air fryer basket. Pausing to shake the pan halfway through the cooking time, air fry for 15 to 20 minutes until crisp. Serve with any juices that accumulate in the bottom of the air fryer, sprinkled with the sesame seeds and sliced scallion.

Per Serving:
calories: 173 | fat: 14g | protein: 12g | carbs: 3g | fiber: 1g | sodium: 49mg

Roasted Portobello Mushrooms with Kale and Red Onion

Prep time: 15 minutes | Cook time: 30 minutes | Serves 4

- ¼ cup white wine vinegar
- 3 tablespoons extra-virgin olive oil, divided
- ½ teaspoon honey
- ¾ teaspoon kosher salt, divided
- ¼ teaspoon freshly ground black pepper
- 4 large (4 to 5 ounces / 113 to 142 g each) portobello mushrooms, stems removed
- 1 red onion, julienned
- 2 garlic cloves, minced
- 1 (8-ounce / 227-g) bunch kale, stemmed and chopped small
- ¼ teaspoon red pepper flakes
- ¼ cup grated Parmesan or Romano cheese

1. Line a baking sheet with parchment paper or foil. In a medium bowl, whisk together the vinegar, 1½ tablespoons of the olive oil, honey, ¼ teaspoon of the salt, and the black pepper. Arrange the mushrooms on the baking sheet and pour the marinade over them. Marinate for 15 to 30 minutes. 2. Meanwhile, preheat the oven to 400°F (205°C). 3. Bake the mushrooms for 20 minutes, turning over halfway through. 4. Heat the remaining 1½ tablespoons olive oil in a large skillet or ovenproof sauté pan over medium-high heat. Add the onion and the remaining ½ teaspoon salt and sauté until golden brown, 5 to 6 minutes. Add the garlic and sauté for 30 seconds. Add the kale and red pepper flakes and sauté until the kale cooks down, about 5 minutes. 5. Remove the mushrooms from the oven and increase the temperature to broil. 6. Carefully pour the liquid from the baking sheet into the pan with the kale mixture; mix well. 7. Turn the mushrooms over so that the stem side is facing up. Spoon some of the kale mixture on top of each mushroom. Sprinkle 1 tablespoon Parmesan cheese on top of each. 8. Broil until golden brown, 3 to 4 minutes.

Per Serving:
calories: 200 | fat: 13g | protein: 8g | carbs: 16g | fiber: 4g | sodium: 365mg

Pesto Vegetable Skewers

Prep time: 30 minutes | Cook time: 8 minutes | Makes 8 skewers

1 medium zucchini, trimmed and cut into ½-inch slices
½ medium yellow onion, peeled and cut into 1-inch squares
1 medium red bell pepper, seeded and cut into 1-inch squares
16 whole cremini mushrooms
⅓ cup basil pesto
½ teaspoon salt
¼ teaspoon ground black pepper

1. Divide zucchini slices, onion, and bell pepper into eight even portions. Place on 6-inch skewers for a total of eight kebabs. Add 2 mushrooms to each skewer and brush kebabs generously with pesto. 2. Sprinkle each kebab with salt and black pepper on all sides, then place into ungreased air fryer basket. Adjust the temperature to 375°F (191°C) and air fry for 8 minutes, turning kebabs halfway through cooking. Vegetables will be browned at the edges and tender-crisp when done. Serve warm.

Per Serving:
calories: 75 | fat: 6g | protein: 3g | carbs: 4g | fiber: 1g | sodium: 243mg

Asparagus and Mushroom Farrotto

Prep time: 20 minutes | Cook time: 45 minutes | Serves 2

1½ ounces (43 g) dried porcini mushrooms
1 cup hot water
3 cups low-sodium vegetable stock
2 tablespoons olive oil
½ large onion, minced (about 1 cup)
1 garlic clove
1 cup diced mushrooms (about 4 ounces / 113-g)
¾ cup farro
½ cup dry white wine
½ teaspoon dried thyme
4 ounces (113 g) asparagus, cut into ½-inch pieces (about 1 cup)
2 tablespoons grated Parmesan cheese
Salt

1. Soak the dried mushrooms in the hot water for about 15 minutes. When they're softened, drain the mushrooms, reserving the liquid. (I like to strain the liquid through a coffee filter in case there's any grit.) Mince the porcini mushrooms. 2. Add the mushroom liquid and vegetable stock to a medium saucepan and bring it to a boil. Reduce the heat to low just to keep it warm. 3. Heat the olive oil in a Dutch oven over high heat. Add the onion, garlic, and mushrooms, and sauté for 10 minutes. 4. Add the farro to the Dutch oven and sauté it for 3 minutes to toast. 5. Add the wine, thyme, and one ladleful of the hot mushroom and chicken stock. Bring it to a boil while stirring the farro. Do not cover the pot while the farro is cooking. 6. Reduce the heat to medium. When the liquid is absorbed, add another ladleful or two at a time to the pot, stirring occasionally, until the farro is cooked through. Keep an eye on the heat, to make sure it doesn't cook too quickly. 7. When the farro is al dente, add the asparagus and another ladleful of stock. Cook for another 3 to 5 minutes, or until the asparagus is softened. 8. Stir in Parmesan cheese and season with salt.

Per Serving:
calories: 341 | fat: 16g | protein: 13g | carbs: 26g | fiber: 5g | sodium: 259mg

Greek Frittata with Tomato-Olive Salad

Prep time: 10 minutes | Cook time: 25 minutes | Serves 4 to 6

Frittata:
2 tablespoons olive oil
6 scallions, thinly sliced
4 cups (about 5 ounces / 142 g) baby spinach leaves
8 eggs
¼ cup whole-wheat breadcrumbs, divided
1 cup (about 3 ounces / 85 g) crumbled feta cheese
¾ teaspoon salt
¼ teaspoon freshly ground black pepper

Tomato-Olive Salad:
2 tablespoons olive oil
1 tablespoon lemon juice
¼ teaspoon dried oregano
½ teaspoon salt
¼ teaspoon freshly ground black pepper
1 pint cherry, grape, or other small tomatoes, halved
3 pepperoncini, stemmed and chopped
½ cup coarsely chopped pitted Kalamata olives

1. Preheat the oven to 450°F (235°C). 2. Heat the olive oil in an oven-safe skillet set over medium-high heat. Add the scallions and spinach and cook, stirring frequently, for about 4 minutes, until the spinach wilts. 3. In a medium bowl, whisk together the eggs, 2 tablespoons breadcrumbs, cheese, ¾ cup water, salt, and pepper. Pour the egg mixture into the skillet with the spinach and onions and stir to mix. Sprinkle the remaining 2 tablespoons of breadcrumbs evenly over the top. Bake the frittata in the preheated oven for about 20 minutes, until the egg is set and the top is lightly browned. 4. While the frittata is cooking, make the salad. In a medium bowl, whisk together the olive oil, lemon juice, oregano, salt, and pepper. Add the tomatoes, pepperoncini, and olives and toss to mix well. 5. Invert the frittata onto a serving platter and slice it into wedges. Serve warm or at room temperature with the tomato-olive salad.

Per Serving:
calories: 246 | fat: 19g | protein: 11g | carbs: 8g | fiber: 1g | sodium: 832mg

Caprese Eggplant Stacks

Prep time: 5 minutes | Cook time: 12 minutes | Serves 4

1 medium eggplant, cut into ¼-inch slices
2 large tomatoes, cut into ¼-inch slices
4 ounces (113 g) fresh Mozzarella, cut into ½-ounce / 14-g slices
2 tablespoons olive oil
¼ cup fresh basil, sliced

1. In a baking dish, place four slices of eggplant on the bottom. Place a slice of tomato on top of each eggplant round, then Mozzarella, then eggplant. Repeat as necessary. 2. Drizzle with olive oil. Cover dish with foil and place dish into the air fryer basket. 3. Adjust the temperature to 350°F (177°C) and bake for 12 minutes. 4. When done, eggplant will be tender. Garnish with fresh basil to serve.

Per Serving:
calories: 97 | fat: 7g | protein: 2g | carbs: 8g | fiber: 4g | sodium: 11mg

Cheese Stuffed Zucchini

Prep time: 20 minutes | Cook time: 8 minutes | Serves 4

1 large zucchini, cut into four pieces	parsley, roughly chopped
2 tablespoons olive oil	1 heaping tablespoon coriander, minced
1 cup Ricotta cheese, room temperature	2 ounces (57 g) Cheddar cheese, preferably freshly grated
2 tablespoons scallions, chopped	1 teaspoon celery seeds
1 heaping tablespoon fresh	½ teaspoon salt
	½ teaspoon garlic pepper

1. Cook your zucchini in the air fryer basket for approximately 10 minutes at 350ºF (177ºC). Check for doneness and cook for 2-3 minutes longer if needed. 2. Meanwhile, make the stuffing by mixing the other items. 3. When your zucchini is thoroughly cooked, open them up. Divide the stuffing among all zucchini pieces and bake an additional 5 minutes.

Per Serving:
calories: 242 | fat: 20g | protein: 12g | carbs: 5g | fiber: 1g | sodium: 443mg

Stuffed Portobellos

Prep time: 10 minutes | Cook time: 8 minutes | Serves 4

3 ounces (85 g) cream cheese, softened	leaves
½ medium zucchini, trimmed and chopped	4 large portobello mushrooms, stems removed
¼ cup seeded and chopped red bell pepper	2 tablespoons coconut oil, melted
1½ cups chopped fresh spinach	½ teaspoon salt

1. In a medium bowl, mix cream cheese, zucchini, pepper, and spinach. 2. Drizzle mushrooms with coconut oil and sprinkle with salt. Scoop ¼ zucchini mixture into each mushroom. 3. Place mushrooms into ungreased air fryer basket. Adjust the temperature to 400ºF (204ºC) and air fry for 8 minutes. Portobellos will be tender and tops will be browned when done. Serve warm.

Per Serving:
calories: 151 | fat: 13g | protein: 4g | carbs: 6g | fiber: 2g | sodium: 427mg

Turkish Red Lentil and Bulgur Kofte

Prep time: 10 minutes | Cook time: 45 minutes | Serves 4

⅓ cup olive oil, plus 2 tablespoons, divided, plus more for brushing	2 tablespoons tomato paste
	1 teaspoon ground cumin
1 cup red lentils	¼ cup finely chopped flat-leaf parsley
½ cup bulgur	3 scallions, thinly sliced
1 teaspoon salt	Juice of ½ lemon
1 medium onion, finely diced	

1. Preheat the oven to 400°F(205ºC). 2. Brush a large, rimmed baking sheet with olive oil. 3. In a medium saucepan, combine the lentils with 2 cups water and bring to a boil. Reduce the heat to low and cook, stirring occasionally, for about 15 minutes, until the lentils are tender and have soaked up most of the liquid. Remove from the heat, stir in the bulgur and salt, cover, and let sit for 15 minutes or so, until the bulgur is tender. 4. Meanwhile, heat ⅓ cup olive oil in a medium skillet over medium-high heat. Add the onion and cook, stirring frequently, until softened, about 5 minutes. Stir in the tomato paste and cook for 2 minutes more. Remove from the heat and stir in the cumin. 5. Add the cooked onion mixture to the lentil-bulgur mixture and stir to combine. Add the parsley, scallions, and lemon juice and stir to mix well. 6. Shape the mixture into walnut-sized balls and place them on the prepared baking sheet. Brush the balls with the remaining 2 tablespoons of olive oil and bake for 15 to 20 minutes, until golden brown. Serve hot.

Per Serving:
calories: 460 | fat: 25g | protein: 16g | carbs: 48g | fiber: 19g | sodium: 604mg

Quinoa with Almonds and Cranberries

Prep time: 15 minutes | Cook time: 0 minutes | Serves 4

2 cups cooked quinoa	½ teaspoon ground cumin
⅓ teaspoon cranberries or currants	½ teaspoon turmeric
	¼ teaspoon ground cinnamon
¼ cup sliced almonds	¼ teaspoon freshly ground black pepper
2 garlic cloves, minced	
1¼ teaspoons salt	

1. In a large bowl, toss the quinoa, cranberries, almonds, garlic, salt, cumin, turmeric, cinnamon, and pepper and stir to combine. Enjoy alone or with roasted cauliflower.

Per Serving:
calories: 194 | fat: 6g | protein: 7g | carbs: 31g | fiber: 4g | sodium: 727mg

Three-Cheese Zucchini Boats

Prep time: 15 minutes | Cook time: 20 minutes | Serves 2

2 medium zucchini	cheese
1 tablespoon avocado oil	¼ teaspoon dried oregano
¼ cup low-carb, no-sugar-added pasta sauce	¼ teaspoon garlic powder
	½ teaspoon dried parsley
¼ cup full-fat ricotta cheese	2 tablespoons grated vegetarian Parmesan cheese
¼ cup shredded Mozzarella	

1. Cut off 1 inch from the top and bottom of each zucchini. Slice zucchini in half lengthwise and use a spoon to scoop out a bit of the inside, making room for filling. Brush with oil and spoon 2 tablespoons pasta sauce into each shell. 2. In a medium bowl, mix ricotta, Mozzarella, oregano, garlic powder, and parsley. Spoon the mixture into each zucchini shell. Place stuffed zucchini shells into the air fryer basket. 3. Adjust the temperature to 350ºF (177ºC) and air fry for 20 minutes. 4. To remove from the basket, use tongs or a spatula and carefully lift out. Top with Parmesan. Serve immediately.

Per Serving:
calories: 208 | fat: 14g | protein: 12g | carbs: 11g | fiber: 3g | sodium: 247mg

Cauliflower Steak with Gremolata

Prep time: 15 minutes | Cook time: 25 minutes | Serves 4

2 tablespoons olive oil
1 tablespoon Italian seasoning
1 large head cauliflower, outer leaves removed and sliced lengthwise through the core into thick "steaks"
Salt and freshly ground black pepper, to taste
¼ cup Parmesan cheese

Gremolata:
1 bunch Italian parsley (about 1 cup packed)
2 cloves garlic
Zest of 1 small lemon, plus 1 to 2 teaspoons lemon juice
½ cup olive oil
Salt and pepper, to taste

1. Preheat the air fryer to 400°F (204°C). 2. In a small bowl, combine the olive oil and Italian seasoning. Brush both sides of each cauliflower "steak" generously with the oil. Season to taste with salt and black pepper. 3. Working in batches if necessary, arrange the cauliflower in a single layer in the air fryer basket. Pausing halfway through the cooking time to turn the "steaks," air fry for 15 to 20 minutes until the cauliflower is tender and the edges begin to brown. Sprinkle with the Parmesan and air fry for 5 minutes longer. 4. To make the gremolata: In a food processor fitted with a metal blade, combine the parsley, garlic, and lemon zest and juice. With the motor running, add the olive oil in a steady stream until the mixture forms a bright green sauce. Season to taste with salt and black pepper. Serve the cauliflower steaks with the gremolata spooned over the top.

Per Serving:
calories: 336 | fat: 30g | protein: 7g | carbs: 15g | fiber: 5g | sodium: 340mg

Rustic Vegetable and Brown Rice Bowl

Prep time: 15 minutes | Cook time: 20 minutes | Serves 4

Nonstick cooking spray
2 cups broccoli florets
2 cups cauliflower florets
1 (15-ounce / 425-g) can chickpeas, drained and rinsed
1 cup carrots sliced 1 inch thick
2 to 3 tablespoons extra-virgin olive oil, divided
Salt
Freshly ground black pepper
2 to 3 tablespoons sesame seeds, for garnish

2 cups cooked brown rice
For the Dressing:
3 to 4 tablespoons tahini
2 tablespoons honey
1 lemon, juiced
1 garlic clove, minced
Salt
Freshly ground black pepper

1. Preheat the oven to 400°F (205°C). Spray two baking sheets with cooking spray. 2. Cover the first baking sheet with the broccoli and cauliflower and the second with the chickpeas and carrots. Toss each sheet with half of the oil and season with salt and pepper before placing in oven. 3. Cook the carrots and chickpeas for 10 minutes, leaving the carrots still just crisp, and the broccoli and cauliflower for 20 minutes, until tender. Stir each halfway through cooking. 4. To make the dressing, in a small bowl, mix the tahini, honey, lemon juice, and garlic. Season with salt and pepper and set aside. 5. Divide the rice into individual bowls, then layer with vegetables and drizzle dressing over the dish.

Per Serving:
calories: 454 | fat: 18g | protein: 12g | carbs: 62g | fiber: 11g | sodium: 61mg

Chapter 12 Vegetables and Sides

Rustic Cauliflower and Carrot Hash

Prep time: 10 minutes | Cook time: 10 minutes | Serves 4

3 tablespoons extra-virgin olive oil
1 large onion, chopped
1 tablespoon garlic, minced
2 cups carrots, diced
4 cups cauliflower pieces, washed
1 teaspoon salt
½ teaspoon ground cumin

1. In a large skillet over medium heat, cook the olive oil, onion, garlic, and carrots for 3 minutes. 2. Cut the cauliflower into 1-inch or bite-size pieces. Add the cauliflower, salt, and cumin to the skillet and toss to combine with the carrots and onions. 3. Cover and cook for 3 minutes. 4. Toss the vegetables and continue to cook uncovered for an additional 3 to 4 minutes. 5. Serve warm.

Per Serving:
calories: 159 | fat: 11g | protein: 3g | carbs: 15g | fiber: 5g | sodium: 657mg

Ratatouille

Prep time: 15 minutes | Cook time: 20 minutes | Serves 2 to 3

2 cups ¾-inch cubed peeled eggplant
1 small red, yellow, or orange bell pepper, stemmed, seeded, and diced
1 cup cherry tomatoes
6 to 8 cloves garlic, peeled and halved lengthwise
3 tablespoons olive oil
1 teaspoon dried oregano
½ teaspoon dried thyme
1 teaspoon kosher salt
½ teaspoon black pepper

1. In a medium bowl, combine the eggplant, bell pepper, tomatoes, garlic, oil, oregano, thyme, salt, and pepper. Toss to combine. 2. Place the vegetables in the air fryer basket. Set the air fryer to 400°F (204°C) for 20 minutes, or until the vegetables are crisp-tender.

Per Serving:
calories: 161 | fat: 14g | protein: 2g | carbs: 9g | fiber: 3g | sodium: 781mg

Roasted Broccolini with Garlic and Romano

Prep time: 5 minutes | Cook time: 10 minutes | Serves 2

1 bunch broccolini (about 5 ounces / 142 g)
1 tablespoon olive oil
½ teaspoon garlic powder
¼ teaspoon salt
2 tablespoons grated Romano cheese

1. Preheat the oven to 400°F(205°C) and set the oven rack to the middle position. Line a sheet pan with parchment paper or foil. 2. Slice the tough ends off the broccolini and place in a medium bowl. Add the olive oil, garlic powder, and salt and toss to combine. Arrange broccolini on the lined sheet pan. 3. Roast for 7 minutes, flipping pieces over halfway through the roasting time. 4. Remove the pan from the oven and sprinkle the cheese over the broccolini. With a pair of tongs, carefully flip the pieces over to coat all sides. Return to the oven for another 2 to 3 minutes, or until the cheese melts and starts to turn golden.

Per Serving:
calories: 114 | fat: 9g | protein: 4g | carbs: 5g | fiber: 2g | sodium: 400mg

Tingly Chili-Roasted Broccoli

Prep time: 5 minutes | Cook time: 10 minutes | Serves 2

12 ounces (340 g) broccoli florets
2 tablespoons Asian hot chili oil
1 teaspoon ground Sichuan peppercorns (or black pepper)
2 garlic cloves, finely chopped
1 (2-inch) piece fresh ginger, peeled and finely chopped
Kosher salt and freshly ground black pepper, to taste

1. In a bowl, toss together the broccoli, chili oil, Sichuan peppercorns, garlic, ginger, and salt and black pepper to taste. 2. Transfer to the air fryer and roast at 375°F (191°C), shaking the basket halfway through, until lightly charred and tender, about 10 minutes. Remove from the air fryer and serve warm.

Per Serving:
calories: 141 | fat: 9g | protein: 5g | carbs: 13g | fiber: 5g | sodium: 57mg

Sweet and Crispy Roasted Pearl Onions

Prep time: 5 minutes | Cook time: 18 minutes | Serves 3

1 (14½-ounce / 411-g) package frozen pearl onions (do not thaw)
2 tablespoons extra-virgin olive oil
2 tablespoons balsamic vinegar
2 teaspoons finely chopped fresh rosemary
½ teaspoon kosher salt
¼ teaspoon black pepper

1. In a medium bowl, combine the onions, olive oil, vinegar, rosemary, salt, and pepper until well coated. 2. Transfer the onions to the air fryer basket. Set the air fryer to 400°F (204°C) for 18 minutes, or until the onions are tender and lightly charred, stirring once or twice during the cooking time.

Per Serving:
calories: 145 | fat: 9g | protein: 2g | carbs: 15g | fiber: 2g | sodium: 396mg

Spiced Honey-Walnut Carrots

Prep time: 5 minutes | Cook time: 12 minutes | Serves 6

1 pound (454 g) baby carrots
2 tablespoons olive oil
¼ cup raw honey
¼ teaspoon ground cinnamon
¼ cup black walnuts, chopped

1. Preheat the air fryer to 360°F(182°C). 2. In a large bowl, toss the baby carrots with olive oil, honey, and cinnamon until well coated. 3. Pour into the air fryer and roast for 6 minutes. Shake the basket, sprinkle the walnuts on top, and roast for 6 minutes more. 4. Remove the carrots from the air fryer and serve.

Per Serving:
calories: 142 | fat: 8g | protein: 2g | carbs: 18g | fiber: 3g | sodium: 60mg

Crispy Roasted Red Potatoes with Garlic, Rosemary, and Parmesan

Prep time: 10 minutes | Cook time: 55 minutes | Serves 2

12 ounces (340 g) red potatoes (3 to 4 small potatoes)
1 tablespoon olive oil
½ teaspoon garlic powder
¼ teaspoon salt
1 tablespoon grated Parmesan cheese
1 teaspoon minced fresh rosemary (from 1 sprig)

1. Preheat the oven to 425°F(220°C) and set the rack to the bottom position. Line a baking sheet with parchment paper. (Do not use foil, as the potatoes will stick.) 2. Scrub the potatoes and dry them well. Dice into 1-inch pieces. 3. In a mixing bowl, combine the potatoes, olive oil, garlic powder, and salt. Toss well to coat. 4. Lay the potatoes on the parchment paper and roast for 10 minutes. Flip the potatoes over and return to the oven for 10 more minutes. 5. Check the potatoes to make sure they are golden brown on the top and bottom. Toss them again, turn the heat down to 350°F(180°C), and roast for 30 minutes more. 6. When the potatoes are golden, crispy, and cooked through, sprinkle the Parmesan cheese over them and toss again. Return to the oven for 3 minutes to let the cheese melt a bit. 7. Remove from the oven and sprinkle with the fresh rosemary.

Per Serving:
calories: 193 | fat: 8g | protein: 5g | carbs: 28g | fiber: 3g | sodium: 334mg

Walnut and Freekeh Pilaf

Prep time: 15 minutes | Cook time: 15 minutes | Serves 4

2½ cups freekeh
3 tablespoons extra-virgin olive oil, divided
2 medium onions, diced
¼ teaspoon ground cinnamon
¼ teaspoon ground allspice
5 cups chicken stock
½ cup chopped walnuts
Salt
Freshly ground black pepper
½ cup plain, unsweetened, full-fat Greek yogurt
1½ teaspoons freshly squeezed lemon juice
½ teaspoon garlic powder

1. In a small bowl, soak the freekeh covered in cold water for 5 minutes. Drain and rinse the freekeh, then rinse one more time. 2. In a large sauté pan or skillet, heat 2 tablespoons oil, then add the onions and cook until fragrant. Add the freekeh, cinnamon, and allspice. Stir periodically for 1 minute. 3. Add the stock and walnuts and season with salt and pepper. Bring to a simmer. 4. Cover and reduce the heat to low. Cook for 15 minutes. Once freekeh is tender, remove from the heat and allow to rest for 5 minutes. 5. In a small bowl, combine the yogurt, lemon juice, and garlic powder. You may need to add salt to bring out the flavors. Add the yogurt mixture to the freekeh and serve immediately.

Per Serving:
calories: 653 | fat: 25g | protein: 23g | carbs: 91g | fiber: 12g | sodium: 575mg

Heirloom Tomato Basil Soup

Prep time: 15 minutes | Cook time: 15 minutes | Serves 4

1 tablespoon olive oil
1 small onion, peeled and diced
1 stalk celery, sliced
8 medium heirloom tomatoes, seeded and quartered
¼ cup julienned fresh basil
½ teaspoon salt
3 cups low-sodium chicken broth
1 cup heavy cream
1 teaspoon ground black pepper

1. Press the Sauté button on the Instant Pot® and heat oil. Add onion and celery and cook until translucent, about 5 minutes. Add tomatoes and cook for 3 minutes, or until tomatoes are tender and start to break down. Add basil, salt, and broth. Press the Cancel button. 2. Close lid, set steam release to Sealing, press the Manual button, and set time to 7 minutes. When the timer beeps, quick-release the pressure until the float valve drops and then open lid. 3. Add cream and pepper. Purée soup with an immersion blender, or purée in batches in a blender. Ladle into bowls and serve warm.

Per Serving:
calories: 282 | fat: 24g | protein: 4g | carbs: 9g | fiber: 1g | sodium: 466mg

Green Beans with Pine Nuts and Garlic

Prep time: 10 minutes | Cook time: 20 minutes | Serves 4 to 6

1 pound (454 g) green beans, trimmed
1 head garlic (10 to 12 cloves), smashed
2 tablespoons extra-virgin olive oil
½ teaspoon kosher salt
¼ teaspoon red pepper flakes
1 tablespoon white wine vinegar
¼ cup pine nuts, toasted

1. Preheat the oven to 425°F (220°C). Line a baking sheet with parchment paper or foil. 2. In a large bowl, combine the green beans, garlic, olive oil, salt, and red pepper flakes and mix together. Arrange in a single layer on the baking sheet. Roast for 10 minutes, stir, and roast for another 10 minutes, or until golden brown. 3. Mix the cooked green beans with the vinegar and top with the pine nuts.

Per Serving:
calories: 165 | fat: 13g | protein: 4g | carbs: 12g | fiber: 4g | sodium: 150mg

Spicy Grilled Veggie Pita

Prep time: 10 minutes | Cook time: 15 minutes | Serves 4

4 pita breads
2 tablespoons olive oil
2 garlic cloves, minced
1 zucchini, sliced
1 red bell pepper, cut into strips
½ red onion, sliced
½ cup plain full-fat Greek yogurt
1 teaspoon harissa
1 large tomato, sliced
Sea salt
Freshly ground black pepper

1. Toast the pitas in a skillet over medium-high heat for 3 to 4 minutes per side, then remove from the heat and set aside. 2. In the same skillet, combine the olive oil and garlic and sauté over medium-high heat for 2 minutes. Add the zucchini, bell pepper, and onion and sauté for 5 to 6 minutes, until softened. Remove from the heat. 3. While the vegetables are cooking, in a small bowl, mix the yogurt and harissa. 4. Halve the pitas crosswise and open each half to form a pocket. Add 1 tablespoon of the yogurt mixture to each pita pocket and spread it over the inside. Spoon the cooked vegetable mixture into the pockets and top with the tomatoes. Season with salt and black pepper. 5. Serve the pitas with the extra sauce on the side.

Per Serving:
calories: 215 | fat: 10g | protein: 5g | carbs: 27g | fiber: 5g | sodium: 244mg

Braised Radishes with Sugar Snap Peas and Dukkah

Prep time: 20 minutes | Cook time: 5 minutes | Serves 4

¼ cup extra-virgin olive oil, divided
1 shallot, sliced thin
3 garlic cloves, sliced thin
1½ pounds (680 g) radishes, 2 cups greens reserved, radishes trimmed and halved if small or quartered if large
½ cup water
½ teaspoon table salt
8 ounces (227 g) sugar snap peas, strings removed, sliced thin on bias
8 ounces (227 g) cremini mushrooms, trimmed and sliced thin
2 teaspoons grated lemon zest plus 1 teaspoon juice
1 cup plain Greek yogurt
½ cup fresh cilantro leaves
3 tablespoons dukkah

1. Using highest sauté function, heat 2 tablespoons oil in Instant Pot until shimmering. Add shallot and cook until softened, about 2 minutes. Stir in garlic and cook until fragrant, about 30 seconds. Stir in radishes, water, and salt. Lock lid in place and close pressure release valve. Select high pressure cook function and cook for 1 minute. 2. Turn off Instant Pot and quick-release pressure. Carefully remove lid, allowing steam to escape away from you. Stir in snap peas, cover, and let sit until heated through, about 3 minutes. Add radish greens, mushrooms, lemon zest and juice, and remaining 2 tablespoons oil and gently toss to combine. Season with salt and pepper to taste. 3. Spread ¼ cup yogurt over bottom of 4 individual serving plates. Using slotted spoon, arrange vegetable mixture on top and sprinkle with cilantro and dukkah. Serve.

Per Serving:
calories: 310 | fat: 23g | protein: 10g | carbs: 17g | fiber: 5g | sodium: 320mg

Eggplant Caponata

Prep time: 20 minutes | Cook time: 5 minutes | Serves 8

¼ cup extra-virgin olive oil
¼ cup white wine
2 tablespoons red wine vinegar
1 teaspoon ground cinnamon
1 large eggplant, peeled and diced
1 medium onion, peeled and diced
1 medium green bell pepper, seeded and diced
1 medium red bell pepper, seeded and diced
2 cloves garlic, peeled and minced
1 (14½-ounce / 411-g) can diced tomatoes
3 stalks celery, diced
½ cup chopped oil-cured olives
½ cup golden raisins
2 tablespoons capers, rinsed and drained
½ teaspoon salt
½ teaspoon ground black pepper

1. Place all ingredients in the Instant Pot®. Stir well to mix. Close lid, set steam release to Sealing, press the Manual button, and set time to 5 minutes. 2. When the timer beeps, quick-release the pressure until the float valve drops. Open the lid and stir well. Serve warm or at room temperature.

Per Serving:
calories: 90 | fat: 1g | protein: 2g | carbs: 17g | fiber: 4g | sodium: 295mg

Zucchini Fritters with Manchego and Smoked Paprika Yogurt

Prep time: 10 minutes | Cook time: 10 minutes | Serves 4 to 6

6 small zucchini, grated on the large holes of a box grater
1¼ teaspoons salt, divided
1 cup plain Greek yogurt
2 teaspoons smoked paprika
Juice of ½ lemon
4 ounces (113 g) manchego cheese, grated
¼ cup finely chopped fresh parsley
4 scallions, thinly sliced
3 eggs, beaten
½ cup all-purpose flour
¼ teaspoon freshly ground black pepper
Neutral-flavored oil (such as grapeseed, safflower, or sunflower seed) for frying

1. Put the grated zucchini in a colander. Sprinkle 1 teaspoon of salt over the top and then toss to combine. Let sit over the sink for at least 20 minutes to drain. Transfer the zucchini to a clean dishtowel and squeeze out as much of the water as you can. 2. Meanwhile, make the yogurt sauce. In a small bowl, stir together the yogurt, smoked paprika, lemon juice, and the remaining ¼ teaspoon of salt. 3. In a large bowl, combine the zucchini, cheese, parsley, scallions, eggs, flour, and pepper and stir to mix. 4. Fill a large saucepan with ½ inch of oil and heat over medium-high heat. When the oil is very hot, drop the batter in by rounded tablespoons, cooking 4 or 5 fritters at a time, flattening each dollop with the back of the spoon. Cook until golden on the bottom, about 2 minutes, then flip and cook on the second side until golden, about 2 minutes more. Transfer the cooked fritters to a plate lined with paper towels to drain and repeat until all of the batter has been cooked.

Per Serving:
calories: 237 | fat: 14g | protein: 11g | carbs: 18g | fiber: 3g | sodium: 655mg

Roasted Harissa Carrots

Prep time: 10 minutes | Cook time: 15 minutes | Serves 4

1 pound (454 g) carrots, peeled and sliced into 1-inch-thick rounds
2 tablespoons extra-virgin olive oil
2 tablespoons harissa
1 teaspoon honey
1 teaspoon ground cumin
½ teaspoon kosher salt
½ cup fresh parsley, chopped

1. Preheat the oven to 450°F (235°C). Line a baking sheet with parchment paper or foil. 2. In a large bowl, combine the carrots, olive oil, harissa, honey, cumin, and salt. Arrange in a single layer on the baking sheet. Roast for 15 minutes. Remove from the oven, add the parsley, and toss together.

Per Serving:
calories: 120 | fat: 8g | protein: 1g | carbs: 13g | fiber: 4g | sodium: 255mg

Brown Rice and Vegetable Pilaf

Prep time: 20 minutes | Cook time: 5 hours | Makes 9 (¾-cup) servings

1 onion, minced
1 cup sliced cremini mushrooms
2 carrots, sliced
2 garlic cloves, minced
1½ cups long-grain brown rice
2½ cups vegetable broth
½ teaspoon salt
½ teaspoon dried marjoram leaves
⅛ teaspoon freshly ground black pepper
⅓ cup grated Parmesan cheese

1. In the slow cooker, combine the onion, mushrooms, carrots, garlic, and rice. 2. Add the broth, salt, marjoram, and pepper, and stir. 3. Cover and cook on low for 5 hours, or until the rice is tender and the liquid is absorbed. 4. Stir in the cheese and serve.

Per Serving:
calories: 68 | fat: 1g | protein: 2g | carbs: 12g | net carbs: 11g | sugars: 2g | fiber: 1g | sodium: 207mg | cholesterol: 3mg

Wild Mushroom Soup

Prep time: 30 minutes | Cook time: 16 minutes | Serves 8

3 tablespoons olive oil
1 stalk celery, diced
1 medium carrot, peeled and diced
½ medium yellow onion, peeled and diced
1 clove garlic, peeled and minced
1 (8-ounce / 227-g) container hen of the woods mushrooms, sliced
1 (8-ounce / 227-g) container porcini or chanterelle mushrooms, sliced
2 cups sliced shiitake mushrooms
2 tablespoons dry sherry
4 cups vegetable broth
2 cups water
1 tablespoon chopped fresh tarragon
½ teaspoon salt
½ teaspoon ground black pepper

1. Press the Sauté button on the Instant Pot® and heat oil. Add celery, carrot, and onion. Cook, stirring often, until softened, about 5 minutes. Add garlic and cook 30 seconds until fragrant, then add mushrooms and cook until beginning to soften, about 5 minutes. 2. Add sherry, broth, water, tarragon, salt, and pepper to pot, and stir well. Press the Cancel button. Close lid, set steam release to Sealing, press the Manual button, and set time to 5 minutes. 3. When the timer beeps, let pressure release naturally, about 15 minutes. Press the Cancel button, open lid, and stir well. Serve hot.

Per Serving:
calories: 98 | fat: 6g | protein: 1g | carbs: 11g | fiber: 2g | sodium: 759mg

Garlicky Broccoli Rabe with Artichokes

Prep time: 5 minutes | Cook time: 10 minutes | Serves 4

2 pounds (907 g) fresh broccoli rabe
½ cup extra-virgin olive oil, divided
3 garlic cloves, finely minced
1 teaspoon salt
1 teaspoon red pepper flakes
1 (13¾-ounce / 390-g) can artichoke hearts, drained and quartered
1 tablespoon water
2 tablespoons red wine vinegar
Freshly ground black pepper

1. Trim away any thick lower stems and yellow leaves from the broccoli rabe and discard. Cut into individual florets with a couple inches of thin stem attached. 2. In a large skillet, heat ¼ cup olive oil over medium-high heat. Add the trimmed broccoli, garlic, salt, and red pepper flakes and sauté for 5 minutes, until the broccoli begins to soften. Add the artichoke hearts and sauté for another 2 minutes. 3. Add the water and reduce the heat to low. Cover and simmer until the broccoli stems are tender, 3 to 5 minutes. 4. In a small bowl, whisk together remaining ¼ cup olive oil and the vinegar. Drizzle over the broccoli and artichokes. Season with ground black pepper, if desired.

Per Serving:
calories: 341 | fat: 28g | protein: 11g | carbs: 18g | fiber: 12g | sodium: 750mg

Air-Fried Okra

Prep time: 10 minutes | Cook time: 10 minutes | Serves 4

1 egg
½ cup almond milk
½ cup crushed pork rinds
¼ cup grated Parmesan cheese
¼ cup almond flour
1 teaspoon garlic powder
¼ teaspoon freshly ground black pepper
½ pound (227 g) fresh okra, stems removed and chopped into 1-inch slices

1. Preheat the air fryer to 400°F (204°C). 2. In a shallow bowl, whisk together the egg and milk. 3. In a second shallow bowl, combine the pork rinds, Parmesan, almond flour, garlic powder, and black pepper. 4. Working with a few slices at a time, dip the okra into the egg mixture followed by the crumb mixture. Press lightly to ensure an even coating. 5. Working in batches if necessary, arrange the okra in a single layer in the air fryer basket and spray lightly with olive oil. Pausing halfway through the cooking time to turn the okra, air fry for 10 minutes until tender and golden brown. Serve warm.

Per Serving:
calories: 200 | fat: 16g | protein: 6g | carbs: 8g | fiber: 2g | sodium: 228mg

Radish Chips

Prep time: 10 minutes | Cook time: 5 minutes | Serves 4

- 2 cups water
- 1 pound (454 g) radishes
- ¼ teaspoon onion powder
- ¼ teaspoon paprika
- ½ teaspoon garlic powder
- 2 tablespoons coconut oil, melted

1. Place water in a medium saucepan and bring to a boil on stovetop. 2. Remove the top and bottom from each radish, then use a mandoline to slice each radish thin and uniformly. You may also use the slicing blade in the food processor for this step. 3. Place the radish slices into the boiling water for 5 minutes or until translucent. Remove them from the water and place them into a clean kitchen towel to absorb excess moisture. 4. Toss the radish chips in a large bowl with remaining ingredients until fully coated in oil and seasoning. Place radish chips into the air fryer basket. 5. Adjust the temperature to 320ºF (160ºC) and air fry for 5 minutes. 6. Shake the basket two or three times during the cooking time. Serve warm.

Per Serving:
calories: 81 | fat: 7g | protein: 1g | carbs: 5g | fiber: 2g | sodium: 27mg

Five-Spice Roasted Sweet Potatoes

Prep time: 10 minutes | Cook time: 12 minutes | Serves 4

- ½ teaspoon ground cinnamon
- ¼ teaspoon ground cumin
- ¼ teaspoon paprika
- 1 teaspoon chile powder
- ⅛ teaspoon turmeric
- ½ teaspoon salt (optional)
- Freshly ground black pepper, to taste
- 2 large sweet potatoes, peeled and cut into ¾-inch cubes (about 3 cups)
- 1 tablespoon olive oil

1. In a large bowl, mix together cinnamon, cumin, paprika, chile powder, turmeric, salt, and pepper to taste. 2. Add potatoes and stir well. 3. Drizzle the seasoned potatoes with the olive oil and stir until evenly coated. 4. Place seasoned potatoes in a baking pan or an ovenproof dish that fits inside your air fryer basket. 5. Cook for 6 minutes at 390ºF (199ºC), stop, and stir well. 6. Cook for an additional 6 minutes.

Per Serving:
calories: 14 | fat: 3g | protein: 1g | carbs: 14g | fiber: 2g | sodium: 327mg

Indian Eggplant Bharta

Prep time: 15 minutes | Cook time: 20 minutes | Serves 4

- 1 medium eggplant
- 2 tablespoons vegetable oil
- ½ cup finely minced onion
- ½ cup finely chopped fresh tomato
- 2 tablespoons fresh lemon juice
- 2 tablespoons chopped fresh cilantro
- ½ teaspoon kosher salt
- ⅛ teaspoon cayenne pepper

1. Rub the eggplant all over with the vegetable oil. Place the eggplant in the air fryer basket. Set the air fryer to 400ºF (204ºC) for 20 minutes, or until the eggplant skin is blistered and charred. 2. Transfer the eggplant to a resealable plastic bag, seal, and set aside for 15 to 20 minutes (the eggplant will finish cooking in the residual heat trapped in the bag). 3. Transfer the eggplant to a large bowl. Peel off and discard the charred skin. Roughly mash the eggplant flesh. Add the onion, tomato, lemon juice, cilantro, salt, and cayenne. Stir to combine.

Per Serving:
calories: 105 | fat: 7g | protein: 2g | carbs: 11g | fiber: 5g | sodium: 295mg

Sesame Carrots and Sugar Snap Peas

Prep time: 10 minutes | Cook time: 16 minutes | Serves 4

- 1 pound (454 g) carrots, peeled sliced on the bias (½-inch slices)
- 1 teaspoon olive oil
- Salt and freshly ground black pepper, to taste
- ⅓ cup honey
- 1 tablespoon sesame oil
- 1 tablespoon soy sauce
- ½ teaspoon minced fresh ginger
- 4 ounces (113 g) sugar snap peas (about 1 cup)
- 1½ teaspoons sesame seeds

1. Preheat the air fryer to 360ºF (182ºC). 2. Toss the carrots with the olive oil, season with salt and pepper and air fry for 10 minutes, shaking the basket once or twice during the cooking process. 3. Combine the honey, sesame oil, soy sauce and minced ginger in a large bowl. Add the sugar snap peas and the air-fried carrots to the honey mixture, toss to coat and return everything to the air fryer basket. 4. Turn up the temperature to 400ºF (204ºC) and air fry for an additional 6 minutes, shaking the basket once during the cooking process. 5. Transfer the carrots and sugar snap peas to a serving bowl. Pour the sauce from the bottom of the cooker over the vegetables and sprinkle sesame seeds over top. Serve immediately.

Per Serving:
calories: 202 | fat: 6g | protein: 2g | carbs: 37g | fiber: 4g | sodium: 141mg

Spicy Roasted Bok Choy

Prep time: 10 minutes | Cook time: 7 to 10 minutes | Serves 4

- 2 tablespoons olive oil
- 2 tablespoons reduced-sodium coconut aminos
- 2 teaspoons sesame oil
- 2 teaspoons chili-garlic sauce
- 2 cloves garlic, minced
- 1 head (about 1 pound / 454 g) bok choy, sliced lengthwise into quarters
- 2 teaspoons black sesame seeds

1. Preheat the air fryer to 400ºF (204ºC). 2. In a large bowl, combine the olive oil, coconut aminos, sesame oil, chili-garlic sauce, and garlic. Add the bok choy and toss, massaging the leaves with your hands if necessary, until thoroughly coated. 3. Arrange the bok choy in the basket of the air fryer. Pausing about halfway through the cooking time to shake the basket, air fry for 7 to 10 minutes until the bok choy is tender and the tips of the leaves begin to crisp. 4. Remove from the basket and let cool for a few minutes before coarsely chopping. Serve sprinkled with the sesame seeds.

Per Serving:
calories: 145 | fat: 13g | protein: 4g | carbs: 6g | fiber: 3g | sodium: 176mg

Couscous-Stuffed Eggplants

Prep time: 10 minutes | Cook time: 45 minutes | Serves 4

2 medium eggplants (about 8 ounces / 227 g each)
1 tablespoon olive oil
⅓ cup whole-wheat couscous
3 tablespoons diced dried apricots
4 scallions, thinly sliced
1 large tomato, seeded and diced
2 tablespoons chopped fresh mint leaves
1 tablespoon chopped, toasted pine nuts
1 tablespoon lemon juice
½ teaspoon salt
¼ teaspoon freshly ground black pepper

1. Preheat the oven to 400°F (205°C). 2. Halve the eggplants lengthwise and score the cut sides with a knife, cutting all the way through the flesh but being careful not to cut through the skin. Brush the cut sides with the olive oil and place the eggplant halves, cut-side up, on a large, rimmed baking sheet. Roast in the preheated oven for about 20 to 30 minutes, until the flesh is softened. 3. While the eggplant is roasting, place the couscous in a small saucepan or heat-safe bowl and cover with boiling water. Cover and let stand until the couscous is tender and has absorbed the water, about 10 minutes. 4. When the eggplants are soft, remove them from the oven (don't turn the oven off) and scoop the flesh into a large bowl, leaving a bit of eggplant inside the skin so that the skin holds its shape. Be cautious not to break the skin. Chop or mash the eggplant flesh and add the couscous, dried apricots, scallions, tomato, mint, pine nuts, lemon juice, salt, and pepper and stir to mix well. 5. Spoon the couscous mixture into the eggplant skins and return them to the baking sheet. Bake in the oven for another 15 minutes or so, until heated through. Serve hot.

Per Serving:
calories: 146 | fat: 5g | protein: 4g | carbs: 22g | fiber: 6g | sodium: 471mg

Cretan Roasted Zucchini

Prep time: 15 minutes | Cook time: 1 hour 15 minutes | Serves 2

6 small zucchini (no longer than 6 inches), washed and ends trimmed
3 garlic cloves, thinly sliced
2 medium tomatoes, chopped, or 1 (15-ounce / 425-g) can crushed tomatoes
⅓ cup extra virgin olive oil
½ teaspoon salt
½ teaspoon freshly ground black pepper
2 tablespoons chopped fresh parsley, divided
Coarse sea salt, for serving (optional)

1. Preheat the oven to 350°F (180°C). 2. Make a long, lengthwise slit in each zucchini that reaches about halfway through. (Do not cut the zucchini all the way through.) Stuff each zucchini with the sliced garlic. 3. Transfer the tomatoes to an oven-safe casserole dish, and nestle the zucchini between the tomatoes. Drizzle the olive oil over the zucchini and tomatoes. 4. Sprinkle the salt, black pepper, and 1 tablespoon of the parsley over the zucchini and tomatoes. Turn the zucchini gently so they are covered in the olive oil. 5. Transfer to the oven and cook for 1 hour 15 minutes or until the skins are soft and the edges have browned. 6. Carefully remove the dish from the oven and sprinkle the remaining parsley and sea salt, if using, over the top. Store covered in the refrigerator for up to 3 days.

Per Serving:
calories: 406 | fat: 37g | protein: 6g | carbs: 18g | fiber: 5g | sodium: 619mg

Roasted Broccoli with Tahini Yogurt Sauce

Prep time: 15 minutes | Cook time: 30 minutes | Serves 4

For the Broccoli:
1½ to 2 pounds (680 to 907 g) broccoli, stalk trimmed and cut into slices, head cut into florets
1 lemon, sliced into ¼-inch-thick rounds
3 tablespoons extra-virgin olive oil
½ teaspoon kosher salt
¼ teaspoon freshly ground black pepper
For the Tahini Yogurt Sauce:
½ cup plain Greek yogurt
2 tablespoons tahini
1 tablespoon lemon juice
¼ teaspoon kosher salt
1 teaspoon sesame seeds, for garnish (optional)

Make the Broccoli: 1. Preheat the oven to 425°F (220°C). Line a baking sheet with parchment paper or foil. 2. In a large bowl, gently toss the broccoli, lemon slices, olive oil, salt, and black pepper to combine. Arrange the broccoli in a single layer on the prepared baking sheet. Roast 15 minutes, stir, and roast another 15 minutes, until golden brown. Make the Tahini Yogurt Sauce: 3. In a medium bowl, combine the yogurt, tahini, lemon juice, and salt; mix well. 4. Spread the tahini yogurt sauce on a platter or large plate and top with the broccoli and lemon slices. Garnish with the sesame seeds (if desired).

Per Serving:
calories: 245 | fat: 16g | protein: 12g | carbs: 20g | fiber: 7g | sodium: 305mg

Cauliflower Steaks with Creamy Tahini Sauce

Prep time: 10 minutes | Cook time: 45 minutes | Serves 4

¼ cup olive oil
4 garlic cloves, minced
1 teaspoon sea salt
1 teaspoon freshly ground black pepper
2 large heads cauliflower, stem end trimmed (core left intact) and cut from top to bottom into thick slabs
½ cup tahini
Juice of 1 lemon
¼ cup chopped fresh Italian parsley

1. Preheat the oven to 400°F (205°C). Line a baking sheet with parchment paper. 2. In a small bowl, combine the olive oil, garlic, salt, and pepper. Brush this mixture on both sides of the cauliflower steaks and place them in a single layer on the baking sheet. Drizzle any remaining oil mixture over the cauliflower steaks. Bake for 45 minutes, or until the cauliflower is soft. 3. While the steaks are baking, in a small bowl, stir together the tahini and lemon juice. Season with salt and pepper. 4. Remove the cauliflower steaks from the oven and transfer them to four plates. Drizzle the lemon tahini sauce evenly over the cauliflower and garnish with the parsley. Serve.

Per Serving:
calories: 339 | fat: 30g | protein: 8g | carbs: 15g | fiber: 6g | sodium: 368mg

Toasted Pita Wedges

Prep time: 5 minutes | Cook time: 12 minutes | Makes 32 wedges

4 whole-wheat pita rounds	¼ teaspoon paprika
1 tablespoon olive oil	Sea salt and freshly ground pepper, to taste
1 teaspoon garlic powder	

1. Preheat oven to 400°F (205°C). 2. Cut the pita rounds into 8 wedges each, and lay on a parchment-lined baking sheet in an even layer. 3. Drizzle with olive oil, and sprinkle with garlic powder and paprika. Season with sea salt and freshly ground pepper. 4. Bake for 10–12 minutes, until wedges are lightly browned and crisp. Allow to cool completely before serving for crisper wedges.

Per Serving:
4 wedges: calories: 102 | fat: 3g | protein: 3g | carbs: 18g | fiber: 2g | sodium: 142mg

Caramelized Eggplant with Harissa Yogurt

Prep time: 10 minutes | Cook time: 15 minutes | Serves 2

1 medium eggplant (about ¾ pound / 340 g), cut crosswise into ½-inch-thick slices and quartered	black pepper, to taste
	½ cup plain yogurt (not Greek)
	2 tablespoons harissa paste
	1 garlic clove, grated
2 tablespoons vegetable oil	2 teaspoons honey
Kosher salt and freshly ground	

1. In a bowl, toss together the eggplant and oil, season with salt and pepper, and toss to coat evenly. Transfer to the air fryer and air fry at 400°F (204°C), shaking the basket every 5 minutes, until the eggplant is caramelized and tender, about 15 minutes. 2. Meanwhile, in a small bowl, whisk together the yogurt, harissa, and garlic, then spread onto a serving plate. 3. Pile the warm eggplant over the yogurt and drizzle with the honey just before serving.

Per Serving:
calories: 247 | fat: 16g | protein: 5g | carbs: 25g | fiber: 8g | sodium: 34mg

Braised Fennel

Prep time: 10 minutes | Cook time: 50 minutes | Serves 4

2 large fennel bulbs	leaves and stalks separated
¼ cup extra-virgin avocado oil or ghee, divided	1 cup water
	3 tablespoons fresh lemon juice
1 small shallot or red onion	Salt and black pepper, to taste
1 clove garlic, sliced	¼ cup extra-virgin olive oil, to drizzle
4 to 6 thyme sprigs	
1 small bunch fresh parsley,	

1. Cut off the fennel stalks where they attach to the bulb. Reserve the stalks. Cut the fennel bulb in half, trim the hard bottom part, and cut into wedges. 2. Heat a saucepan greased with 2 tablespoons of the avocado oil over medium-high heat. Sauté the shallot, garlic, thyme sprigs, parsley stalks, and hard fennel stalks for about 5 minutes. Add the water, bring to a boil, and simmer over medium heat for 10 minutes. Remove from the heat, set aside for 10 minutes, and then strain the stock, discarding the aromatics. 3. Preheat the oven to 350°F (180°C) fan assisted or 400°F (205°C) conventional. 4. Heat an ovenproof skillet greased with the remaining 2 tablespoons of avocado oil over medium-high heat and add the fennel wedges. Sear until caramelized, about 5 minutes, turning once. Pour the stock and the lemon juice over the fennel wedges, and season with salt and pepper. Loosely cover with a piece of aluminum foil. Bake for about 30 minutes. When done, the fennel should be easy to pierce with the tip of a knife. 5. Remove from the oven and scatter with the chopped parsley leaves and drizzle with the olive oil. To store, let cool and refrigerate for up to 5 days.

Per Serving:
calories: 225 | fat: 20g | protein: 2g | carbs: 12g | fiber: 5g | sodium: 187mg

Honey and Spice Glazed Carrots

Prep time: 5 minutes | Cook time: 5 minutes | Serves 4

4 large carrots, peeled and sliced on the diagonal into ½-inch-thick rounds	½ cup honey
	1 tablespoon red wine vinegar
	1 tablespoon chopped flat-leaf parsley
1 teaspoon ground cinnamon	
1 teaspoon ground ginger	1 tablespoon chopped cilantro
3 tablespoons olive oil	2 tablespoons toasted pine nuts

1. Bring a large saucepan of lightly salted water to a boil and add the carrots. Cover and cook for about 5 minutes, until the carrots are just tender. Drain in a colander, then transfer to a medium bowl. 2. Add the cinnamon, ginger, olive oil, honey, and vinegar and toss to combine well. Add the parsley and cilantro and toss again to incorporate. Garnish with the pine nuts. Serve immediately or let cool to room temperature.

Per Serving:
calories: 281 | fat: 14g | protein: 1g | carbs: 43g | fiber: 2g | sodium: 48mg

Mediterranean Zucchini Boats

Prep time: 5 minutes | Cook time: 10 minutes | Serves 4

1 large zucchini, ends removed, halved lengthwise	¼ cup feta cheese
	1 tablespoon balsamic vinegar
6 grape tomatoes, quartered	1 tablespoon olive oil
¼ teaspoon salt	

1. Use a spoon to scoop out 2 tablespoons from center of each zucchini half, making just enough space to fill with tomatoes and feta. 2. Place tomatoes evenly in centers of zucchini halves and sprinkle with salt. Place into ungreased air fryer basket. Adjust the temperature to 350°F (177°C) and roast for 10 minutes. When done, zucchini will be tender. 3. Transfer boats to a serving tray and sprinkle with feta, then drizzle with vinegar and olive oil. Serve warm.

Per Serving:
calories: 92 | fat: 6g | protein: 3g | carbs: 8g | fiber: 2g | sodium: 242mg

Rice Pilaf with Dill

Prep time: 15 minutes | Cook time: 25 minutes | Serves 6

2 tablespoons olive oil
1 carrot, finely chopped (about ¾ cup)
2 leeks, halved lengthwise, washed, well drained, and sliced in half-moons
½ teaspoon salt
¼ teaspoon freshly ground black pepper
2 tablespoons chopped fresh dill
1 cup low-sodium vegetable broth or water
½ cup basmati rice

1. In a 2-or 3-quart saucepan, heat the olive oil over medium heat. Add the carrot, leeks, salt, pepper, and 1 tablespoon of the dill. Cover and cook for 6 to 8 minutes, stirring once, to soften all the vegetables but not brown them. 2. Add the broth or water and bring to a boil. Stir in the rice, reduce the heat to maintain a simmer, cover, and cook for 15 minutes. Remove from the heat; let stand, covered, for 10 minutes. 3. Fluff the rice with fork. Stir in the remaining 1 tablespoon dill and serve.

Per Serving:
1 cup: calories: 100 | fat: 7g | protein: 2g | carbs: 11g | fiber: 4g | sodium: 209mg

Zucchini-Eggplant Gratin

Prep time: 10 minutes |Cook time: 20 minutes| Serves: 6

1 large eggplant, finely chopped (about 5 cups)
2 large zucchini, finely chopped (about 3¾ cups)
¼ teaspoon freshly ground black pepper
¼ teaspoon kosher or sea salt
3 tablespoons extra-virgin olive oil, divided
1 tablespoon all-purpose flour
¾ cup 2% milk
⅓ cup plus 2 tablespoons grated Parmesan cheese, divided
1 cup chopped tomato (about 1 large tomato)
1 cup diced or shredded fresh mozzarella (about 4 ounces / 113 g)
¼ cup fresh basil leaves

1. Preheat the oven to 425ºF (220ºC). 2. In a large bowl, toss together the eggplant, zucchini, pepper, and salt. 3. In a large skillet over medium-high heat, heat 1 tablespoon of oil. Add half the veggie mixture to the skillet. Stir a few times, then cover and cook for 5 minutes, stirring occasionally. Pour the cooked veggies into a baking dish. Place the skillet back on the heat, add 1 tablespoon of oil, and repeat with the remaining veggies. Add the veggies to the baking dish. 4. While the vegetables are cooking, heat the milk in the microwave for 1 minute. Set aside. 5. Place a medium saucepan over medium heat. Add the remaining tablespoon of oil and flour, and whisk together for about 1 minute, until well blended. 6. Slowly pour the warm milk into the oil mixture, whisking the entire time. Continue to whisk frequently until the mixture thickens a bit. Add ⅓ cup of Parmesan cheese, and whisk until melted. Pour the cheese sauce over the vegetables in the baking dish and mix well. 7. Gently mix in the tomatoes and mozzarella cheese. Roast in the oven for 10 minutes, or until the gratin is almost set and not runny. Garnish with the fresh basil leaves and the remaining 2 tablespoons of Parmesan cheese before serving.

Per Serving:
calories: 176 | fat: 9g | protein: 11g | carbs: 14g | fiber: 5g | sodium: 362mg

Puréed Cauliflower Soup

Prep time: 15 minutes | Cook time: 11 minutes | Serves 6

2 tablespoons olive oil
1 medium onion, peeled and chopped
1 stalk celery, chopped
1 medium carrot, peeled and chopped
3 sprigs fresh thyme
4 cups cauliflower florets
2 cups vegetable stock
½ cup half-and-half
¼ cup low-fat plain Greek yogurt
2 tablespoons chopped fresh chives

1. Press the Sauté button on the Instant Pot® and heat oil. Add onion, celery, and carrot. Cook until just tender, about 6 minutes. Add thyme, cauliflower, and stock. Stir well, then press the Cancel button. 2. Close lid, set steam release to Sealing, press the Manual button, and set time to 5 minutes. When the timer beeps, let pressure release naturally, about 15 minutes. 3. Open lid, remove and discard thyme stems, and with an immersion blender, purée soup until smooth. Stir in half-and-half and yogurt. Garnish with chives and serve immediately.

Per Serving:
calories: 113 | fat: 7g | protein: 3g | carbs: 9g | fiber: 2g | sodium: 236mg

Crispy Green Beans

Prep time: 5 minutes | Cook time: 8 minutes | Serves 4

2 teaspoons olive oil
½ pound (227 g) fresh green beans, ends trimmed
¼ teaspoon salt
¼ teaspoon ground black pepper

1. In a large bowl, drizzle olive oil over green beans and sprinkle with salt and pepper. 2. Place green beans into ungreased air fryer basket. Adjust the temperature to 350ºF (177ºC) and set the timer for 8 minutes, shaking the basket two times during cooking. Green beans will be dark golden and crispy at the edges when done. Serve warm.

Per Serving:
calories: 33 | fat: 3g | protein: 1g | carbs: 3g | fiber: 1g | sodium: 147mg

Garlic and Herb Roasted Grape Tomatoes

Prep time: 10 minutes | Cook time: 45 minutes | Serves 2

1 pint grape tomatoes
10 whole garlic cloves, skins removed
¼ cup olive oil
½ teaspoon salt
1 fresh rosemary sprig
1 fresh thyme sprig

1. Preheat oven to 350ºF(180ºC). 2. Toss tomatoes, garlic cloves, oil, salt, and herb sprigs in a baking dish. 3. Roast tomatoes until they are soft and begin to caramelize, about 45 minutes. 4. Remove herbs before serving.

Per Serving:
calories: 271 | fat: 26g | protein: 3g | carbs: 12g | fiber: 3g | sodium: 593mg

Tahini-Lemon Kale

Prep time: 5 minutes | Cook time: 15 minutes | Serves 2 to 4

¼ cup tahini	4 cups packed torn kale leaves
¼ cup fresh lemon juice	(stems and ribs removed and
2 tablespoons olive oil	leaves torn into palm-size
1 teaspoon sesame seeds	pieces; about 4 ounces / 113 g)
½ teaspoon garlic powder	Kosher salt and freshly ground
¼ teaspoon cayenne pepper	black pepper, to taste

1. In a large bowl, whisk together the tahini, lemon juice, olive oil, sesame seeds, garlic powder, and cayenne until smooth. Add the kale leaves, season with salt and black pepper, and toss in the dressing until completely coated. Transfer the kale leaves to a cake pan. 2. Place the pan in the air fryer and roast at 350°F (177°C), stirring every 5 minutes, until the kale is wilted and the top is lightly browned, about 15 minutes. Remove the pan from the air fryer and serve warm.

Per Serving:
calories: 221 | fat: 21g | protein: 5g | carbs: 8g | fiber: 3g | sodium: 32mg

Sesame-Ginger Broccoli

Prep time: 10 minutes | Cook time: 15 minutes | Serves 4

3 tablespoons toasted sesame oil	½ teaspoon kosher salt
2 teaspoons sesame seeds	½ teaspoon black pepper
1 tablespoon chili-garlic sauce	1 (16-ounce / 454-g) package frozen broccoli florets (do not thaw)
2 teaspoons minced fresh ginger	

1. In a large bowl, combine the sesame oil, sesame seeds, chili-garlic sauce, ginger, salt, and pepper. Stir until well combined. Add the broccoli and toss until well coated. 2. Arrange the broccoli in the air fryer basket. Set the air fryer to 325°F (163°C) for 15 minutes, or until the broccoli is crisp, tender, and the edges are lightly browned, gently tossing halfway through the cooking time.

Per Serving:
calories: 143 | fat: 11g | protein: 4g | carbs: 9g | fiber: 4g | sodium: 385mg

Easy Greek Briami (Ratatouille)

Prep time: 15 minutes | Cook time: 40 minutes | Serves 6

2 russet potatoes, cubed	1 teaspoon dried oregano
½ cup Roma tomatoes, cubed	½ teaspoon salt
1 eggplant, cubed	½ teaspoon black pepper
1 zucchini, cubed	¼ teaspoon red pepper flakes
1 red onion, chopped	⅓ cup olive oil
1 red bell pepper, chopped	1 (8-ounce / 227-g) can tomato paste
2 garlic cloves, minced	
1 teaspoon dried mint	¼ cup vegetable broth
1 teaspoon dried parsley	¼ cup water

1. Preheat the air fryer to 320°F (160°C). 2. In a large bowl, combine the potatoes, tomatoes, eggplant, zucchini, onion, bell pepper, garlic, mint, parsley, oregano, salt, black pepper, and red pepper flakes. 3. In a small bowl, mix together the olive oil, tomato paste, broth, and water. 4. Pour the oil-and-tomato-paste mixture over the vegetables and toss until everything is coated. 5. Pour the coated vegetables into the air fryer basket in an even layer and roast for 20 minutes. After 20 minutes, stir well and spread out again. Roast for an additional 10 minutes, then repeat the process and cook for another 10 minutes.

Per Serving:
calories: 239 | fat: 13g | protein: 5g | carbs: 31g | fiber: 7g | sodium: 250mg

Roasted Garlic

Prep time: 5 minutes | Cook time: 20 minutes | Makes 12 cloves

1 medium head garlic	2 teaspoons avocado oil

1. Remove any hanging excess peel from the garlic but leave the cloves covered. Cut off ¼ of the head of garlic, exposing the tips of the cloves. 2. Drizzle with avocado oil. Place the garlic head into a small sheet of aluminum foil, completely enclosing it. Place it into the air fryer basket. 3. Adjust the temperature to 400°F (204°C) and air fry for 20 minutes. If your garlic head is a bit smaller, check it after 15 minutes. 4. When done, garlic should be golden brown and very soft. 5. To serve, cloves should pop out and easily be spread or sliced. Store in an airtight container in the refrigerator up to 5 days. You may also freeze individual cloves on a baking sheet, then store together in a freezer-safe storage bag once frozen.

Per Serving:
calories: 8 | fat: 1g | protein: 0g | carbs: 0g | fiber: 0g | sodium: 0mg

Nordic Stone Age Bread

Prep time: 10 minutes | Cook time: 1 hour | Serves 14

½ cup flaxseeds	chopped
½ cup chia seeds	½ cup pecans or walnuts
½ cup sesame seeds	1 teaspoon salt, or to taste
¼ cup pumpkin seeds	1 teaspoon coarse black pepper
¼ cup sunflower seeds	4 large eggs
½ cup whole almonds, chopped	½ cup extra-virgin olive oil or melted ghee
½ cup blanched hazelnuts,	

1. Preheat the oven to 285°F (140°C) fan assisted or 320°F (160°C) conventional. Line a loaf pan with parchment paper. 2. In a mixing bowl, combine all of the dry ingredients. Add the eggs and olive oil and stir through until well combined. Pour the dough into the loaf pan. Transfer to the oven and bake for about 1 hour or until the top is crisp. 3. Remove from the oven and let cool slightly in the pan before transferring to a wire rack to cool completely before slicing. Store at room temperature for up to 3 days loosely covered with a kitchen towel, refrigerate for up to 10 days, or freeze for up to 3 months.

Per Serving:
calories: 251 | fat: 23g | protein: 7g | carbs: 7g | fiber: 5g | sodium: 192mg

Roasted Vegetables with Lemon Tahini

Prep time: 15 minutes | Cook time: 25 minutes | Serves 4

For the Dressing:
½ cup tahini
½ cup water, as needed
3 tablespoons freshly squeezed lemon juice
Sea salt
For the Vegetables:
8 ounces (227 g) baby potatoes, halved
8 ounces (227 g) baby carrots
1 head cauliflower, cored and cut into large chunks
2 red bell peppers, quartered
1 zucchini, cut into 1-inch pieces
¼ cup olive oil
1½ teaspoons garlic powder
¼ teaspoon dried oregano
¼ teaspoon dried thyme
Sea salt
Freshly ground black pepper
Red pepper flakes (optional)

Make the Dressing: 1. In a small bowl, stir together the tahini, water, and lemon juice until well blended. 2. Taste, season with salt, and set aside. Make the Vegetables: 3. Preheat the oven to 425°F(220°C). Line a baking sheet with parchment paper. 4. Place the potatoes in a microwave-safe bowl with 3 tablespoons water, cover with a paper plate, and microwave on high for 4 minutes. Drain any excess water. 5. Transfer the potatoes to a large bowl and add the carrots, cauliflower, bell peppers, zucchini, olive oil, garlic powder, oregano, and thyme. Season with salt and black pepper. 6. Spread the vegetables in a single layer on the prepared baking sheet and roast until fork-tender and a little charred, about 25 minutes. 7. Transfer the vegetables to a large bowl and add the dressing and red pepper flakes, if desired. Toss to coat. 8. Serve the roasted vegetables alongside your favorite chicken or fish dish.

Per Serving:
calories: 412 | fat: 30g | protein: 9g | carbs: 31g | fiber: 9g | sodium: 148mg

Brussels Sprouts with Pecans and Gorgonzola

Prep time: 10 minutes | Cook time: 25 minutes | Serves 4

½ cup pecans
1½ pounds (680 g) fresh Brussels sprouts, trimmed and quartered
2 tablespoons olive oil
Salt and freshly ground black pepper, to taste
¼ cup crumbled Gorgonzola cheese

1. Spread the pecans in a single layer of the air fryer and set the heat to 350°F (177°C). Air fry for 3 to 5 minutes until the pecans are lightly browned and fragrant. Transfer the pecans to a plate and continue preheating the air fryer, increasing the heat to 400°F (204°C). 2. In a large bowl, toss the Brussels sprouts with the olive oil and season with salt and black pepper to taste. 3. Working in batches if necessary, arrange the Brussels sprouts in a single layer in the air fryer basket. Pausing halfway through the baking time to shake the basket, air fry for 20 to 25 minutes until the sprouts are tender and starting to brown on the edges. 4. Transfer the sprouts to a serving bowl and top with the toasted pecans and Gorgonzola. Serve warm or at room temperature.

Per Serving:
calories: 253 | fat: 18g | protein: 9g | carbs: 17g | fiber: 8g | sodium: 96mg

Roasted Fennel with Za'atar

Prep time: 10 minutes | Cook time: 30 minutes | Serves 4

4 fennel bulbs, quartered
1 tablespoon olive oil
1 tablespoon za'atar seasoning
¼ teaspoon salt

1. Preheat the oven to 425°F (220°C). 2. In a large bowl, toss the fennel bulbs with the olive oil, za'atar, and salt. Spread them on a large baking sheet and roast for 25 to 30 minutes, tossing once after 15 minutes, until softened and caramelized.

Per Serving:
calories: 109 | fat: 3g | protein: 3g | carbs: 18g | fiber: 7g | sodium: 422mg

Polenta with Mushroom Bolognese

Prep time: 5 minutes | Cook time: 25 minutes | Serves 4

2 (8-ounce / 227-g) packages white button mushrooms
3 tablespoons extra-virgin olive oil, divided
1½ cups finely chopped onion (about ¾ medium onion)
½ cup finely chopped carrot (about 1 medium carrot)
4 garlic cloves, minced (about 2 teaspoons)
1 (18-ounce / 510-g) tube plain polenta, cut into 8 slices
¼ cup tomato paste
1 tablespoon dried oregano, crushed between your fingers
¼ teaspoon ground nutmeg
¼ teaspoon kosher or sea salt
¼ teaspoon freshly ground black pepper
½ cup dry red wine
½ cup whole milk
½ teaspoon sugar

1. Put half the mushrooms in a food processor bowl and pulse about 15 times until finely chopped but not puréed, similar to the texture of ground meat. Repeat with the remaining mushrooms and set aside. (You can also use the food processor to chop the onion, carrot, and garlic, instead of chopping with a knife.) 2. In a large stockpot over medium-high heat, heat 2 tablespoons of oil. Add the onion and carrot and cook for 5 minutes, stirring occasionally. Add the mushrooms and garlic and cook for 5 minutes, stirring frequently. 3. While the vegetables are cooking, add the remaining 1 tablespoon of oil to a large skillet and heat over medium-high heat. Add 4 slices of polenta to the skillet and cook for 3 to 4 minutes, until golden; flip and cook for 3 to 4 minutes more. Remove the polenta from the skillet, place it on a shallow serving dish, and cover with aluminum foil to keep warm. Repeat with the remaining 4 slices of polenta. 4. To the mushroom mixture in the stockpot, add the tomato paste, oregano, nutmeg, salt, and pepper and stir. Continue cooking for another 2 to 3 minutes, until the vegetables have softened and begun to brown. Add the wine and cook for 1 to 2 minutes, scraping up any bits from the bottom of the pan while stirring with a wooden spoon. Cook until the wine is nearly all evaporated. Lower the heat to medium. 5. Meanwhile, in a small, microwave-safe bowl, mix the milk and sugar together and microwave on high for 30 to 45 seconds, until very hot. Slowly stir the milk into the mushroom mixture and simmer for 4 more minutes, until the milk is absorbed. To serve, pour the mushroom veggie sauce over the warm polenta slices.

Per Serving:
calories: 313 | fat: 12g | protein: 7g | carbs: 41g | fiber: 4g | sodium: 467mg

Balsamic Beets

Prep time: 15 minutes | Cook time: 3 to 4 hours | Serves 8

Cooking spray or 1 tablespoon extra-virgin olive oil
3 pounds (1.4 kg) beets, scrubbed, peeled, and cut into wedges
2 garlic cloves, minced
1 cup white grape or apple juice
½ cup balsamic vinegar
1 tablespoon honey
2 fresh thyme sprigs
1 teaspoon kosher salt, plus more for seasoning
½ teaspoon freshly ground black pepper, plus more for seasoning
1 tablespoon cold water
1 tablespoon cornstarch

1. Use the cooking spray or olive oil to coat the inside (bottom and sides) of the slow cooker. Add the beets, garlic, juice, vinegar, honey, thyme, salt, and pepper. Stir to combine. Cover and cook on high for 3 to 4 hours. 2. About 10 minutes before serving, combine the water and cornstarch in a small bowl, stirring until no lumps remain. Add to the slow cooker and continue to cook for 10 minutes, or until the sauce thickens. 3. Discard the thyme. Season with additional salt and pepper, as needed. Serve.

Per Serving:
calories: 129 | fat: 2g | protein: 3g | carbs: 26g | net carbs: 21g | sugars: 19g | fiber: 5g | sodium: 429mg | cholesterol: 0mg

Grilled Vegetables

Prep time: 15 minutes | Cook time: 8 minutes | Serves 4

4 carrots, peeled and cut in half
2 onions, quartered
1 zucchini, cut into ½-inch rounds
1 red bell pepper, seeded and cut into cubes
¼ cup olive oil
Sea salt and freshly ground pepper, to taste
Balsamic vinegar

1. Heat the grill to medium-high. 2. Brush the vegetables lightly with olive oil, and season with sea salt and freshly ground pepper. 3. Place the carrots and onions on the grill first because they take the longest. Cook the vegetables for 3–4 minutes on each side. 4. Transfer to a serving dish, and drizzle with olive oil and balsamic vinegar.

Per Serving:
calories: 209 | fat: 14g | protein: 3g | carbs: 20g | fiber: 6g | sodium: 92mg

Mushrooms with Goat Cheese

Prep time: 10 minutes | Cook time: 10 minutes | Serves 4

3 tablespoons vegetable oil
1 pound (454 g) mixed mushrooms, trimmed and sliced
1 clove garlic, minced
¼ teaspoon dried thyme
½ teaspoon black pepper
4 ounces (113 g) goat cheese, diced
2 teaspoons chopped fresh thyme leaves (optional)

1. In a baking pan, combine the oil, mushrooms, garlic, dried thyme, and pepper. Stir in the goat cheese. Place the pan in the air fryer basket. Set the air fryer to 400°F (204°C) for 10 minutes, stirring halfway through the cooking time. 2. Sprinkle with fresh thyme, if desired.

Per Serving:
calories: 218 | fat: 19g | protein: 10g | carbs: 4g | fiber: 1g | sodium: 124mg

Roasted Cherry Tomato Caprese

Prep time: 15 minutes | Cook time: 30 minutes | Serves 4

2 pints (about 20 ounces / 567 g) cherry tomatoes
6 thyme sprigs
6 garlic cloves, smashed
2 tablespoons extra-virgin olive oil
½ teaspoon kosher salt
8 ounces (227 g) fresh, unsalted Mozzarella, cut into bite-size slices
¼ cup basil, chopped or cut into ribbons
Loaf of crusty whole-wheat bread, for serving

1. Preheat the oven to 350°F (180°C). Line a baking sheet with parchment paper or foil. 2. Put the tomatoes, thyme, garlic, olive oil, and salt into a large bowl and mix together. Place on the prepared baking sheet in a single layer. Roast for 30 minutes, or until the tomatoes are bursting and juicy. 3. Place the Mozzarella on a platter or in a bowl. Pour all the tomato mixture, including the juices, over the Mozzarella. Garnish with the basil. 4. Serve with crusty bread.

Per Serving:
calories: 250 | fat: 17g | protein: 17g | carbs: 9g | fiber: 2g | sodium: 157mg

Mediterranean Lentil Sloppy Joes

Prep time: 5 minutes | Cook time: 15 minutes | Serves: 4

1 tablespoon extra-virgin olive oil
1 cup chopped onion (about ½ medium onion)
1 cup chopped bell pepper, any color (about 1 medium bell pepper)
2 garlic cloves, minced (about 1 teaspoon)
1 (15-ounce / 425-g) can lentils, drained and rinsed
1 (14½-ounce / 411-g) can low-sodium or no-salt-added diced tomatoes, undrained
1 teaspoon ground cumin
1 teaspoon dried thyme
¼ teaspoon kosher or sea salt
4 whole-wheat pita breads, split open
1½ cups chopped seedless cucumber (1 medium cucumber)
1 cup chopped romaine lettuce

1. In a medium saucepan over medium-high heat, heat the oil. Add the onion and bell pepper and cook for 4 minutes, stirring frequently. Add the garlic and cook for 1 minute, stirring frequently. Add the lentils, tomatoes (with their liquid), cumin, thyme, and salt. Turn the heat to medium and cook, stirring occasionally, for 10 minutes, or until most of the liquid has evaporated. 2. Stuff the lentil mixture inside each pita. Lay the cucumbers and lettuce on top of the lentil mixture and serve.

Per Serving:
calories: 530 | fat: 6g | protein: 31g | carbs: 93g | fiber: 17g | sodium: 292mg

Dandelion Greens

Prep time: 10 minutes | Cook time: 1 minute | Serves 6

- 4 pounds (1.8 kg) dandelion greens, stalks cut and discarded, and greens washed
- ½ cup water
- ¼ cup extra-virgin olive oil
- ¼ cup lemon juice
- ½ teaspoon salt
- ½ teaspoon ground black pepper

1. Add dandelion greens and water to the Instant Pot®. Close lid, set steam release to Sealing, press the Manual button, and set time to 1 minute. When the timer beeps, quick-release the pressure until the float valve drops. Open lid and drain well. 2. Combine olive oil, lemon juice, salt, and pepper in a small bowl. Pour over greens and toss to coat.

Per Serving:
calories: 39 | fat: 12g | protein: 1g | carbs: 7g | fiber: 3g | sodium: 253mg

Broccoli Salad

Prep time: 5 minutes | Cook time: 7 minutes | Serves 4

- 2 cups fresh broccoli florets, chopped
- 1 tablespoon olive oil
- ¼ teaspoon salt
- ⅛ teaspoon ground black pepper
- ¼ cup lemon juice, divided
- ¼ cup shredded Parmesan cheese
- ¼ cup sliced roasted almonds

1. In a large bowl, toss broccoli and olive oil together. Sprinkle with salt and pepper, then drizzle with 2 tablespoons lemon juice. 2. Place broccoli into ungreased air fryer basket. Adjust the temperature to 350ºF (177ºC) and set the timer for 7 minutes, shaking the basket halfway through cooking. Broccoli will be golden on the edges when done. 3. Place broccoli into a large serving bowl and drizzle with remaining lemon juice. Sprinkle with Parmesan and almonds. Serve warm.

Per Serving:
calories: 76 | fat: 5g | protein: 3g | carbs: 5g | fiber: 1g | sodium: 273mg

Individual Asparagus and Goat Cheese Frittatas

Prep time: 15 minutes | Cook time: 15 minutes | Serves 4

- 1 tablespoon extra-virgin olive oil
- 8 ounces (227 g) asparagus, trimmed and sliced ¼ inch thick
- 1 red bell pepper, stemmed, seeded, and chopped
- 2 shallots, minced
- 2 ounces (57 g) goat cheese, crumbled (½ cup)
- 1 tablespoon minced fresh tarragon
- 1 teaspoon grated lemon zest
- 8 large eggs
- ½ teaspoon table salt

1. Using highest sauté function, heat oil in Instant Pot until shimmering. Add asparagus, bell pepper, and shallots; cook until softened, about 5 minutes. Turn off Instant Pot and transfer vegetables to bowl. Stir in goat cheese, tarragon, and lemon zest. 2. Arrange trivet included with Instant Pot in base of now-empty insert and add 1 cup water. Spray four 6-ounce ramekins with vegetable oil spray. Beat eggs, ¼ cup water, and salt in large bowl until thoroughly combined. Divide vegetable mixture between prepared ramekins, then pour egg mixture over top (you may have some left over). Set ramekins on trivet. Lock lid in place and close pressure release valve. Select high pressure cook function and cook for 10 minutes. 3. Turn off Instant Pot and quick-release pressure. Carefully remove lid, allowing steam to escape away from you. Using tongs, transfer ramekins to wire rack and let cool slightly. Run paring knife around inside edge of ramekins to loosen frittatas, then invert onto individual serving plates. Serve.

Per Serving:
calories: 240 | fat: 16g | protein: 17g | carbs: 6g | fiber: 2g | sodium: 500mg

Spanish Green Beans

Prep time: 10 minutes | Cook time: 20 minutes | Serves 4

- ¼ cup extra-virgin olive oil
- 1 large onion, chopped
- 4 cloves garlic, finely chopped
- 1 pound (454 g) green beans, fresh or frozen, trimmed
- 1½ teaspoons salt, divided
- 1 (15-ounce / 425-g) can diced tomatoes
- ½ teaspoon freshly ground black pepper

1. In a large pot over medium heat, heat the olive oil, onion, and garlic; cook for 1 minute. 2. Cut the green beans into 2-inch pieces. 3. Add the green beans and 1 teaspoon of salt to the pot and toss everything together; cook for 3 minutes. 4. Add the diced tomatoes, remaining ½ teaspoon of salt, and black pepper to the pot; continue to cook for another 12 minutes, stirring occasionally. 5. Serve warm.

Per Serving:
calories: 200 | fat: 14g | protein: 4g | carbs: 18g | fiber: 6g | sodium: 844mg

Mini Moroccan Pumpkin Cakes

Prep time: 10 minutes | Cook time: 10 minutes | Serves 6

- 2 cups cooked brown rice
- 1 cup pumpkin purée
- ½ cup finely chopped walnuts
- 3 tablespoons olive oil, divided
- ½ medium onion, diced
- ½ red bell pepper, diced
- 1 teaspoon ground cumin
- Sea salt and freshly ground pepper, to taste
- 1 teaspoon hot paprika or a pinch of cayenne

1. Combine the rice, pumpkin, and walnuts in a large bowl; set aside. 2. In a medium skillet, heat the olive oil over medium heat, add the onion and bell pepper, and cook until soft, about 5 minutes. 3. Add the cumin to the onions and bell peppers. Add onion mixture to the rice mixture. 4. Mix thoroughly and season with sea salt, freshly ground pepper, and paprika or cayenne. 5. In a large skillet, heat 2 tablespoons of olive oil over medium heat. 6. Form the rice mixture into 1-inch patties and add them to the skillet. Cook until both sides are browned and crispy. 7. Serve with Greek yogurt or tzatziki on the side.

Per Serving:
calories: 193 | fat: 12g | protein: 3g | carbs: 20g | fiber: 3g | sodium: 6mg

Cauliflower Steaks Gratin

Prep time: 10 minutes | Cook time: 13 minutes | Serves 2

1 head cauliflower	thyme leaves
1 tablespoon olive oil	3 tablespoons grated
Salt and freshly ground black pepper, to taste	Parmigiano-Reggiano cheese
½ teaspoon chopped fresh	2 tablespoons panko bread crumbs

1. Preheat the air fryer to 370ºF (188ºC). 2. Cut two steaks out of the center of the cauliflower. To do this, cut the cauliflower in half and then cut one slice about 1-inch thick off each half. The rest of the cauliflower will fall apart into florets, which you can roast on their own or save for another meal. 3. Brush both sides of the cauliflower steaks with olive oil and season with salt, freshly ground black pepper and fresh thyme. Place the cauliflower steaks into the air fryer basket and air fry for 6 minutes. Turn the steaks over and air fry for another 4 minutes. Combine the Parmesan cheese and panko bread crumbs and sprinkle the mixture over the tops of both steaks and air fry for another 3 minutes until the cheese has melted and the bread crumbs have browned. Serve this with some sautéed bitter greens and air-fried blistered tomatoes.

Per Serving:
calories: 192 | fat: 10g | protein: 9g | carbs: 21g | fiber: 6g | sodium: 273mg

Vegetable Terrine

Prep time: 30 minutes | Cook time: 5 to 7 hours | Serves 6

1 small eggplant, thinly sliced lengthwise	4 large tomatoes, sliced
2 green bell peppers, halved, seeded, and sliced	1 teaspoon sea salt
	¼ teaspoon freshly ground black pepper
2 red bell peppers, halved, seeded, and sliced	Nonstick cooking spray
1 portobello mushroom, cut into ¼-inch-thick slices	1 cup grated Parmesan cheese
	2 tablespoons extra-virgin olive oil
1 zucchini, thinly sliced lengthwise	1 tablespoon red wine vinegar
1 large red onion, cut into ¼-inch-thick rounds	2 teaspoons freshly squeezed lemon juice
	1 teaspoon dried basil
2 yellow squash, thinly sliced lengthwise	1 garlic clove, minced

1. Season the eggplant, green and red bell peppers, mushroom, zucchini, onion, squash, and tomatoes with salt and black pepper, but keep all the vegetables separate. 2. Generously coat a slow-cooker insert with cooking spray, or line the bottom and sides with parchment paper or aluminum foil. 3. Starting with half of the eggplant, line the bottom of the prepared slow cooker with overlapping slices. Sprinkle with 2 tablespoons of Parmesan cheese. 4. Add a second layer using half of the green and red bell peppers. Sprinkle with 2 more tablespoons of Parmesan cheese. 5. Add a third layer using half of the mushroom slices. Sprinkle with 2 more tablespoons of Parmesan cheese. 6. Add a fourth layer using half of the zucchini slices. Sprinkle with 2 more tablespoons of Parmesan cheese. 7. Add a fifth layer using half of the red onion slices. Sprinkle with another 2 tablespoons of Parmesan cheese. 8. Add a sixth layer using half of the yellow squash slices. Sprinkle with 2 more tablespoons of Parmesan cheese. 9. Add a final seventh layer with half of the tomato slices. Sprinkle with 2 more tablespoons of Parmesan cheese. 10. Repeat the layering with the remaining vegetables and Parmesan cheese in the same order until all of the vegetables have been used. 11. In a small bowl, whisk together the olive oil, vinegar, lemon juice, basil, and garlic until combined. Pour the mixture over the vegetables. Top with any remaining Parmesan cheese. 12. Cover the cooker and cook for 5 to 7 hours on Low heat. 13. Let cool to room temperature before slicing and serving.

Per Serving:
calories: 217 | fat: 11g | protein: 12g | carbs: 24g | fiber: 7g | sodium: 725mg

Greek Garlic Dip

Prep time: 10 minutes | Cook time: 30 minutes | Serves 4

2 potatoes (about 1 pound / 454 g), peeled and quartered	juice
	4 garlic cloves, minced
½ cup olive oil	Sea salt
¼ cup freshly squeezed lemon	Freshly ground black pepper

1. Place the potatoes in a large saucepan and fill the pan three-quarters full with water. Bring the water to a boil over medium-high heat, then reduce the heat to medium and cook the potatoes until fork-tender, 20 to 30 minutes. 2. While the potatoes are boiling, in a medium bowl, stir together the olive oil, lemon juice, and garlic; set aside. 3. Drain the potatoes and return them to the saucepan. Pour in the oil mixture and mash with a potato masher or a fork until well combined and smooth. Taste and season with salt and pepper. Serve.

Per Serving:
calories: 334 | fat: 27g | protein: 3g | carbs: 22g | fiber: 3g | sodium: 47mg

Lemon-Rosemary Beets

Prep time: 10 minutes | Cook time: 8 hours | Serves 7

2 pounds (907 g) beets, peeled and cut into wedges	1 tablespoon apple cider vinegar
2 tablespoons fresh lemon juice	¾ teaspoon sea salt
2 tablespoons extra-virgin olive oil	½ teaspoon black pepper
	2 sprigs fresh rosemary
2 tablespoons honey	½ teaspoon lemon zest

1. Place the beets in the slow cooker. 2. Whisk the lemon juice, extra-virgin olive oil, honey, apple cider vinegar, salt, and pepper together in a small bowl. Pour over the beets. 3. Add the sprigs of rosemary to the slow cooker. 4. Cover and cook on low for 8 hours, or until the beets are tender. 5. Remove and discard the rosemary sprigs. Stir in the lemon zest. Serve hot.

Per Serving:
calories: 111 | fat: 4g | protein: 2g | carbs: 18g | fiber: 4g | sodium: 351mg

Roasted Brussels Sprouts with Tahini-Yogurt Sauce

Prep time: 10 minutes | Cook time: 35 minutes | Serves 4

1 pound (454 g) Brussels sprouts, trimmed and halved lengthwise
6 tablespoons extra-virgin olive oil, divided
1 teaspoon salt, divided
½ teaspoon garlic powder
¼ teaspoon freshly ground black pepper
¼ cup plain whole-milk Greek yogurt
¼ cup tahini
Zest and juice of 1 lemon

1. Preheat the oven to 425°F (220°C). Line a baking sheet with aluminum foil or parchment paper and set aside. 2. Place the Brussels sprouts in a large bowl. Drizzle with 4 tablespoons olive oil, ½ teaspoon salt, the garlic powder, and pepper and toss well to coat. 3. Place the Brussels sprouts in a single layer on the baking sheet, reserving the bowl, and roast for 20 minutes. Remove from the oven and give the sprouts a toss to flip. Return to the oven and continue to roast until browned and crispy, another 10 to 15 minutes. Remove from the oven and return to the reserved bowl. 4. In a small bowl, whisk together the yogurt, tahini, lemon zest and juice, remaining 2 tablespoons olive oil, and remaining ½ teaspoon salt. Drizzle over the roasted sprouts and toss to coat. Serve warm.

Per Serving:
calories: 330 | fat: 29g | protein: 7g | carbs: 15g | fiber: 6g | sodium: 635mg

Braised Cauliflower

Prep time: 10 minutes | Cook time: 35 minutes | Serves 3

½ cup extra virgin olive oil
1 medium head cauliflower (about 2 pounds / 907 g), washed and cut into medium-sized florets
1 medium russet or white potato, cut into 1-inch pieces
¼ teaspoon freshly ground black pepper
3 allspice berries
1 cinnamon stick
3 cloves
2 tablespoons tomato paste
1 teaspoon fine sea salt
¾ cup hot water

1. Add the olive oil to a large pot over medium heat. When the oil begins to shimmer, add the cauliflower, potatoes, black pepper, allspice berries, cinnamon stick, and cloves. Sauté for 4 minutes or until the cauliflower begins to brown. 2. Add the tomato paste and sea salt. Continue heating, using a wooden spoon to swirl the tomato paste around the pan until the color changes to a brick red. 3. Add the hot water and stir gently. Reduce the heat to low, cover, and simmer for about 30 minutes or until the cauliflower is tender and the sauce has thickened. (If the sauce is still watery, remove the lid and simmer until the sauce has thickened.) Remove the allspice berries, cinnamon stick, and cloves. 4. Remove the cauliflower from the heat and set it aside to cool for at least 10 minutes before serving. When ready to serve, transfer the cauliflower to a large serving bowl and spoon the sauce over the top. Store covered in the refrigerator for up to 3 days.

Per Serving:
calories: 406 | fat: 36g | protein: 4g | carbs: 19g | fiber: 3g | sodium: 813mg

Gorgonzola Sweet Potato Burgers

Prep time: 10 minutes |Cook time: 15 minutes| Serves: 4

1 large sweet potato (about 8 ounces / 227 g)
2 tablespoons extra-virgin olive oil, divided
1 cup chopped onion (about ½ medium onion)
1 cup old-fashioned rolled oats
1 large egg
1 tablespoon balsamic vinegar
1 tablespoon dried oregano
1 garlic clove
¼ teaspoon kosher or sea salt
½ cup crumbled Gorgonzola or blue cheese (about 2 ounces / 57 g)
Salad greens or 4 whole-wheat rolls, for serving (optional)

1. Using a fork, pierce the sweet potato all over and microwave on high for 4 to 5 minutes, until tender in the center. Cool slightly, then slice in half. 2. While the sweet potato is cooking, in a large skillet over medium-high heat, heat 1 tablespoon of oil. Add the onion and cook for 5 minutes, stirring occasionally. 3. Using a spoon, carefully scoop the sweet potato flesh out of the skin and put the flesh in a food processor. Add the onion, oats, egg, vinegar, oregano, garlic, and salt. Process until smooth. Add the cheese and pulse four times to barely combine. With your hands, form the mixture into four (½-cup-size) burgers. Place the burgers on a plate, and press to flatten each to about ¾-inch thick. 4. Wipe out the skillet with a paper towel, then heat the remaining 1 tablespoon of oil over medium-high heat until very hot, about 2 minutes. Add the burgers to the hot oil, then turn the heat down to medium. Cook the burgers for 5 minutes, flip with a spatula, then cook an additional 5 minutes. Enjoy as is or serve on salad greens or whole-wheat rolls.

Per Serving:
calories: 337 | fat: 16g | protein: 13g | carbs: 38g | fiber: 6g | sodium: 378mg

Steamed Cauliflower with Olive Oil and Herbs

Prep time: 10 minutes | Cook time: 0 minutes | Serves 6

1 head cauliflower, cut into florets (about 6 cups)
1 cup water
4 tablespoons olive oil
1 clove garlic, peeled and minced
2 tablespoons chopped fresh oregano
1 teaspoon chopped fresh thyme leaves
1 teaspoon chopped fresh sage
¼ teaspoon salt
¼ teaspoon ground black pepper

1. Place cauliflower florets in a steamer basket. Place the rack in the Instant Pot®, add water, then top with the steamer basket. Close lid, set steam release to Sealing, press the Manual button, and set time to 0 minutes. 2. While cauliflower cooks, prepare the dressing. Whisk together olive oil, garlic, oregano, thyme, sage, salt, and pepper. 3. When the timer beeps, quick-release the pressure until the float valve drops. Press the Cancel button and open lid. Carefully transfer cauliflower to a serving bowl and immediately pour dressing over cauliflower. Carefully toss to coat. Let stand for 5 minutes. Serve hot.

Per Serving:
calories: 105 | fat: 9g | protein: 0g | carbs: 0g | fiber: 2g | sodium: 128mg

Cucumbers with Feta, Mint, and Sumac

Prep time: 15 minutes | Cook time: 0 minutes | Serves 4

1 tablespoon extra-virgin olive oil
1 tablespoon lemon juice
2 teaspoons ground sumac
½ teaspoon kosher salt
2 hothouse or English cucumbers, diced
¼ cup crumbled feta cheese
1 tablespoon fresh mint, chopped
1 tablespoon fresh parsley, chopped
⅛ teaspoon red pepper flakes

1. In a large bowl, whisk together the olive oil, lemon juice, sumac, and salt. Add the cucumber and feta cheese and toss well. 2. Transfer to a serving dish and sprinkle with the mint, parsley, and red pepper flakes.

Per Serving:
calories: 85 | fat: 6g | protein: 3g | carbs: 8g | fiber: 1g | sodium: 230mg

Savory Butternut Squash and Apples

Prep time: 20 minutes | Cook time: 4 hours | Serves 10

1 (3-pound / 1.4-kg) butternut squash, peeled, seeded, and cubed
4 cooking apples (granny smith or honeycrisp work well), peeled, cored, and chopped
¾ cup dried currants
½ sweet yellow onion such as vidalia, sliced thin
1 tablespoon ground cinnamon
1½ teaspoons ground nutmeg

1. Combine the squash, apples, currants, and onion in the slow cooker. Sprinkle with the cinnamon and nutmeg. 2. Cook on high for 4 hours, or until the squash is tender and cooked through. Stir occasionally while cooking.

Per Serving:
calories: 114 | fat: 0g | protein: 2g | carbs: 28g | fiber: 6g | sodium: 8mg

Greek Fasolakia (Green Beans)

Prep time: 10 minutes | Cook time: 6 to 8 hours | Serves 6

2 pounds (907 g) green beans, trimmed
1 (15-ounce / 425-g) can no-salt-added diced tomatoes, with juice
1 large onion, chopped
4 garlic cloves, chopped
Juice of 1 lemon
1 teaspoon dried dill
1 teaspoon ground cumin
1 teaspoon dried oregano
1 teaspoon sea salt
½ teaspoon freshly ground black pepper
¼ cup feta cheese, crumbled

1. In a slow cooker, combine the green beans, tomatoes and their juice, onion, garlic, lemon juice, dill, cumin, oregano, salt, and pepper. Stir to mix well. 2. Cover the cooker and cook for 6 to 8 hours on Low heat. 3. Top with feta cheese for serving.

Per Serving:
calories: 94 | fat: 2g | protein: 5g | carbs: 18g | fiber: 7g | sodium: 497mg

Sautéed Mustard Greens and Red Peppers

Prep time: 10 minutes | Cook time: 5 minutes | Serves 4

1 tablespoon olive oil
½ red pepper, diced
2 cloves garlic, minced
1 bunch mustard greens
Sea salt and freshly ground pepper, to taste
1 teaspoon white wine vinegar

1. Heat olive oil in a large saucepan over medium heat. Add bell pepper and garlic, and sauté for 1 minute, stirring often. 2. Add greens to pan and immediately cover to begin steaming. Set a timer for 2 minutes. 3. After 1 minute, lift lid and stir greens well, then immediately put lid back on for remaining minute. Remove the lid, season with sea salt and freshly ground pepper, sprinkle with vinegar, and serve.

Per Serving:
calories: 42 | fat: 4g | protein: 1g | carbs: 2g | fiber: 1g | sodium: 7mg

Beet and Watercress Salad with Orange and Dill

Prep time: 20 minutes | Cook time: 8 minutes | Serves 4

2 pounds (907 g) beets, scrubbed, trimmed, and cut into ¾-inch pieces
½ cup water
1 teaspoon caraway seeds
½ teaspoon table salt
1 cup plain Greek yogurt
1 small garlic clove, minced to paste
5 ounces (142 g) watercress, torn into bite-size pieces
1 tablespoon extra-virgin olive oil, divided, plus extra for drizzling
1 tablespoon white wine vinegar, divided
1 teaspoon grated orange zest plus 2 tablespoons juice
¼ cup hazelnuts, toasted, skinned, and chopped
¼ cup coarsely chopped fresh dill
Coarse sea salt

1. Combine beets, water, caraway seeds, and table salt in Instant Pot. Lock lid in place and close pressure release valve. Select high pressure cook function and cook for 8 minutes. Turn off Instant Pot and quick-release pressure. Carefully remove lid, allowing steam to escape away from you. 2. Using slotted spoon, transfer beets to plate; set aside to cool slightly. Combine yogurt, garlic, and 3 tablespoons beet cooking liquid in bowl; discard remaining cooking liquid. In large bowl toss watercress with 2 teaspoons oil and 1 teaspoon vinegar. Season with table salt and pepper to taste. 3. Spread yogurt mixture over surface of serving dish. Arrange watercress on top of yogurt mixture, leaving 1-inch border of yogurt mixture. Add beets to now-empty large bowl and toss with orange zest and juice, remaining 2 teaspoons vinegar, and remaining 1 teaspoon oil. Season with table salt and pepper to taste. Arrange beets on top of watercress mixture. Drizzle with extra oil and sprinkle with hazelnuts, dill, and sea salt. Serve.

Per Serving:
calories: 240 | fat: 15g | protein: 9g | carbs: 19g | fiber: 5g | sodium: 440mg

Chapter 13 Salads

Simple Insalata Mista (Mixed Salad) with Honey Balsamic Dressing

Prep time: 15 minutes | Cook time: 0 minutes | Serves 2

For the Dressing:
¼ cup balsamic vinegar
¼ cup olive oil
1 tablespoon honey
1 teaspoon Dijon mustard
¼ teaspoon salt, plus more to taste
¼ teaspoon garlic powder
Pinch freshly ground black pepper
For the Salad:
4 cups chopped red leaf lettuce
½ cup cherry or grape tomatoes, halved
½ English cucumber, sliced in quarters lengthwise and then cut into bite-size pieces
Any combination fresh, torn herbs (parsley, oregano, basil, chives, etc.)
1 tablespoon roasted sunflower seeds

Make the Dressing: Combine the vinegar, olive oil, honey, mustard, salt, garlic powder, and pepper in a jar with a lid. Shake well. Make the Salad: 1. In a large bowl, combine the lettuce, tomatoes, cucumber, and herbs. 2. Toss well to combine. 3. Pour all or as much dressing as desired over the tossed salad and toss again to coat the salad with dressing. 4. Top with the sunflower seeds.

Per Serving:
calories: 339 | fat: 26g | protein: 4g | carbs: 24g | fiber: 3g | sodium: 171mg

Easy Greek Salad

Prep time: 10 minutes | Cook time: 0 minutes | Serves 4 to 6

1 head iceberg lettuce
1 pint (2 cups) cherry tomatoes
1 large cucumber
1 medium onion
½ cup extra-virgin olive oil
¼ cup lemon juice
1 teaspoon salt
1 clove garlic, minced
1 cup Kalamata olives, pitted
1 (6-ounce / 170-g) package feta cheese, crumbled

1. Cut the lettuce into 1-inch pieces and put them in a large salad bowl. 2. Cut the tomatoes in half and add them to the salad bowl. 3. Slice the cucumber into bite-size pieces and add them to the salad bowl. 4. Thinly slice the onion and add it to the salad bowl. 5. In another small bowl, whisk together the olive oil, lemon juice, salt, and garlic. Pour the dressing over the salad and gently toss to evenly coat. 6. Top the salad with the Kalamata olives and feta cheese and serve.

Per Serving:
calories: 297 | fat: 27g | protein: 6g | carbs: 11g | fiber: 3g | sodium: 661mg

Citrus Fennel Salad

Prep time: 15 minutes | Cook time: 0 minutes | Serves 2

For the Dressing:
2 tablespoons fresh orange juice
3 tablespoons olive oil
1 tablespoon blood orange vinegar, other orange vinegar, or cider vinegar
1 tablespoon honey
Salt
Freshly ground black pepper
For the Salad:
2 cups packed baby kale
1 medium navel or blood orange, segmented
½ small fennel bulb, stems and leaves removed, sliced into matchsticks
3 tablespoons toasted pecans, chopped
2 ounces (57 g) goat cheese, crumbled

Make the Dressing: Combine the orange juice, olive oil, vinegar, and honey in a small bowl and whisk to combine. Season with salt and pepper. Set the dressing aside. Make the Salad: 1. Divide the baby kale, orange segments, fennel, pecans, and goat cheese evenly between two plates. 2. Drizzle half of the dressing over each salad.

Per Serving:
calories: 502 | fat: 39g | protein: 13g | carbs: 31g | fiber: 6g | sodium: 158mg

Greek Potato Salad

Prep time: 15 minutes | Cook time: 15 to 18 minutes | Serves 6

1½ pounds (680 g) small red or new potatoes
½ cup olive oil
⅓ cup red wine vinegar
1 teaspoon fresh Greek oregano
4 ounces (113 g) feta cheese, crumbled, if desired, or 4 ounces (113 g) grated Swiss cheese (for a less salty option)
1 green bell pepper, seeded and chopped (1¼ cups)
1 small red onion, halved and thinly sliced (generous 1 cup)
½ cup Kalamata olives, pitted and halved

1. Put the potatoes in a large saucepan and add water to cover. Bring the water to a boil and cook until tender, 15 to 18 minutes. Drain and set aside until cool enough to handle. 2. Meanwhile, in a large bowl, whisk together the olive oil, vinegar, and oregano. 3. When the potatoes are just cool enough to handle, cut them into 1-inch pieces and add them to the bowl with the dressing. Toss to combine. Add the cheese, bell pepper, onion, and olives and toss gently. Let stand for 30 minutes before serving.

Per Serving:
calories: 315 | fat: 23g | protein: 5g | carbs: 21g | fiber: 3g | sodium: 360mg

Italian Summer Vegetable Barley Salad

Prep time: 1 minutes | Cook time: 25 to 45 minutes | Serves 4

1 cup uncooked barley (hulled or pearl)	chopped
3 cups water	15 Kalamata olives, pitted and sliced or chopped
¾ teaspoon fine sea salt, divided	¼ cup chopped fresh parsley
1 teaspoon plus 3 tablespoons extra virgin olive oil, divided	¼ cup chopped fresh basil
3 tablespoons fresh lemon juice	1 cup cherry tomatoes, halved
2 medium zucchini, washed and	½ teaspoon freshly ground black pepper

1. Place the barley in a medium pot and add 3 cups of water and ¼ teaspoon of the sea salt. Bring to a boil over high heat, then reduce the heat to low. Simmer for 25–40 minutes, depending on the type of barley you're using, adding small amounts of hot water if the barley appears to be drying out. Cook until the barley is soft but still chewy, then transfer to a mesh strainer and rinse with cold water. 2. Empty the rinsed barley into a large bowl, drizzle 1 teaspoon of the olive oil over the top, fluff with a fork, and then set aside. 3. In a small bowl, combine the remaining 3 tablespoons of olive oil and the lemon juice. Whisk until the dressing thickens. 4. In a large bowl, combine the barley, zucchini, olives, parsley, and basil. Toss and then add the cherry tomatoes, remaining ½ teaspoon of sea salt, and black pepper. Toss gently, drizzle the dressing over the top, and continue tossing until the ingredients are coated with the dressing. Serve promptly. Store covered in the refrigerator for up to 3 days.

Per Serving:
calories: 308 | fat: 13g | protein: 7g | carbs: 45g | fiber: 10g | sodium: 614mg

Beets with Goat Cheese and Chermoula

Prep time: 10 minutes | Cook time: 40 minutes | Serves 4

6 beets, trimmed	1 teaspoon smoked paprika
Chermoula:	½ teaspoon kosher salt
1 cup fresh cilantro leaves	¼ teaspoon chili powder (optional)
1 cup fresh flat-leaf parsley leaves	¼ cup extra-virgin olive oil
¼ cup fresh lemon juice	2 ounces (57 g) goat cheese, crumbled
3 cloves garlic, minced	
2 teaspoons ground cumin	

1. Preheat the oven to 400°F(205°C). 2. Wrap the beets in a piece of foil and place on a baking sheet. Roast until the beets are tender enough to be pierced with a fork, 30 to 40 minutes. When cool enough to handle, remove the skins and slice the beets into ¼' rounds. Arrange the beet slices on a large serving platter. 3. To make the chermoula: In a food processor, pulse the cilantro, parsley, lemon juice, garlic, cumin, paprika, salt, and chili powder (if using) until the herbs are just coarsely chopped and the ingredients are combined. Stir in the oil. 4. To serve, dollop the chermoula over the beets and scatter the cheese on top.

Per Serving:
calories: 249 | fat: 19g | protein: 6g | carbs: 15g | fiber: 5g | sodium: 472mg

No-Mayo Florence Tuna Salad

Prep time: 10 minutes | Cook time: 0 minutes | Serves 4

4 cups spring mix greens	olives
1 (15-ounce / 425-g) can cannellini beans, drained	¼ cup thinly sliced scallions, both green and white parts
2 (5-ounce / 142-g) cans water-packed, white albacore tuna, drained (I prefer Wild Planet brand)	3 tablespoons extra-virgin olive oil
	½ teaspoon dried cilantro
⅔ cup crumbled feta cheese	2 or 3 leaves thinly chopped fresh sweet basil
½ cup thinly sliced sun-dried tomatoes	1 lime, zested and juiced
¼ cup sliced pitted kalamata	Kosher salt
	Freshly ground black pepper

1. In a large bowl, combine greens, beans, tuna, feta, tomatoes, olives, scallions, olive oil, cilantro, basil, and lime juice and zest. Season with salt and pepper, mix, and enjoy!

Per Serving:
1 cup: calories: 355 | fat: 19g | protein: 22g | carbs: 25g | fiber: 8g | sodium: 744mg

Superfood Salmon Salad Bowl

Prep time: 5 minutes | Cook time: 10 minutes | Serves 2

Salmon:	Salad:
2 fillets wild salmon	½ medium cucumber, diced
Salt and black pepper, to taste	1 cup sugar snap peas, sliced into matchsticks
2 teaspoons extra-virgin avocado oil	½ small red bell pepper, sliced
Dressing:	⅓ cup pitted Kalamata olives, halved
1 tablespoon capers	2 sun-dried tomatoes, chopped
1 teaspoon Dijon or whole-grain mustard	1 medium avocado, diced
1 tablespoon apple cider vinegar or fresh lemon juice	3 tablespoons chopped fresh herbs, such as dill, chives, parsley, and/or basil
3 tablespoons extra-virgin olive oil	1 tablespoon pumpkin seeds
1 teaspoon coconut aminos	1 tablespoon sunflower seeds
Salt and black pepper, to taste	

1. Make the salmon: Season the salmon with salt and pepper. Heat a pan greased with the avocado oil over medium heat. Add the salmon, skin-side down, and cook for 4 to 5 minutes. Flip and cook for 1 to 2 minutes or until cooked through. Remove from the heat and transfer to a plate to cool. Remove the skin from the salmon and flake into chunks. 2. Make the dressing: Mix all the dressing ingredients together in a small bowl. Set aside. 3. Make the salad: Place the cucumber, sugar snap peas, bell pepper, olives, sun-dried tomatoes, avocado, and herbs in a mixing bowl, and combine well. Add the flaked salmon. Dry-fry the seeds in a pan placed over medium-low heat until lightly golden. Allow to cool, then add to the bowl. Drizzle with the prepared dressing and serve. This salad can be stored in the fridge for up to 1 day.

Per Serving:
calories: 660 | fat: 54g | protein: 31g | carbs: 18g | fiber: 9g | sodium: 509mg

Israeli Salad with Nuts and Seeds

Prep time: 15 minutes | Cook time: 0 minutes | Serves 4

- ¼ cup pine nuts
- ¼ cup shelled pistachios
- ¼ cup coarsely chopped walnuts
- ¼ cup shelled pumpkin seeds
- ¼ cup shelled sunflower seeds
- 2 large English cucumbers, unpeeled and finely chopped
- 1 pint cherry tomatoes, finely chopped
- ½ small red onion, finely chopped
- ½ cup finely chopped fresh flat-leaf Italian parsley
- ¼ cup extra-virgin olive oil
- 2 to 3 tablespoons freshly squeezed lemon juice (from 1 lemon)
- 1 teaspoon salt
- ¼ teaspoon freshly ground black pepper
- 4 cups baby arugula

1. In a large dry skillet, toast the pine nuts, pistachios, walnuts, pumpkin seeds, and sunflower seeds over medium-low heat until golden and fragrant, 5 to 6 minutes, being careful not to burn them. Remove from the heat and set aside. 2. In a large bowl, combine the cucumber, tomatoes, red onion, and parsley. 3. In a small bowl, whisk together olive oil, lemon juice, salt, and pepper. Pour over the chopped vegetables and toss to coat. 4. Add the toasted nuts and seeds and arugula and toss with the salad to blend well. Serve at room temperature or chilled.

Per Serving:
calories: 404 | fat: 36g | protein: 10g | carbs: 16g | fiber: 5g | sodium: 601mg

Roasted Cauliflower Salad with Tahini-Yogurt Dressing

Prep time: 10 minutes | Cook time: 35 minutes | Serves 8 to 10

- 10 cups cauliflower florets (1- to 2-inch florets, from 1 to 2 heads)
- 1½ tablespoons olive oil
- ¾ teaspoon kosher salt, divided
- ½ cup walnuts
- ½ cup yogurt
- ¼ cup tahini, at room temperature
- ¼ cup lemon juice, plus more to taste
- ¼ cup water
- 1 tablespoon honey
- ¼ cup chopped fresh dill
- 1 tablespoon minced shallot

1. Preheat the oven to 450°F(235°C). 2. On a large baking sheet, toss the cauliflower with the olive oil and ¼ teaspoon of the salt. Spread the cauliflower out in a single layer and roast in the preheated oven for about 30 minutes, until it is tender and browned on the bottom. Place the cooked cauliflower in a large bowl and set aside to cool while you prepare the rest of the salad. 3. Toast the walnuts in a skillet over medium heat until fragrant and golden, about 5 minutes. Chop and set aside. 4. In a blender or food processor, combine the yogurt, tahini, lemon juice, water, and honey and process until smooth. If the mixture is too thick, add a tablespoon or two of additional water. 5. Add the dill, shallot, and the remaining ½ teaspoon of salt to the cauliflower and toss to combine. Add the dressing and toss again to coat well. 6. Serve the salad at room temperature, garnished with the toasted walnuts.

Per Serving:
calories: 153 | fat: 10g | protein: 6g | carbs: 12g | fiber: 4g | sodium: 249mg

Quinoa with Zucchini, Mint, and Pistachios

Prep time: 20 to 30 minutes | Cook time: 20 minutes | Serves 4

For the Quinoa:
- 1½ cups water
- 1 cup quinoa
- ¼ teaspoon kosher salt

For the Salad:
- 2 tablespoons extra-virgin olive oil
- 1 zucchini, thinly sliced into rounds
- 6 small radishes, sliced
- 1 shallot, julienned
- ¾ teaspoon kosher salt
- ¼ teaspoon freshly ground black pepper
- 2 garlic cloves, sliced
- Zest of 1 lemon
- 2 tablespoons lemon juice
- ¼ cup fresh mint, chopped
- ¼ cup fresh basil, chopped
- ¼ cup pistachios, shelled and toasted

Make the Quinoa: Bring the water, quinoa, and salt to a boil in a medium saucepan. Reduce to a simmer, cover, and cook for 10 to 12 minutes. Fluff with a fork. Make the Salad: 1. Heat the olive oil in a large skillet or sauté pan over medium-high heat. Add the zucchini, radishes, shallot, salt, and black pepper, and sauté for 7 to 8 minutes. Add the garlic and cook 30 seconds to 1 minute more. 2. In a large bowl, combine the lemon zest and lemon juice. Add the quinoa and mix well. Add the cooked zucchini mixture and mix well. Add the mint, basil, and pistachios and gently mix.

Per Serving:
calories: 220 | fat: 12g | protein: 6g | carbs: 25g | fiber: 5g | sodium: 295mg

Tabbouleh

Prep time: 15 minutes | Cook time: 12 minutes | Serves 4 to 6

- 1 cup water
- ½ cup dried bulgur
- ½ English cucumber, quartered lengthwise and sliced
- 2 tomatoes on the vine, diced
- 2 scallions, chopped
- Juice of 1 lemon
- 2 cups coarsely chopped fresh Italian parsley
- ⅓ cup coarsely chopped fresh mint leaves
- 1 garlic clove
- ¼ cup extra-virgin olive oil
- Sea salt
- Freshly ground black pepper

1. In a medium saucepan, combine the water and bulgur and bring to a boil over medium heat. Reduce the heat to low, cover, and cook until the bulgur is tender, about 12 minutes. Drain off any excess liquid, fluff the bulgur with a fork, and set aside to cool. 2. In a large bowl, toss together the bulgur, cucumber, tomatoes, scallions, and lemon juice. 3. In a food processor, combine the parsley, mint, and garlic and process until finely chopped. 4. Add the chopped herb mixture to the bulgur mixture and stir to combine. Add the olive oil and stir to incorporate. 5. Season with salt and pepper and serve.

Per Serving:
calories: 215 | fat: 14g | protein: 4g | carbs: 21g | fiber: 5g | sodium: 66mg

Roasted Cauliflower "Steak" Salad

Prep time: 10 minutes | Cook time: 50 minutes | Serves 4

2 tablespoons olive oil, divided
2 large heads cauliflower (about 3 pounds / 1.4 kg each), trimmed of outer leaves
2 teaspoons za'atar
1½ teaspoons kosher salt, divided
1¼ teaspoons ground black pepper, divided
1 teaspoon ground cumin
2 large carrots
8 ounces (227 g) dandelion greens, tough stems removed
½ cup low-fat plain Greek yogurt
2 tablespoons tahini
2 tablespoons fresh lemon juice
1 tablespoon water
1 clove garlic, minced

1. Preheat the oven to 450°F(235°C). Brush a large baking sheet with some of the oil. 2. Place the cauliflower on a cutting board, stem side down. Cut down the middle, through the core and stem, and then cut two 1'-thick "steaks" from the middle. Repeat with the other cauliflower head. Set aside the remaining cauliflower for another use. Brush both sides of the steaks with the remaining oil and set on the baking sheet. 3. Combine the za'atar, 1 teaspoon of the salt, 1 teaspoon of the pepper, and the cumin. Sprinkle on the cauliflower steaks. Bake until the bottom is deeply golden, about 30 minutes. Flip and bake until tender, 10 to 15 minutes. 4. Meanwhile, set the carrots on a cutting board and use a vegetable peeler to peel them into ribbons. Add to a large bowl with the dandelion greens. 5. In a small bowl, combine the yogurt, tahini, lemon juice, water, garlic, the remaining ½ teaspoon salt, and the remaining ¼ teaspoon pepper. 6. Dab 3 tablespoons of the dressing onto the carrot-dandelion mix. With a spoon or your hands, massage the dressing into the mix for 5 minutes. 7. Remove the steaks from the oven and transfer to individual plates. Drizzle each with 2 tablespoons of the dressing and top with 1 cup of the salad.

Per Serving:
calories: 214 | fat: 12g | protein: 9g | carbs: 21g | fiber: 7g | sodium: 849mg

Riviera Tuna Salad

Prep time: 15 minutes | Cook time: 0 minutes | Serves 4

¼ cup olive oil
¼ cup balsamic vinegar
½ teaspoon minced garlic
¼ teaspoon dried oregano
Sea salt and freshly ground pepper, to taste
2 tablespoons capers, drained
4–6 cups baby greens
1 (6-ounce / 170-g) can solid white albacore tuna, drained
1 cup canned garbanzo beans, rinsed and drained
¼ cup low-salt olives, pitted and quartered
2 Roma tomatoes, chopped

1. To make the vinaigrette, whisk together the olive oil, balsamic vinegar, garlic, oregano, sea salt, and pepper until emulsified. 2. Stir in the capers. Refrigerate for up to 6 hours before serving. 3. Place the baby greens in a salad bowl or on individual plates, and top with the tuna, beans, olives, and tomatoes. 4. Drizzle the vinaigrette over all, and serve immediately.

Per Serving:
calories: 300 | fat: 19g | protein: 16g | carbs: 17g | fiber: 5g | sodium: 438mg

Bacalhau and Black-Eyed Pea Salad

Prep time: 10 minutes | Cook time: 10 minutes | Serves 4

1 pound (454 g) bacalhau (salt cod) fillets
¼ cup olive oil, plus 1 tablespoon, divided
3 tablespoons white wine vinegar
1 teaspoon salt
¼ teaspoon freshly ground black pepper
1 (15-ounce / 425-g) can black-eyed peas, drained and rinsed
1 small yellow onion, halved and thinly sliced crosswise
1 small clove garlic, minced
¼ cup chopped fresh flat-leaf parsley leaves, divided

1. Rinse the cod under cold running water to remove any surface salt. Place the fish pieces in a large nonreactive pot, cover with water and refrigerate (covered) for 24 hours, changing the water several times. 2. Pour off the water, refill the pot with clean water and gently boil the cod until it flakes easily with a fork, about 7 to 10 minutes (or longer), depending on the thickness. Drain and set aside to cool. 3. To make the dressing, whisk together the oil, vinegar, salt, and pepper in a small bowl. 4. In a large bowl, combine the beans, onion, garlic, and ¾ of the parsley. Add the dressing and mix to coat well. Stir in the salt cod, cover, and chill in the refrigerator for at least 2 hours to let the flavors meld. Let sit on the countertop for 30 minutes before serving. 5. Serve garnished with the remaining parsley.

Per Serving:
calories: 349 | fat: 18g | protein: 32g | carbs: 16g | fiber: 4g | sodium: 8mg

Roasted Golden Beet, Avocado, and Watercress Salad

Prep time: 15 minutes | Cook time: 1 hour | Serves 4

1 bunch (about 1½ pounds / 680 g) golden beets
1 tablespoon extra-virgin olive oil
1 tablespoon white wine vinegar
½ teaspoon kosher salt
¼ teaspoon freshly ground black pepper
1 bunch (about 4 ounces / 113 g) watercress
1 avocado, peeled, pitted, and diced
¼ cup crumbled feta cheese
¼ cup walnuts, toasted
1 tablespoon fresh chives, chopped

1. Preheat the oven to 425°F (220°C). Wash and trim the beets (cut an inch above the beet root, leaving the long tail if desired), then wrap each beet individually in foil. Place the beets on a baking sheet and roast until fully cooked, 45 to 60 minutes depending on the size of each beet. Start checking at 45 minutes; if easily pierced with a fork, the beets are cooked. 2. Remove the beets from the oven and allow them to cool. Under cold running water, slough off the skin. Cut the beets into bite-size cubes or wedges. 3. In a large bowl, whisk together the olive oil, vinegar, salt, and black pepper. Add the watercress and beets and toss well. Add the avocado, feta, walnuts, and chives and mix gently.

Per Serving:
calories: 235 | fat: 16g | protein: 6g | carbs: 21g | fiber: 8g | sodium: 365mg

Tuna Niçoise

Prep time: 15 minutes | Cook time: 20 minutes | Serves 4

- 1 pound (454 g) small red or fingerling potatoes, halved
- 1 pound (454 g) green beans or haricots verts, trimmed
- 1 head romaine lettuce, chopped or torn into bite-size pieces
- ½ pint cherry tomatoes, halved
- 8 radishes, thinly sliced
- ½ cup olives, pitted (any kind you like)
- 2 (5-ounce / 142-g) cans no-salt-added tuna packed in olive oil, drained
- 8 anchovies (optional)

1. Fill a large pot fitted with a steamer basket with 2 to 3 inches of water. Put the potatoes in the steamer basket and lay the green beans on top of the potatoes. Bring the water to a boil over high heat, lower the heat to low and simmer, cover, and cook for 7 minutes, or until the green beans are tender but crisp. Remove the green beans and continue to steam the potatoes for an additional 10 minutes. 2. Place the romaine lettuce on a serving platter. Group the potatoes, green beans, tomatoes, radishes, olives, and tuna in different areas of the platter. If using the anchovies, place them around the platter.

Per Serving:
calories: 315 | fat: 9g | protein: 28g | carbs: 33g | fiber: 9g | sodium: 420mg

Wilted Kale Salad

Prep time: 10 minutes | Cook time: 5 minutes | Serves 4

- 2 heads kale
- 1 tablespoon olive oil, plus 1 teaspoon
- 2 cloves garlic, minced
- 1 cup cherry tomatoes, sliced
- Sea salt and freshly ground pepper, to taste
- Juice of 1 lemon

1. Rinse and dry kale. 2. Tear the kale into bite-sized pieces. 3. Heat 1 tablespoon of the olive oil in a large skillet, and add the garlic. Cook for 1 minute and then add the kale. 4. Cook just until wilted, then add the tomatoes. 5. Cook until tomatoes are softened, then remove from heat. 6. Place tomatoes and kale in a bowl, and season with sea salt and freshly ground pepper. 7. Drizzle with remaining olive oil and lemon juice, serve, and enjoy.

Per Serving:
calories: 153 | fat: 6g | protein: 10g | carbs: 23g | fiber: 9g | sodium: 88mg

Dakos (Cretan Salad)

Prep time: 7 minutes | Cook time: 00 minutes | Serves 1

- 1 medium ripe tomato (any variety)
- 2 whole-grain crispbreads or rusks (or 1 slice toasted whole-grain, wheat, or barley bread)
- 1 tablespoon plus 1 teaspoon extra virgin olive oil
- Pinch of kosher salt
- 1½ ounces (43 g) crumbled feta
- 2 teaspoons capers, drained
- 2 Kalamata olives, pitted
- Pinch of dried oregano

1. Slice a thin round off the bottom of the tomato. Hold the tomato from the stem side and begin grating the tomato over a plate, using the largest holes of the grater. Grate until only the skin of the tomato remains, then discard the skin. Use a fine mesh strainer to drain the liquid from the grated tomato. 2. Place the crisps on a plate, one next to the other, and sprinkle with a few drops of water. Drizzle 1 tablespoon of the olive oil over the crisps and then top the crisps with the grated tomato, ensuring the crisps are thoroughly covered with the tomato. 3. Sprinkle the kosher salt over the tomato, then layer the crumbled feta over the top. Top with the capers and olives, and sprinkle the oregano over the top and drizzle with the remaining 1 teaspoon of olive oil. Serve promptly. (This salad is best served fresh.)

Per Serving:
calories: 346 | fat: 24g | protein: 12g | carbs: 21g | fiber: 4g | sodium: 626mg

Pistachio-Parmesan Kale-Arugula Salad

Prep time: 20 minutes | Cook time: 0 minutes | Serves: 6

- 6 cups raw kale, center ribs removed and discarded, leaves coarsely chopped
- ¼ cup extra-virgin olive oil
- 2 tablespoons freshly squeezed lemon juice (from about 1 small lemon)
- ½ teaspoon smoked paprika
- 2 cups arugula
- ⅓ cup unsalted shelled pistachios
- 6 tablespoons grated Parmesan or Pecorino Romano cheese

1. In a large salad bowl, combine the kale, oil, lemon juice, and smoked paprika. With your hands, gently massage the leaves for about 15 seconds or so, until all are thoroughly coated. Let the kale sit for 10 minutes. 2. When you're ready to serve, gently mix in the arugula and pistachios. Divide the salad among six serving bowls, sprinkle 1 tablespoon of grated cheese over each, and serve.

Per Serving:
calories: 150 | fat: 14g | protein: 4g | carbs: 5g | fiber: 1g | sodium: 99mg

447. Marinated Greek Salad with Oregano and Goat Cheese

Prep time: 10 minutes | Cook time: 0 minutes | Serves 4

- ½ cup white wine vinegar
- 1 small garlic clove, minced
- 1 teaspoon crumbled dried Greek oregano
- ½ teaspoon salt
- ¼ teaspoon freshly ground black pepper
- 2 Persian cucumbers, sliced thinly
- 4 to 6 long, skinny red or yellow banana peppers or other mild peppers
- 1 medium red onion, cut into rings
- 1 pint mixed small heirloom tomatoes, halved
- 2 ounces (57 g) crumbled goat cheese or feta

1. In a large, nonreactive (glass, ceramic, or plastic) bowl, whisk together the vinegar, garlic, oregano, salt, and pepper. Add the cucumbers, peppers, and onion and toss to mix. Cover and refrigerate for at least 1 hour. 2. Add the tomatoes to the bowl and toss to coat. Serve topped with the cheese.

Per Serving:
calories: 98 | fat: 4g | protein: 4g | carbs: 13g | fiber: 3g | sodium: 460mg

Italian White Bean Salad with Bell Peppers

Prep time: 15 minutes | Cook time: 0 minutes | Serves 4

- 2 tablespoons extra-virgin olive oil
- 2 tablespoons white wine vinegar
- ½ shallot, minced
- ½ teaspoon kosher salt
- ¼ teaspoon freshly ground black pepper
- 3 cups cooked cannellini beans, or 2 (15-ounce / 425-g) cans no-salt-added or low-sodium cannellini beans, drained and rinsed
- 2 celery stalks, diced
- ½ red bell pepper, diced
- ¼ cup fresh parsley, chopped
- ¼ cup fresh mint, chopped

1. In a large bowl, whisk together the olive oil, vinegar, shallot, salt, and black pepper. 2. Add the beans, celery, red bell pepper, parsley, and mint; mix well.

Per Serving:
calories: 300 | fat: 8g | protein: 15g | carbs: 46g | fiber: 11g | sodium: 175mg

Citrusy Spinach Salad

Prep time: 10 minutes | Cook time: 5 minutes | Serves 4

- 1 large ripe tomato
- 1 medium red onion
- ½ teaspoon fresh lemon zest
- 3 tablespoons balsamic vinegar
- ¼ cup extra-virgin olive oil
- ½ teaspoon salt
- 1 pound (454 g) baby spinach, washed, stems removed

1. Dice the tomato into ¼-inch pieces and slice the onion into long slivers. 2. In a small bowl, whisk together the lemon zest, balsamic vinegar, olive oil, and salt. 3. Put the spinach, tomatoes, and onions in a large bowl. Pour the dressing over the salad and lightly toss to coat.

Per Serving:
calories: 172 | fat: 14g | protein: 4g | carbs: 10g | fiber: 4g | sodium: 389mg

Insalata Caprese

Prep time: 5 minutes | Cook time: 0 minutes | Serves 2

- 2 firm medium tomatoes (any variety), cut into ¼-inch slices
- ¼ teaspoon kosher salt
- 8 fresh basil leaves
- 7 ounces (198 g) fresh mozzarella, cut into ¼-inch slices
- ¼ teaspoon dried oregano
- 3 teaspoons extra virgin olive oil

1. Place the sliced tomatoes on a cutting board and sprinkle them with the kosher salt. Set aside. 2. Arrange 4 basil leaves in a circular pattern on a large, round serving plate. (Tear the leaves into 2 pieces if they're large.) 3. Assemble the tomato slices and mozzarella slices on top of the basil leaves, alternating a tomato slice and then a mozzarella slice, adding a basil leaf between every 3–4 slices of tomato and mozzarella. 4. Sprinkle the oregano over the top and then drizzle the olive oil over the entire salad. Serve promptly. (This salad is best served fresh.)

Per Serving:
calories: 361 | fat: 24g | protein: 28g | carbs: 8g | fiber: 2g | sodium: 313mg

Valencia-Inspired Salad

Prep time: 5 minutes | Cook time: 0 minutes | Serves 4

- 2 small oranges, peeled, thinly sliced, and pitted
- 1 small blood orange, peeled, thinly sliced, and pitted
- 1 (7-ounce / 198-g) bag butter lettuce
- ½ English cucumber, thinly sliced into rounds
- 1 (6-ounce / 170-g) can pitted black olives, halved
- 1 small shallot, thinly sliced (optional)
- ¼ cup raw hulled pumpkin seeds
- 8 slices Manchego cheese, roughly broken
- 2 to 3 tablespoons extra-virgin olive oil
- Juice of 1 orange

1. In a large bowl, toss together the oranges, lettuce, cucumber, olives, shallot (if desired), pumpkin seeds, and cheese until well mixed. Evenly divide the mixture among four plates. 2. Drizzle the salads with the olive oil and orange juice. Serve.

Per Serving:
calories: 419 | fat: 31g | protein: 17g | carbs: 22g | fiber: 5g | sodium: 513mg

Arugula and Fennel Salad with Fresh Basil

Prep time: 5 minutes | Cook time: 0 minutes | Serves 4

- 3 tablespoons olive oil
- 3 tablespoons lemon juice
- 1 teaspoon honey
- ½ teaspoon salt
- 1 medium bulb fennel, very thinly sliced
- 1 small cucumber, very thinly sliced
- 2 cups arugula
- ¼ cup toasted pine nuts
- ½ cup crumbled feta cheese
- ¼ cup julienned fresh basil leaves

1. In a medium bowl, whisk together the olive oil, lemon juice, honey, and salt. Add the fennel and cucumber and toss to coat and let sit for 10 minutes or so. 2. Put the arugula in a large salad bowl. Add the marinated cucumber and fennel, along with the dressing, to the bowl and toss well. Serve immediately, sprinkled with pine nuts, feta cheese, and basil.

Per Serving:
calories: 237 | fat: 21g | protein: 6g | carbs: 11g | fiber: 3g | sodium: 537mg

Asparagus Salad

Prep time: 10 minutes | Cook time: 0 minutes | Serves 4

- 1 pound (454 g) asparagus
- Sea salt and freshly ground pepper, to taste
- 4 tablespoons olive oil
- 1 tablespoon balsamic vinegar
- 1 tablespoon lemon zest

1. Either roast the asparagus or, with a vegetable peeler, shave it into thin strips. 2. Season to taste. 3. Toss with the olive oil and vinegar, garnish with a sprinkle of lemon zest, and serve.

Per Serving:
calories: 146 | fat: 14g | protein: 3g | carbs: 5g | fiber: 3g | sodium: 4mg

Tricolor Tomato Summer Salad

Prep time: 10 minutes | Cook time: 0 minutes | Serves 3 to 4

¼ cup while balsamic vinegar
2 tablespoons Dijon mustard
1 tablespoon sugar
½ teaspoon freshly ground black pepper
½ teaspoon garlic salt
¼ cup extra-virgin olive oil
1½ cups chopped orange, yellow, and red tomatoes
½ cucumber, peeled and diced
1 small red onion, thinly sliced
¼ cup crumbled feta (optional)

1. In a small bowl, whisk the vinegar, mustard, sugar, pepper, and garlic salt. Next, slowly whisk in the olive oil. 2. In a large bowl, add the tomatoes, cucumber, and red onion. Add the dressing. Toss once or twice, and serve with feta crumbles (if using) on top.

Per Serving:
calories: 246 | fat: 18g | protein: 1g | carbs: 19g | fiber: 2g | sodium: 483mg

Turkish Shepherd'S Salad

Prep time: 15 minutes | Cook time: 0 minutes | Serves 6

¼ cup extra-virgin olive oil
2 tablespoons apple cider vinegar
2 tablespoons lemon juice
½ teaspoon kosher salt
¼ teaspoon ground black pepper
3 plum tomatoes, seeded and chopped
2 cucumbers, seeded and chopped
1 red bell pepper, seeded and chopped
1 green bell pepper, seeded and chopped
1 small red onion, chopped
⅓ cup pitted black olives (such as kalamata), halved
½ cup chopped fresh flat-leaf parsley
¼ cup chopped fresh mint
¼ cup chopped fresh dill
6 ounces (170 g) feta cheese, cubed

1. In a small bowl, whisk together the oil, vinegar, lemon juice, salt, and black pepper. 2. In a large serving bowl, combine the tomatoes, cucumber, bell peppers, onion, olives, parsley, mint, and dill. Pour the dressing over the salad, toss gently, and sprinkle with the cheese.

Per Serving:
calories: 238 | fat: 20g | protein: 6g | carbs: 10g | fiber: 2g | sodium: 806mg

French Lentil Salad with Parsley and Mint

Prep time: 20 minutes | Cook time: 25 minutes | Serves 6

For the Lentils:
1 cup French lentils
1 garlic clove, smashed
1 dried bay leaf
For the Salad:
2 tablespoons extra-virgin olive oil
2 tablespoons red wine vinegar
½ teaspoon ground cumin
½ teaspoon kosher salt
¼ teaspoon freshly ground black pepper
2 celery stalks, diced small
1 bell pepper, diced small
½ red onion, diced small
¼ cup fresh parsley, chopped
¼ cup fresh mint, chopped

Make the Lentils: 1. Put the lentils, garlic, and bay leaf in a large saucepan. Cover with water by about 3 inches and bring to a boil. Reduce the heat, cover, and simmer until tender, 20 to 30 minutes. 2. Drain the lentils to remove any remaining water after cooking. Remove the garlic and bay leaf. Make the Salad: 3. In a large bowl, whisk together the olive oil, vinegar, cumin, salt, and black pepper. Add the celery, bell pepper, onion, parsley, and mint and toss to combine. 4. Add the lentils and mix well.

Per Serving:
calories: 200 | fat: 8g | protein: 10g | carbs: 26g | fiber: 10g | sodium: 165mg

Italian Tuna and Olive Salad

Prep time : 5 minutes | Cook time: 0 minutes | Serves 4

¼ cup olive oil
3 tablespoons white wine vinegar
1 teaspoon salt
1 cup pitted green olives
1 medium red bell pepper, seeded and diced
1 small clove garlic, minced
2 (6-ounce / 170-g) cans or jars tuna in olive oil, well drained
Several leaves curly green or red lettuce

1. In a large bowl, whisk together the olive oil, vinegar, and salt. 2. Add the olives, bell pepper, and garlic to the dressing and toss to coat. Stir in the tuna, cover, and chill in the refrigerator for at least 1 hour to let the flavors meld. 3. To serve, line a serving bowl with the lettuce leaves and spoon the salad on top. Serve chilled.

Per Serving:
calories: 339 | fat: 24g | protein: 25g | carbs: 4g | fiber: 2g | sodium: 626mg

Red Pepper, Pomegranate, and Walnut Salad

Prep time: 5 minutes | Cook time: 40 minutes | Serves 4

2 red bell peppers, halved and seeded
1 teaspoon plus 2 tablespoons olive oil
4 teaspoons pomegranate molasses, divided
2 teaspoons fresh lemon juice
¼ teaspoon kosher salt
⅛ teaspoon ground black pepper
4 plum tomatoes, halved, seeded, and chopped
¼ cup walnut halves, chopped
¼ cup chopped fresh flat-leaf parsley

1. Preheat the oven to 450°F(235°C). 2. Brush the bell peppers all over with 1 teaspoon of the oil and place cut side up on a large rimmed baking sheet. Drizzle 2 teaspoons of the pomegranate molasses in the cavities of the bell peppers. Roast the bell peppers until they have softened and the skins have charred, turning once during cooking, 30 to 40 minutes. Remove from the oven and cool to room temperature. Remove the skins and chop the peppers coarsely. 3. In a large bowl, whisk together the lemon juice, salt, black pepper, the remaining 2 tablespoons oil, and the remaining 2 teaspoons pomegranate molasses. Add the bell peppers, tomatoes, walnuts, and parsley and toss gently to combine. Serve at room temperature.

Per Serving:
calories: 166 | fat: 13g | protein: 2g | carbs: 11g | fiber: 3g | sodium: 153mg

Moroccan Tomato and Roasted Chile Salad

Prep time: 15 minutes | Cook time: 0 minutes | Serves 6

2 large green bell peppers	1 small bunch flat-leaf parsley, chopped
1 hot red chili Fresno or jalapeño pepper	4 tablespoons olive oil
4 large tomatoes, peeled, seeded, and diced	1 teaspoon ground cumin
	Juice of 1 lemon
1 large cucumber, peeled and diced	Sea salt and freshly ground pepper, to taste

1. Preheat broiler on high. Broil all of the peppers and chilies until the skin blackens and blisters. 2. Place the peppers and chilies in a paper bag. Seal and set aside to cool. Combine the rest of the ingredients in a medium bowl and mix well. 3. Take peppers and chilies out from the bag and remove the skins. Seed and chop the peppers and add them to the salad. 4. Season with sea salt and freshly ground pepper. 5. Toss to combine and let sit for 15–20 minutes before serving.

Per Serving:
calories: 128 | fat: 10g | protein: 2g | carbs: 10g | fiber: 3g | sodium: 16mg

Powerhouse Arugula Salad

Prep time: 10 minutes | Cook time: 0 minutes | Serves 4

4 tablespoons extra-virgin olive oil	¼ teaspoon freshly ground black pepper
Zest and juice of 2 clementines or 1 orange (2 to 3 tablespoons)	8 cups baby arugula
	1 cup coarsely chopped walnuts
1 tablespoon red wine vinegar	1 cup crumbled goat cheese
½ teaspoon salt	½ cup pomegranate seeds

1. In a small bowl, whisk together the olive oil, zest and juice, vinegar, salt, and pepper and set aside. 2. To assemble the salad for serving, in a large bowl, combine the arugula, walnuts, goat cheese, and pomegranate seeds. Drizzle with the dressing and toss to coat.

Per Serving:
calories: 448 | fat: 41g | protein: 11g | carbs: 13g | fiber: 4g | sodium: 647mg

Watermelon Burrata Salad

Prep time: 10 minutes | Cook time: 0 minutes | Serves 4

2 cups cubes or chunks watermelon	4 fresh basil leaves, sliced chiffonade-style (roll up leaves of basil, and slice into thin strips)
1½ cups small burrata cheese balls, cut into medium chunks	
1 small red onion or 2 shallots, thinly sliced into half-moons	1 tablespoon lemon zest
¼ cup olive oil	Salt and freshly ground black pepper, to taste
¼ cup balsamic vinegar	

1. In a large bowl, mix all the ingredients. Refrigerate until chilled before serving.

Per Serving:
1 cup: calories: 224 | fat: 14g | protein: 14g | carbs: 12g | fiber: 1g | sodium: 560mg

Wild Greens Salad with Fresh Herbs

Prep time: 10 minutes | Cook time: 20 minutes | Serves 6 to 8

¼ cup olive oil	or apple cider vinegar
2 pounds (907 g) dandelion greens, tough stems removed and coarsely chopped	1 tablespoon fresh thyme, chopped
	2 cloves garlic, minced
1 small bunch chicory, trimmed and coarsely chopped	½ teaspoon kosher salt
	½ teaspoon ground black pepper
1 cup chopped fresh flat-leaf parsley, divided	¼ cup almonds or walnuts, coarsely chopped
1 cup chopped fresh mint, divided	2 tablespoons chopped fresh chives or scallion greens
½ cup water	
2 tablespoons red wine vinegar	1 tablespoon chopped fresh dill

1. In a large pot over medium heat, warm the oil. Add the greens, half of the parsley, half of the mint, the water, vinegar, thyme, garlic, salt, and pepper. Reduce the heat to a simmer and cook until the greens are very tender, about 20 minutes. 2. Meanwhile, in a small skillet over medium heat, toast the nuts until golden and fragrant, 5 to 8 minutes. Remove from the heat. 3. If serving immediately, stir the chives or scallion greens, dill, and the remaining parsley and mint into the pot. If serving as a cool or cold salad, allow to come to room temperature or refrigerate until cold before stirring in the fresh herbs. Top with the toasted nuts before serving.

Per Serving:
calories: 190 | fat: 13g | protein: 6g | carbs: 17g | fiber: 7g | sodium: 279mg

Pipirrana (Spanish Summer Salad)

Prep time: 15 minutes | Cook time: 0 minutes | Serves 2

1 medium red onion, diced	Pinch of ground cumin
2 large tomatoes, cut into small cubes	½ teaspoon salt plus a pinch for the garlic paste
1 large Persian or mini cucumber, cut into small cubes	3 tablespoons extra virgin olive oil plus a few drops for the garlic paste
1 large green bell pepper, seeded and diced	
2 garlic cloves, minced	2 tablespoons red wine vinegar

1. Place the onions in a small bowl filled with water. Set aside to soak. 2. Place the tomatoes, cucumber, and bell pepper in a medium bowl. Drain the onions and then combine them with the rest of the vegetables. Mix well. 3. In a mortar or small bowl, combine the garlic, cumin, a pinch of salt, and a few drops of olive oil, then roll or mash the ingredients until a paste is formed. 4. In another small bowl, combine 3 tablespoons of the olive oil, vinegar, and ½ teaspoon of the salt. Add the garlic paste and mix well. 5. Add the dressing to the salad and mix well. 6. Cover and refrigerate for 30 minutes before serving. Store in the refrigerator for up to 2 days.

Per Serving:
calories: 274 | fat: 21g | protein: 4g | carbs: 20g | fiber: 6g | sodium: 600mg

Zucchini and Ricotta Salad

Prep time: 5 minutes | Cook time: 2 minutes | Serves 1

2 teaspoons raw pine nuts
5 ounces (142 g) whole-milk ricotta cheese
1 tablespoon chopped fresh mint
1 teaspoon chopped fresh basil
1 tablespoon chopped fresh parsley
Pinch of fine sea salt
1 medium zucchini, very thinly sliced horizontally with a mandoline slicer
Pinch of freshly ground black pepper

For the Dressing:
1½ tablespoons extra virgin olive oil
1 tablespoon fresh lemon juice
Pinch of fine sea salt
Pinch of freshly ground black pepper

1. Add the pine nuts to a small pan placed over medium heat. Toast the nuts, turning them frequently, for 2 minutes or until golden. Set aside. 2. In a food processor, combine the ricotta, mint, basil, parsley, and a pinch of sea salt. Process until smooth and then set aside. 3. Make the dressing by combining the olive oil and lemon juice in a small bowl. Use a fork to stir rapidly until the mixture thickens, then add a pinch of sea salt and a pinch of black pepper. Stir again. 4. Place the sliced zucchini in a medium bowl. Add half of the dressing, and toss to coat the zucchini. 5. To serve, place half of the ricotta mixture in the center of a serving plate, then layer the zucchini in a circle, covering the cheese. Add the rest of the cheese in the center and on top of the zucchini, then sprinkle the toasted pine nuts over the top. Drizzle the remaining dressing over the top, and finish with a pinch of black pepper. Store covered in the refrigerator for up to 1 day.

Per Serving:
calories: 504 | fat: 43g | protein: 19g | carbs: 13g | fiber: 3g | sodium: 136mg

Traditional Greek Salad

Prep time: 10 minutes | Cook time: 0 minutes | Serves 4

2 large English cucumbers
4 Roma tomatoes, quartered
1 green bell pepper, cut into 1- to 1½-inch chunks
¼ small red onion, thinly sliced
4 ounces (113 g) pitted Kalamata olives
¼ cup extra-virgin olive oil

2 tablespoons freshly squeezed lemon juice
1 tablespoon red wine vinegar
1 tablespoon chopped fresh oregano or 1 teaspoon dried oregano
¼ teaspoon freshly ground black pepper
4 ounces (113 g) crumbled traditional feta cheese

1. Cut the cucumbers in half lengthwise and then into ½-inch-thick half-moons. Place in a large bowl. 2. Add the quartered tomatoes, bell pepper, red onion, and olives. 3. In a small bowl, whisk together the olive oil, lemon juice, vinegar, oregano, and pepper. Drizzle over the vegetables and toss to coat. 4. Divide between salad plates and top each with 1 ounce (28 g) of feta.

Per Serving:
calories: 256 | fat: 22g | protein: 6g | carbs: 11g | fiber: 3g | sodium: 476mg

Melon Caprese Salad

Prep time: 20 minutes |Cook time: 0 minutes| Serves: 6

1 cantaloupe, quartered and seeded
½ small seedless watermelon
1 cup grape tomatoes
2 cups fresh mozzarella balls (about 8 ounces / 227 g)
⅓ cup fresh basil or mint leaves, torn into small pieces

2 tablespoons extra-virgin olive oil
1 tablespoon balsamic vinegar
¼ teaspoon freshly ground black pepper
¼ teaspoon kosher or sea salt

1. Using a melon baller or a metal, teaspoon-size measuring spoon, scoop balls out of the cantaloupe. You should get about 2½ to 3 cups from one cantaloupe. (If you prefer, cut the melon into bite-size pieces instead of making balls.) Put them in a large colander over a large serving bowl. 2. Using the same method, ball or cut the watermelon into bite-size pieces; you should get about 2 cups. Put the watermelon balls in the colander with the cantaloupe. 3. Let the fruit drain for 10 minutes. Pour the juice from the bowl into a container to refrigerate and save for drinking or adding to smoothies. Wipe the bowl dry, and put in the cut fruit. 4. Add the tomatoes, mozzarella, basil, oil, vinegar, pepper, and salt to the fruit mixture. Gently mix until everything is incorporated and serve.

Per Serving:
calories: 297 | fat: 12g | protein: 14g | carbs: 39g | fiber: 3g | sodium: 123mg

Chapter 14 Desserts

Strawberry-Pomegranate Molasses Sauce

Prep time: 10 minutes | Cook time: 5 minutes | Serves 6

3 tablespoons olive oil
¼ cup honey
2 pints strawberries, hulled and halved
1 to 2 tablespoons pomegranate molasses
2 tablespoons chopped fresh mint
Greek yogurt, for serving

1. In a medium saucepan, heat the olive oil over medium heat. Add the strawberries; cook until their juices are released. Stir in the honey and cook for 1 to 2 minutes. Stir in the molasses and mint. Serve warm over Greek yogurt.

Per Serving:
calories: 189 | fat: 7g | protein: 4g | carbs: 24g | fiber: 3g | sodium: 12mg

Cherry-Stuffed Apples

Prep time: 15 minutes | Cook time: 4 hours | Serves 2

3 apples
1 tablespoon freshly squeezed lemon juice
⅓ cup dried cherries
2 tablespoons apple cider
2 tablespoons honey
¼ cup water

1. Cut about half an inch off the top of each of the apples, and peel a small strip of the skin away around the top. 2. Using a small serrated spoon or melon baller, core the apples, making sure not to go through the bottom. Drizzle with the lemon juice. 3. Fill the apples with the dried cherries. Carefully spoon the cider and honey into the apples. 4. Place the apples in the slow cooker. Pour the water around the apples. 5. Cover and cook on low for 4 hours, or until the apples are soft, and serve.

Per Serving:
calories: 227 | fat: 1g | protein: 1g | carbs: 60g | net carbs: 53g | sugars: 49g | fiber: 7g | sodium: 6mg | cholesterol: 0mg

Poached Apricots and Pistachios with Greek Yogurt

Prep time: 2 minutes | Cook time: 18 minutes | Serves 4

½ cup orange juice
2 tablespoons brandy
2 tablespoons honey
¾ cup water
1 cinnamon stick
12 dried apricots
⅓ cup 2% Greek yogurt
2 tablespoons mascarpone cheese
2 tablespoons shelled pistachios

1. Place a saucepan over medium heat and add the orange juice, brandy, honey, and water. Stir to combine, then add the cinnamon stick. 2. Once the honey has dissolved, add the apricots. Bring the mixture to a boil, then cover, reduce the heat to low, and simmer for 15 minutes. 3. While the apricots are simmering, combine the Greek yogurt and mascarpone cheese in a small serving bowl. Stir until smooth, then set aside. 4. When the cooking time for the apricots is complete, uncover, add the pistachios, and continue simmering for 3 more minutes. Remove the pan from the heat. 5. To serve, divide the Greek yogurt–mascarpone cheese mixture into 4 serving bowls and top each serving with 3 apricots, a few pistachios, and 1 teaspoon of the syrup. The apricots and syrup can be stored in a jar at room temperature for up to 1 month.

Per Serving:
calories: 146 | fat: 3g | protein: 4g | carbs: 28g | fiber: 4g | sodium: 62mg

Creamy Rice Pudding

Prep time: 5 minutes | Cook time: 45 minutes | Serves 6

1¼ cups long-grain rice
5 cups whole milk
1 cup sugar
1 tablespoon rose water or orange blossom water
1 teaspoon cinnamon

1. Rinse the rice under cold water for 30 seconds. 2. Put the rice, milk, and sugar in a large pot. Bring to a gentle boil while continually stirring. 3. Turn the heat down to low and let simmer for 40 to 45 minutes, stirring every 3 to 4 minutes so that the rice does not stick to the bottom of the pot. 4. Add the rose water at the end and simmer for 5 minutes. 5. Divide the pudding into 6 bowls. Sprinkle the top with cinnamon. Cool for at least 1 hour before serving. Store in the fridge.

Per Serving:
calories: 394 | fat: 7g | protein: 9g | carbs: 75g | fiber: 1g | sodium: 102mg

Greek Yogurt Ricotta Mousse

Prep time: 1 hour 5 minutes | Cook time: 0 minutes | Serves 4

9 ounces (255 g) full-fat ricotta cheese
4½ ounces (128 g) 2% Greek yogurt
3 teaspoons fresh lemon juice
½ teaspoon pure vanilla extract
2 tablespoons granulated sugar

1. Combine all of the ingredients in a food processor. Blend until smooth, about 1 minute. 2. Divide the mousse between 4 serving glasses. Cover and transfer to the refrigerator to chill for 1 hour before serving. Store covered in the refrigerator for up to 4 days.

Per Serving:
calories: 156 | fat: 8g | protein: 10g | carbs: 10g | fiber: 0g | sodium: 65mg

Pears with Blue Cheese and Walnuts

Prep time: 10 minutes | Cook time: 0 minutes | Serves 1

1 to 2 pears, cored and sliced into 12 slices
¼ cup blue cheese crumbles
12 walnut halves
1 tablespoon honey

1. Lay the pear slices on a plate, and top with the blue cheese crumbles. Top each slice with 1 walnut, and drizzle with honey. 2. Serve and enjoy!

Per Serving:
calories: 420 | fat: 29g | protein: 12g | carbs: 35g | fiber: 6g | sodium: 389mg

Olive Oil Ice Cream

Prep time: 5 minutes | Cook time: 25 minutes | Serves 8

4 large egg yolks
⅓ cup powdered sugar-free sweetener (such as stevia or monk fruit extract)
2 cups half-and-half or 1 cup heavy whipping cream and 1 cup whole milk
1 teaspoon vanilla extract
⅛ teaspoon salt
¼ cup light fruity extra-virgin olive oil

1. Freeze the bowl of an ice cream maker for at least 12 hours or overnight. 2. In a large bowl, whisk together the egg yolks and sugar-free sweetener. 3. In a small saucepan, heat the half-and-half over medium heat until just below a boil. Remove from the heat and allow to cool slightly. 4. Slowly pour the warm half-and-half into the egg mixture, whisking constantly to avoid cooking the eggs. Return the eggs and cream to the saucepan over low heat. 5. Whisking constantly, cook over low heat until thickened, 15 to 20 minutes. Remove from the heat and stir in the vanilla extract and salt. Whisk in the olive oil and transfer to a glass bowl. Allow to cool, cover, and refrigerate for at least 6 hours. 6. Freeze custard in an ice cream maker according to manufacturer's directions.

Per Serving:
calories: 168 | fat: 15g | protein: 2g | carbs: 8g | fiber: 0g | sodium: 49mg

Chocolate Lava Cakes

Prep time: 5 minutes | Cook time: 15 minutes | Serves 2

2 large eggs, whisked
¼ cup blanched finely ground almond flour
½ teaspoon vanilla extract
2 ounces (57 g) low-carb chocolate chips, melted

1. In a medium bowl, mix eggs with flour and vanilla. Fold in chocolate until fully combined. 2. Pour batter into two ramekins greased with cooking spray. Place ramekins into air fryer basket. Adjust the temperature to 320°F (160°C) and bake for 15 minutes. Cakes will be set at the edges and firm in the center when done. Let cool 5 minutes before serving.

Per Serving:
calories: 313 | fat: 23g | protein: 11g | carbs: 16g | fiber: 5g | sodium: 77mg

Karithopita (Greek Juicy Walnut Cake)

Prep time: 10 minutes | Cook time: 30 minutes | Serves 8

¼ cup extra virgin olive oil plus 1 teaspoon for brushing
½ cup walnut halves
¼ cup granulated sugar
¼ cup brown sugar
1 egg
1 tablespoon pure vanilla extract
¼ cup orange juice, strained
½ cup all-purpose flour
¼ cup whole-wheat flour
¼ teaspoon baking powder
¼ teaspoon baking soda
¼ teaspoon ground cinnamon
Syrup:
⅓ cup water
¼ cup granulated sugar
1 cinnamon stick
1 tablespoon orange juice

1. Preheat the oven to 350°F (180°C). Brush an 8 × 4-inch loaf pan with 1 teaspoon of the olive oil, and then line the pan with parchment paper. 2. Prepare the syrup by combining the water, sugar, and cinnamon stick in a small pan placed over medium heat. Bring to a boil and then boil for 2 minutes, then remove the pan from the heat. Remove the cinnamon stick, add the orange juice, then stir and set aside to cool. 3. Pulse the walnuts in a food processor until you achieve a cornmeal-like consistency. (Do not over-grind.) 4. In a large bowl, combine ¼ cup of the olive oil, the granulated sugar, and the brown sugar. Stir until the sugar is dissolved, then add the egg. Add the vanilla extract and orange juice. Mix well. 5. In a small bowl, combine the all-purpose flour and whole-wheat flour with the baking powder, baking soda, and cinnamon. 6. Add the flour mixture to the olive oil mixture and mix just until the flour has been incorporated. Add ¼ cup of the ground walnuts and mix until they are distributed throughout the batter. 7. Pour the batter into the prepared pan. Bake for 25–30 minutes or until a toothpick inserted into the cake comes out clean. 8. Use a toothpick to poke 8 holes across the top of the cake and then pour the syrup over the entire surface of the cake. Sprinkle the remaining ground walnuts over the top, and then set the cake aside to rest for 30 minutes before cutting it in equal-sized 1-inch slices. Store in an airtight container in the refrigerator for up to 5 days.

Per Serving:
calories: 240 | fat: 12g | protein: 3g | carbs: 30g | fiber: 1g | sodium: 52mg

Avocado-Orange Fruit Salad

Prep time: 10 minutes | Cook time: 0 minutes | Serves 5 to 6

2 large Gala apples, chopped
2 oranges, segmented and chopped
⅓ cup sliced almonds
½ cup honey
1 tablespoon extra-virgin olive oil
½ teaspoon grated orange zest
1 large avocado, semi-ripened, medium diced

1. In a large bowl, combine the apples, oranges, and almonds. Mix gently. 2. In a small bowl, whisk the honey, oil, and orange zest. Set aside. 3. Drizzle the orange zest mix over the fruit salad and toss. Add the avocado and toss gently one more time.

Per Serving:
calories: 296 | fat: 12g | protein: 3g | carbs: 51g | fiber: 7g | sodium: 4mg

Date and Honey Almond Milk Ice Cream

Prep time: 10 minutes | **Cook time:** 5 minutes | **Serves 4**

¾ cup (about 4 ounces/ 113 g) pitted dates
¼ cup honey
½ cup water
2 cups cold unsweetened almond milk
2 teaspoons vanilla extract

1. Combine the dates and water in a small saucepan and bring to a boil over high heat. Remove the pan from the heat, cover, and let stand for 15 minutes. 2. In a blender, combine the almond milk, dates, the date soaking water, honey, and the vanilla and process until very smooth. 3. Cover the blender jar and refrigerate the mixture until cold, at least 1 hour. 4. Transfer the mixture to an electric ice cream maker and freeze according to the manufacturer's instructions. 5. Serve immediately or transfer to a freezer-safe storage container and freeze for 4 hours (or longer). Serve frozen.

Per Serving:
calories: 106 | fat: 2g | protein: 1g | carbs: 23g | fiber: 3g | sodium: 92mg

Grilled Pineapple and Melon

Prep time: 10 minutes | **Cook time:** 7 minutes | **Serves 4**

8 fresh pineapple rings, rind removed
8 watermelon triangles, with rind
1 tablespoon honey
½ teaspoon freshly ground black pepper

1. Preheat an outdoor grill or a grill pan over high heat. 2. Drizzle the fruit slices with honey and sprinkle one side of each piece with pepper. Grill for 5 minutes, turn, and grill for another 2 minutes. Serve.

Per Serving:
calories: 244 | fat: 1g | protein: 4g | carbs: 62g | fiber: 4g | sodium: 7mg

Peaches Poached in Rose Water

Prep time: 15 minutes | **Cook time:** 1 minute | **Serves 6**

1 cup water
1 cup rose water
¼ cup wildflower honey
8 green cardamom pods, lightly crushed
1 teaspoon vanilla bean paste
6 large yellow peaches, pitted and quartered
½ cup chopped unsalted roasted pistachio meats

1. Add water, rose water, honey, cardamom, and vanilla to the Instant Pot®. Whisk well, then add peaches. Close lid, set steam release to Sealing, press the Manual button, and set time to 1 minute. 2. When the timer beeps, quick-release the pressure until the float valve drops. Press the Cancel button and open lid. Allow peaches to stand for 10 minutes. Carefully remove peaches from poaching liquid with a slotted spoon. 3. Slip skins from peach slices. Arrange slices on a plate and garnish with pistachios. Serve warm or at room temperature.

Per Serving:
calories: 145 | fat: 3g | protein: 2g | carbs: 28g | fiber: 2g | sodium: 8mg

Pumpkin-Ricotta Cheesecake

Prep time: 25 minutes | **Cook time:** 45 minutes | **Serves 10 to 12**

1 cup almond flour
½ cup butter, melted
1 (14½-ounce / 411-g) can pumpkin purée
8 ounces (227 g) cream cheese, at room temperature
½ cup whole-milk ricotta cheese
½ to ¾ cup sugar-free sweetener
4 large eggs
2 teaspoons vanilla extract
2 teaspoons pumpkin pie spice
Whipped cream, for garnish (optional)

1. Preheat the oven to 350°F(180°C). Line the bottom of a 9-inch springform pan with parchment paper. 2. In a small bowl, combine the almond flour and melted butter with a fork until well combined. Using your fingers, press the mixture into the bottom of the prepared pan. 3. In a large bowl, beat together the pumpkin purée, cream cheese, ricotta, and sweetener using an electric mixer on medium. 4. Add the eggs, one at a time, beating after each addition. Stir in the vanilla and pumpkin pie spice until just combined. 5. Pour the mixture over the crust and bake until set, 40 to 45 minutes. 6. Allow to cool to room temperature. Refrigerate for at least 6 hours before serving. 7. Serve chilled, garnishing with whipped cream, if desired.

Per Serving:
calories: 230 | fat: 21g | protein: 6g | carbs: 5g | fiber: 1g | sodium: 103mg

Chocolate Turtle Hummus

Prep time: 15 minutes | **Cook time:** 0 minutes | **Serves 2**

For the Caramel:
2 tablespoons coconut oil
1 tablespoon maple syrup
1 tablespoon almond butter
Pinch salt
For the Hummus:
½ cup chickpeas, drained and rinsed
2 tablespoons unsweetened cocoa powder
1 tablespoon maple syrup, plus more to taste
2 tablespoons almond milk, or more as needed, to thin
Pinch salt
2 tablespoons pecans

Make the caramel 1. put the coconut oil in a small microwave-safe bowl. If it's solid, microwave it for about 15 seconds to melt it. 2. Stir in the maple syrup, almond butter, and salt. 3. Place the caramel in the refrigerator for 5 to 10 minutes to thicken. Make the hummus 1. In a food processor, combine the chickpeas, cocoa powder, maple syrup, almond milk, and pinch of salt, and process until smooth. Scrape down the sides to make sure everything is incorporated. 2. If the hummus seems too thick, add another tablespoon of almond milk. 3. Add the pecans and pulse 6 times to roughly chop them. 4. Transfer the hummus to a serving bowl and when the caramel is thickened, swirl it into the hummus. Gently fold it in, but don't mix it in completely. 5. Serve with fresh fruit or pretzels.

Per Serving:
calories: 321 | fat: 22g | protein: 7g | carbs: 30g | fiber: 6g | sodium: 100mg

Creamy Spiced Almond Milk

Prep time: 5 minutes | Cook time: 1 minute | Serves 6

1 cup raw almonds
5 cups filtered water, divided
1 teaspoon vanilla bean paste
½ teaspoon pumpkin pie spice

1. Add almonds and 1 cup water to the Instant Pot®. Close lid, set steam release to Sealing, press the Manual button, and set time to 1 minute. 2. When the timer beeps, quick-release the pressure until the float valve drops. Press the Cancel button and open lid. Strain almonds and rinse under cool water. Transfer to a high-powered blender with remaining 3.cups water. Purée for 2 minutes on high speed. 4. Pour mixture into a nut milk bag set over a large bowl. Squeeze bag to extract all liquid. Stir in vanilla and pumpkin pie spice. Transfer to a Mason jar or sealed jug and refrigerate for 8 hours. Stir or shake gently before serving.

Per Serving:
calories: 86 | fat: 8g | protein: 3g | carbs: 3g | fiber: 2g | sodium: 0mg

Frozen Raspberry Delight

Prep time: 10 minutes | Cook time: 0 minutes | Serves 2

3 cups frozen raspberries
1 peach, peeled and pitted
1 mango, peeled and pitted
1 teaspoon honey

1. Add all ingredients to a blender and purée, only adding enough water to keep the mixture moving and your blender from overworking itself. 2. Freeze for 10 minutes to firm up if desired.

Per Serving:
calories: 237 | fat: 2g | protein: 4g | carbs: 57g | fiber: 16g | sodium: 4mg

Fresh Figs with Chocolate Sauce

Prep time: 5 minutes | Cook time: 0 minutes | Serves 4

¼ cup honey
2 tablespoons cocoa powder
8 fresh figs

1. Combine the honey and cocoa powder in a small bowl, and mix well to form a syrup. 2. Cut the figs in half and place cut side up. Drizzle with the syrup and serve.

Per Serving:
calories: 112 | fat: 1g | protein: 1g | carbs: 30g | fiber: 3g | sodium: 3mg

Grilled Stone Fruit with Whipped Ricotta

Prep time: 10 minutes |Cook time: 10 minutes| Serves: 4

Nonstick cooking spray
4 peaches or nectarines (or 8 apricots or plums), halved and pitted
2 teaspoons extra-virgin olive oil
¾ cup whole-milk ricotta
cheese
1 tablespoon honey
¼ teaspoon freshly grated nutmeg
4 sprigs mint, for garnish (optional)

1. Spray the cold grill or a grill pan with nonstick cooking spray. Heat the grill or grill pan to medium heat. 2. Place a large, empty bowl in the refrigerator to chill. 3. Brush the fruit all over with the oil. Place the fruit cut-side down on the grill or pan and cook for 3 to 5 minutes, or until grill marks appear. (If you're using a grill pan, cook in two batches.) Using tongs, turn the fruit over. Cover the grill (or the grill pan with aluminum foil) and cook for 4 to 6 minutes, until the fruit is easily pierced with a sharp knife. Set aside to cool. 4. Remove the bowl from the refrigerator and add the ricotta. Using an electric beater, beat the ricotta on high for 2 minutes. Add the honey and nutmeg and beat for 1 more minute. Divide the warm (or room temperature) fruit among 4 serving bowls, top with the ricotta mixture, and a sprig of mint (if using) and serve.

Per Serving:
calories: 180 | fat: 9g | protein: 7g | carbs: 21g | fiber: 3g | sodium: 39mg

Toasted Almonds with Honey

Prep time: 15 minutes | Cook time: 5 minutes | Serves 4

½ cup raw almonds
3 tablespoons good-quality
honey, plus more if desired

1. Fill a medium saucepan three-quarters full with water and bring to a boil over high heat. Add the almonds and cook for 1 minute. Drain the almonds in a fine-mesh sieve and rinse them under cold water to cool and stop the cooking. Remove the skins from the almonds by rubbing them in a clean kitchen towel. Place the almonds on a paper towel to dry. 2. In the same saucepan, combine the almonds and honey and cook over medium heat until the almonds get a little golden, 4 to 5 minutes. Remove from the heat and let cool completely, about 15 minutes, before serving or storing.

Per Serving:
calories: 151 | fat: 9g | protein: 4g | carbs: 17g | fiber: 2g | sodium: 1mg

Grilled Peaches with Greek Yogurt

Prep time: 5 minutes | Cook time: 30 minutes | Serves 4

4 ripe peaches, halved and pitted
2 tablespoons olive oil
1 teaspoon ground cinnamon,
plus extra for topping
2 cups plain full-fat Greek yogurt
¼ cup honey, for drizzling

1. Preheat the oven to 350°F (180°C). 2. Place the peaches in a baking dish, cut-side up. 3. In a small bowl, stir together the olive oil and cinnamon, then brush the mixture over the peach halves. 4. Bake the peaches for about 30 minutes, until they are soft. 5. Top the peaches with the yogurt and drizzle them with the honey, then serve.

Per Serving:
calories: 259 | fat: 11g | protein: 6g | carbs: 38g | fiber: 3g | sodium: 57mg

Poached Pears with Greek Yogurt and Pistachio

Prep time: 10 minutes | Cook time: 3 minutes | Serves 8

2 cups water
1¾ cups apple cider
¼ cup lemon juice
1 cinnamon stick
1 teaspoon vanilla bean paste
4 large Bartlett pears, peeled
1 cup low-fat plain Greek yogurt
½ cup unsalted roasted pistachio meats

1. Add water, apple cider, lemon juice, cinnamon, vanilla, and pears to the Instant Pot®. Close lid, set steam release to Sealing, press the Manual button, and set time to 3 minutes. 2. When the timer beeps, quick-release the pressure until the float valve drops. Press the Cancel button and open lid. With a slotted spoon remove pears to a plate and allow to cool to room temperature. 3. To serve, carefully slice pears in half with a sharp paring knife and scoop out core with a melon baller. Lay pear halves on dessert plates or in shallow bowls. Top with yogurt and garnish with pistachios. Serve immediately.

Per Serving:
calories: 181 | fat: 7g | protein: 7g | carbs: 23g | fiber: 4g | sodium: 11mg

Ricotta Cheesecake

Prep time: 2 minutes | Cook time: 45 to 50 minutes | Serves 12

2 cups skim or fat-free ricotta cheese (one 15-ounce / 425-g container)
1¼ cups sugar
1 teaspoon vanilla extract
6 eggs
Zest of 1 orange

1. Preheat the oven to 375°F (190°C). Grease an 8-inch square baking pan with butter or cooking spray. 2. In a medium bowl, stir together the ricotta and sugar. Add the eggs one at a time until well incorporated. Stir in the vanilla and orange zest. 3. Pour the batter into the prepared pan. Bake for 45 to 50 minutes, until set. Let cool in the pan for 20 minutes. Serve warm.

Per Serving:
calories: 160 | fat: 5g | protein: 12g | carbs: 15g | fiber: 0g | sodium: 388mg

Apricot and Mint No-Bake Parfait

Prep time: 10 minutes | Cook time: 0 minutes | Serves 6

4 ounces (113 g) Neufchâtel or other light cream cheese
1 (7-ounce / 198-g) container 2% Greek yogurt
½ cup plus 2 tablespoons sugar
2 teaspoons vanilla extract
1 tablespoon fresh lemon juice
1 pound (454 g) apricots, rinsed, pitted, and cut into bite-size pieces
2 tablespoons finely chopped fresh mint, plus whole leaves for garnish if desired

1. In the bowl of a stand mixer fitted with the paddle attachment, beat the Neufchâtel cheese and yogurt on low speed until well combined, about 2 minutes, scraping down the bowl as needed. Add ½ cup of the sugar, the vanilla, and the lemon juice. Mix until smooth and free of lumps, 2 to 3 minutes; set aside. 2. In a medium bowl, combine the apricots, mint, and remaining 2 tablespoons sugar. Stir occasionally, waiting to serve until after the apricots have released their juices and have softened. 3. Line up six 6-to 8-ounce (170-to 227-g) glasses. Using an ice cream scoop, spoon 3 to 4 tablespoons of the cheesecake mixture evenly into the bottom of each glass. (Alternatively, transfer the cheesecake mixture to a piping bag or a small zip-top bag with one corner snipped and pipe the mixture into the glasses.) Add a layer of the same amount of apricots to each glass. Repeat so you have two layers of cheesecake mixture and two layers of the apricots, ending with the apricots.) Garnish with the mint, if desired, and serve.

Per Serving:
calories: 132 | fat: 2g | protein: 5g | carbs: 23g | fiber: 2g | sodium: 35mg

S'mores

Prep time: 5 minutes | Cook time: 30 seconds | Makes 8 s'mores

Oil, for spraying
8 graham cracker squares
2 (1½-ounce / 43-g) chocolate bars
4 large marshmallows

1. Line the air fryer basket with parchment and spray lightly with oil. 2. Place 4 graham cracker squares in the prepared basket. 3. Break the chocolate bars in half and place 1 piece on top of each graham cracker. Top with 1 marshmallow. 4. Air fry at 370°F (188°C) for 30 seconds, or until the marshmallows are puffed and golden brown and slightly melted. 5. Top with the remaining graham cracker squares and serve.

Per Serving:
calories: 154 | fat: 7g | protein: 2g | carbs: 22g | fiber: 2g | sodium: 75mg

Tahini Baklava Cups

Prep time: 10 minutes | Cook time: 25 minutes | Serves 8

1 box (about 16) mini phyllo dough cups, thawed
⅓ cup tahini
¼ cup shelled pistachios or walnuts, chopped, plus more for garnish
4 tablespoons honey, divided
1 teaspoon ground cinnamon
Pinch of kosher salt
½ teaspoon rosewater (optional)

1. Preheat the oven to 350°F (180°C). Remove the phyllo cups from the packaging and place on a large rimmed baking sheet. 2. In a small bowl, stir together the tahini, nuts, 1 tablespoon of the honey, the cinnamon, and salt. Divide this mixture among the phyllo cups and top each with a few more nuts. Bake until golden and warmed through, 10 minutes. Remove from the oven and cool for 5 minutes. 3. Meanwhile, in a small saucepan or in a microwaveable bowl, stir together the remaining 3 tablespoons honey and the rosewater, if using, and heat until warmed, about 5 minutes over medium heat o

Per Serving:
calories: 227 | fat: 9g | protein: 5g | carbs: 32g | fiber: 2g | sodium: 195mg

Mascarpone and Fig Crostini

Prep time: 10 minutes | Cook time: 10 minutes | Serves 6 to 8

1 long French baguette
4 tablespoons (½ stick) salted butter, melted
1 (8-ounce / 227-g) tub mascarpone cheese
1 (12-ounce / 340-g) jar fig jam

1. Preheat the oven to 350°F(180ºC). 2. Slice the bread into ¼-inch-thick slices. 3. Arrange the sliced bread on a baking sheet and brush each slice with the melted butter. 4. Put the baking sheet in the oven and toast the bread for 5 to 7 minutes, just until golden brown. 5. Let the bread cool slightly. Spread about a teaspoon or so of the mascarpone cheese on each piece of bread. 6. Top with a teaspoon or so of the jam. Serve immediately.

Per Serving:
calories: 445 | fat: 24g | protein: 3g | carbs: 48g | fiber: 5g | sodium: 314mg

Greek Yogurt with Honey and Pomegranates

Prep time: 5 minutes | Cook time: 0 minutes | Serves 4

4 cups plain full-fat Greek yogurt
½ cup pomegranate seeds
¼ cup honey
Sugar, for topping (optional)

1. Evenly divide the yogurt among four bowls. Evenly divide the pomegranate seeds among the bowls and drizzle each with the honey. 2. Sprinkle each bowl with a pinch of sugar, if desired, and serve.

Per Serving:
calories: 232 | fat: 8g | protein: 9g | carbs: 33g | fiber: 1g | sodium: 114mg

Roasted Plums with Nut Crumble

Prep time: 5 minutes | Cook time: 25 minutes | Serves 4

¼ cup honey
¼ cup freshly squeezed orange juice
4 large plums, halved and pitted
¼ cup whole-wheat pastry flour
1 tablespoon pure maple sugar
1 tablespoon nuts, coarsely chopped (your choice; I like almonds, pecans, and walnuts)
1½ teaspoons canola oil
½ cup plain Greek yogurt

1. Preheat the oven to 400°F (205ºC). Combine the honey and orange juice in a square baking dish. Place the plums, cut-side down, in the dish. Roast about 15 minutes, and then turn the plums over and roast an additional 10 minutes, or until tender and juicy. 2. In a medium bowl, combine the flour, maple sugar, nuts, and canola oil and mix well. Spread on a small baking sheet and bake alongside the plums, tossing once, until golden brown, about 5 minutes. Set aside until the plums have finished cooking. 3. Serve the plums drizzled with pan juices and topped with the nut crumble and a dollop of yogurt.

Per Serving:
calories: 175 | fat: 3g | protein: 4g | carbs: 36g | fiber: 2g | sodium: 10mg

Lemon Fool

Prep time: 25minutes |Cook time: 5 minutes| Serves: 4

1 cup 2% plain Greek yogurt
1 medium lemon
¼ cup cold water
1½ teaspoons cornstarch
3½ tablespoons honey, divided
⅔ cup heavy (whipping) cream
Fresh fruit and mint leaves, for serving (optional)

1. Place a large glass bowl and the metal beaters from your electric mixer in the refrigerator to chill. Add the yogurt to a medium glass bowl, and place that bowl in the refrigerator to chill as well. 2. Using a Microplane or citrus zester, zest the lemon into a medium, microwave-safe bowl. Halve the lemon, and squeeze 1 tablespoon of lemon juice into the bowl. Add the water and cornstarch, and stir well. Whisk in 3 tablespoons of honey. Microwave the lemon mixture on high for 1 minute; stir and microwave for an additional 10 to 30 seconds, until the mixture is thick and bubbling. 3. Remove the bowl of yogurt from the refrigerator, and whisk in the warm lemon mixture. Place the yogurt back in the refrigerator. 4. Remove the large chilled bowl and the beaters from the refrigerator. Assemble your electric mixer with the chilled beaters. Pour the cream into the chilled bowl, and beat until soft peaks form—1 to 3 minutes, depending on the freshness of your cream. 5. Take the chilled yogurt mixture out of the refrigerator. Gently fold it into the whipped cream using a rubber scraper; lift and turn the mixture to prevent the cream from deflating. Chill until serving, at least 15 minutes but no longer than 1 hour. 6. To serve, spoon the lemon fool into four glasses or dessert dishes and drizzle with the remaining ½ tablespoon of honey. Top with fresh fruit and mint, if desired.

Per Serving:
calories: 172 | fat: 8g | protein: 4g | carbs: 22g | fiber: 1g | sodium: 52mg

Red Wine–Poached Figs with Ricotta and Almond

Prep time: 5 minutes | Cook time: 1 minute | Serves 4

2 cups water
2 cups red wine
¼ cup honey
1 cinnamon stick
1 star anise
1 teaspoon vanilla bean paste
12 dried mission figs
1 cup ricotta cheese
1 tablespoon confectioners' sugar
¼ teaspoon almond extract
1 cup toasted sliced almonds

1. Add water, wine, honey, cinnamon, star anise, and vanilla to the Instant Pot® and whisk well. Add figs, close lid, set steam release to Sealing, press the Manual button, and set time to 1 minute. 2. When the timer beeps, quick-release the pressure until the float valve drops. Press the Cancel button and open lid. With a slotted spoon, transfer figs to a plate and set aside to cool for 5 minutes. 3. In a small bowl, mix together ricotta, sugar, and almond extract. Serve figs with a dollop of sweetened ricotta and a sprinkling of almonds.

Per Serving:
calories: 597 | fat: 21g | protein: 13g | carbs: 56g | fiber: 9g | sodium: 255mg

Cucumber-Lime Popsicles

Prep time: 5 minutes | **Cook time:** 0 minutes | **Serves 4 to 6**

2 cups cold water
1 cucumber, peeled
¼ cup honey
Juice of 1 lime

1. In a blender, purée the water, cucumber, honey, and lime juice. Pour into popsicle molds, freeze, and enjoy on a hot summer day!

Per Serving:
calories: 49 | fat: 0g | protein: 0g | carbs: 13g | fiber: 0g | sodium: 3mg

Almond Rice Pudding

Prep time: 5 minutes | **Cook time:** 45 minutes | **Serves 8**

1 cup Arborio rice
¼ teaspoon kosher salt
5 cups unsweetened almond milk
2 tablespoons chopped preserved lemon or dried lemons
½ cup sugar
2 teaspoons vanilla extract
2 tablespoons slivered almonds, toasted (optional)

1. In a medium saucepan, combine the rice, salt, and 2 cups water. Bring to a boil. Reduce the heat to low-medium, cover the pan with the lid ajar, and cook until the water has been almost completely absorbed, 6 to 8 minutes, stirring occasionally. 2. Stir in the almond milk, sugar, dried or preserved lemon, and vanilla. Bring the mixture to a simmer, stirring occasionally, and cook until the rice is tender and the mixture has thickened, 30 to 35 minutes. Let cool slightly before serving. 3. Serve warm, topped with toasted almonds, if desired.

Per Serving:
calories: 203 | fat: 10g | protein: 9g | carbs: 23g | fiber: 4g | sodium: 146mg

Honey-Vanilla Apple Pie with Olive Oil Crust

Prep time: 10 minutes | **Cook time:** 45 minutes | **Serves 8**

For the crust:
¼ cup olive oil
1½ cups whole-wheat flour
½ teaspoon sea salt
2 tablespoons ice water
For the filling:
4 large apples of your choice, peeled, cored, and sliced
Juice of 1 lemon
1 tablespoon pure vanilla extract
1 tablespoon honey
½ teaspoon sea salt
Olive oil

Make the crust: 1. Put the olive oil, flour, and sea salt in a food processor and process until dough forms. 2. Slowly add the water and pulse until you have a stiff dough. 3. Form the dough into 2 equal-sized balls, wrap in plastic wrap, and put in the refrigerator while you make the filling. Make the filling: 1. Combine the apples, lemon juice, vanilla, honey, and sea salt in a large bowl. 2. Stir and allow to sit for at least 10 minutes. Preheat oven to 400ºF (205ºC). 3. Roll 1 crust out on a lightly floured surface. Transfer to a 9-inch pie plate and top with filling. 4. Roll the other ball of dough out and put on top of the pie. Cut a few slices in the top to vent the pie, and lightly brush the top of the pie with olive oil. 5. Bake for 45 minutes, or until top is browned and apples are bubbly. 6. Allow to cool completely before slicing and serving with your favorite frozen yogurt.

Per Serving:
calories: 208 | fat: 8g | protein: 3g | carbs: 34g | fiber: 5g | sodium: 293mg

Golden Coconut Cream Pops

Prep time: 5 minutes | **Cook time:** 0 minutes | **Makes 8 cream pops**

1½ cups coconut cream
½ cup coconut milk
4 egg yolks
2 teaspoons ground turmeric
1 teaspoon ground ginger
1 teaspoon cinnamon
1 teaspoon vanilla powder or 1 tablespoon unsweetened vanilla extract
¼ teaspoon ground black pepper
Optional: low-carb sweetener, to taste

1. Place all of the ingredients in a blender (including the optional sweetener) and process until well combined. Pour into eight ⅓-cup (80 ml) ice pop molds. Freeze until solid for 3 hours, or until set. 2. To easily remove the ice pops from the molds, fill a pot as tall as the ice pops with warm (not hot) water and dip the ice pop molds in for 15 to 20 seconds. Remove the ice pops from the molds and then freeze again. Store in the freezer in a resealable bag for up to 3 months.

Per Serving:
calories: 219 | fat: 21g | protein: 3g | carbs: 5g | fiber: 2g | sodium: 9mg

Greek Island Almond Cocoa Bites

Prep time: 5 minutes | **Cook time:** 0 minutes | **Serves 6**

½ cup roasted, unsalted whole almonds (with skins)
3 tablespoons granulated sugar, divided
1½ teaspoons unsweetened cocoa powder
1¼ tablespoons unseasoned breadcrumbs
¾ teaspoon pure vanilla extract
1½ teaspoons orange juice

1. Place the almonds in a food processor and process until you have a coarse ground texture. 2. In a medium bowl, combine the ground almonds, 2 tablespoons sugar, the cocoa powder, and the breadcrumbs. Mix well. 3. In a small bowl, combine the vanilla extract and orange juice. Stir and then add the mixture to the almond mixture. Mix well. 4. Measure out a teaspoon of the mixture. Squeeze the mixture with your hand to make the dough stick together, then mold the dough into a small ball. 5. Add the remaining tablespoon of the sugar to a shallow bowl. Roll the balls in the sugar until covered, then transfer the bites to an airtight container. Store covered at room temperature for up to 1 week.

Per Serving:
calories: 102 | fat: 6g | protein: 3g | carbs: 10g | fiber: 2g | sodium: 11mg

Koulourakia (Olive Oil Cinnamon Cookies)

Prep time: 25 minutes | Cook time: 25 to 30 minutes | Serves 15

¼ cup extra virgin olive oil
¼ cup granulated sugar
¼ cup orange juice, strained
1¼ cups all-purpose flour plus extra if needed
¼ teaspoon baking powder
¼ teaspoon baking soda
¼ teaspoon ground cinnamon
Cinnamon-Sugar Coating:
1½ tablespoons granulated sugar
¾ teaspoon ground cinnamon

1. Preheat the oven to 350°F (180°C). Line a large baking sheet with parchment paper. 2. In a large bowl, combine the olive oil, sugar, and orange juice. Mix with a rubber spatula until the sugar has completely dissolved. 3. In a small bowl, combine the flour, baking powder, baking soda, and cinnamon. Stir to combine. 4. Gradually add the flour mixture to the olive oil mixture while gently mixing and folding with the spatula until a smooth, shiny, pliable dough that does not stick to your hands is formed. Pick up the dough with your hands and fold it once or twice to make sure it has the proper consistency. If the dough is still sticky, add more flour in small amounts. (Be careful not to add more flour than needed.) Cover the dough with plastic wrap and set it aside to rest for 5 minutes at room temperature. 5. While the dough is resting, make the cinnamon-sugar coating by combining the sugar and cinnamon in a small bowl and mixing well. 6. When the dough is rested, coat your fingers with a few drops of olive oil and begin shaping the cookies by taking about 1 teaspoon of the dough and rolling it out into a thin cord about 6 inches long, then set it aside. Continue the process until you have 10–12 cords, then dip each cord in the cinnamon-sugar mixture and fold it in half and twist it into a braid, or shape it into a ring or spiral. Place the cookies on the prepared baking sheet, and bake for 12–15 minutes or until golden brown. 7. While the first batch is baking, begin shaping the next batch. Once the first batch is done baking, remove the pan from the oven and let them sit for 5 minutes before transferring them to a wire rack to cool completely. Repeat the process with the remaining dough. Store in an airtight container for up to 3 weeks.

Per Serving:
calories: 90 | fat: 4g | protein: 1g | carbs: 13g | fiber: 0g | sodium: 22mg

Red-Wine Poached Pears

Prep time: 10 minutes | Cook time: 20 minutes | Serves 2

2 cups red wine, such as Merlot or Zinfandel, more if necessary
2 firm pears, peeled
2 to 3 cardamom pods, split
1 cinnamon stick
2 peppercorns
1 bay leaf

1. Put all ingredients in a large pot and bring to a boil. Make sure the pears are submerged in the wine. 2. Reduce heat and simmer for 15–20 minutes until the pears are tender when poked with a fork. 3. Remove the pears from the wine, and allow to cool. 4. Bring the wine to a boil, and cook until it reduces to a syrup. 5. Strain and drizzle the pears with the warmed syrup before serving.

Per Serving:
calories: 268 | fat: 0g | protein: 1g | carbs: 22g | fiber: 6g | sodium: 0mg

Lemon Coconut Cake

Prep time: 5 minutes | Cook time: 40 minutes | Serves 9

Base:
6 large eggs, separated
⅓ cup melted ghee or virgin coconut oil
1 tablespoon fresh lemon juice
Zest of 2 lemons
2 cups almond flour
½ cup coconut flour
¼ cup collagen powder
1 teaspoon baking soda
1 teaspoon vanilla powder or 1 tablespoon unsweetened vanilla extract
Optional: low-carb sweetener, to taste
Topping:
½ cup unsweetened large coconut flakes
1 cup heavy whipping cream or coconut cream
¼ cup mascarpone, more heavy whipping cream, or coconut cream
½ teaspoon vanilla powder or 1½ teaspoons unsweetened vanilla extract

1. Preheat the oven to 285°F (140°C) fan assisted or 320°F (160°C) conventional. Line a baking tray with parchment paper (or use a silicone tray). A square 8 × 8–inch (20 × 20 cm) or a rectangular tray of similar size will work best. 2. To make the base: Whisk the egg whites in a bowl until stiff peaks form. In a separate bowl, whisk the egg yolks, melted ghee, lemon juice, and lemon zest. In a third bowl, mix the almond flour, coconut flour, collagen, baking soda, vanilla and optional sweetener. 3. Add the whisked egg yolk–ghee mixture into the dry mixture and combine well. Gently fold in the egg whites, trying not to deflate them. 4. Pour into the baking tray. Bake for 35 to 40 minutes, until lightly golden on top and set inside. Remove from the oven and let cool completely before adding the topping. 5. To make the topping: Preheat the oven to 350°F (175°C) fan assisted or 380°F (195°C) conventional. Place the coconut flakes on a baking tray and bake for 2 to 3 minutes. Remove from the oven and set aside to cool. 6. Once the cake is cool, place the cream, mascarpone, and vanilla in a bowl. Whip until soft peaks form. Spread on top of the cooled cake and top with the toasted coconut flakes. 7. To store, refrigerate for up to 5 days or freeze for up to 3 months. Coconut flakes will soften in the fridge. If you want to keep them crunchy, sprinkle on top of each slice before serving.

Per Serving:
calories: 342 | fat: 31g | protein: 9g | carbs: 10g | fiber: 4g | sodium: 208mg

Apple and Brown Rice Pudding

Prep time: 10 minutes | Cook time: 20 minutes | Serves 6

2 cups almond milk
1 cup long-grain brown rice
½ cup golden raisins
1 Granny Smith apple, peeled, cored, and chopped
¼ cup honey
1 teaspoon vanilla extract
½ teaspoon ground cinnamon

1. Place all ingredients in the Instant Pot®. Stir to combine. Close lid, set steam release to Sealing, press the Manual button, and set time to 20 minutes. 2. When the timer beeps, let pressure release naturally for 15 minutes, then quick-release the remaining pressure. Press the Cancel button and open lid. Serve warm or at room temperature.

Per Serving:
calories: 218 | fat: 2g | protein: 3g | carbs: 51g | fiber: 4g | sodium: 54mg

Dried Fruit Compote

Prep time: 15 minutes | Cook time: 8 minutes | Serves 6

8 ounces (227 g) dried apricots, quartered
8 ounces (227 g) dried peaches, quartered
1 cup golden raisins
1½ cups orange juice
1 cinnamon stick
4 whole cloves

1. Place all ingredients in the Instant Pot®. Stir to combine. Close lid, set steam release to Sealing, press the Manual button, and set time to 3 minutes. When the timer beeps, let pressure release naturally, about 20 minutes. Press the Cancel button and open lid. 2. Remove and discard cinnamon stick and cloves. Press the Sauté button and simmer for 5–6 minutes. Serve warm or allow to cool, and then cover and refrigerate for up to a week.

Per Serving:
calories: 258 | fat: 0g | protein: 4g | carbs: 63g | fiber: 5g | sodium: 7mg

Greek Yogurt Chocolate "Mousse" with Berries

Prep time: 15 minutes | Cook time: 0 minutes | Serves 4

2 cups plain Greek yogurt
¼ cup heavy cream
¼ cup pure maple syrup
3 tablespoons unsweetened cocoa powder
2 teaspoons vanilla extract
¼ teaspoon kosher salt
1 cup fresh mixed berries
¼ cup chocolate chips

1. Place the yogurt, cream, maple syrup, cocoa powder, vanilla, and salt in the bowl of a stand mixer or use a large bowl with an electric hand mixer. Mix at medium-high speed until fluffy, about 5 minutes. 2. Spoon evenly among 4 bowls and put in the refrigerator to set for at least 15 minutes. 3. Serve each bowl with ¼ cup mixed berries and 1 tablespoon chocolate chips.

Per Serving:
calories: 300 | fat: 11g | protein: 16g | carbs: 35g | fiber: 3g | sodium: 60mg

Steamed Dessert Bread

Prep time: 5 minutes | Cook time: 1 hour | Serves 8

½ cup all-purpose flour
½ cup stone-ground cornmeal
½ cup whole-wheat flour
½ teaspoon baking powder
¼ teaspoon salt
¼ teaspoon baking soda
½ cup maple syrup
½ cup buttermilk
1 large egg
1 cup water

1. Grease the inside of a 6-cup heatproof pudding mold or baking pan. 2. Add flour, cornmeal, whole-wheat flour, baking powder, salt, and baking soda to a medium mixing bowl. Stir to combine. Add maple syrup, buttermilk, and egg to another mixing bowl or measuring cup. Whisk to mix and then pour into the flour mixture. Mix until a thick batter is formed. 3. Pour enough batter into prepared baking pan to fill it three-quarters full. 4. Butter one side of a piece of heavy-duty aluminum foil large enough to cover the top of the baking dish. Place the foil butter side down over the pan and crimp the edges to seal. 5. Add water to the Instant Pot® and place the rack inside. Fold a long piece of aluminum foil in half lengthwise. Lay foil over rack to form a sling. Place pan on rack so it rests on the sling. 6. Close lid, set steam release to Sealing, press the Manual button, set time to 1 hour, and press the Adjust button and set pressure to Low. When the timer beeps, let pressure release naturally, about 25 minutes. 7. Open lid, lift pan from Instant Pot® using the sling, and place on a cooling rack. Remove foil. Test bread with a toothpick. If the toothpick comes out wet, place the foil over the pan and return it to the Instant Pot® to cook for 10 additional minutes. If the bread is done, use a knife to loosen it and invert it onto the cooling rack. Serve warm.

Per Serving:
calories: 175 | fat: 1g | protein: 4g | carbs: 37g | fiber: 2g | sodium: 102mg

Minty Cantaloupe Granita

Prep time: 10 minutes | Cook time: 5 minutes | Serves 4

½ cup plus 2 tablespoons honey
¼ cup water
2 tablespoons fresh mint leaves, plus more for garnish
1 medium cantaloupe (about 4 pounds/ 1.8 kg) peeled, seeded, and cut into 1-inch chunks

1. In a small saucepan set over low heat, combine the honey and water and cook, stirring, until the honey has fully dissolved. Stir in the mint and remove from the heat. Set aside to cool. 2. In a food processor, process the cantaloupe until very smooth. Transfer to a medium bowl. Remove the mint leaves from the syrup and discard them. Pour the syrup into the cantaloupe purée and stir to mix. 3. Transfer the mixture into a 7-by-12-inch glass baking dish and freeze, stirring with a fork every 30 minutes, for 3 to 4 hours, until it is frozen, but still grainy. Serve chilled, scooped into glasses and garnished with mint leaves.

Per Serving:
calories: 174 | fat: 0g | protein: 1g | carbs: 47g | fiber: 1g | sodium: 9mg

Red Grapefruit Granita

Prep time: 5 minutes | Cook time: 0 minutes | Serves 4 to 6

3 cups red grapefruit sections
1 cup freshly squeezed red grapefruit juice
¼ cup honey
1 tablespoon freshly squeezed lime juice
Fresh basil leaves for garnish

1. Remove as much pith (white part) and membrane as possible from the grapefruit segments. 2. Combine all ingredients except the basil in a blender or food processor and pulse just until smooth. 3. Pour the mixture into a shallow glass baking dish and place in the freezer for 1 hour. Stir with a fork and freeze for another 30 minutes, then repeat. To serve, scoop into small dessert glasses and garnish with fresh basil leaves.

Per Serving:
calories: 94 | fat: 0g | protein: 1g | carbs: 24g | fiber: 1g | sodium: 1mg

Pears Poached in Pomegranate and Wine

Prep time: 5 minutes | Cook time: 60 minutes | Serves 4

4 ripe, firm Bosc pears, peeled, left whole, and stems left intact
1½ cups pomegranate juice
1 cup sweet, white dessert wine, such as vin santo
½ cup pomegranate seeds (seeds from about ½ whole fruit)

1. Slice off a bit of the bottom of each pear to create a flat surface so that the pears can stand upright. If desired, use an apple corer to remove the cores of the fruit, working from the bottom. 2. Lay the pears in a large saucepan on their sides and pour the juice and wine over the top. Set over medium-high heat and bring to a simmer. Cover the pan, reduce the heat, and let the pears simmer, turning twice, for about 40 minutes, until the pears are tender. Transfer the pears to a shallow bowl, leaving the cooking liquid in the saucepan. 3. Turn the heat under the saucepan to high and bring the poaching liquid to a boil. Cook, stirring frequently, for about 15 to 20 minutes, until the liquid becomes thick and syrupy and is reduced to about ½ cup. 4. Spoon a bit of the syrup onto each of 4 serving plates and top each with a pear, sitting it upright. Drizzle a bit more of the sauce over the pears and garnish with the pomegranate seeds. Serve immediately.

Per Serving:
calories: 208 | fat: 0g | protein: 1g | carbs: 46g | fiber: 7g | sodium: 7mg

Pomegranate-Quinoa Dark Chocolate Bark

Prep time: 10 minutes |Cook time: 10 minutes| Serves: 6

Nonstick cooking spray
½ cup uncooked tricolor or regular quinoa
½ teaspoon kosher or sea salt
8 ounces (227 g) dark chocolate or 1 cup dark chocolate chips
½ cup fresh pomegranate seeds

1. In a medium saucepan coated with nonstick cooking spray over medium heat, toast the uncooked quinoa for 2 to 3 minutes, stirring frequently. Do not let the quinoa burn. Remove the pan from the stove, and mix in the salt. Set aside 2 tablespoons of the toasted quinoa to use for the topping. 2. Break the chocolate into large pieces, and put it in a gallon-size zip-top plastic bag. Using a metal ladle or a meat pounder, pound the chocolate until broken into smaller pieces. (If using chocolate chips, you can skip this step.) Dump the chocolate out of the bag into a medium, microwave-safe bowl and heat for 1 minute on high in the microwave. Stir until the chocolate is completely melted. Mix the toasted quinoa (except the topping you set aside) into the melted chocolate. 3. Line a large, rimmed baking sheet with parchment paper. Pour the chocolate mixture onto the sheet and spread it evenly until the entire pan is covered. Sprinkle the remaining 2 tablespoons of quinoa and the pomegranate seeds on top. Using a spatula or the back of a spoon, press the quinoa and the pomegranate seeds into the chocolate. 4. Freeze the mixture for 10 to 15 minutes, or until set. Remove the bark from the freezer, and break it into about 2-inch jagged pieces. Store in a sealed container or zip-top plastic bag in the refrigerator until ready to serve.

Per Serving:
calories: 290 | fat: 17g | protein: 5g | carbs: 29g | fiber: 6g | sodium: 202mg

Olive Oil Greek Yogurt Brownies

Prep time: 5 minutes | Cook time: 25 minutes | Serves 9

¼ cup extra virgin olive oil
¾ cup granulated sugar
1 teaspoon pure vanilla extract
2 eggs
¼ cup 2% Greek yogurt
½ cup all-purpose flour
⅓ cup unsweetened cocoa powder
¼ teaspoon salt
¼ teaspoon baking powder
⅓ cup chopped walnuts

1. Preheat the oven to 350°F (180°C) and line a 9-inch square baking pan with wax paper. 2. In a small bowl, combine the olive oil and sugar. Stir until well combined, then add the vanilla extract and mix well. 3. In another small bowl, beat the eggs and then add them to the olive oil mixture. Mix well. Add the yogurt and mix again. 4. In medium bowl, combine the flour, cocoa powder, salt, and baking powder, then mix well. Add the olive oil mixture to the dry ingredients and mix well, then add the walnuts and mix again. 5. Carefully pour the brownie mixture into the prepared pan and use a spatula to smooth the top. Transfer to the oven and bake for 25 minutes. 6. Set the brownies aside to cool completely. Lift the wax paper to remove the brownies from the pan. Remove the paper and cut the brownies into 9 squares. Store at room temperature in an airtight container for up to 2 days.

Per Serving:
calories: 198 | fat: 10g | protein: 4g | carbs: 25g | fiber: 2g | sodium: 85mg

Dark Chocolate Bark with Fruit and Nuts

Prep time: 15 minutes | Cook time: 0 minutes | Serves 2

2 tablespoons chopped nuts (almonds, pecans, walnuts, hazelnuts, pistachios, or any combination of those)
3 ounces (85 g) good-quality dark chocolate chips (about ⅔ cup)
¼ cup chopped dried fruit (apricots, blueberries, figs, prunes, or any combination of those)

1. Line a sheet pan with parchment paper. 2. Place the nuts in a skillet over medium-high heat and toast them for 60 seconds, or just until they're fragrant. 3. Place the chocolate in a microwave-safe glass bowl or measuring cup and microwave on high for 1 minute. Stir the chocolate and allow any unmelted chips to warm and melt. If necessary, heat for another 20 to 30 seconds, but keep a close eye on it to make sure it doesn't burn. 4. Pour the chocolate onto the sheet pan. Sprinkle the dried fruit and nuts over the chocolate evenly and gently pat in so they stick. 5. Transfer the sheet pan to the refrigerator for at least 1 hour to let the chocolate harden. 6. When solid, break into pieces. Store any leftover chocolate in the refrigerator or freezer.

Per Serving:
calories: 284 | fat: 16g | protein: 4g | carbs: 39g | fiber: 2g | sodium: 2mg

Chocolate Hazelnut "Powerhouse" Truffles

Prep time: 5 minutes | Cook time: 50 minutes | Makes 12 truffles

Filling:
1¾ cups blanched hazelnuts, divided
½ cup coconut butter
4 tablespoons butter or ¼ cup virgin coconut oil
¼ cup collagen powder
¼ cup raw cacao powder

1 teaspoon vanilla powder or cinnamon
Optional: low-carb sweetener, to taste
Chocolate Coating:
2½ ounces (71 g) 100% dark chocolate
1 ounce (28 g) cacao butter
Pinch of salt

1. Preheat the oven to 285°F (140°C) fan assisted or 320°F (160°C) conventional. 2. To make the filling: Spread the hazelnuts on a baking tray and roast for 40 to 50 minutes, until lightly golden. Remove from the oven and let cool for a few minutes. 3. Place 1 cup of the roasted hazelnuts in a food processor. Process for 1 to 2 minutes, until chunky. Add the coconut butter, butter, collagen powder, cacao powder, vanilla, and sweetener, if using. Process again until well combined. Place the dough in the fridge to set for 1 hour. 4. Reserve 12 hazelnuts for filling and crumble the remaining hazelnuts unto small pieces. 5. To make the chocolate coating: Line a baking tray with parchment. Melt the dark chocolate and cacao butter in a double boiler, or use a heatproof bowl placed over a small saucepan filled with 1 cup of water, placed over medium heat. Remove from the heat and let cool to room temperature before using for coating. Alternatively, use a microwave and melt in short 10- to 15-second bursts until melted, stirring in between. 6. Remove the dough from the fridge and use a spoon to scoop about 1 ounce (28 g) of the dough. Press one whole hazelnut into the center and use your hands to wrap the dough around to create a truffle. Place in the freezer for about 15 minutes. 7. Gently pierce each very cold truffle with a toothpick or a fork. Working one at a time, hold the truffle over the melted chocolate and spoon the chocolate over it to coat completely. Turn the toothpick as you work until the coating is solidified. Place the coated truffles on the lined tray and drizzle any remaining coating over them. Before they become completely solid, roll them in the chopped nuts. Refrigerate the coated truffles for at least 15 minutes to harden. 8. Keep refrigerated for up to 1 week or freeze for up to 3 months.

Per Serving:
calories: 231 | fat: 22g | protein: 4g | carbs: 8g | fiber: 4g | sodium: 3mg

Chapter 15 Staples, Sauces, Dips, and Dressings

Creamy Grapefruit-Tarragon Dressing

Prep time: 5 minutes | Cook time: 0 minutes | Serves 4 to 6

½ cup avocado oil mayonnaise
2 tablespoons Dijon mustard
1 teaspoon dried tarragon or 1 tablespoon chopped fresh tarragon
Zest and juice of ½ grapefruit (about 2 tablespoons juice)
½ teaspoon salt
¼ teaspoon freshly ground black pepper
1 to 2 tablespoons water (optional)

1. In a large mason jar or glass measuring cup, combine the mayonnaise, Dijon, tarragon, grapefruit zest and juice, salt, and pepper and whisk well with a fork until smooth and creamy. If a thinner dressing is preferred, thin out with water.

Per Serving:
calories: 49 | fat: 4g | protein: 0g | carbs: 4g | fiber: 0g | sodium: 272mg

Parsley-Mint Sauce

Prep time: 5 minutes | Cook time: 0 minutes | Serves 6

½ cup fresh flat-leaf parsley
1 cup fresh mint leaves
2 garlic cloves, minced
2 scallions (green onions), chopped
2 tablespoons pomegranate molasses
¼ cup olive oil
1 tablespoon fresh lemon juice

1. Combine all the ingredients in a blender and blend until smooth. Transfer to an airtight container and refrigerate until ready to use. Can be refrigerated for 1 day.

Per Serving:
calories: 90 | fat: 9g | protein: 1g | carbs: 2g | fiber: 0g | sodium: 5mg

Pickled Turnips

Prep time: 5 minutes | Cook time: 0 minutes | Serves 2

1 pound (454 g) turnips, washed well, peeled, and cut into 1-inch batons
1 small beet, roasted, peeled, and cut into 1-inch batons
2 garlic cloves, smashed
1 teaspoon dried Turkish oregano
3 cups warm water
½ cup red wine vinegar
½ cup white vinegar

1. In a jar, combine the turnips, beet, garlic, and oregano. Pour the water and vinegars over the vegetables, cover, then shake well and put it in the refrigerator. The turnips will be pickled after 1 hour.

Per Serving:
calories: 3 | fat: 0g | protein: 1g | carbs: 0g | fiber: 0g | sodium: 6mg

Kidney Bean Dip with Cilantro, Cumin, and Lime

Prep time: 10 minutes | Cook time: 30 minutes | Serves 16

1 cup dried kidney beans, soaked overnight and drained
4 cups water
3 cloves garlic, peeled and crushed
¼ cup roughly chopped cilantro, divided
¼ cup extra-virgin olive oil
1 tablespoon lime juice
2 teaspoons grated lime zest
1 teaspoon ground cumin
½ teaspoon salt

1. Place beans, water, garlic, and 2 tablespoons cilantro in the Instant Pot®. Close the lid, set steam release to Sealing, press the Bean button, and cook for the default time of 30 minutes. 2. When the timer beeps, let pressure release naturally, about 20 minutes. Press the Cancel button, open lid, and check that beans are tender. Drain off excess water and transfer beans to a medium bowl. Gently mash beans with potato masher or fork until beans are mashed but chunky. Add oil, lime juice, lime zest, cumin, salt, and remaining 2 tablespoons cilantro and stir to combine. Serve warm or at room temperature.

Per Serving:
calories: 65 | fat: 3g | protein: 2g | carbs: 7g | fiber: 2g | sodium: 75mg

Berry and Honey Compote

Prep time: 5 minutes | Cook time: 15 minutes | Serves 2 to 3

½ cup honey
¼ cup fresh berries
2 tablespoons grated orange zest

1. In a small saucepan, heat the honey, berries, and orange zest over medium-low heat for 2 to 5 minutes, until the sauce thickens, or heat for 15 seconds in the microwave. Serve the compote drizzled over pancakes, muffins, or French toast.

Per Serving:
calories: 272 | fat: 0g | protein: 1g | carbs: 74g | fiber: 1g | sodium: 4mg

Lemon Tahini Dressing

Prep time: 5 minutes | Cook time: 0 minutes | Makes ½ cup

¼ cup tahini
3 tablespoons lemon juice
3 tablespoons warm water
¼ teaspoon kosher salt
¼ teaspoon pure maple syrup
¼ teaspoon ground cumin
⅛ teaspoon cayenne pepper

1. In a medium bowl, whisk together the tahini, lemon juice, water, salt, maple syrup, cumin, and cayenne pepper until smooth. Place in the refrigerator until ready to serve. Store any leftovers in the refrigerator in an airtight container up to 5 days.

Per Serving:
2 tablespoons: calories: 90 | fat: 7g | protein: 3g | carbs: 5g | fiber: 1g | sodium: 80mg

White Bean Hummus

Prep time: 10 minutes | Cook time: 30 minutes | Serves 12

⅔ cup dried white beans, rinsed and drained
3 cloves garlic, peeled and crushed
¼ cup olive oil
1 tablespoon lemon juice
½ teaspoon salt

1. Place beans and garlic in the Instant Pot® and stir well. Add enough cold water to cover ingredients. Close lid, set steam release to Sealing, press the Manual button, and set time to 30 minutes. 2. When the timer beeps, let pressure release naturally, about 20 minutes. Press the Cancel button and open lid. Use a fork to check that beans are tender. Drain off excess water and transfer beans to a food processor. 3. Add oil, lemon juice, and salt to the processor and pulse until mixture is smooth with some small chunks. Transfer to a storage container and refrigerate for at least 4 hours. Serve cold or at room temperature. Store in the refrigerator for up to one week.

Per Serving:
calories: 57 | fat: 5g | protein: 1g | carbs: 3g | fiber: 1g | sodium: 99mg

Versatile Sandwich Round

Prep time: 5 minutes | Cook time: 2 minutes | Serves 1

3 tablespoons almond flour
1 tablespoon extra-virgin olive oil
1 large egg
½ teaspoon dried rosemary,
oregano, basil, thyme, or garlic powder (optional)
¼ teaspoon baking powder
⅛ teaspoon salt

1. In a microwave-safe ramekin, combine the almond flour, olive oil, egg, rosemary (if using), baking powder, and salt. Mix well with a fork. 2. Microwave for 90 seconds on high. 3. Slide a knife around the edges of ramekin and flip to remove the bread. 4. Slice in half with a serrated knife if you want to use it to make a sandwich.

Per Serving:
calories: 354 | fat: 33g | protein: 12g | carbs: 6g | fiber: 3g | sodium: 388mg

Tomatillo Salsa

Prep time: 5 minutes | Cook time: 15 minutes | Serves 4

12 tomatillos
2 fresh serrano chiles
1 tablespoon minced garlic
1 cup chopped fresh cilantro leaves
1 tablespoon vegetable oil
1 teaspoon kosher salt

1. Remove and discard the papery husks from the tomatillos and rinse them under warm running water to remove the sticky coating. 2. Place the tomatillos and peppers in a baking pan. Place the pan in the air fryer basket. Air fry at 350ºF (177ºC) for 15 minutes. 3. Transfer the tomatillos and peppers to a blender, add the garlic, cilantro, vegetable oil, and salt, and blend until almost smooth. (If not using immediately, omit the salt and add it just before serving.) 4. Serve or store in an airtight container in the refrigerator for up to 10 days.

Per Serving:
calories: 68 | fat: 4g | protein: 1g | carbs: 7g | fiber: 2g | sodium: 585mg

Vinaigrette

Prep time: 5 minutes | Cook time: 0 minutes | Serves 4

2 tablespoons balsamic vinegar
2 large garlic cloves, minced
1 teaspoon dried rosemary, crushed
¼ teaspoon freshly ground black pepper
¼ cup olive oil

1. In a small bowl, whisk together the vinegar, garlic, rosemary, and pepper. While whisking, slowly stream in the olive oil and whisk until emulsified. Store in an airtight container in the refrigerator for up to 3 days.

Per Serving:
1 cup: calories: 129 | fat: 1g | protein: 3g | carbs: 0g | fiber: 0g | sodium: 2mg

Maltese Sun-Dried Tomato and Mushroom Dressing

Prep time: 10 minutes | Cook time: 5 minutes | Serves 4

⅓ cup olive oil (use a combination of olive oil and sun-dried tomato oil, if they were packed in oil)
8 ounces (227 g) mushrooms, sliced
3 tablespoons red wine vinegar
Freshly ground black pepper, to taste
½ cup sun-dried tomatoes, drained (if they are packed in oil, reserve the oil) and chopped

1. In a medium skillet, heat 2 tablespoons of the olive oil (or mixed olive oil and sun-dried tomato packing oil) over high heat. Add the mushrooms and cook, stirring, until they have released their liquid. 2. Add vinegar and season with pepper. Remove from the heat and add the remaining oil and the sun-dried tomatoes.

Per Serving:
1 cup: calories: 190 | fat: 18g | protein: 3g | carbs: 6g | fiber: 2g | sodium: 21mg

Lemon-Yogurt Sauce

Prep time: 5 minutes | Cook time: 0 minutes | Makes about 1 cup

1 cup plain whole-milk yogurt	plus 2 tablespoons juice
1 teaspoon grated lemon zest	1 garlic clove, minced

1. Whisk all ingredients together in bowl and season with salt and pepper to taste. Cover and refrigerate for at least 30 minutes to allow flavors to meld. (Sauce can be refrigerated for up to 4 days.)

Per Serving:
¼ cup: calories: 40 | fat: 2g | protein: 2g | carbs: 4g | fiber: 0g | sodium: 28mg

Olive Mint Vinaigrette

Prep time: 5 minutes | Cook time: 0 minutes | Makes ½ cup

¼ cup white wine vinegar	¼ cup extra-virgin olive oil
¼ teaspoon honey	¼ cup olives, pitted and minced
¼ teaspoon kosher salt	2 tablespoons fresh mint, minced
¼ teaspoon freshly ground black pepper	

1. In a bowl, whisk together the vinegar, honey, salt, and black pepper. Add the olive oil and whisk well. Add the olives and mint, and mix well. Store any leftovers in the refrigerator in an airtight container for up to 5 days.

Per Serving:
2 tablespoons: calories: 135 | fat: 15g | protein: 0g | carbs: 1g | fiber: 0g | sodium: 135mg

Skinny Cider Dressing

Prep time: 5 minutes | Cook time: 0 minutes | Serves 2

2 tablespoons apple cider vinegar	⅓ lemon, zested
⅓ lemon, juiced	Salt
	Freshly ground black pepper

1. In a jar, combine the vinegar, lemon juice, and zest. Season with salt and pepper, cover, and shake well.

Per Serving:
calories: 2 | fat: 0g | protein: 0g | carbs: 1g | fiber: 0g | sodium: 0mg

Pepper Sauce

Prep time: 10 minutes | Cook time: 20 minutes | Makes 4 cups

2 red hot fresh chiles, seeded	2 garlic cloves, peeled
2 dried chiles	2 cups water
½ small yellow onion, roughly chopped	2 cups white vinegar

1. In a medium saucepan, combine the fresh and dried chiles, onion, garlic, and water. Bring to a simmer and cook for 20 minutes, or until tender. Transfer to a food processor or blender. 2. Add the vinegar and blend until smooth.

Per Serving:
1 cup: calories: 41 | fat: 0g | protein: 1g | carbs: 5g | fiber: 1g | sodium: 11mg

Olive Tapenade

Prep time: 10 minutes | Cook time: 0 minutes | Makes about 1 cup

¾ cup pitted brine-cured green or black olives, chopped fine	1 tablespoon capers, rinsed and minced
1 small shallot, minced	1½ teaspoons red wine vinegar
2 tablespoons extra-virgin olive oil	1 teaspoon minced fresh oregano

1. Combine all ingredients in bowl. (Tapenade can be refrigerated for up to 1 week.)

Per Serving:
¼ cup: calories: 92 | fat: 9g | protein: 0g | carbs: 2g | fiber: 1g | sodium: 236mg

Simple Vinaigrette

Prep time: 5 minutes | Cook time: 0 minutes | Makes 1 cup

½ cup extra-virgin olive oil	1 teaspoon dried herbs (oregano, rosemary, parsley, or thyme)
¼ cup red wine vinegar or freshly squeezed lemon juice	½ teaspoon salt
1 tablespoon Dijon mustard	½ teaspoon freshly ground black pepper
1 small garlic clove, finely minced (optional)	

1. In a glass Mason jar with a lid, combine the olive oil, vinegar, Dijon, garlic (if using), herbs, salt, and pepper and shake until well combined. Store in the refrigerator and bring to room temperature before serving. Be sure to shake the dressing well before using as the oil and vinegar will naturally separate.

Per Serving:
¼ cup: calories: 246 | fat: 27g | protein: 0g | carbs: 1g | fiber: 0g | sodium: 336mg

Herbed Oil

Prep time: 5 minutes | Cook time: 0 minutes | Serves 2

½ cup extra-virgin olive oil	leaves
1 teaspoon dried basil	2 teaspoons dried oregano
1 teaspoon dried parsley	⅛ teaspoon salt
1 teaspoon fresh rosemary	

1. Pour the oil into a small bowl and stir in the basil, parsley, rosemary, oregano, and salt while whisking the oil with a fork.

Per Serving:
calories: 486 | fat: 54g | protein: 1g | carbs: 2g | fiber: 1g | sodium: 78mg

Italian Dressing

Prep time: 5 minutes | Cook time: 0 minutes | Serves 12

¼ cup red wine vinegar
½ cup extra-virgin olive oil
¼ teaspoon salt
¼ teaspoon freshly ground black pepper
1 teaspoon dried Italian seasoning
1 teaspoon Dijon mustard
1 garlic clove, minced

1. In a small jar, combine the vinegar, olive oil, salt, pepper, Italian seasoning, mustard, and garlic. Close with a tight-fitting lid and shake vigorously for 1 minute. 2. Refrigerate for up to 1 week.

Per Serving:
calories: 82 | fat: 9g | protein: 0g | carbs: 0g | fiber: 0g | sodium: 71mg

Cucumber Yogurt Dip

Prep time: 5 minutes | Cook time: 0 minutes | Serves 2 to 3

1 cup plain, unsweetened, full-fat Greek yogurt
½ cup cucumber, peeled, seeded, and diced
1 tablespoon freshly squeezed lemon juice
1 tablespoon chopped fresh mint
1 small garlic clove, minced
Salt and freshly ground black pepper, to taste

1. In a food processor, combine the yogurt, cucumber, lemon juice, mint, and garlic. Pulse several times to combine, leaving noticeable cucumber chunks. 2. Taste and season with salt and pepper.

Per Serving:
calories: 55 | fat: 3g | protein: 3g | carbs: 5g | fiber: 0g | sodium: 38mg

Appendix 1: Measurement Conversion Chart

MEASUREMENT CONVERSION CHART

VOLUME EQUIVALENTS (DRY)

US STANDARD	METRIC (APPROXIMATE)
1/8 teaspoon	0.5 mL
1/4 teaspoon	1 mL
1/2 teaspoon	2 mL
3/4 teaspoon	4 mL
1 teaspoon	5 mL
1 tablespoon	15 mL
1/4 cup	59 mL
1/2 cup	118 mL
3/4 cup	177 mL
1 cup	235 mL
2 cups	475 mL
3 cups	700 mL
4 cups	1 L

VOLUME EQUIVALENTS (LIQUID)

US STANDARD	US STANDARD (OUNCES)	METRIC (APPROXIMATE)
2 tablespoons	1 fl.oz.	30 mL
1/4 cup	2 fl.oz.	60 mL
1/2 cup	4 fl.oz.	120 mL
1 cup	8 fl.oz.	240 mL
1 1/2 cup	12 fl.oz.	355 mL
2 cups or 1 pint	16 fl.oz.	475 mL
4 cups or 1 quart	32 fl.oz.	1 L
1 gallon	128 fl.oz.	4 L

TEMPERATURES EQUIVALENTS

FAHRENHEIT(F)	CELSIUS(C) (APPROXIMATE)
225 °F	107 °C
250 °F	120 °C
275 °F	135 °C
300 °F	150 °C
325 °F	160 °C
350 °F	180 °C
375 °F	190 °C
400 °F	205 °C
425 °F	220 °C
450 °F	235 °C
475 °F	245 °C
500 °F	260 °C

WEIGHT EQUIVALENTS

US STANDARD	METRIC (APPROXIMATE)
1 ounce	28 g
2 ounces	57 g
5 ounces	142 g
10 ounces	284 g
15 ounces	425 g
16 ounces (1 pound)	455 g
1.5 pounds	680 g
2 pounds	907 g

Appendix 2: The Dirty Dozen and Clean Fifteen

The Dirty Dozen and Clean Fifteen

The Environmental Working Group (EWG) is a nonprofit, nonpartisan organization dedicated to protecting human health and the environment Its mission is to empower people to live healthier lives in a healthier environment. This organization publishes an annual list of the twelve kinds of produce, in sequence, that have the highest amount of pesticide residue-the Dirty Dozen-as well as a list of the fifteen kinds of produce that have the least amount of pesticide residue-the Clean Fifteen.

THE DIRTY DOZEN

- The 2016 Dirty Dozen includes the following produce. These are considered among the year's most important produce to buy organic:

Strawberries	Spinach
Apples	Tomatoes
Nectarines	Bell peppers
Peaches	Cherry tomatoes
Celery	Cucumbers
Grapes	Kale/collard greens
Cherries	Hot peppers

- The Dirty Dozen list contains two additional items kale/collard greens and hot peppers-because they tend to contain trace levels of highly hazardous pesticides.

THE CLEAN FIFTEEN

- The least critical to buy organically are the Clean Fifteen list. The following are on the 2016 list:

Avocados	Papayas
Corn	Kiw
Pineapples	Eggplant
Cabbage	Honeydew
Sweet peas	Grapefruit
Onions	Cantaloupe
Asparagus	Cauliflower
Mangos	

- Some of the sweet corn sold in the United States are made from genetically engineered (GE) seedstock. Buy organic varieties of these crops to avoid GE produce.

Made in United States
North Haven, CT
10 April 2023

35268944R00080